Cases in Operations Management

Analysis and Action

Cases in

Operations

Management

Analysis and

Action

W. Earl Sasser

Kim B. Clark

David A. Garvin

Margaret B. W. Graham

Ramchandran Jaikumar

David H. Maister

all of
Harvard University

1982
IRWIN
Homewood, Illinois 60430

ISBN 0-256-02903-2

Library of Congress Catalog Card No. 82–80419

Printed in the United States of America

6 7 8 9 0 ML 9 8 7 6

Acknowledgments

The cases in this book were developed for and used extensively in the required Production and Operations Management (POM) course at the Harvard Graduate School of Business Administration. This course has had a long and successful history at the school, and this volume is the result not only of the efforts of the authors (all of whom have been responsible for teaching the course in recent years) but of many of our numerous POM colleagues, past and present, who have influenced the direction and content of our efforts.

Particular thanks must be expressed to those colleagues who contributed cases not written or supervised by one of us. We here express our gratitude to William J. Abernathy for *Max-Able Medical Clinic;* to Michael Beer and Bert Spector for *Sedalia Engine;* to William K. Holstein for *Arrow Diagramming Exercise, Kool King,* and *Space Constructors* and (together with T. J. R. Johnson and L. A. Bennigson) for *Fabritek;* to Frank Leonard for *Hank Kolb;* to Paul W. Marshall for *Planets* II; to Jeffrey G. Miller for *Granger Transmission* and (together with R. Paul Olsen) for *National Cranberry Cooperative;* to Richard S. Rosenbloom for *Lowell Steel Corporation* and (together with W. H. Hart) for *Blitz Company;* to C. Wickham Skinner (together with Frank Leonard) for *Kalamazoo* and (together with A. R. Dooley) for *Sunshine Builders;* and to Steven C. Wheelwright for *Insight Optical, Chaircraft (R), Corning Glass Works, Texas Instruments: TPD* (with Rod White), *Cross River Products* (with Eleanor Latimer), and *Sorenson Research* (with Gary Crocker).

Gratitude is also due to those individuals who helped one or more of us with other cases: J. R. Klug *(Benihana of Tokyo);* David Rikert *(McDonald's Corporation, Burger King Corporation, Swift River Box Company, Sof-Optics,* and *Boise Cascade);* R. T. Lund *(Walton Manufacturing);* Robert D. Turner *(FBO, Inc.);* and A. Pigneri and Shauna Doyle *(University Health Services).*

Since some of the cases used in this book are disguised we cannot publicly express our thanks to all of the managers of the firms described here. Nevertheless, we are deeply in their debt because without their cooperation in sharing their experiences with us, this book would not have been possible.

We wish to express our gratitude to the President and Fellows of Harvard College, by whom most of the cases in this volume are individually copyrighted, and to the General Electric Company for permission to include the *Master Operations Scheduling Game.*

We would also like to express our thanks to the Harvard Graduate School of Business Administration and its Dean, John A. McArthur, for providing the opportunity and resources to develop the materials included here. We have all benefited greatly, as academics and teachers, from the classroom discussions of these cases with our M.B.A. and executive students and thank them all for helping to make our teaching experiences as fulfilling as they have been.

Finally, we especially want to thank Conny Doty whose patience and organization helped bring this project to a successful conclusion.

W. E. S.
K. C.
D. A. G.
M. B. W. G.
R. J.
D. H. M.

Contents

Introduction

In a recent bestseller, *The Soul of a New Machine*,[1] the story is told of a crack young team of engineers who designed and built a new computer at the Data General Corporation. The manager of the group, Tom West, did not design a single element of the machine, nor did he perform any soldering or assembly or write any of the basic computer code. Yet at the end of the project, many participants felt that the new machine was West's creation. It was he, after all, who set the objectives and targets for the group; selected and recruited the human, financial, and physical resources for the task; organized and allocated these resources to different parts of the project; and established the schedule and provided the motivation for the group to meet it. West did not "build" the machine in any physical sense, but in many ways, it was *his*. Without him, Data General's new computer, if one had been produced at all, would undoubtedly have been a very different machine.

While the full extent of Tom West's contribution is difficult to assess, his experience at Data General does illustrate the fundamental contribution and challenges of the operating manager. Such a manager must define the task to be accomplished; must marshal the resources necessary to accomplish it; and must allocate, monitor, direct, motivate, control, evaluate, and supervise the efforts of others in bringing the task to successful completion. Above all else, management (and especially operations management) remains the art of getting things done.

Throughout history, it has been clear that a nation's economic success is determined not only by its access to valuable natural resources but also by its ability to manage those resources well—to combine the materials, machines, and manpower available to produce, as efficiently as possible, the

---

[1] Tracy Kidder (Boston: Little, Brown, 1981).

products and services demanded by society. Just as 18th-century Britain carved out the world's most advanced economy from a small island with a few natural resources, so today have countries such as Japan acquired great wealth, not through an abundance of grain, oil, or other minerals but through their ability to purchase those resources from others and to then employ them more productively than their competitors.

What is true of nations is equally true of business enterprises. A company that is able to produce goods and services that meet the market's needs while employing fewer resources than its competitors will attract customers and flourish. An efficient operation will attract additional investment, leading to further growth. In order to achieve such success, however, good operations management—the ability to transform, efficiently and effectively, basic raw materials into useful outputs—is an absolute necessity.

An example will illustrate the importance of operations management. According to recent estimates, in 1979 the Ford Motor Company had an employee cost per vehicle of $2,464, while Toyo Kogyo, a Japanese automaker, incurred only $491 in employee cost per vehicle.[2] At the same time, Ford incurred book-value capital costs of $3,048 per vehicle; the comparable figure for Toyo Kogyo was $1,639.[3] During this period, typical work in process inventories per vehicle were $536 in the United States; in Japan, they averaged $80.[4] These differences reflect operating decisions—planning, design, and execution—and illustrate well the potential impact of good operations management. Not surprisingly, Toyo Kogyo was a far more profitable company than Ford during this time.

Nor is the importance of operations management confined to the automobile industry. For virtually any company in any industry, the vast majority of employees are likely to be engaged in production and delivery. Most of the firm's capital assets are similarly under the control of its operating managers, as are a large proportion of the firm's expenditures on machines, energy, labor, and materials. Operations management, it should be clear, is an extremely important field.

The cases in this volume are designed to expose students to the choices, challenges, opportunities, and constraints faced by operating managers and to help them develop the understanding, skills, and judgment necessary to function effectively in those roles. A diverse set of industries is represented in these cases, ranging from steel making and watch manufacture to airplane refueling and fast-food delivery. The decisions faced by the managers in this book are similarly diverse—dealing with a work force, choosing between alternative methods of producing a product, and deciding whether, when,

[2] Abernathy, Clark and Kantrow, "The New Industrial Competition," *Harvard Business Review*, September–October 1981, pp. 80–81.

[3] *The Competitive Status of the U.S. Auto Industry* (Report of the automotive panel—National Academy of Engineering, National Academy of Science), forthcoming 1982.

[4] Ibid.

and where to keep inventories. However, while the contexts, decisions, and themes vary considerably, the underlying issue remains the same—the manager who must act. As the title of this volume indicates, this book is not just about operations but about *operations management;* not just about operations analysis but about analysis as the basis for decision making and action.

Historically, operations management has been viewed as the domain of the engineer, requiring a detailed mastery of technical knowledge in order to make important operating decisions. This belief was widely held in industry and in educational institutions and was reflected in the topics included in most training programs for operating managers: time-and-motion studies, industrial engineering, and analysis of plant layout. Later, the application of sophisticated mathematical analyses to operating problems became popular. New and powerful techniques for controlling inventories, scheduling production, and balancing capacities were developed, and the belief soon spread, in both academia and industry, that the operating managers *had* to be trained in mathematical methods.

Neither of these views is correct. Certainly, industrial engineering and mathematical analysis are important, and the modern business enterprise cannot afford to ignore them. But engineering and mathematical studies can be (and are) performed by staff specialists; they are not the job of the manager. As the real-life situations described in these pages illustrate, when all of the technical analyses have been performed, there virtually always remains a management decision (or, rather, set of decisions) to be taken by the individual with *line management* responsibility for the effective functioning of the operating unit. This volume is about those decisions. Students that attempt to understand and deal with the problems here will not need to be engineers or mathematicians. Nor will the cases here necessarily help the students to become better engineers or mathematicians. Rather, our aim is to help students to become more effective managers.

We hope this will be accomplished by making students aware of the major elements of an operating system; by helping them understand the range of choices open to managers; by exposing the interconnections between different aspects of operating systems; and by constantly giving practice in decision making in the face of complexity, ambiguity, and annoying real-world detail. These cases do not pose problems such as "What is the best way to manage inventories?" or "How can production be scheduled?" or "How can you motivate employees" although we hope that students will begin to develop answers to these questions. Rather, for each of these cases, the same critical question should be asked: "What can be done, if anything, to make this operation run more effectively or efficiently?"

The concepts of efficiency and effectiveness are important and worthy of some discussion. *Efficiency* is the simpler (and more familiar) notion and refers to the avoidance of waste in the transformation of the inputs to a productive system (usually categorized as labor, materials, capital, and energy) into useful outputs (finished products of good quality produced on time). Since inputs and outputs are normally measured in different units (labor in worker-hours, materials in tons, cubic feet, or items, energy in kilowatt-hours, etc.) all units are usually converted to monetary amounts for ease of comparison. Efficiency thus relates the value of the output of an operation to the total cost of its inputs. If the same value of output can be produced at a lower cost by varying the combination of inputs (or by managing them better), then the system being employed is not perfectly efficient. Ultimately, questions of efficiency come down to issues of costs and cost control. It is usually on questions of this sort that the technical specialist has the most to contribute.

However, low cost is not the only desired output from an operation. It must not only be efficient but also effective. In the most basic terms, *effectiveness* means getting the right job done and getting all of the job done: meeting (or exceeding) all of the performance characteristics desired. There can be many noncost performance goals for an operating system, but four are of particular interest because of their wide applicability: quality, response time, flexibility to volume changes, and flexibility to product mix changes. There are always choices available among different ways to design and manage an operating system. The system that produces the product at lowest cost (i.e., is technically efficient), for example, may not be the system that produces the most consistent quality. Similarly, the low cost system, because of long production runs, may result in such lengthy lead times that orders cannot be delivered for some weeks after they have been placed. The system that results in the highest quality may suffer from the disadvantage that it can only operate at a steady pace and cannot respond (except at substantial cost penalty) to dramatic increases or decreases in demand, while the system that has the best (fastest?) response time may only be able to handle standard products and may not be good at dealing with special orders or other variations in the mix of products produced. Faced with these alternatives, how is one to decide which is the "best" system? The most effective system?

The answers to these questions will always depend on the context and will always be the domain of the operating manager rather than the technical specialist. The reason for this is that the answers require a thorough understanding of the competitive needs of the firm. As a result, the first question that must be asked when dealing with any operating issue is "What do we as a company have to do well to succeed?" Only when this agenda has been set (a task for managers, not technicians) can the effectiveness of the operation be assessed. As the student works through the cases in this volume, we hope that these considerations will be constantly borne in mind.

The cases in this book are designed to encourage students to deal with the operating system as a unified whole. A good manager will examine all aspects of a problem before reaching a decision on a course of action and will review each situation from a variety of different perspectives. As a broad framework within which to develop this point of view, let us consider the structure of an operating system. Figure 1 describes a typical operating process by means of a "process flow diagram." As in most such diagrams, major activities are indicated by rectangles and inventories by triangles.

FIGURE 1
A Process Flow Diagram

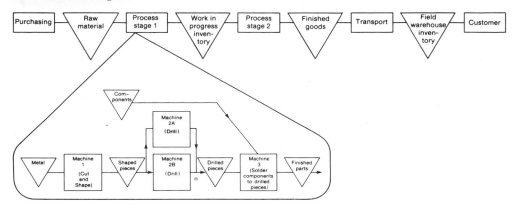

The first step in this process is to acquire the raw materials necessary to make the product. This activity results in an inventory of raw materials from which the first stages of the process draw as production is scheduled. Preliminary operating processes (parts fabrication, for example) result in work in process (WIP) inventory which is further worked upon in later operating stages (various assembly operations, perhaps) in order to produce finished goods inventory. This inventory may be transported to field warehouses, to bring it closer to the market, and delivered to customers from these remote locations.

Figure 1 presents only the broadest outlines of an operating process. We could (if it were of interest) go into finer detail (as shown) and draw a similar diagram to study the activities and events that take place within a single phase of the operation. The more-detailed description reveals a choice to be made: some shaped pieces are drilled on machine 2A and some on machine 2B. The process flow diagram can thus reveal variations in the flow of work through the operation. The level of detail required in the process description will depend upon the problem to be addressed. The diagram can be used to ask such questions as: What is the capacity of each stage in the process? What is the typical rate of output? How long does it take for an item to pass through each stage? How much inventory is there in the system?

As useful as process flow descriptions such as Figure 1 may be, they reveal only part of the *physical system* of production. They involve only materials and machines. An operating system, however, is much more than just a physical system. A *people system* is involved as well. How, for example, is the work force allocated? At what stages are the most people employed? Where are the most highly skilled tasks? How finely divided are the tasks? Do people work in groups or individually? In appraising an operating system, these questions are as important as those involving materials and machinery.

An operating system may also be represented as a *financial or monetary system*. One can ask where in the process most costs are incurred and what types of expenditures are involved. Which parts of the operation, for example, require large capital investments? Where are costs fixed and where variable? What is the value of the materials and work in progress and finished goods inventory at various stages?

Finally, an operation may be regarded as an *information system*. What information must the work force have to do their jobs? Where, to keep the system running, must operating decisions be made, (e.g., produce model X today and model Y tomorrow)? What information must managers and workers have in order to make these decisions? How is the information collected, assembled, and communicated? A good understanding of the information flows and decision systems is essential to a full understanding of an operating system.

Throughout this introduction, we have referred in general terms to "production processes," "operations," and "operating systems." So far, we have discussed these concepts in very general terms. However, while every production process is unique in certain respects, a number of general categories can be identified. In combination, these categories provide a useful way of thinking about production systems, for they highlight differences of great interest to management. Different types of processes, for example, often have very different operating characteristics, requiring different skills and sensitivities. In some cases, labor relations and worker supervision will be critical, while in others, capacity utilization and machine downtime will be more important. Recognition of these differences is an important first step in ensuring that an operating system performs effectively.

Production processes can be distinguished from one another on several dimensions, but one in particular is of paramount importance: the degree of variability (or customization) in the products or services that the system is required to produce at any one time. At one extreme lies the project-type operation designed to produce a highly customized, unique, one-of-a-kind item. Activities must be carefully coordinated, including planning, design, purchasing, and production. The scheduling and sequencing of tasks, therefore, becomes of primary importance. At any one time, a given worker or work group might be devoting most of its attention to a single project. Over the course of a year, however, the work group is likely to be involved in a wide variety of different projects, adapting its activities and procedures to the specific needs of the project at hand.

It is important to recognize that services as well as manufactured products qualify as projects, as do certain special-purpose activities undertaken within a firm. The launching of a new product's advertising campaign, for example, can be considered a project, as can a targeted research and development program. Other examples of this type of production process include major construction projects like dams or highways, customized products like racing cars or oceangoing vessels, and highly engineered products like satellites or missiles.

Compared to projects, *job shop* operations typically involve the production not of a single item but of a small number of a wide variety of products (usually grouped together in batches or lots). The degree of customization in the product or service is still high, but the set of activities to be performed has a greater degree of regularity and predictability. However, not all products produced will have to be worked on by all of the available machines and work groups. Different products will follow different paths through the production process. In a hospital emergency room, for example, which is representative of a job shop, some patients will receive X rays, others blood transfusions, and still others surgical treatment, yet all will first be processed by a receiving nurse. Because of these different sequences and the varying amounts of time involved at each step, different loads are imposed on different pieces of equipment, and work in process inventories may build up, occasionally appearing in different parts of the system. Overall, labor content and worker skills are high, general-purpose machinery is often employed, and workers may be trained to operate several different pieces of equipment.

Batch processes are often quite similar to job shops, for they, too, involve small production volumes. They are distinguished from job shops by their larger lot sizes (the number of units being worked on simultaneously at a given work station), the greater standardizaton of their products, and the greater commonality of the required tasks. Batch processes involve greater similarity among the units produced and require less flexibility to product variation. Their limited volumes per product, however, preclude the efficient use of assembly lines.

Both services and manufactured products fall under these headings. Examples of job shops include general-purpose machine shops, automobile repair shops, manufacturers of specialty furniture, and custom dressmakers, while examples of batch processes include bookbinderies, the manufacturers of complex electronic equipment, and musical instruments makers.

Of all production systems, *line flows* and *continuous processes* typically produce products in the largest volumes. Standardization becomes critical, and some products, like oil, chemicals, or paper, are relatively undifferentiated bulk commodities. In many continuous processes, raw and in-process materials are automatically transported throughout the plant, with little worker contact. Along the way, the material is processed or chemically transformed—in furnaces, separators, mixers, and the like—

gradually attaining its final, salable form. Often the only responsibility of workers in these plants is the monitoring of dials and gauges controlling the process flow. Line-flow processes are also highly automated, although some of them, like fast-food restaurants, employ a more labor-intensive process. In either case, tasks are defined narrowly, and the division of labor is high. The production process is broken down into relatively simple operations, with workers normally specializing in a small number of tasks (except in those continuous processes where workers spend most of their time monitoring equipment, in which case they may have rather broad responsibilities). Repetition and simplicity are essential features of each activity. The different stages of the production process are tightly interconnected, with partially completed products often flowing uninterruptedly (typically on a moving assembly line) from one step to the next. The same production sequence is normally followed by most products.

One implication of the preceding discussion is that different production processes possess characteristics that make them more or less suitable for different competitive environments. No single process is likely to be appropriate in all circumstances. A continuous process, for example, because of its lack of flexibility, is unlikely to be especially effective in a market where customized, low-volume products are the norm, just as a job shop is unlikely to be the best way to produce a commodity item.

This suggests that product and process characteristics are often complementary, with processes chosen to match the key features of the markets that they serve. Different processes do different things well and should be chosen accordingly. Projects and job shops, for example, would be most appropriate where low-volume, relatively expensive products predominated and buyers were more concerned with performance and quality than with price. These production processes, after all, are often extremely time-consuming and typically require highly skilled labor. Line flows and continuous processes, on the other hand, would be better suited to markets where standardized, high-volume production was the norm and buyers were especially price sensitive. The advantage of these systems lies in their ability to employ capital-intensive techniques to produce similar products relatively cheaply. Batch processes would fall somewhere between these two extremes, being suitable for volumes less than those typical of line flows and greater than those typical of job shops, while still allowing for some standardization of the product.

An example may be helpful here. Consider how various types of automobiles are manufactured. While we typically think of automobile assembly as a line-flow process—Henry Ford being the father of the modern assembly line—mass production techniques are not always appropriate. A racing car for the Indianapolis 500 or a special-order Rolls Royce is unlikely to be assembled by this means. Their low product volumes, attention to quality and performance, and buyers' insensitivity to price all argue in favor of other methods. Project techniques would probably be most appropriate for constructing the racing car, while a job shop or batch process would best serve the needs of Rolls Royce assembly. More automated processes, designed for standardized chassis and bodies, provide little flexibility and would be inappropriate here. The usual advantage of such capital-intensive techniques—their ability to produce large product volumes at comparatively low cost—does not match the demands of the racing car or Rolls Royce markets.

At the other extreme, a "world car" is now in the offing, with the same basic automobile being sold in a number of different countries. Efforts to tap these global markets have led to further standardization of automobile and engine designs. In these circumstances, continuous processes become increasingly desirable, for greater standardization implies higher volumes, fewer changeovers, and a reduced need for flexibility. Cost reduction becomes critical, putting a premium on capital-intensive techniques. Nissan, for example, a major Japanese automaker, has pursued this goal by using industrial robots to assemble automobiles, a degree of automation now considered desirable because of the changed nature of the product and the market.

It is important to recognize that the particular production processes employed by firms do not simply reflect the limits imposed by technology. As our discussion of the automobile industry makes clear, managers have considerable discretion in choosing among production techniques, for the same product can usually be produced in a number of different ways. The choice among these alternatives has an important bearing on the likely success or failure of a firm and on the tasks required of management to compete effectively. In general, a production process has been well chosen if it matches the firm's strategy, the demands of the market, and the features of the external environment in which the firm finds itself.

The broad categorization of process types presented here is best viewed as part of a continuous spectrum (Figure 2). Because not all operations fit neatly into one or the other of the five major process types, they should be thought of as elements of a spectrum, blending into one another without sharp divisions. However, in wrestling with the cases in this volume, it is important for students to consider which process type a given operation resembles most closely. The reason for this is that there are significant differences between process types in the characteristics of the people system, the physical system, the information system, and the monetary system. Some broad generalizations are offered below:

FIGURE 2
The Process Spectrum

Projects $\longleftrightarrow$ Job shops $\longleftrightarrow$ Batch processes $\longleftrightarrow$ Line flows $\longleftrightarrow$ Continuous processes xviii

The People System

As one moves along the spectrum from projects to continuous processes:

Labor content per dollar value of the product decreases.

The required labor skills fall. Craft skills are often required by projects or job shops, while line flows, because of their increased division of labor, involve simpler and more repetitive tasks. For many continuous processes, however, higher skill levels are required because of the "art" and judgment involved in monitoring or controlling the process. In the extreme case of a fully automated continuous process, no direct labor would be involved.

Training times fall, although continuous processes may again be an exception to the general pattern.

The degree of worker discretion (e.g., control over the pace of the process) declines.

disagree?

Staff needs (for quality control, capacity planning, new product development, etc.) become important relative to line supervision.

The Physical System

As one moves along the spectrum from projects to continuous processes:

Equipment becomes less general purpose and more dedicated to performing a limited number of functions efficiently.

The flow of materials through the operation follows a more regular and predictable path (fewer choices or alternatives).

Capital utilization tends to be high, and the process operates at a high, steady pace.

Raw materials inventories tend to increase in size in order to ensure constant availability to keep the process running at a steady pace. However, steady purchases can reduce the size of inventories on hand at any given time.

Work in process inventories decrease in size, since materials and products spend little time waiting between stages of the process.

Finished goods inventories are larger (on average) since they are used to "buffer" the steady pace.

The Information and Decision Systems

As one moves along the spectrum from projects to continuous processes:

Long-term issues such as capacity planning, facilities location, technological change, and long-range forecasting become more important than day-to-day operating considerations.

Monthly and daily scheduling becomes less complex because of the limited variation in job sequences and tasks.

Quality control becomes more formal.

Information flows and coordination between workers and management become less important, simplifying the monitoring of production flows.

The Monetary System

As one moves along the spectrum from projects to continuous process:

Payment systems tend to shift from piece rates to hourly wages and, occasionally, to weekly or monthly salaries.

The cost structure of the operation tends to have a higher proportion of fixed costs and lower proportion of variable costs.

Control of capital and material costs tend to be more critical to financial success than labor costs.

The generalizations offered here are but a sample of the differences to be found in comparing production processes. As students work through the cases in this volume they will be able to develop their own insights and basis for comparison. It should be noted, however, that, while the choice of the appropriate process design to deliver the desired product or service characteristics may determine some part of the management task, it is only the first step in operations management. Once a process design has been chosen, many other decisions remain, for operating systems do not exist in static settings. Much of operations management, in fact, is concerned with dealing with variability, uncertainty, and contingencies.

The sources of variation and uncertainty are many: the overall demand for output may dramatically increase or decrease over time; the mix of products to be produced may shift; deliveries from vendors may be late; worker productivity may, for a host of reasons, decline or improve sharply; a new technology may become available; or quality problems may suddenly appear. These contingencies fall under a variety of different headings; among the most important are aggregate capacity planning, scheduling, operations control, inventory and materials management, technology choice, work-force management, and quality assurance. Numerous examples of each are contained in the cases that follow. Few problems, of course, fall exclusively under any one of these headings. A problem that appears to be primarily concerned with difficulties in work-force management (the people system) may find its solution in changes in materials flow (the physical system) or in the kinds of information that managers and workers collect and use (the information system). A new machine introduced into the physical system may have implications for production scheduling (the information and decision systems), for how employees are compensated (the monetary system), and for training and recruitment of the work force (the people system). The task of the operations manager is to ensure that all these systems are in balance and that when changes occur, equilibrium is quickly restored. The cases that follow present a variety of situations in which managers are required to deal with the uncertainties and variability characteristic of the real world of operations management. By working through the cases here, we hope that students will develop a sense of the excitement, challenge, and opportunity that the field of operations management provides.

Blitz Company

In October 1961, Mr. Alfred Jodal, president of the Blitz Company, was reviewing the company's position prior to planning 1962 operations.[1]

THE MARKET

The Blitz Company manufactured electrical circuit boards to the specifications of a variety of electronic manufacturers. Each board consisted of a thin sheet of insulating material with thin metal strips (conductors) bonded to its surface. The insulating sheet acted as a structural member and supported electrical components and fragile conductors which connected the components into an electrical network. A typical example of the products produced by the company was a circuit board consisting of a 4- by 2- by $1/_{16}$-inch plastic plate with 18 separate conductors bonded on its surface, as shown in Exhibit 1. In the customer's plant, assemblers positioned electronic components in the holes on the board, soldered them in place, and installed the assembly in final products such as two-way radios, electronic instruments, and radar equipment. Because circuit boards reduced the labor required in assembling and wiring electrical components, lessened the chances of human errors in assembly, and reduced the size of completed assemblies, the market for circuit boards had grown rapidly since World War II.

Competitive Advantages

Since the start of operations in 1959, the Blitz Company had specialized in making circuit boards for experimental devices and for pilot production

---

[1] All figures have been disguised.

1

EXHIBIT 1
A Typical Circuit Board in Its Stages of Fabrication

Figure a.   The raw material is a plastic sheet with a copper
veneer.

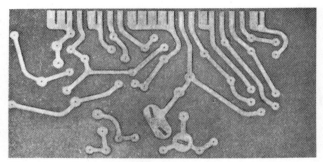

Figure b.   After etching and shearing, only plated conductors
are left on the plastic sheet.

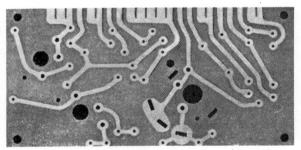

Figure c.   The finished circuit board has been shaped to final
dimensions in a stamping operation and drilled.

runs. Earning statements and a balance sheet are shown in Exhibits 2 and
3. Most of the company's managers were engineers with substantial experience in the electronics industry. Mr. Jodal and the firm's design engineer,
Mr. Krebs, had invented several of the company's processing methods and
had patented applications, processes, and modifications of some commer-

EXHIBIT 2

BLITZ COMPANY
Summary of Profit and Loss Statements

	September 1961	100%	August 1961	100%	July 1961	100%	January–June 1961	100%	1960	1959
Net sales*	$33,201		$34,689		$16,089		$ 78,585		$93,837	$50,778
Direct material:										
Beginning in-process inventory	8,277	24.9	4,743	13.7	3,906	24.3	3,162	4.0	2,511	1,209
From stock and purchases	5,766	17.4	12,462	35.9	4,557	28.3	22,971	29.2	25,947	14,136
Chemicals, film, and supplies	2,325	7.0	3,627	10.5	2,418	15.0	10,044	12.5	6,603	3,999
Shop wages and foreman's salary	6,231	18.5	5,859	16.9	3,906	24.3	22,692	28.9	29,016	16,275
Overtime wages	279	0.8	1,023	2.9	0	0.0	1,023	1.3	n.a.	n.a.
Other expenses†	1,488	4.5	1,116	3.2	930	5.8	6,231	7.9	7,254	3,534
Total	24,366	73.4	28,830	83.1	15,717	97.7	66,123	84.1	71,331	39,153
Less closing in-process direct material	(6,603)	19.9	(8,277)	23.9	(4,743)	29.5	(3,906)	5.0	(3,162)	(2,511)
Cost of goods manufactured	17,763	53.5	20,553	59.2	10,974	68.2	62,217	79.2	68,169	36,642
Gross profit	15,438	46.5	14,136	40.8	5,115	31.8	16,368	20.8	25,668	14,136
Less company overhead:										
Salaries (administrative, engineering, and office)	4,836	14.6	5,487	15.8	4,278	26.6	25,482	32.4	26,784	11,346
Other (rent, interest, telephone, utilities, etc.)	837	2.5	930	2.7	651	4.1	4,371	5.6	7,812	2,883
Profit or (loss) before taxes	$ 9,765	29.4%	$ 7,719	22.3%	$ 186	1.2%	$(13,485)	(17.2%)	$ (8,928)	$ (93)

* Recorded on day of shipment.
† Includes water, heat, power, payroll taxes, group insurance, and depreciation ($279 month in 1961).
n.a. = Not available.
Source: Company records.

EXHIBIT 3

BLITZ COMPANY
Balance Sheet
September 30, 1961

Assets

Current assets:
Cash...................		$13,299
Accounts receivable...........		53,196
Inventory:		
Raw material..............	$ 2,976	
Supplies..................	2,232	
In process................	6,603	11,811
Prepaid expenses..............		2,325
Total current assets........		$ 80,631

	Cost	Depre-ciation	
Fixed assets:			
Buildings...................	$14,880	$ 1,953	
Machinery..................	15,531	3,162	
Small tools.................	2,325	2,232	
Office equipment.............	3,627	651	
	36,363	7,998	
Total fixed assets..........			28,365
Total assets...................			$108,996

Liabilities

Current liabilities:		
Accounts payable.............	$24,180	
Commissions...............	6,231	
Taxes payable...............	3,069	
Notes payable...............	14,229	
Total current liabilities.....		$ 47,709
Long-term notes...............		2,604
Net worth:		
Capital stock................	63,519	
Deficit 1/1/61................	(9,021)	
Profit for year...............	4,185	58,683
Total liabilities and net worth.....		$108,996

Source: Company records.

cial machinery. The president believed that the Blitz Company was therefore more adept than its competitors in anticipating and resolving the problems inherent in new designs and production techniques.

MANUFACTURING PROCESS

The manufacturing process was divided into three stages: preparation, image transfer, and fabrication. In the first stage, patterns, jigs, and fixtures were produced and raw material was prepared for processing. The next step, image transfer, yielded a sheet of plastic with appropriate conductors bonded on the surface. In the final stage, this material was transformed into shaped, drilled, and finished circuit boards. The most common sequence of operations is listed in Exhibit 4.

Preparation Stage

The pattern used in the image transfer stage was made by photographing the customer's blueprint and producing a "panel" negative showing a number of the circuits in actual size, side by side, on a 12- by 18-inch film. This negative was then used in conjunction with a light-sensitive chemical (KPR), as described later in the case. In other preparatory steps, simple drilling jigs and fixtures and routing fixtures for the fabrication operations were made using bench drills, a circular saw, a band saw, and hand tools. Stamping dies, when required, were obtained from subcontractors.

The principal raw material used by the company consisted of plastic panels with a thin sheet of copper facing bonded to one surface. This material was usually purchased in sheets of desired thickness measuring approximately 48 by 36 inches. In the preparation stage, these sheets were inspected visually for flaws and were then cut on a shear into smaller panels measuring approximately 12 by 18 inches. The panel's exact dimensions were chosen by the operator so that the maximum number of circuit boards could be obtained from the sheets. Location holes, used to facilitate positioning in later processes, were then drilled in each panel.

Image Transfer

In the image-transferring process, the panels were washed, dipped into a solution of a light-sensitive chemical (KPR), and baked. A panel negative was then laid over the KPR-coated copper surface and the assembly was exposed to ultraviolet light for two minutes. A finishing dip in a solvent removed that portion of the KRP coating which had been covered by the dark portions of the negative and had not been exposed to the ultra-violet light. After this step, the areas of the panel's copper surface corresponding to the desired conductors remained bare.

EXHIBIT 4

Operation	Standard Production Times (minutes)		September's Production		September's Total Standard Production (minutes)			(hours)
	Setup	Run	Orders	Circuits	Setup	Run	Total	Total
Photograph	29	0	59	4,690	1,710	0	1,710	28.5
Inspect and shear	20	0.5*	60	5,740	1,200	360	1,560	26.0
Drill (location holes)	10	0.5*	60	5,740	600	360	960	16.0
KPR	1	10*	60	5,740	60	7,200	7,260	121.0
Touch-up and inspect	10	3*	60	5,740	600	2,150	2,750	45.8
Plate	10	5*	52	5,616	520	3,510	4,030	67.2
Etch	10	4*	59	5,739	590	2,870	3,460	57.7
Shear (into circuit boards)	10	0.5*	56	5,828	560	360	920	15.3
Drill (location holes)	10	0.5†	53	5,709	530	2,855	3,385	56.4
Configuration:								
Rout	50†	1†	49	2,380	2,450	2,380	4,830	80.5
Punch press	150	0.6†	4	3,329	600	2,000	2,600	43.3
Drill holes:								
Green pantographic	50†	0.05 per hole	8	1,879§	400	9,400	9,800	163.3
Manual	15	0.10 per hole	40	494	600	4,940	5,540	92.3
Epoxy painting	50†	1†	8	1,000	400	1,000	1,400	23.7
Stake:								
Eyelet	20	0.07 per eye	14	487	280	340	620	10.3
Terminals	20	0.15 per term	3	257	60	40	100	1.7
Solder	30	1.5†	8	1,233	240	1,850	2,090	34.8
Inspect and pack	10	1.5†	60	5,740	600	8,610	9,210	153.5
Total					12,000	50,225	62,225	1,037.3

* Per panel.
† Per circuit board.
‡ Includes time for jigs and fixtures.
§ Only lots of more than 100 boards were drilled on this machine. This time is for each board. It was estimated by assuming more than one board would be drilled at a time.
Assumptions: Eight circuit boards per panel; 100 holes per circuit board; 10 eyelets and 1 terminal per circuit board.
Source: Prepared by case writer from company production records and standard times estimated by Mr. Jodal.

Next, the bare surfaces (conductors) were protected with a metal plating. The plater inspected each panel, touching up voids in the remaining KPR coating and removing any excess, and then inserted it into a 50-gallon plating tank where a 0.001-inch-thick coating of lead-tin alloy or other metal was deposited on the panel's bare surfaces. In the following etching operation, the plated panels were placed in rubber-coated racks and successively submerged in a coating solvent, a rinse solution, an acid bath, and another rinse. The acid ate away the unprotected copper, thus producing a sheet of plastic with a pattern of plated conductors on its surface.

Fabrication

Subsequently, the etched panels were cut into individual circuit boards on the same shear used previously to cut the plastic sheet into panels. Two location holes were then drilled in each circuit board on a bench press.

Each individual board was then reduced to the desired final size and shape either by die-stamping in a 20-ton punch press or by shaping on a routing machine. The operator of the routing machine (which was similar to a vertical milling machine) placed each circuit board on a fixture which controlled the way it was fed into the cutting tool.

On the average, 100 holes were drilled in each circuit board using either ordinary bench drill presses or the company's modified Green pantographic drill press.[2] An operator using the pantographic press could drill as many as three circuit boards simultaneously by stacking them on top of each other in a fixture positioned on the machine's worktable. The location of all the drilled holes was controlled by a master pattern (a plastic plate with the proper hole pattern drilled in it) mounted alongside the worktable. To position the tool and drill the circuit boards, the operator simply inserted the machine's follower stylus successively into each of the pattern's holes.

After drilling, some circuit boards were coated with an epoxy resin in a painting process to inhibit damage caused by corrosion, scratching, and rough handling.

To assemble eyelets and terminals in the holes of the circuit boards, an operator sat before a simple staking machine and placed the hole to receive an eyelet or terminal on the machine's anvil. Eyelets were fed and positioned automatically, and terminals were positioned manually.

In the soldering operation, each circuit was dipped into a vat of molten solder for a few seconds.

In final inspection, any production employee who had run out of his ordinary work visually checked each finished board for omitted operations, scratches, and poor workmanship. Items passing inspection were wrapped in kraft paper and deposited in a shipping container.

Although the work normally progressed through the sequence of operations described, some orders bypassed two or three operations. For exam-

---

[2] Occasionally these holes were punched out in the preceding stamping operation.

ple, some initial operations were omitted when the customer supplied precut boards or negatives; others were omitted when the customer preferred to do them in his own shop. Occasionally an order was sent ahead and then returned to continue through the normal sequence of processes.

Supervision

Supervisory responsibility for various phases of production was shared by three men: Joseph Hadler, the expediter; Alexander Krebs, the design engineeer; and Michael Beck, the shop foreman. Messrs. Hadler and Krebs reported to the president; Mr. Beck reported to Mr. Krebs.

Mr. Hadler had been hired in August 1961. He kept track of orders in process and initiated action if an order failed to progress through manufacturing satisfactorily. When the foreman's daily progress report (showing the last operation performed on each order) indicated a delay, Mr. Hadler investigated and usually secured the missing supplies or instructions, told the foreman to start the job moving again, or called the customer and advised him of possible late delivery. On average, Mr. Hadler investigated from two to three slow orders each day. In addition, he conferred with the sales manager and president to determine how many small special orders (usually having a four-day delivery date) should be sent into processing.

Mr. Krebs's primary duties were to inspect the customer's blueprints and requirements in order to locate design errors, to determine the best means of processing, and to identify unusual production problems. In addition, he commonly spent 10 hours a week talking with shop employees about these problems and others that cropped up in processing.

Mr. Beck, the foreman, was in charge of all other aspects of manufacturing from the time he received a shop order and blueprints until he shipped the order. In total, Mr. Beck supervised the activities of 20 production employees. Four of these were lead men who spent about 10 percent of their time instructing people in their areas or advising the foreman on various problems.

The Shop Employees

The shop was nonunion, and employees were paid an hourly wage averaging $1.72 per hour. They used simple, manually controlled apparatus to perform light, short-cycle, repetitive tasks and commonly performed two or three different operations every week. Only the photographing, plating, and etching operations were not traded among a number of workers. The photographer alone used the company's camera and darkroom to produce and develop negatives used in image application. The plater and etcher exchanged jobs between themselves, but not with other employees. The usual pattern of work was such that most workers interrupted their tasks from seven to nine times a day to secure more work from another room, to seek advice on a problem, or to deliver completed work to the foreman's desk or other storage area.

Judgment and experience were important in the photographing, plating, and etching processes since the operators had to compensate for such factors as changes in the shop's temperature and the slow deterioration of the chemical action in various solutions. In the other operations, some care was required to position both tools and workpieces accurately and to prevent scratching or marring of the circuit boards. To reduce the chance of damage in transport, panels and circuit boards were moved and stored between operations in racks holding as many as 15 pieces. Some typical operations are shown in Exhibit 5.

Order Processing

As the first step in the preparation of a factory order, Mr. Jodal and Mr. Krebs estimated material and labor costs. These estimates were then used in preparing a bid for the customer. If the customer subsequently accepted the bid, the Blitz Company would promise delivery in three weeks for orders of less than 1,000 boards and five weeks for larger orders. The estimate sheet and blueprint were then pulled from the files by a secretary and delivered to Mr. Krebs, who wrote out detailed material specifications (there were 30 types used by the company) and a factory order showing the delivery date, the number of circuits, the material specifications, and the sequence of operations. The order was then sent to the treasurer, who required one or two days to locate the needed raw material at a low price and to order it. (The materials used in September are shown in Exhibit 8.) A secretary then entered the order in a log and sent the blueprint and factory order to the foreman. Most orders reached the foreman about four days after the bid had been accepted.

Occasionally the president or sales manager promised delivery within four days in order to satisfy the customer's urgent need. These rush orders were expedited by Mr. Krebs. As soon as the order was received, he wrote material specifications, gave the foreman a factory order and a blueprint, and instructed the treasurer to secure material for delivery on the same or following day.

When the foreman, Mike Beck, received a factory order, he used his own judgment in scheduling preparatory work. Usually Mr. Beck delayed his scheduling decision for several days until the raw material arrived from the vendor. He then estimated the labor required in each step, examined the work in process at critical points, estimated the difficulties in meeting the new order's shipping date, weighed the sales manager's priority on orders already in process, guessed at the possibilities of these orders being held up, and then decided when to schedule the order. The foreman spent much of his time determining when to move jobs ahead of others during process and when to shift workers from one operation to another.

EXHIBIT 5
Typical Shop Operations

Figure a. The photographer is inspecting and retouching a panel
negative before sending it on to the image transferring
operations.

Figure b. The plater is examining a panel during the plating operations.
Panels in process appear behind him.

EXHIBIT 5 (*concluded*)

Figure c.   An operator is shaping some circuit boards to
their final configuration and dimensions on the
routing machine.

Figure d.   Two employees are drilling holes in
circuit boards on bench drill presses.

Until a job was shipped, the factory order and blueprints were kept by the foreman, who gave them to any worker requiring information. A ticket denoting the factory order number was kept with the first rack of material as it moved through processing.

Facilities and Layout

When the company moved to its present location in January 1960, Mr. Jodal had chosen a production layout which he felt minimized installation

EXHIBIT 6

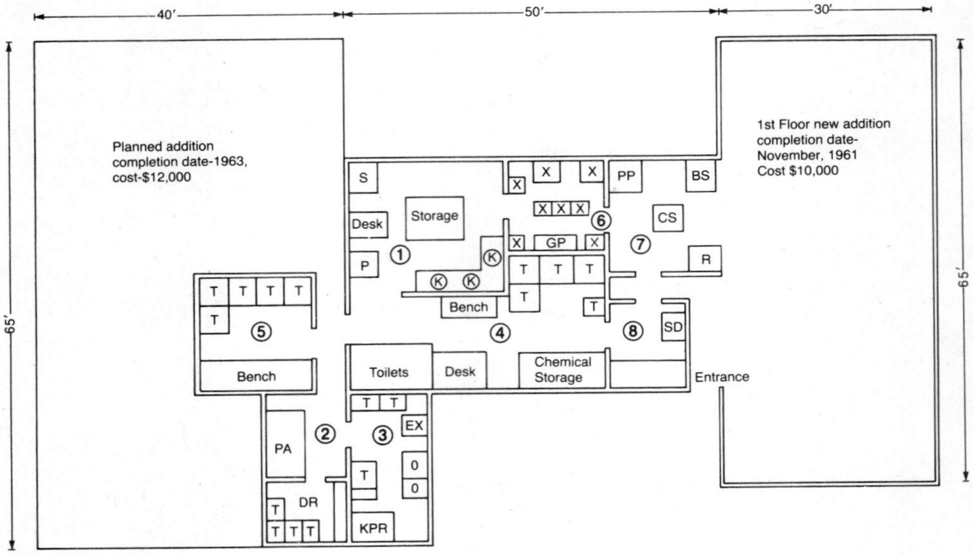

LEGEND

Areas

1. Miscellaneous—foreman's desk, shear, staking, packaging, inspections.
2. Photographic.
3. KPR image application.
4. Touch-up and plating.
5. Etching.
6. Drilling.
7. Other machining operations.
8. Dip solder and research and development laboratory.

Equipment

BS—Band saw.
CS—Circular saw.
DR—Darkroom.
EX—Ultraviolet light exposure table.
GP—Green pantographic press.
K—Eyelet and terminal staking machines.
KPR—KPR tank.
O—Oven.

P—Packing bench.
PA—Photographic apparatus.
PP—Punch press.
R—Routing machine.
S—Shear.
SD—Solder tank.
T—Tanks.
X—Manual drill press.

costs, preserved the life of expensive machines, and isolated the operations' diverse environments (Exhibit 6).[3] Cost had been an important consideration because the company had committed most of its funds for equipment and had not been able to attract outside capital. The plating apparatus had cost about $5,000, while the photographic equipment, the Green pantographic drill press, and the punch press were purchased for approximately $1,500 each. The company had paid an average of $300 apiece for the shear, eight bench-drill presses, the routing machine, band saw, and circular saw; and less than $3,000 (total) for all the other equipment.

Mr. Jodal had spent $1,000 to install the partitions for isolating the production processes. (Recent inquiries indicated that removing these and

_____

[3] This plan shows the location of the addition to the plant due for completion in 1961 as well as a possible second addition projected for 1963.

putting up six other ones would cost about $3,000.) The plating and etching processes, which released acid vapors, had been located far from the machining operations to prevent excessive corrosion of the machine tools. Similarly, the machining operations, which created dust, had been separated from the photography, KPR, plating, and etching processes, which were sensitive to dust and dirt. After a year and a half, neither the machine tools nor the photographic equipment exhibited signs of corrosion. Similarly, dust from the machining areas had not contaminated other processes, although no doors had been installed to seal the passages between the process areas. In October 1961, the company was fully utilizing the space in its existing plant. An 1,800-square-foot addition was due to be completed in November.

CURRENT OPERATING PROBLEMS

In assessing the company's operating position, Mr. Jodal was most concerned about the current difficulties which he described as production bottleneck, performance, quality, and delivery problems.

Production Bottleneck   *Trying to do batch processing in job shop?*

The bottleneck was perplexing because it shifted almost daily from one operation to another, without pattern. Anticipating where work would pile up in the shop on a given day had proven difficult because individual orders imposed varying work loads on each operation. These variations stemmed from differences in order size, from orders bypassing some operations, and from differences in circuit designs. Also contributing to fluctuations were the four-day rush orders (usually three a week), orders requiring rework at one or two operations, and work delayed in process pending a customer's delivery of special eyelets and terminals or a design change (one to nine a week). Approximately one fourth of the jobs delayed in process were held as a result of telephone calls from the customers' engineers who had encountered a problem. Then, any time from one day to two weeks later, the customer would relay permission to complete the order as originally specified or give new specifications. About an equal number of jobs were stopped as a result of processing problems or mistakes made in operations which could be overcome by a specification change. These orders were held until Mr. Krebs could secure permission to deviate from the customer's original specifications.

During the past several months, the foreman had found compensating for these variations increasingly difficult because he had no accurate way of predicting where work would pile up or run out, or of assessing the future effects of any corrective action. A recent Wednesday's events were typical. Early in the morning, three men engaged in manual drilling had run out of work. The foreman, therefore, shifted them to other tasks until other boards could be expedited to the drilling operation. In this case, the foreman decided to meet the situation by expediting two orders which required work in only one or two operations preceding drilling. By midmorning one of the men transferred away from drilling had completed his new assignment and had to be given a different job. In the afternoon, by which time the expedited orders had reached the drilling operation, the foreman found that two employees assigned to certain of the steps which had been bypassed by the expedited orders had run out of work.

Only the small orders (10 circuit boards or less) seemed to pose no scheduling problems. Such orders were always assigned to a senior employee, Arthur Dief, who carried each order from step to step, doing the work himself or having someone else perform it. Dief consistently met delivery deadlines, even on four-day rush orders, and his reject rate was usually zero.

Performance and Methods

Mr. Jodal realized that it was impossible to evaluate shop productivity precisely. However, during his daily trips through the shop he had noticed that several of the machines were idle more often than he would have expected. In commenting on the summary of productive labor shown in Exhibit 4, the president noted that total standard labor hours did not include time which was spent reworking or replacing circuits which failed inspection or were returned by customers. In addition, he believed that the time required to move boards from one operation to another and between elements within an operation was not adequately reflected in the standards. The time standards used in Exhibit 4 were based in part on a synthesis of what they knew to be the standards applied in competing firms (from whom they had hired various workers and supervisors) and in part based on judgments made by Mr. Jodal and Mr. Krebs after long experience gained in performing and observing those jobs in the Blitz Company. In preparing time estimates for bid preparation, Mr. Jodal actually used figures which were substantially above those standards.

The president felt, however, that the job methods in use were far from ideal and that the standards did not reflect improvements which could probably be made in almost any job in the shop. As a specific example, he cited the plating operation. The plater worked at a desk inspecting (touching up) panels and then carried the panels to plating tanks 18 feet away, inserted them, and returned to inspect more panels. He interrupted his work at the desk every three or four minutes to inspect the panels in one of the tanks. Mr. Krebs thought that the plater sometimes spent 15 percent of his time simply walking between the desk and the tanks.

Mr. Jodal suspected that methods improvements were not being introduced because the current pressure for output, the constant shifting of men from job to job, and other immediate problems inhibited experimentation with new ideas. Furthermore, job improvements often seemed, in retrospect, to have created more problems than they solved. For example, those infrequent cases in which improvements had substantially increased production at one station often resulted in work piling up at the following operations. The foreman was then forced to reschedule orders and reassign workers, thus adding to the general confusion and occasionally creating personal friction.

Quality and Delivery Problems

Mr. Sacks, who joined the company as the sales manager in April 1961, was concerned about recent failures in maintaining quality standards and in meeting promised delivery dates. Since August, customer returns had increased from 4 percent to about 8 percent and shipments had averaged nine days late. Mr. Sacks felt that a continuation of these conditions would impede his hope of increasing the present sales volume and achieving the company's sales goals. The sales goals shown in Exhibit 7 had been developed by a local consulting firm in November 1960, after a month's study of the potential market. The sales manager predicted that volume would reach only $600,000 in 1964 if he began promising four-week deliveries on small orders, as four competitors were quoting. If, on the other hand, the com-

EXHIBIT 7

BLITZ COMPANY
Pro Forma Profit and Loss Statements
Prepared by Rothchilde and Rommel, Inc.—Management Consultants
on November 21, 1960
($000)

	1961		1962		1963		1964	
Net sales	$199	100%	$336	100%	$521	100%	$823	100%
Direct material	45	22.4	75	22.4	116	22.3	181	22.0
Chemicals, film, and supplies	17	8.4	32	9.4	56	10.7	74	9.0
Wages and foreman's salary	50	25.2	88	26.3	135	25.9	214	26.0
Other expenses*	11	5.6	18	5.3	28	5.4	47	5.6
Cost of goods sold	123	61.7	213	63.4	335	64.3	516	62.6
Gross profit	76	38.3	123	36.6	186	35.7	307	37.3
Company overhead: Salaries (administrative, engineering, and office)	42	21.0	56	16.6	79	15.2	130	15.8
Other overhead (rent, interest, utilities, etc.)	13	6.5	20	5.8	28	5.4	42	5.1
Profit before taxes	21	10.8	47	14.1	79	15.2	135	16.4

* Water, heat, power, depreciation, etc.
Source: Company records.

pany were able to regain its pre-August delivery performance, Mr. Sacks felt sales should exceed $1.5 million in 1964. Both Mr. Sacks and Mr. Jodal believed that the company should continue to bid only for low-volume, special circuit-board business. Their sales estimates, therefore, were based on an order-size profile similar to that actually produced in September 1961, as shown in Exhibit 8.

Quality

Mr. Jodal was also concerned about the present inspection system in which formal inspections of raw material and finished boards were supple-

EXHIBIT 8
The Order Size and Number of Orders Processed during September 1961

Order Size (number of circuit boards in each order)	Raw Material Code Letters	Number of Orders	Total Number of Circuit Boards
1	A,B,D,E	7	7
2	A,B,F,H	6	12
3	B,D	2	6
4	A,B,C,F,H	11	44
5	A,D	2	10
6	B,C	2	12
10	B,D,E	3	30
11	D,F	2	22
12	A,J,K	3	36
14	A,E,G	3	42
20	D	1	20
40	B,K	2	80
50	C,E	2	100
60	C	1	60
84	J	1	84
100	C	1	100
113	E	1	113
136	C	1	136
140	F	1	140
154	A	1	154
200	D	1	200
229	E	1	229
252	A	1	252
800	G	1	800
1,000	D,M	2	2,000
1,050	A	1	1,050
		60	5,739

Source: Company records.

mented by each worker's informal examination of the units as they moved through processing. The president felt that any effort to specify quality standards more exactly and to enforce them more rigorously might not be feasible because the standards varied from customer to customer and even from order to order. For example, in one recent episode a customer's engineers had praised the quality of the Blitz Company's work on one order even though the boards were scratched and marred and had one or two holes located out of tolerance. A week later, other engineers at the same company had rejected 25 apparently perfect boards because one conductor on each had a single 0.005- by 0.010-inch nick in it.

One tenth of the boards returned were damaged or out of tolerance. The remainder were returned because the Blitz Company had failed to perform one or two required operations. These boards were reprocessed and shipped within one or two days. The company's preshipment reject rate in September amounted to 7 percent, of which 4 percent were total losses and 3 percent were missing operations.

Deliveries

Mr. Jodal had always emphasized a shipping policy aimed at clearing all the work possible out of the shop prior to the end of each month. As a result, substantially fewer shipments were made in the first half of each month than in the second half, as shown in Exhibit 9. Actual deliveries in August, September, and the first part of October had averaged 10, 8, and 9 days late, respectively. During the period, the company had continued its historical practice of quoting three weeks' delivery on orders of less than 1,000 circuit boards and five weeks on larger orders. In August, when deliveries climbed to a volume of $34,700, eight new people had been added to the production force. Mr. Jodal observed that the eight workers had developed some skill by the second week in August but believed that they would require three months to become as skilled as the company's more senior employees.

18

EXHIBIT 9
Value of Actual Shipments in September 1961

Date	Daily	Cumulative
1	$ 2,957	$ 2,957
4	(316)*	2,641
5	1,079	3,720
6	451	4,171
7	592	4,763
8	2,242	7,005
11	637	7,642
12	(182)	7,460
13	681	8,141
14	1,576	9,717
15	(39)	9,678
18	1,051	10,729
19	3,515	14,244
20	2,678	16,922
21	1,479	18,401
22	605	19,006
25	47	19,053
26	(353)	18,700
27	(2,121)	16,579
28	4,771	21,350
29	11,851	33,201

* Negative shipments, shown by parentheses, indicate that receipts returned for rework or refabrication exceeded shipments.

Source: Company records.

CASE 2

Benihana of Tokyo

"Some restaurateurs like myself have more fun than others," said Hiroaki (Rocky) Aoki, youthful president of Benihana of Tokyo. From 1964 to 1972, he had gone from a deficit net worth to becoming president of a chain of 15 restaurants which grossed over $12 million per year. He sported a $4,000 sapphire ring, maintained a $250,000 home, kept five cars including three Rolls Royces. One wall of his office was completely covered with photographs of Rocky with famous personalities who have eaten at a Benihana. Rocky firmly believed, "In America, money is always available if you work hard."

BACKGROUND

Benihana was basically a steakhouse with a difference—the food was cooked in front of the customer by native Japanese chefs and the decor was that of an authentically detailed Japanese country inn. From a humble 40-seat unit opened in midtown Manhattan in 1964, Benihana had grown to a chain of 15 units across the country. Nine were company-owned stores: New York (3); San Francisco; Chicago; Encino and Marina del Rey, California; Portland, Oregon; and Honolulu. Five were franchised: Boston; Fort Lauderdale; Beverly Hills; Seattle; and Harrisburg, Pennsylvania. The most recent store, Las Vegas, was operated as a joint venture with Hilton Hotels Corporation. Rocky, who was a former Olympic wrestler, described his success as follows:

> In 1959, I came to the United States on a tour with my university wrestling team. I was 20 at the time. When I reached New York, it was love at first sight! I was convinced that there were more opportunities for me in America than in Japan. In fact, the minute I was able to forget that I was Japanese, my success began. I decided to enroll in the School of Restaurant Management

at City College basically because I knew that in the restaurant business I'd never go hungry. I earned money those early years by washing dishes, driving an ice cream truck, and acting as a tour guide. Most importantly, I spent three years making a systematic analysis of the U.S. restaurant market. What I discovered was that Americans enjoy eating in exotic surroundings but are deeply mistrustful of exotic foods. Also I learned that people very much enjoy watching their food being prepared. So I took $10,000 I had saved by 1963 and borrowed $20,000 more to open my first unit on the West Side and tried to apply all that I had learned.

The origins of the Benihana of Tokyo actually dated back to 1935. That was when Yunosuke Aoki (Rocky's father) opened the first of his chain of restaurants in Japan. He called it Benihana, after the small red flower that grew wild near the front door of the restaurant.

The elder Aoki ("Papasan"), like his son who was to follow in the family tradition, was a practical and resourceful restaurateur. In 1958, concerned about rising costs and increased competition, he first incorporated the hibachi table concept into his operations. Rocky borrowed this method of cooking from his father and commented as follows:

> One of the things I learned in my analysis, for example, was that the number one problem of the restaurant industry in the United States is the shortage of skilled labor. By eliminating the need for a conventional kitchen with the hibachi table arrangement, the only "skilled" person I need is the chef. I can give an unusual amount of attentive service and still keep labor cost to 10 percent to 12 percent of gross sales (food and beverage), depending whether a unit is at full volume. In addition, I was able to turn practically the entire restaurant into productive dining space. Only about 22 percent of the total space of a unit is back-of-the-house, including preparation areas, dry and refrigerated storage, employee dressing rooms, and office space. Normally a restaurant requires 30 percent of its total space as back-of-the-house.
>
> The other thing I discovered was that food storage and waste contribute greatly to the overhead of the typical restaurant. By reducing my menu to only three simple "Middle American" entrees—steak, chicken, and shrimp—I have virtually no waste and can cut food costs to between 30 and 35 percent of food sales depending on the price of meat.
>
> Finally, I insist on historical authenticity. The walls, ceilings, beams, artifacts, and decorative lights of a Benihana are all from Japan. The building materials are gathered from old houses there, carefully disassembled and shipped in pieces to the United States where they are reassembled by one of my father's two crews of Japanese carpenters.

Rocky's first unit on the West Side was such a success that it paid for itself in six months. He then built in 1966 a second unit three blocks away on the East Side simply to cater to the overflow of the Benihana West. The Benihana East quickly developed a separate clientele and prospered. In 1967, Barron Hilton, who had eaten at a Benihana, approached Rocky concerning the possibility of locating a unit in the Marina Towers in Chicago. Rocky flew to Chicago, rented a car, and while driving to meet Mr. Hilton saw a vacant site. He immediately stopped, called the owner, and signed a lease the next day. Needless to say, a Benihana didn't go into the Marina Towers.

The Chicago unit had proven to be the company's largest money maker in 1972. It was an instant success and grossed approximately $1.3 million per year. The food and beverage split was 70 percent and 30 percent; and management was able to keep food (30 percent), beverage (20 percent),

EXHIBIT 1
Operating Statistics for a Typical Service Restaurant

	Ranges (percent)	Benihana
Sales:		
Food	70.0–80.0	70
Beverage	20.0–30.0	30
Total sales	100.0	
Cost of sales:		
Food cost (raw food from suppliers; percent of food sales)	38.0–48.0	30–35%
Beverage cost (percent of beverage sales)	25.0–30.0	20%
Total cost of sales	35.0–45.0	
Gross profit	55.0–65.0	
Operating expenses:		
Controllable expense:		
Payroll	30.0–35.0	10%
Employee benefits	3.0–5.0	
Employee meals	1.0–2.0	
Laundry, linen, uniforms	1.5–2.0	
Replacements	0.5–1.0	
Supplies (guest)	1.0–1.5	
Menus and printing	0.25–0.5	
Miscellaneous contract expense (cleaning, garbage, extermination, equipment rental)	1.0–2.0	
Music and entertainment (where applicable)	0.5–1.0	
Advertising and promotion	0.75–2.0	10%
Utilities	1.0–2.0	
Management salary	2.0–6.0	
Administration expense (including legal and accounting)	0.75–2.0	
Repairs and maintenance	1.0–2.0	
Occupation expense:		
Rent	4.5–9.0	5%
Taxes (real estate and personal property)	0.5–1.5	
Insurance	0.75–1.0	
Interest	0.3–1.0	
Depreciation	2.0–4.0	
Franchise royalties (where applicable)	3.0–6.0	
Total operating expenses	55.0–65.0	
Net profit before income tax	0.5–9.0	

Source: Bank of America *Small Business Reporter*, vol. 8, no. 2, 1968.

EXHIBIT 2

A typical Benihana floor plan

2   Towel washer by Hamilton.
3   Worktable, custom.
4   Worktable, custom.
5   Three compartment sink, custom.
6   Double overshelf, custom.
6   Double slant overshelf, custom.
8   Rice stocker, custom.
9   Rice cooker.
10 Range with oven by Vulcan Hart.
11 Stock pot stove by Vulcan Hart.
12 Swing faucet.
13 Exhaust hood, custom.
15 Reach-in refrigerator by Traulsen.
16 Scale by Howe Richardson.
17 Combination walk-in cooler-freezer by Bally.
18 Adjustable modular shelving by Market Forge.
19 Adjustable modular shelving by Market Forge.
20 Shelf, custom.
21 Dishwasher with electric booster by Champion.
22 Soiled-dish table with pre-rinse sink, custom.
23 Slant overshelf, custom.
24 Clean-dish table, custom.
25 Exhaust hood, custom.
26 Double wallshelf, custom.
27 Twin soup urn by Cecilware.
28 Single tea urn by Cecilware.
29 Towel warmer.
30 Water station with sink, custom.
31 Rice warmer.
32 Utility table, custom.
33 Double wallshelf, custom.

34 Two-compartment sink, custom.
35 Overshelf, custom.
46 Worktable, custom.
37 Open-front cold cast with adjustable shelves by Tyler.
38 Double overshelf, custom.
39 Pre-check register, by NCR.
40 Utility table with Dipperwell, custom.
41 Double overshelf, custom.
42 Ice cream dipping cabinet by Schaefer.
43 Ice cream storage cabinet by Schaefer.
44 Double wallshelf, custom.
45 Reach-in freezer by Traulsen.
46 Ice cube maker by Kold Draft.
47 Ice crusher by Scotsman.
48 Adjustable modular shelving by Market Forge.
49 Pass-through refrigerator by Traulsen.
50 Sake warmer.
51 Cash register by NCR.
52 Underbar workboard by Perlick.
54 Back bar refrigerator by Perlick.
56 Underbar bottle cooler by Perlick.
57 Remote soda system dispensing station by Perlick.
58 Remote soda system power pak with stand by Perlick.
59 Pre-check register by NCR.
60 Cash register by NCR.
61 Shelving, custom.
62 Glasswasher by Dorex.
63 Time clock.
64 Telephone shelf booth.
65 Platform truck by Roll A. Liss.
66 Utility table, custom.

labor (10 percent), advertising (10 percent), and rent (5 percent) expense percentages of sales at relatively low levels.[1] Operating statistics for a typical service restaurant are included in Exhibit 1.

The fourth unit was located in San Francisco, and the fifth was a joint venture with International Hotel in Las Vegas in 1969. By this time literally hundreds of people were clamoring for franchises. Rocky sold a total of six franchises until he decided in 1970 that it would be much more to his advantage to own rather than to franchise additional stores. Following are the franchises that were granted: Puerto Rico (not successful due to economic turndown); Harrisburg, Pennsylvania; Ft. Lauderdale; Portland (company bought the unit back); Seattle; Beverly Hills; and Boston.

The decision to stop franchising occurred because of a number of problems. First, all the franchises were bought by investors, none of whom had any restaurant experience. Second, it was difficult for the American in-

[1] Food and beverage percentages are based on food and beverage revenues, respectively. Labor, advertising, and rent percentages are based on total revenue.

EXHIBIT 2 (*concluded*)

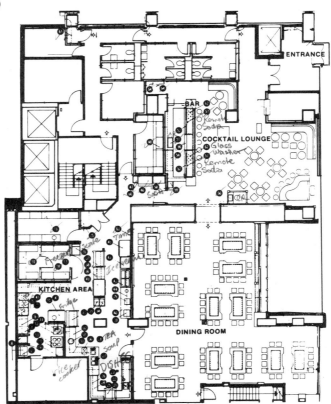

vestor to relate to a predominantly native Japanese staff. Finally, control was considerably more difficult to maintain with a franchisee than with a company-employee manager. During the period to 1970, several groups attempted to imitate the Benihana success. One group, including several individuals with an intimate knowledge of the Benihana operation, set up a competing concept in very close proximity to an existing Benihana unit. However, they folded within the year. Bolstered by the confidence that the Benihana success could not be easily replicated, management felt that one of the classic pressures to franchise was eliminated, i.e., the desire to expand rapidly to preempt competitors.

The proportion of the total space devoted to the bar (lounge) holding area indicated when the unit was built. When Rocky opened his first unit, he saw the business as primarily food-service sales. The Benihana West had a tiny bar which seated about eight and had no lounge area. Rocky quickly learned that the amount of bar space was insufficient, and in the second unit, Benihana East, he doubled the size of the bar/lounge area. But since the whole unit was larger, the ratio of space was not too different. A typical floor plan is included as Exhibit 2.

Rocky's third Manhattan operation, called Benihana Palace, opened in 1970. Here, the lounge area was enormous, even in ratio to size. Beverage revenues bore out the wisdom of the design. At Benihana West, beverage sales represented about 18 percent of total sales. At East, they ran 20 to 22 percent. And at the Palace, they ran a handsome 30 to 33 percent of total sales. The beverage cost averaged 20 percent of beverage sales.

The heart of the "show biz" was in the dining area. The "teppanyaki" table was comprised of a steel griddle plate with a 9½-inch wooden ledge bordering it to hold the ware. It was gas fired. Above every table was an exhaust hood to remove cooking steam and odors and much of the heat from the griddle. Service was by a chef and waitress; each such team handled two regular tables.

The four food items (steak, filet mignon, chicken, and shrimp) could either be had as a single entree item or in combinations. A full dinner had three, with the shrimp as appetizer. The accompaniments were unvaried: bean sprouts, zucchini, fresh mushrooms, onions, and rice, cooked on the grill.

Normally, a customer could come in, be seated, have dinner, and be on his way out in 45 minutes, if need be. The average turnover including drinks was 1 hour, up to 1½ hours in slow periods.

The average check, including food and beverage, ran about $6 at lunch, about $10 at dinner. These figures included a drink (average price $1.50) at lunch, an average of one-plus at dinner.

The big purchase was meat. Only USDA prime grade, tightly specified tenderloin and boneless strip loins were used. The steaks were further trimmed in-house. Only a bit of fat at the tail was left, and this was for effect. When the chef started cooking the meat, he dramatically trimmed this part off and pushed it aside before cubing the remaining meat.

The hours of operation for the 15 units varied according to local requirements. All were open for lunch and dinner, though not necessarily every day for each. Lunch business was considered important; overall it accounted for about 30 to 40 percent of the total dollar volume despite a significantly lower check average. Essentially the same menu items were served for both meals; the lower menu price average at lunch reflected smaller portions and fewer combinations.

SITE SELECTION

Because of the importance of lunch-time business, Benihana had one basic criterion for site selection—high traffic. Management wanted to be sure that a lot of people were nearby or going by both at lunch and at dinner. Rent normally ran 5–7 percent of sales for 5,000–6,000 square feet of floor space. Most units were located in a predominately business district, though some had easy access to residential area. Shopping center locations were considered, but none accepted as of 1972.

TRAINING

Because the chefs were considered by Benihana to be a key to its success, they were very highly trained. All were young and single native Japanese, and all "certified," which meant that they had completed a formal apprenticeship. They were then given a course in Japan in the English language and American manner as well as the Benihana form of cooking, which was mostly showmanship. The chefs were brought to the United States under a "trade treaty" agreement.

Training of the chefs within the United States was a continuous process also. In addition to the competition among the chefs to perfect their art in hopes of becoming the chief chef, there was also a traveling chef who inspected each unit periodically as well as being involved in the grand opening of new units.

While Benihana found it relatively difficult to attract chefs and other personnel from Japan due to the general level of prosperity there as well as competition from other restaurants bidding for their talents, once in the United States they were generally not anxious to leave. This was due to several factors. One was the rapidity with which they could rise in the U.S. Benihana operation versus the rather rigid hierarchy based on class, age, and education they would face in Japan. A second and major factor was the paternal attitude that Benihana took toward all its employees. While personnel were well paid in a tangible sense, a large part of the compensation was intangible based on job security and a total commitment of Benihana to the well-being of its employees. As a result, turnover of personnel within the United States was very low, although most did eventually return to Japan. To fully appreciate the Benihana success, one must appreciate the unique combination of Japanese paternalism in an American setting. Or, as Rocky put it, "At Benihana we combine Japanese workers with American management techniques."

ORGANIZATION AND CONTROL

Each restaurant carried a simple management structure. It had a manager ($15,000 per year), an assistant manager ($12,000 per year), and two to three "front men" ($9,000 per year) who might be likened to maitre d's. These latter were really potential managers in training. All managers reported to the manager of operations, Allen Saito, who, in turn, reported to Bill Susha, vice president in charge of operations and business development (see Exhibit 3).

Susha came with Benihana in 1971, following food and beverage experience with Hilton, Loew's, and the Flagship Hotel division of American Airlines. He described his job as follows:

> I see management growth as a priority objective. My first step was to establish some sort of control system by introducing sales goals and budgets.

EXHIBIT 3
Organization, 1972

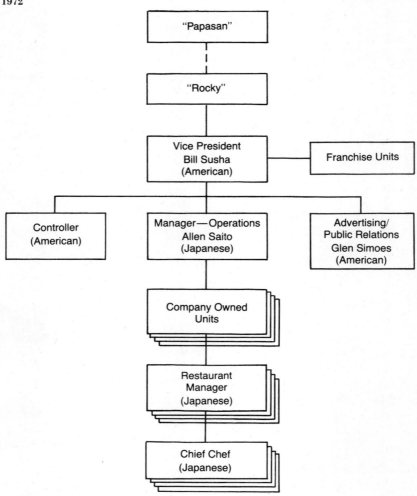

At the most recent manager workshop meeting in New York, with managers attending from all over the country, I asked each to project his sales goal on an annual basis, then break it out by month, then by week, then by day. After I reached agreement with a manager on the individual quota figures, I instituted a bonus plan. Any unit that exceeds its quota on any basis (daily, weekly, monthly, yearly) will get a proportionate bonus, which will be prorated across the entire staff of the unit. I've also built up an accounting staff and controller to monitor our costs. It's been a slow but steady process. We have to be very careful to balance our needs for control with the amount of overhead we can stand. We can justify extra "front men" standing around in the units. At the corporate level, however, we have to be very careful. In fact, at present the company is essentially being run by three people—Rocky, myself, and Allen Saito.

ADVERTISING POLICY

Rocky considered that a vitally import factor in Benihana's success was a substantial investment in creative advertising and public relations. The company invested 8–10 percent of its gross sales on communications with the public.

Glen Simoes, the director of advertising and public relations, summed it up as follows:

> We deliberately try to be different and original in our advertising approach. We never place advertisements on the entertainment pages of newspapers on the theory that they would be lost among the countless other restaurant advertisements.
>
> We have a visual product to sell. Therefore, Benihana utilizes outstanding visuals in its ads. The accompanying copy is contemporary, sometimes offbeat. A recent full-page advertisement which appeared in *The New York Times, Women's Wear Daily,* and *New York Magazine* did not contain the word restaurant. We also conduct a considerable amount of market research to be sure we know who our customers really are.

Exhibit 4 shows the results of Benihana's market research. The Benihana advertising philosophy is summarized in Exhibit 5. Exhibits 6, 7, and 8 are examples of Benihana advertising copy.

FUTURE EXPANSION

Bill Susha summed up the future of Benihana as he saw it:

> I think the biggest problem facing us now is how to expand. We tried franchising and decided to discontinue the program for several reasons. Most of our franchisees were businessmen looking for investment opportunities and did not really know and understand the restaurant business; this was a problem. The Japanese staff we provided were our people, and we have obligations to them that the franchisee could not or would not cope with which at the time made us unhappy. The uniqueness of our operation in the hands of novices to the business made control more difficult, and finally, we found it more profitable to own and operate the restaurants ourselves.
>
> Presently, we are limited to opening only five units a year because that is as fast as the two crews of Japanese carpenters we have can work. We are facing a decision and weighing the advantages and disadvantages of going into hotels with our type of restaurant. We are presently in two Hilton Hotels (Las Vegas and Honolulu) and have recently signed an agreement with Canadian Pacific Hotels. What we have done in these deals is to put "teeth" in the agreements so that we are not at the mercy of the hotel company's management.

EXHIBIT 4

WHAT THE CUSTOMERS THINK

Every food-service operator thinks he knows why customers come to his operation. Benihana, which has served 2¼ million customers in eight years, a high percentage of which were repeat business, thought it knew.

But when he joined as vice president of operations 1½ years ago, Bill Susha wanted to be sure the hallowed presumptions were true.

He devised a questionnaire and arranged that it be handed to departing customers. A remarkable number took the time to fill out and return the form.

The percentage figures shown here are averages of six stores. While there were many variations from unit to unit, the general thrust was constant, so the six-store figures have been averaged to save space.

The six units included the three in New York City, plus Chicago; Encino, California; and Portland, Oregon. The questions and averages are as follows:

Are you from out of town?

Yes	38.6%
No	61.4

Here on:

Business	38.7%
Pleasure	61.3

Do you live in the area?

Live	16.0%
Work	35.9
Both	45.1

Have you been to a Benihana in another city?

Yes	22.9%
No	77.3

How did you learn of us?

Newspaper	4.0%
Magazine	6.9
Radio	4.6
Recommended	67.0
TV show	1.0
Walk by	5.0
Other	11.5

Is this your first visit?

Yes	34.3%
No	65.7

What persuaded you to come?

Good food	46.7%
Service	8.2
Preparation	13.1
Atmosphere	13.3
Recommendation	5.7
Other	13.1

Would you consider yourself a lunch or dinner customer?

Lunch	17.3%
Dinner	59.0
Both	23.7

Which aspect of our restaurant would would you highlight?

Food	38.2%
Atmosphere	13.0
Preparation	24.6
Service	16.3
Different	2.2
Friendly	2.4
Other	3.3

How frequently do you come to Benihana?

Once a week or more	12.1%
Once a month or more	32.5
Once a year or more	55.6

Age:

10–20	4.2%
21–30	28.3
31–40	32.0
41–50	21.4
51–60	10.1
60 and over	4.0

Sex:

Male	71.4%
Female	28.6

EXHIBIT 4 (*concluded*)

Food was:

Good	2.0%
Satisfactory	20.1
Excellent.	77.9

Portions were:

Satisfactory	21.8%
Good	33.0
Excellent.	45.4

Service was

Satisfactory	9.8%
Good	21.5
Excellent.	71.3

Atmosphere is:

Satisfactory	6.3%
Good	29.9
Excellent.	63.2

Income:

$7,500–$10,000	16.8%
$10,000–$15,000	14.2
$15,000–$20,000	17.3
$20,000–$25,000	15.0
$25,000–$40,000	17.9
$40,000 and over.	18.7

Occupation:

Managerial	23.0%
Professional	20.6
White collar.	36.9
Student.	6.9
Housewife	5.0
Unskilled	1.1

Further, one of our biggest constraints is staff. Each unit requires approximately 30 people who are all Oriental. Six to eight of these are highly trained chefs.

Finally, there is the cost factor. Each new unit costs us a minimum of $300,000. My feeling is that we should confine ourselves to the major cities, like Atlanta, Dallas, St. Louis, etc., in the near future. Then we can use all these units to expand into the suburbs.

We've been highly tempted to try to grow too fast without really considering the full implications of the move. One example was the franchise thing, but we found it unsatisfactory. Another example is that a large international banking organization offered to make a major investment in us which would have allowed us to grow at a terrific rate. But when we looked at the amount of control and autonomy we'd have to give up, it just wasn't worth it, at least in my mind.

Another thing I'm considering is whether it's worth it to import every item used in construction from Japan to make a Benihana 100 percent "authentic." Does an American really appreciate it, and is it worth the cost? We could use material available here and achieve substantially the same effect. Also is it worth it to use Japanese carpenters and pay union carpenters to sit and watch? All these things could reduce our construction costs by 50 percent and allow us to expand much faster.

Rocky described his perception of where the firm should go as follows:

I see three principal areas for growth: United States, overseas, and Japan. In the United States, we need to expand into the primary marketing areas Bill talked about that do not have a Benihana. But I think through our franchises we also learned that secondary markets such as Harrisburg, Pennsylvania, and Portland, Oregon, also have potential. While their volume potential obviously will not match that of a primary market, these smaller units offer

EXHIBIT 5
Summary of Benihana Marketing Philosophy

NO ICKY, STICKY, SLIMY STUFF

"Part of what makes Benihana successful," Rocky Aoki believes, "is our advertising and promotion. It's different, and it makes us seem different to people."

Indeed it is, and does. Much of the credit belongs to Glen Simoes, the hip director of advertising and public relations for Benihana of Tokyo. With a background mostly in financial public relations, Simoes joined the chain a little over two years ago to help open the flagship Benihana Palace. Since then, he's created a somewhat novel, all-embracing public relations program that succeeds on many levels.

"My basic job," he explains, "is guardian of the image. The image is that of a dynamic chain of Japanese restaurants with phenomenal growth." Keeping the image bright means exposure. Part of the exposure is a brilliant advertising campaign; part is publicity.

Each has its own function. Advertising is handled by Kracauer and Marvin, an outside agency, under Simoes' supervision and guidance. Its function is to bring in new customers.

"Our ads," Simoes points out, "are characterized by a bold headline statement and an illustration that make you want to read on. The copy itself is fairly clever and cute. If it works properly, it will keep you reading until you get the message—which is to persuade a stranger to come into Benihana.

"The ads are designed to still fears about icky, sticky, slimy stuff," he adds. "We reassure folks that they will get wholesome, familiar food, with unusual, unique, and delicious preparation, served in a fun atmosphere. We want to intrigue the people celebrating an anniversary or taking Aunt Sally out to dinner. A Japanese restaurant would normally never cross their minds. We're saying we're a fun place to try, and there's no slithery, fishy stuff.

"We have an impact philosophy. We go for full pages in national publications on a now-and-then basis, rather than a regular schedule of small ads. We want that impact to bring the stranger into Benihana for the first time. After that, the restaurant will bring him back again and again, and he will bring his friends."

"We do a good media mix," Simoes concludes. "We advertise in each of the cities in which we operate. Within each market we aim for two people: the resident, of course, but even more, the tourist-visitor. With them you know you're always talking to new people. We appear in city entertainment guides and work with convention and visitor bureaus to go after groups and conventions."

The second factor is publicity. Here, the intent is not the quantity of mentions or exposure, but the type. As Simoes sees it, "We are building. Each mention is a building block. Some are designed to bring customers into the store. Some are designed to bring us prospective financing, or suppliers, or friends, or whatever. We work many ways against the middle. And the middle is the company, the people, Rocky, the growth, and all of it put together that makes the image."

Publicity takes many forms, it's media stories and TV demonstrations. Simoes cites clipping and viewing services to prove that every day of the year something about Benihana appears either in print or on radio or TV, a record he believes is unique. Publicity is department store demonstrations, catering to celebrities, hosting youth groups, sending matchboxes to conventions and chopsticks to ladies clubs,

EXHIBIT 5 (*concluded*)

scheduling Rocky for interviews, and paying publicists to provide one-liners to columnists.

But no engine runs without fuel. And Rocky believes that advertising and promotion are a good investment. He believes so strongly, in fact, that he puts an almost unprecedented $1 million a year into advertising, and probably half that again into promotion, for a total expenditure of nearly 8 percent of gross sales in this area.

A few months back, Simoes, wholeheartedly pitching his company to a skeptical magazine writer, said heatedly there are "at least 25 reasons people come to Benihana." Challenged on the spot, he came back a few days later with a list of 31. They are: (1) the quality of the food; (2) the presentation of the food; (3) the preparation of the food; (4) the showmanship of the chef; (5) the taste of the food; (6) authenticity of construction; (7) authenticity of decor; (8) continuity of Japanese flavor throughout; (9) communal dining; (10) service—constant attention; (11) youthfulness of staff; (12) frequent presence of celebrities; (13) excitement created by frequent promotions; (14) type of cuisine; (15) moderate price; (16) the uniqueness of appeal to the five senses; (17) the recent growth in popularity of things Japanese; (18) quick service; (19) unusual advertising concept; (20) publicity; (21) no stringent dress requirements; (22) recommendations from friends; (23) the basic meal is low calorie; (24) banquet and party facilities; (25) the presence of Rocky Aoki, himself; (26) chance to meet people of the opposite sex; (27) the presence of many Japanese customers (about 20 percent); (28) locations in major cities giving a radiation effect; (29) acceptance of all major credit cards; (30) the informality of the dining experience; and (31) the use of the restaurant as a business tool.

fewer headaches and generate nice profits. Secondary markets being considered include Cincinnati and Indianapolis.

The third principal area I see for growth is in suburbia. No sites have yet been set, but I think it holds a great potential. A fourth growth area, not given the importance of the others, is further penetration into existing markets. Saturation is not a problem as illustrated by the fact that New York and greater Los Angeles have three units each, all doing well.

We are also considering going public someday. In the meantime, we are moving into joint ventures in Mexico and overseas. Each joint venture is unique in itself. We negotiate each on the basis that will be most advantageous to the parties concerned taking into account the contributions of each party in the form of services and cash. Once this is established, we agreee on a formula for profits and away we go.

Four deals have now been consummated. Three are joint ventures outside the country. An agreement has already been reached to open a Benihana in the Royal York Hotel, Toronto, Canada. This will provide the vanguard for a march across Canada with units in or outside Canadian Pacific Hotels.

Second is a signed agreement for a new unit in Mexico City. From here, negotiations are under way on a new hotel to be built in Acapulco. Benihana stands ready to build and operate a unit in the hotel or, if possible, to take over management of the entire hotel. These units would form a base for expansion throughout Mexico.

The third extraterritorial arrangement was recently signed with David Paradine, Ltd., a British firm of investors headed by TV personality David

Frost. Again, this is a joint venture, with the Paradine group to supply technical assistance, public relations, advertising, and financing, Benihana the management and know-how. This venture hopes ultimately to have Benihana restaurants, not only thoughout Great Britian, but across the Continent.

Rocky also had a number of diversification plans:

> We have entered into an agreement with a firm that is researching and contacting large food processors in an effort to interest them into producing a line of Japanese food products under the Benihana label for retail sale. There has been a great deal of interest, and we are close to concluding a deal.
>
> I worry a lot. Right now we cater to a middle-income audience, not the younger generation. That makes a difference. We charge more, serve better

EXHIBIT 6

Go forth now and cook amongst the Americans.

It's not easy earning the right to feed the people of America.

No, it's no picnic getting admitted to the league of Benihana chefs.

First, you must serve a 2 year apprenticeship in Japan. Then you must be accepted at the Benihana College of Chefs in Tokyo. There you have to spend fifteen gruelling weeks under Master Chef Shinji Fujisaku. You don't graduate unless the Master certifies that you've become an absolute whiz at Benihana's special style of Hibachi cooking (Japanese grill cuisine as opposed to classical Japanese cuisine.)

And what are some of the teachings of the Master?

Well, one of the first has to do with the cutting of the meat. "A Benihana chef is an artist, not a butcher," the Master says. So you must learn to wield a knife with dazzling grace, speed and precision. Your hands should move like Fred Astaire's feet.

You also learn that to a Benihana chef, Hibachi cooking is never solemn. As the Master says "It's an act of pure joy." So joy, really, is what you must bring to the Hibachi table. A joy that the people around you can see and feel. A joy they can catch as you sauté those jumbo shrimps. Or as you dust that chicken with sesame seeds. Or as you slam that pepper shaker against the grill and send the pepper swirling over those glorious chunks of steak.

Perhaps most important of all, is this saying of the Master's: "Benihana has no cooks. Only chefs." Which means that while you should be joyous, you must always strive for perfection. So you learn everything there is to learn about sauces and seasonings. You labor to make your shrimp the most succulent shrimp anyone's ever tasted. Your sirloin the most delicious and juicy. Your every mushroom and bean-sprout a song.

Over and over the Master drills you. Again and again you go through your paces. Fifteen exhausting, perfection-seeking weeks.

But the day comes when you're ready. Ready to bring what you've learned to the people of such faraway places as New York, Chicago and Los Angeles. It's a great moment.

"Sayonara, Honorable Teacher," you say.

"Knock 'em dead, Honorable Graduate," he replies.

BENIHANA of TOKYO

quality, have a better atmosphere and more service. But we are in the planning stages for operations with appeal to the younger generation.

For instance, there is no Japanese quick-service operation in this country. I think we should go into a combination Chinese-Japanese operation like this. We might call the concept "the Orient Express." The unit would also feature a dynamic cooking show exposed to the customers. Our initial projections

EXHIBIT 7

It's a little scary at first. There you are sitting around this enormous table (which turns out to also be a grill) when suddenly he appears. A man dressed like a chef but with the unmistakable air of a samurai warrior.

He bows. Just to be on the safe side, you bow back.

Smiling inscrutably, he takes out a knife. You make a grab for your chopsticks.

He reaches into the cart he's wheeled in. From it he brings out rows of these really beautiful fresh whole shrimps.

Suddenly, the man turns into a kind of whirling dervish. Zip.

Zip, zip...his knife flashes through the rows like lightning. The shrimps (now cut into bite-size morsels) seem to dance to the center of the grill. He presses on. With magnificent, sweeping gestures he adds freshly ground pepper to the shrimps. Then butter. Then soy sauce. The action never stops. He even spins around and throws sesame seeds out from over his shoulder.

At last comes the moment of truth. He flips a sizzling shrimp directly on your plate. You taste it. You have a small fit of ecstasy.

Naturally, that's just the first scene. The show goes on this

way...course after course after course. He performs. You eat. He performs again. You eat again. Steak. Chicken. Mouth-watering vegetables of every variety. You've never had such a feast, you've never seen such choreography.

Finally, it's over. He bows. You sigh. He thanks you. You thank him. He walks off.

If you weren't so full you'd get up and give him a standing ovation.

BENIHANA of TOKYO

New York — Benihana Palace 15 W. 44 St., 682-7120 • Benihana East 120 E. 56 St., 593-1627 • Benihana West 61 W. 56 St., 581-0930
Boston, Harrisburg, Fort Lauderdale, Chicago, Seattle, Portland Ore., San Francisco, Las Vegas, Encino, Beverly Hills, Honolulu, Tokyo.

show margins comparable to our present margins with Benihana of Tokyo. I see a check of about 99 cents. We are negotiating with an oil company to put small units in gas stations. They could be located anywhere—on turnpikes or in the Bronx. I think we should do this very soon. I think I will get a small store in Manhattan and try it out. This is the best kind of market research in the United States. Market research works in other countries, but I don't believe in it here.

The restaurant business is not my only business. I went into producing; I had two unsuccessful Broadway shows. The experience was very expensive, but I learned a great deal and learned it very fast. It's all up to the critics there. In the restaurant business, the critics don't write much about you if you're bad; but even if they do, they can't kill you. On Broadway they can. They did.

EXHIBIT 8

The Mission of Rocky Aoki

When Rocky Aoki, owner of Benihana, came to America six years ago, this was how a great many Americans felt about Japanese food:

(1) It wasn't as good as Chinese food.

(2) It was mostly sukiyaki and soup that tasted like hot brown water.

(3) If you ordered anything besides sukiyaki, you'd wind up with raw, slithery fishy things.

(4) OK, the food was very prettily arranged. But you walked out twice as hungry as when you walked in.

(5) It wasn't as good as Chinese food.

"My task is clear," said Rocky. "I'm going to change the way Americans think about Japanese food. I'm going to introduce America to Hibachi cooking."

(Hibachi cooking or cooking on a grill, is nothing at all like the highly stylized classical Japanese cuisine.)

And so, in 1964, Rocky opened the first Benihana. It broke all the rules. You couldn't get suki-yaki there. Or raw fish. There wasn't even a conventional kitchen. You just sat around this big Hibachi table—a combination grill and dining table—and waited for your chef to appear.

When he did, he came bearing a feast. Basket upon basket of beautiful fresh meat,

poultry and vegetables. Then, right in front of you, he sprang into action. Slicing, seasoning and cooking, he prepared your meal with a speed and skill bordering on wizardry.

It was hard to believe. No exquisitely carved carrot slices. No wispy vegetables arranged in perfect flower patterns. Instead, solid food in abundance. Jumbo shrimps sauteed with lemon. Succulent chunks of steak. Young chicken dusted with sesame seeds. Mushrooms, scallions, beansprouts—served not together in some kind of mish-mash, but individually. It was enough to bring joy to the most jaded gourmet, bliss to the most ravenous appetite.

Well, the first New York Benihana was an enormous success. Within a year, Rocky had to open another one. That too became a smash. Soon Rocky was opening a Benihana in Chicago. And then one in San Francisco. And then another in Las Vegas. Today Rocky has Benihanas all over the United States.

Earlier this year, after opening his third New York Benihana—the Benihana Palace—Rocky Aoki declared: "I'll consider my mission accomplished when everyone in America has tried Hibachi cooking at least once."

Come in and give a nice Japanese boy a break.

BENIHANA of TOKYO

No slithery, fishy things.

I promoted a heavyweight boxing match in Japan. It was successful. I am going into promoting in the entertainment field in Japan. I am doing a Renoir exhibition in Japan with an auction over television. I am thinking about buying a Japanese movie series and bringing it here. I am also thinking of opening a model agency, probably specializing in Oriental models.

But everything always works back to Benihana. For instance, if I open a model agency, I will let the girls come to Benihana to eat. Twenty beautiful girls at the restaurant would mean 400 guys, which would mean 600 girls, and so on.

My philosophy of the restaurant business is simply to make people happy. We do it many ways in Benihana. As we start different types of operations, we will try to do it in other ways. I have no real worries about the future. The United States is the greatest country in the world to make money. Anybody can do it who wants to work hard and make people happy.

Russ Carpenter, a consultant and editor for the magazine, *Institutions/ Volume Feeding,* summed up his perceptions as follows:

I basically see two main problems.

What is Benihana really selling? Is it food, atmosphere, hospitality, a "watering hole" or what? Is having entertainment in the lounge, for example, consistent with the overall image? All the advertising emphasizes the chef and the food, but is that really what the public comes for? I don't know. I'm only raising the questions.

The other thing is how do you hedge your bets? Is Benihana really on the forefront of a trend of the future with their limited menu, cooking in front of you, and Oriental atmosphere, or is it just a fad? This relates to whether it should emphasize restaurant operations only.

Metreke Cards

During the first week in January of 1979, workers in the boxing department of Metreke Cards were using three new methods for packing greeting cards and their envelopes prior to shipment to customers. Two of the methods had been installed in the department during the last two weeks of December by Tom Hayes, the company's only industrial engineer, who left the company on December 31 to take a higher level position with another company.

Conrad Lewis, the plant manager, had received a four-page memorandum from Hayes on December 31. The memorandum outlined the methods work which Hayes had done and gave the production figures in the boxing department for December 28, 29, and 30. This memorandum, along with Hayes's working notes, constituted the written records of Hayes's work which were available to Mr. Lewis.

COMPANY BACKGROUND

Metreke Cards was one of several medium-sized companies in the greeting card industry. Its plant in Atlanta, Georgia, produced greeting cards and also a small amount of gift wrapping materials. Metreke was an integrated producer; it designed, printed, and distributed greeting cards to retail outlets.

In recent years, Metreke's sales had been in excess of $30 million. Approximately half these sales were from "seasonal cards," such as those for generally recognized holidays. Christmas cards accounted for one half of all the seasonal sales. The balance of sales were "everyday cards," such as birthday and get-well cards, which exhibited no seasonal sales pattern. At any one time, the company offered for sale about 4,000 different card designs.

The predominant distribution method in the greeting card industry was direct sale to retail outlets. Like Hallmark Cards, the largest company in the industry, Metreke sold exclusively to retail outlets. Most retailers sold the cards from display racks. It was customary for the rack spaces to be allocated to several card manufacturers, with the retailer deciding what percentage of the rack would be supplied by each manufacturer. It was generally conceded in the industry that sales depended on the rack space allocated to a company by retailers.

THE ATLANTA PLANT

Metreke's Atlanta plant was its only production facility in the United States. The two-story plant building was two years old and was located in a suburban area. The second floor housed the art and verse departments, the photographic department, and some of the administrative offices. Printing and other production departments and the main offices were located on the ground floor.

The production of cards began in the art and verse departments where the creative part of the process took place. Cards were printed on offset presses, using plates prepared by a photographic process. After printing, some cards were embossed, and then all the large sheets on which the cards were printed were cut to obtain the single, unfolded cards. The cards were then sorted by design and automatically folded. After folding, the cards were transported to another area where workers applied special effects and tied ribbons where required. Throughout these operations and those that followed, the operators continually inspected the cards, as they handled them, for dirt, oil smears, off-registered colors, wrinkles, process defects, and other faults.

After the cards were completed, they were packed in wooden crates, each of which contained about 2,000 cards. These wooden crates of cards were held in storage before the final counting and packing. Envelopes were held in a separate inventory. Metreke's major supplier of envelopes was located nearby and could deliver envelopes of a requested size within one week after an order was placed. The envelopes were bundled by the supplier in packs of 12, fastened by a paper band.

Mr. Lewis supervised all the production activities on the ground floor. Approximately 1,000 people worked in the plant. Three subordinates reported directly to Mr. Lewis, each responsible for one part of the production process. Bert Starr, one of the three subordinates, had been hospitalized in December with a heart attack. By early January, his condition had improved enough for him to leave the hospital, but it was uncertain when he might be able to return to work. Starr was in charge of the finishing section which included the operations from special effects application through the final shipment. Slightly more than 300 workers worked in the finishing section. Six section heads reported directly to Starr. In January, they were being supervised by the plant manager. One of these section heads, Joan Jenkins, was in charge of the boxing department.

THE BOXING DEPARTMENT

The boxing department prepared both everyday and seasonal cards for the order-filling department. The cards were received in the boxing department in the wooden crates. Envelope bundles were delivered to the department in sizes corresponding to the cards to be processed. The workers in the department counted the cards and placed them in piles of 12. A bundle of envelopes was placed with each pile. The combined stack of 12 cards and 12 envelopes was then placed in a container, which in turn was placed in a corrugated paper box. The corrugated boxes, called shippers, were used for delivery to the order-filling department.

When the shippers went to the order-filling department, they contained only one card design. The order fillers made up shipments to customers by taking containers of card designs from various shippers as prepared by the boxing department and placing them in a shipper which would go to the customer. Orders typically contained as many as 30 different card designs.

A large inventory of cards was kept in the order-filling department so that the boxing department seldom was required to rush through an order of a particular card. The company manufactured seasonal cards far enough ahead so that the total volume of cards through the boxing department was nearly constant throughout the year. This total volume of cards was expected to approximate 800,000 cards per day during the current year. About 48 percent of the cards processed through the boxing department in a year were seasonal cards, and the balance were everyday cards. This proportion was closely maintained throughout the year.

Because of the even volume of cards passing through the boxing department, the work force was held at about 43 people throughout the year. In the month of January, 22 of these laborers were working on everyday cards. In addition to the 43 workers, the department had five materials handlers. The department worked a 7½-hour day, with two 10-minute breaks, which brought actual production time down to 430 minutes per day. The plant workers were members of a union. Their hourly pay was $3.75 per hour.

Up until July of 1978, the boxing department had used a small cardboard box as the container in which the pile of counted cards and the bundle of envelopes were placed. The boxing operation had been accomplished through the use of a conveyor belt with six work positions. The first worker placed the small open box and its cover on the end of the conveyor belt. The next two workers took cards from wooden crates, counted them into stacks, and placed the stacks on the belt. The next worker on the belt placed envelope bundles on top of each pile of cards. The fifth worker placed the combined pile of envelopes and cards into the box and put the lid on the box. The sixth worker removed the boxes from the conveyor and stacked them.

The stacks of filled boxes were then taken to another area in the department where the labels were applied to the ends of boxes. These labels indicated the number and type of cards in the box. Since most orders were very small, the 12-card box provided an acceptable basic shipping quantity for one card design. The small boxes were packed into shippers for delivery to the order-filling department.

THE PAPER PACKER

In an effort to reduce costs, Metreke introduced a paper "packer" as a substitute for the cardboard box to contain the everyday cards. This packer was used for all everyday cards starting in the previous summer. The packer was a manila envelope, with a flap on the long side. One size packer, 8½ inches long, accommodated 90 percent of the cards in the everyday line, and the balance of the designs fitted in a second size packer, 10 inches long, except for about 10 designs which required a box because of their unusual thickness.

By adopting the packer on everyday cards, Metreke was able to replace 102 sizes of the small boxes with two sizes of packers. Whereas the boxes had required 47 sizes of shippers, the packers could be fitted into two sizes of shippers. Metreke also realized savings by eliminating the hand-labeling operation for everyday cards. The packers could be printed within 24 hours to meet the requirements of runs scheduled in the boxing department.

The packers were not introduced in the seasonal line because Metreke feared retailer resistance. When the dealer received everyday cards, he withdrew the cards and envelopes from the packer, placed some in his display rack, placed the balance into numbered files in rack drawers, and threw away the packer. In seasonal cards, however, the dealers purchased ahead in quantities larger than could be displayed or stored in the drawers in the display rack. The retailer could easily stack the small boxes in his storeroom, but the paper packers would be more difficult to store.

When the packer was introduced in the boxing department in July 1978, the method used for packing was a slight adaptation of the method used previously with the boxes. Two of the department's four conveyors were changed to accommodate the packers. The new worker arrangement is shown in Exhibit 1.

The first worker on the belt inserted a bundle of envelopes in a packer and placed the packer on the belt. The next two workers counted out stacks of cards and placed them on the belt. The fourth worker placed a stack of cards in the packer, and the fifth worker folded over the packer flap, removed the packer from the belt, and put it on a table. The sixth worker took the filled packers from the table and packed them in a shipper.

EXHIBIT 1
Layout for the Six-Operator Belt Method

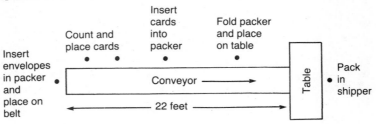

At the time the packers were introduced in the Atlanta plant, Metreke's Canadian affiliate was using the same packer in its boxing department. The Canadian plant was averaging 175 packers per hour for each worker on the line, using the same six-operator method and layout shown in Exhibit 1. Since Metreke had been getting 212 boxes per hour for each worker in the boxing department before shifting to packers, Metreke management was concerned that increased labor costs might offset the savings in changing to the packer. The number of cards contained in either a box or packer was the same.

As the result of a study made by a management trainee, the plant manager authorized two measures intended to reduce costs for filling the packers: one of them based on a simplified manual operation, and the other using a mechanical aid to filling the packers. The first measure was to assign the plant industrial engineer, Tom Hayes, the job of improving the six-operator belt method which was then being used with the packers. The method he developed as a result of this assignment is described below as the "single-operator method." The second measure was the placing of an order for an Aero-Sonic machine. The salesman representing the manufacturer of the Aero-Sonic machine claimed that his company could adapt the machine for use with the packers and that it could produce at a rate of at least 26 packers per minute. On the basis of this claim and the experience of Metreke personnel with other models of the machine, an order was placed for one machine in July 1978.

THE SINGLE-OPERATOR METHOD

As Tom Hayes worked to improve the packing methods, he decided to experiment with a single-operator method. In this arrangement, each laborer worked at a separate table, with all materials supplied to the table by the materials handlers. The materials handlers also took away the finished shippers. Each operator arranged the materials on a table and then filled the packers and placed them in the shipper. Packers, envelopes, and cards were placed by the materials handlers in open boxes along the rear of the

table. The worker first arranged enough packers on the table to fill one
shipper. The operator then placed the same number of envelope bundles
in a loose pile on the right of the packers. The operator reached under the
table to get a shipper from the stack stored there and placed one open
shipper on the table to the left. The operator next reached into the container of cards, took a handful, counted them into stacks of 12, and placed
the stacks on the table beside the envelopes. The operator was then ready
to fill the packers and pack them in the shipper. In his memo and throughout his training of the operators, Hayes emphasized the necessity of ar-
ranging the materials on the table neatly to achieve high output.

Exhibit 2 shows the workplace layout developed by Tom Hayes for the
single-operator method, and Exhibit 3 is Hayes's calculation of the total
time required to fill one shipper, including the operations which were
performed only once in the filling of a shipper. These times were all derived
from Methods-Time Measurement (MTM) standard data (see footnote to
Exhibit 3).

EXHIBIT 2
Layout for the Single-Operator Method

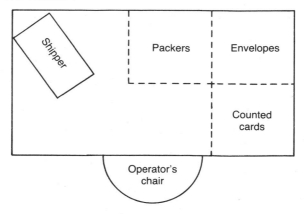

Hayes used the standard times he calculated to set goals for the five
workers he trained in the single-operator method. He began training the
five workers on December 14, and he had given each about six hours of
instruction when they began to use the single-operator method in the
boxing department on December 21. Hayes kept no records of their learning progress during the training, but he estimated that on the last day of
training the slowest operator was producing at the rate of 1,000 packers per
day and the fastest, 1,700 packers. The only production figures which were
kept for the five workers were for December 28, 29, and 30. On those three
days the average production per operator was 1,415, 1,332, and 1,610
packers per day.

EXHIBIT 3
Time Standard for Single-Operator Method

	Element	Element Time* (minutes)	Frequency per Shipper	Normal Time per Shipper (minutes)
1.	Get packers	0.0384	1	0.0384
2.	Get envelopes	0.0425	1	0.0425
3.	Get shipper	0.1088	1	0.1088
4.	Count cards	0.0025	360	0.9000
5.	Fill and pack	0.0698	30	2.0940
6.	Put aside shipper.	0.1088	1	0.1088

3.2925 minutes per shipper
+ 15% personal and
fatigue allowance =
3.7825 minutes per
shipper ÷ 30 packers
per shipper =
0.1261 minutes per
packer.

* All the times were developed using Methods-Time Measurement (MTM). This is a method of developing "synthetic" time standards by breaking down the work into elements, to which predetermined times are assigned. The time assigned to each work element is intended to represent the time required by an average proficient worker at a normal pace without allowance for unavoidable delay, fatigue, or personal time.

THE AERO-SONIC MACHINE

On December 24, the Aero-Sonic machine was delivered to Metreke plant in Atlanta. The billed price to Metreke was $2,400, but the manufacturer said he would not deliver another machine for less than $4,500 because of the difficulties encountered in adapting it to take the Metreke packer.

The Aero-Sonic machine was a flat table, approximately 3 feet by 4 feet, under which were mounted two small fans. The air blast from the fans was directed through a tube to the top of the table. Seventy-five packers were held in a recess in the top of the table so that the packer on top of the pile was just flush with the surface of the table. The packer's open side was pointed toward the air jet. The packer was held in place by two small metal arms inserted into the packer from the open end. The blast of air held the packer open so that with one hand a person could slide a stack of cards and bundle of envelopes into the open mouth of the packer. By continuing the motion, the hand could push the packer and its contents off the two metal arms. The other hand could then take the packer and place it on another table at the side of the Aero-Sonic machine. As the packer left the two metal arms, a spring-loaded device raised the pile of packers to bring the next packer even with the metal arms. The blast of air opened the packer, and

EXHIBIT 4
Layout for Aero-Sonic Machine

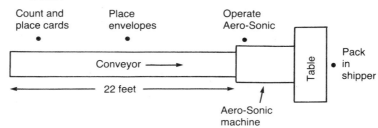

the arms again engaged the edges of the packer. The machine was thus automatically ready for another cycle. An MTM study by Hayes produced an estimated time of 0.0374 minutes to perform this cycle given that envelopes, cards, and packers were available when needed.

Tom Hayes had worked out the layout for the Aero-Sonic machine shown in Exhibit 4 before the machine was delivered, so that he was able to start training the four operators on December 24. The machine was put in production in the boxing department on December 28. In the first three days of production, the four operators on the team using the machine produced 4,065, 6,700, and 6,178 packers per day.

Tom Hayes had estimated (using MTM) that it would take 0.042 minutes to place one bundle of envelopes on the conveyor in the Aero-Sonic method. Similar calculations indicated a time of 0.03 minutes to count and place 12 cards on the conveyor and 0.024 minutes to place a filled packer in a shipper. From these calculations, Hayes decided that the first worker on the conveyor would count and place cards and the second worker would place envelopes.

THE FIRST WEEK IN JANUARY

After the New Year's holiday, Joan Jenkins had 12 laborers working on the single-operator method. Since Tom Hayes was gone and she felt incapable of training the seven workers, she had directed the five operators already trained to teach the others. The operators were deviating from the method developed by Hayes. They were using the same general hand motions, but none of the workers was carefully laying out the work area as planned by Hayes. The workers were particularly sloppy in placing the stacks of counted cards. Occasionally one of the counted stacks of cards would fall over or become entangled with another stack. As a result, the operators lost time when reaching for stacks of cards.

Everyday cards were being processed not only by the 12 single operators but also by one belt running on the Aero-Sonic machine and by a second belt which was used with the 6-operator method. The 6-operator line had never exceeded production of 9,400 packers per day, and its production had been as low as 6,202 packers on December 28. Average production for the belt during December was 9,100 packers per day. These three methods handled all the everyday cards for the boxing department. One materials handler was serving the two belts, and a second materials handler was able to support the 12 single operators. The boxing department's other two belts were being used for the seasonal cards. Six operators worked on each of these belts with the remaining nine workers labeling the boxes and placing them in shippers.

Conrad Lewis had recently discharged Joan Jenkins' assistant in the boxing department, and he had no replacement in mind. In the absence of Bert Starr, Lewis realized he would have to continue to take responsibility for activities in the boxing department.

CASE 4

Fawcett Optical Equipment Company

On May 25, Mr. William Thomas, manager of manufacturing of the Fawcett Optical Equipment Company, was holding a meeting to discuss and evaluate plans for the assembly activities for the KD 780 photoreconnaissance Air Force camera contract. These plans (Exhibit 1) had been developed during April and May by Mr. Robert Phillips, superintendent of the assembly of noncommercial products of the Fawcett factory at Cleveland, Ohio. Mr. Thomas and others at this meeting were not at all certain that Mr. Phillips' plans were feasible. The KD 780 camera job was Fawcett's first defense-product contract in the past decade, and Mr. Thomas was anxious for the manufacturing division to look good on this job to enhance prospects for more business with the Air Force.

EXHIBIT 1
Assembly Schedule

	Assembly Operators Added	Total Operators Available	Effective Labor-Hours Available	Cameras Assembled during Month	Cumulative Total Cameras Assembled
June and July..........	0	4	1,280	2	2
August	25	29	3,440	12	14
September.............	25	54	7,440	59	73
October	0	54	8,640	120	193
November	0	54	8,640	173	366
December	0	54	8,640	223	589
January...............	0	54	8,640*	241*	840*

*Six hundred sixty five effective labor hours available in January will not be needed to achieve the total production of 840 units.
Source: Mr. Robert Phillips' KD 780 Camera Assembly Project File.

The Fawcett Optical Equipment Company of Cleveland, Ohio, designed, manufactured, and sold optical equipment used in laboratories, factories, and medical facilities. Two years earlier, the company had purchased a factory building and some machine tools that had been declared surplus property by the U.S. Department of Defense. These new facilities provided about 25 percent more space and machine capacity than was to be required by optical equipment manufacturing, according to a 10-year forecast of sales. However, the price and especially the location of this former government property were so attractive and Fawcett's former plant space had been so inadequate that the added investment in the surplus plant and machines was easily justified. During the ensuing nine months, the move to the new plant had been completed and operations were running smoothly.

The previous September, Mr. J. F. Pickering, president of the company, had decided to solicit government contracts to manufacture and assemble defense products in order to utilize the extra available plant space and machine tools more fully. No commitments were to be made for Fawcett to design or develop new products because Fawcett's engineers were fully occupied with optical equipment design work. Accordingly, a sales engineer and a production engineer had made a series of calls at various military equipment procurement offices. In December, Fawcett was awarded a prime contract to manufacture 840 model KD 780 night-photo reconnaissance cameras for the Air Force. Fawcett had been chosen among competitive bidders as the alternate prime source of supply of these cameras, which had previously been designed and produced by the Sedgewick Instrument Company.

To prepare Fawcett's quotation for this contract, a group comprised of a manufacturing engineer, a tool engineer, a cost estimator, and a purchasing agent had reviewed and analyzed over 600 Sedgewick Instrument Company drawings of detail and assembly parts of the KD 780 camera. After Fawcett was awarded the contract, these drawings were thoroughly checked to ensure that Fawcett had drawings showing the latest Sedgewick engineering change information. Then, various make-buy decisions had been made, and accordingly materials and tool orders placed with various vendors and/or with the machining and toolmaking departments at the Fawcett plant. Air Force procurement officers had stated they wanted these cameras as soon as possible. The contract stipulated that Fawcett was to ship the first KD 780 cameras in July, and by October, Fawcett was to build up its camera output rate to at least 120 units per month until the 840 cameras had been produced and shipped.

DEVELOPMENT OF MR. PHILLIPS' ASSEMBLY PLAN

By February, Mr. Phillips received copies of the parts lists, assembly drawings, and test specifications, after the various procurement and parts manufacturing planning decisions had been made. Mr. Phillips turned these documents over to the assembly methods engineer on his staff, with instructions to plan the layout of the benches in the assembly area, to design and order necessary tools and fixtures, and to provide estimates of the standard hours per unit required at each assembly work station. The standard hour estimates were prepared by using predetermined methods and time standard data, and by presuming planned assembly work station layouts, methods, and carefully selected and fully trained assembly operators. Assisting the methods engineer were the project foreman and four assembly technicians assigned as a nucleus crew to assemble the first, small production lot of cameras and to "debug" the assembly processing methods. The technicians were later to become working foremen and job leaders of new assembly personnel to be added to the assembly working force, as the assembly output rate was boosted to the minimum rate of 120 units per month. On April 15, the assembly methods planning group advised Mr. Phillips that after the assembly work force were skilled in using the planned methods, each camera would require a total 85 standard labor-hours to assemble completely. The 85 standard labor-hours was the sum of the standard labor-hours per unit for different jobs involved in assembling one camera.

While his assembly methods planning group were engaged in their work, Mr. Phillips concentrated on how to approach the problems of programming the buildup of the assembly work force, and of controlling the rate of buildup in output of the cameras while new personnel were being hired and trained. He anticipated the possibilities of production delays and worker idleness during the entire period of assembling the 840 KD 780 cameras. He had heard of production delay problems in companies producing defense products, in which as much as 95 percent of the units ordered were delayed in shipment to the customer until the last month of a 12-month planned period devoted to producing a particular defense product. This was an experience Mr. Phillips hoped to avoid. He realized that a desirable approach was one enabling him to anticipate a specific quantitative pattern of output during the entire period the cameras were being assembled.

Mr. Phillips had decided that the best approach to his planning problem was to use a learning curve analysis (sometimes called a manufacturing progress function). A few years earlier, he had discovered that this method of quantifying cost experiences was frequently used by the Air Force as a guide in negotiating prices and delivery terms of contracts with manufacturers. Mr. Phillips had investigated a number of pieces of literature on the subject and had talked to people who had used it before; as a result of his investigation and his persistence, Fawcett last year had utilized learning curve analysis fairly successfully to plan inventory and manpower needs for a new line of photo cells.[1]

[1] W. B. Hirschmann, "Profit from the Learning Curve," *Harvard Business Review*, January–February 1964; and W. Abernathy and K. Wayne, "Limits of the Learning Curve," *Harvard Business Review*, September–October 1974.

Learning curve analysis was founded on the premise that as production experience increased (as measured by number of units produced), costs could be reduced on a fairly predictable basis. A general rule of thumb which had been developed through application of the technique suggested that each time output doubled, labor-hours (and therefore costs) could be reduced to between 70 percent and 90 percent of previous levels. As Mr. Phillips had used this method once before, and as this was an Air Force contract, he felt the concept would provide a logical and sound base for planning his assembly operations.

As his first step in adapting the manufacturing progress function to his assembly activities, Mr. Phillips listed pertinent conditions that would affect his assembly program.

1.   After lengthy discussion with his methods engineer and technicians, Mr. Phillips decided that 90 KD 780 cameras would have been assembled by the time the assembly personnel had developed sufficient skill and experience to meet the standard rate of 85 total labor-hours per unit.

2.   Starting with the nucleus crew of four assembly technicians, it was decided that additional assembly personnel could be selected, hired, and effectively trained at the maximum rate of 25 new employees per month. To attempt to train more than 25 new operators would overtax training facilities and personnel, Mr. Phillips believed. The personnel manager, Mr. P. D. Kenworthy, had advised that all additional assembly personnel required for the KD 780 job would have to be recruited from the Cleveland area and would require Fawcett company orientation training as well as job-methods training. During their first month on the KD 780 job, new employees were presumed to be 70 percent efficient (100 percent efficient meant that an operator completed the job in exactly the standard labor-hours set for the assembly tasks assigned for him/her to complete). After the first month, all operators were presumed to be at least 100 percent efficient.

3.   For purposes of developing these plans, Mr. Phillips assumed that there would be 160 assembly operating hours in any calendar month. Since a calendar month contained 4⅓ weeks, this meant that every third month, a "margin of safety" of one week was available as a reserve for contingencies such as material shortages, quality problems, and other delays interfering with the flow of assembly work.

4.   The KD 780 camera contained over 800 parts. Plans for the process specified assembly work to be done at 27 different work stations on four major subassemblies and 35 work stations in the final assembly area. Standard times at these work stations were not uniform, and to ensure reasonable continuity of flow of work, buffer stocks were to be provided and certain operators were to be shifted among several work stations. From these plans, Mr. Phillips estimated that the elapsed time for assembling a camera would be four weeks, two weeks for final and test, and two weeks for subassembly work.

5.   The initial production-lot quantity planned was two cameras—just

enough for the methods engineer and the four assembly technicians to check on the assembly methods, tools, and workplace arrangements in the assembly area. The Air Force desired to make thorough acceptance tests of the performance of the first two units produced by Fawcett.

6.   To use the manufacturing progress function, Mr. Phillips had to make an assumption of the measured rate of progress he could expect the growing labor force to achieve while assembling the 840 KD 780 cameras. He had noted in the literature that an 80–85 percent learning curve was rather widely used in the aircraft industry. Mr. Phillips had realized that to choose a progress rate parameter of 80 percent, 70 percent, or whatever, he would have to use good judgment in extrapolating from past experiences. He therefore examined blueprints, methods specifications, and labor time tickets for several optical equipment products assembled by Fawcett employees in the past. He chose products all of which had some degree of similarity with the KD 780 job with respect to such factors as the numbers of different parts to be assembled, the clearances between parts, the fragility of the parts, the numbers of different assembly operations required, and the total assembly hours required per unit.[2] By plotting learning curves for several such similar assembly activities in the past, Mr. Phillips had determined that the assembly progress-rate parameters for these past jobs had ranged from 70 percent to 75 percent. From this, Mr. Phillips had chosen 72 percent as the expected rate of progress that would be achieved on the KD 780 Air Force camera assembly job.

From these six presumed conditions, Mr. Phillips had developed his assembly production schedule and his direct labor buildup schedule shown in Exhibit 1. The detailed, step-by-step procedure Mr. Phillips followed to determine these schedules is summarized in the Appendix at the end of this case. Mr. Phillips had completed the work of determining these schedules on May 20.

During a regular KD 780 camera job-progress meeting of manufacturing management personnel held on May 25, Mr. Phillips had presented his assembly schedules and had briefly described how he had derived them.

Mr. J. D. Jorgenson, KD 780 camera project cost supervisor: Bob, using your data on labor-hours and total units assembled and some cost figures I have, I estimate that we won't make any money on the KD 780 job until after we have shipped about 450 units. In fact, I don't think we will have absorbed our start-up costs directly incurred on this job until after we've shipped the 300th unit. We're committed to a fixed price on this job you know; we could not get the Air Force to go along with a cost-plus-fixed-fee price.

Mr. Phillip D. Kenworthy, manager of personnel and relations: The union has been after me about wage-incentive procedures for this KD 780 camera assembly job. As you know, we put a newly hired worker on a straight piecework incentive wage after he has been on the job for one month. As I see this learning

[2] The photo-cell product with which Fawcett had used the learning curve analysis previously had not been as complex a product as the KD 780 camera.

curve plan, we have an inevitable "looseness" built into our time standards. I know we regularly use predetermined motion and time standard data, as well as stopwatch time studies for the factory floor, to set piece rates. But if we put these KD 780 assembly personnel on an incentive pay basis too soon, their wages will get out of line with other personnel in the same labor class. If we don't put operators on incentives soon enough, the union will gripe. We don't build the same model of optical equipment in quantities compared to the 840 KD 780 cameras, so there isn't the extensive and uninterrupted opportunity for learning on comparable optical equipment assembly jobs. If all your people are put on incentive wage rates by October, Bob, and if they progress the way you say they will along your 72 percent progress curve, they will be turning out the 840th camera in less than 30 hours. But if they start pegging rates, say, after the 150th camera (when standard hours are 85/66 = 128 percent of actual hours), won't this give you some trouble, Bob?

Mr. Phillips: There is a possible wage inequity problem, Phil, and all I can say is that we'll have to take a good look at our whole wage payment policy and procedure in light of this before our next union contract negotiation. Meanwhile, I'm going to keep my methods engineer alert to keep his methods standards and time standards up to date and to take more initiative in revising methods and time standards. There is nothing in the contract to prevent us from tightening the rates of jobs when we engineer job-methods changes. I'm also going to tell my foreman to encourage our people to exploit this learning opportunity and to assure our people that there will be no tightening of standards when an operator makes methods changes that enable him/her to beat the rates we have set. This is a great chance for us to learn more about a valuable planning tool.

Mr. William Thomas, manager of manufacturing: Bob, this is quite a program you've planned. I had told Mr. Pickering I thought we wouldn't wind up this KD 780 job until May of next year. Now you show us shipping the last unit in January or February. If you're wrong, and we land another Air Force contract to work on in February, we'll really be in a bind. Are you sure you can make this schedule? Another thing, if you've planned that the standard will be 85 labor-hours per unit and the contract states that we have to ship 120 units per month, then I figure we should have a capacity 85 X 120 = 10,200 standard labor-hours per month. Divided by actual hours per month (4 weeks × 40 hours), this is 10,200/160 = 64 operators. Yet you say you can do the whole job with 54 operators. (If this is true with assembly work, I wonder how this idea would go with our parts machining work.)

Mr. Phillips: Bill, I'm convinced we can do this. I'm telling my foremen exactly how I got the 72 percent progress curve, and that I am going to plot their actual progress each week to see how close they come to the curve. All I'll have to do is take the count of cameras coming off the packaging operation and divide this into the total weekly direct labor-hours tallied by the timekeeper. If their actual progress data plot above the curve for direct labor-hours per unit, I'll know something is wrong and find out what it is. I'd like to try to carry out these plans, and I hope you will approve them and give me the support I know I'll need.

APPENDIX: FAWCETT OPTICAL EQUIPMENT COMPANY[3]

1.   General Technical Specifications of the Manufacturing Progress Function.

When empirical data on direct labor-hours per unit are plotted against the production count of units produced, the resulting curve for the KD 780 camera assembly operations appears as shown in Exhibit A–1. The curve depicts a phenomenon which makes strong intuitive sense; that is, *a job requires less effort as more experience is gained and as more methods improvements are made.* As production accumulates, progress continues but at a decreasing rate, because further opportunities to improve the job become less and less obvious. This curve is just one of an almost infinite variety of such curves having the same "family resemblance"; that is, the

EXHIBIT A–1
Graph of the 72 Percent Assembly Progress Curve

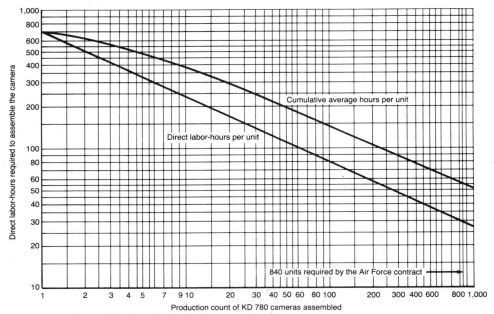

Note: Graphs are plotted on log-log graph paper.
Source: Mr. Robert Phillips KD 780 Camera Assembly Project Files.

---

[3] Summary of the procedure for using the manufacturing progress function to schedule assembly buildup on KD 780 Air Force Night-Photo Reconnaissance Camera. Source: Mr. Robert Phillips' KD 780 Camera Assembly Project File.

direct labor-hours per unit decrease more or less sharply, but always steadily, as the number of units produced increases.

The algebraic statement of this progress phenomenon is:

$$Y_i = ai^{-b}$$

where

Y_i is the direct labor-hours required to produce the ith unit of product.
i is the production count, beginning with the first unit.
a is a parameter of the model which is equal to the labor-hours required
for the first unit, Y_1 (for $i = 1$, $Y_1 = a(1)^{-b} = a$).
b is a measure of the *rate* at which the direct labor-hours per unit are
reduced as the production count increases.

When the labor-hours per unit and production count data are plotted on
logarithmic coordinate graph paper, or when the logarithms of these data
are plotted on conventional arithmetic coordinate graph paper, the curve
becomes a straight line. Algebraically this fact is stated by taking the logarithmic transformation of the equation above:

$$(\log Y_i) = (\log a) - b(\log i)$$

The rate of progress is nominally described by stating the complement
of the percentage reduction in labor-hours per unit when the production
quantity is doubled. This means that if i_2 and i_1 are any two different
production counts and if i_1 always equals 2, then for an 80 percent progress
curve, $b \times 0.322$ because $2^{-0.322} = 0.80$; for a 72 percent progress curve, b
$\times 0.474$ because $2^{-0.474} = 0.72$.

The *cumulative* number of direct labor-hours required to produce n units
may be expressed as:

$$T_n = Y_1 + Y_2 + \cdots + Y_n = \sum_{i=1}^{n} Y_i$$

An approximation of this sum is given by the integral:

$$T_n = \int_0^n Y_i \, di = a\int_0^n i^{-b} \, di \cong a\left(\frac{n^{1-b}}{1-b}\right)$$

Dividing this expression by the cumulative number of units (n) gives an
approximation for the *cumulative average* number of labor-hours:

$$A_n \cong \frac{a}{n}\left(\frac{n^{1-b}}{1-b}\right) \cong \frac{an^{-b}}{1-b} \cong \frac{Yn}{1-b}$$

These approximations typically yield insignificant errors at n values of
100 units or more, but large errors can occur for small values of n.

2. Method of Adapting the Manufacturing Progress Function to Plans for Assembling the KD 780 Camera

a. Assumptions made:
   (1) The standard of 85 hours per camera will be achieved on the 90th camera.
   (2) The rate of progress in assembly methods improvements, and in development of skill by assembly personnel, would conform to a 72 percent progress function (corresponding to a b parameter value of 0.474).

$$Y_i = a\,(i)^{-0.474}$$

b. The assembly progress curve (direct labor-hours per unit): Using log-log graph paper, starting at 85 hours for the 90th unit, a straight line with a slope of -0.474 was drawn through this point. See Exhibit A–1. This implies that 716 hours will be required to assemble the first camera.

c. A cumulative average direct labor-hours curve was also plotted on Exhibit A–1 to ease calculations for the assembly output buildup schedule and for the direct labor buildup schedule. This curve was developed by calculating the cumulative average hours per unit for a variety of values of cumulative output (n) and then plotting them on the graph (Exhibit A–1). Note that the cumulative average curve becomes asymptotically parallel to the unit curve as the number of units completed increase.

The assembly direct labor buildup schedule required that subtotals of the cumulative assembly direct labor-hours be related to cumulative production. These subtotals were easily calculated by multiplying the cumulative average direct labor-hours per unit by the cumulative number of units assembled. Data on cumulative average direct labor-hours per unit were simply read from the curve. (Without having this curve, calculations for the direct labor and output buildup schedules would have been more tedious.) From this curve the following Exhibit could be determined (the actual values shown were computer calculated).

Sample Calculations for Assembly Output and Direct Labor Schedules

June and July:
   Direct labor required for the first two units is approximately 1,240 labor-hours.
   Direct labor available: 4 at 160 hours per month × 2 months = 1,280 labor-hours.

August:
   Direct labor: Add 25 new employees whose efficiency is 70 percent.

25 × 160 × 0.70 =	2,800	
Already available: 4 × 160 =	640	3,440 labor-hours

Sample Calculations (*concluded*)

	Cumulative total labor-hours through August 4,720	
Output:	Comparison of 4,720 with data in column 4 of Exhibit A–2 shows that the 14th unit would have been produced by the end of August. During August, 14 − 2 = 12 units would have been completed.	

September:

Direct labor:
Add 25 new employees—
efficiency 70 percent =   2,800 labor-hours
Already available as of
September 1: 29 × 160 =   4,640
Total labor-hours expended
in September. 7,440
Cumulative total labor-hours
through August 4,720
Cumulative total labor-hours
through September. 12,160

Output:
In Exhibit A–2, comparison of 12,160 with data in column 4 shows that about 73 units would have been produced by the end of September. During September, 73 − 14 = 59 units would have been completed.

October:

Direct labor:
Available as of October 1:
54 × 160 =   8,640   labor-hours
Cumulative total expended
through September. 12,160
Cumulative total labor-hours
expended through October . . . 20,800

Output:
In Exhibit A–2, comparison of 20,800 with data approximately 193 units would have been produced after expending 20,800 labor-hours of assembly labor. During the month of October, 193 − 73 = 120 cameras would have been assembled.

From October through January the output schedule was based on the 8,640 labor-hours available each month and the data in Exhibit A–2.

EXHIBIT A–2
Table of Cumulative Production and Labor-Hour Data

(1) Cumulative Production	(2) Hours This Unit	(3) Cumulative Average Hours per Unit	(4) Cumulative Total Hours (column 1 × column 3)
1	716	716	716
2	516	616	1,232
10	240	371	3,714
12	221	347	4,165
15	198	319	4,780
20	173	285	5,692
40	125	214	8,564
60	103	180	10,806
75	93	163	12,262
100	81	144	14,412
150	67	120	18,054
200	58	106	21,153
250	52	96	23,903
300	48	88	26,402
400	42	77	30,868
500	38	70	34,830
600	35	64	38,431
700	32	60	41,757
800	30	56	44,864
840	29	55	46,055

Texas Instruments—Time Products Division

Efficiency?
Goal Attainment?

By June 1976, production of digital watches at Texas Instruments (TI) was going more smoothly after the somewhat frenetic start-up of the first watch assembly line five months earlier. In the opinion of Peter Bradley, operations manager of TI's Time Products Division (TPD), now was the time to respond to continuing corporate pressures for improved performance, by reviewing the watch assembly operations at the plant in Lubbock, Texas.

COMPANY BACKGROUND

As a technology-based company, Texas Instruments Incorporated (TI) had its headquarters in Dallas, manufactured in 44 plants in 18 countries, and employed 57,930 people worldwide. The company had expanded its products and services from its original geophysical and geological exploration service to include clad-material systems, semiconductor materials and components, control devices, instrument systems, and consumer electronic products. Corporate net sales in 1975 had reached almost $1.4 billion, resulting in net income of $62.1 million. Electrical and electronic products had accounted for 83 percent of these sales. Stated corporate objectives were for $3 billion in sales by the beginning of the 1980s and $10 billion by the end of that decade.

TI had been involved in the early commercial production of transistors in 1952. To create a market for these devices, the company had designed and produced its first commercial transistor radio in 1954. In 1958, the company had developed its first integrated circuit (IC). These unique devices eliminated the need for numerous separate transistors and mechanical connections in an electronic system. Building on this base, TI had developed its semiconductor technology over the years, making it an integral part of many of the company's defense, commercial, and consumer products.

In 1971, TI had announced its "calculator on a chip" which packed more than 6,000 transistors on a tiny silicon chip only a quarter of an inch square. This chip had made it possible for TI to announce in 1972 its entry into the consumer market with the Datamath, a four-function, hand-held calculator. In 1974, an even more complex integrated circuit was introduced as "a general-purpose computer on a chip." This chip had contained both logic and memory functions—the equivalent of 8,000 transistors—on a chip 0.2 of an inch square. In June 1975, TI had announced its entry into a new consumer market, microelectronic digital watches; deliveries of a jewelry line of digital watches had begun in August of that year.

THE WATCH INDUSTRY

The traditional watch, a combination of cogs, levers, springs, and pins, had existed relatively unchanged since the 17th century. A watch driven by a battery-powered electric motor, as opposed to a mainspring, had been introduced in the late 1950s. A few years later, the Bulova Accutron had been the first popularly priced watch to use an innovative timing mechanism—a miniature tuning fork—to drive the hands of the watch. The next major change, the electronic watch, had appeared in the late 1960s and early 1970s.

The electronic watch was a major technological and product change. The combination of a quartz crystal, an integrated circuit (IC), and a power source resulted in an extremely accurate timing mechanism. This advance was achieved by passing a small current through a quartz crystal that oscillated at a predetermined rate of about 32 KHz (32,000 cycles per second). The IC reduced these oscillations to one-second increments and sent the resultant impulse to a stepping motor (for an analog display) or through further IC logic (for a digital display).

Analog electronic watches used conventional hands and dials. On the outside, they resembled a traditional watch; inside, the analog watch used one battery and a less complex, lower cost integrated circuit than that used for digital-readout watches. Digital electronic watches employed solid-state display technology, most commonly light-emitting diodes (LED). To save power, the LED gave a numerical readout of the time only when activated. Less common in 1975, but perhaps with greater market potential, were liquid crystal displays (LCD). The displays of these units reflected ambient light. Because of the lower power requirements, LCDs could display the time continuously. The first digital electronic watches had used LCDs; however, as a result of quality problems and their higher prices, most digital watches used LEDs in 1976. Both types of digital readouts required two batteries.

EXHIBIT 1
Worldwide Electronic Watch Market (units and $ millions)

| | Digital | | | | Analog | | Total | |
| | LED | | LCD | | | | | |
	Units	Dollars	Units	Dollars	Units	Dollars	Units	Dollars
1973	0.1	$ 30	0.3	$ 82.5	1.0	$ 240	1.4	$ 352.5
1974	1.3	60	0.4	50	2.5	500	3.2	610
1975^e.............	2.0	125	0.8	64	4.2	504	7.0	693
1976^e.............	5.5	550	2.2	154	8.5	680	16.2	1,384
1977^e.............	8.0	680	7.0	420	11.0	770	26.0	1,870
1978^e.............	12.5	1,000	12.0	600	15.0	825	39.5	2,425
1980^e.............	22.0	1,100	36.0	1,080	28.0	980	86.0	3,160
1983^e.............	30.0	1,500	45.0	990	42.0	1,260	117.0	3,750

Note: These estimates were prepared prior to TI's entry into the low-priced digital watch market in early 1976.
^{e} = Estimated.
Source: Company records.

Prices of electronic watches had fallen rapidly since their 1970 introduction at $1,000 to $2,000; by 1975, electronic watches were available from more than 50 firms, some for as low as $40 retail. With declining prices, volumes were expected to increase rapidly (Exhibit 1). Forecasts for electronic watches were surrounded by considerable uncertainty. For example, one big question was what kind of display—LCD, LED, analog, or some new technology—would be most popular in the future.

Two major groups were contending for the digital watch market. The first was composed of the manufacturers of traditional timepieces; among these were Timex, Seiko, Benrus, Bulova, Gruen, Elgin, and Waltham. The second included a number of major semiconductor companies—National Semiconductor, Texas Instruments, Fairchild Camera and Instrument, and Litronix. Hughes Aircraft, a major semiconductor producer, had been the major supplier of modules (the "movement" of an electronic watch) to assemblers (often the traditional watch manufacturers) but had not become involved in the final assembly or sale of watches.

Due to the competitive environment and the lack of extensive consumer experience with low-priced digital watches, most observers felt that flexibility to product change was particularly important for success in this market. This was necessary to avoid large inventory write-offs and yet gain market share by meeting demand when it occurred. Minimizing finished goods fluctuations and product mix changes made digital watches a risky market for both traditional watch manufacturers and semiconductor firms.

COMPONENTS OF A DIGITAL WATCH

A digital watch consisted of two parts—the module that functioned as the timekeeping and display mechanism and the case that held the module

(Exhibit 2). The case included a bezel, back cover, lens, and strap. The latest innovation in case construction had been the use of plastic as a low-cost replacement for metal bezels and back covers. The electronic components of digital watches also had changed considerably since the early 1970s, and further innovation was expected.

EXHIBIT 2
Parts of a Digital Electronic Watch

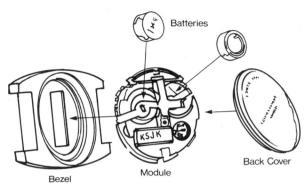

Integrated Circuits (IC). When electronic watches were first developed, both positive-channel metal-oxide semiconductors (PMOS) and complementary metal-oxide semiconductors (CMOS) ICs were considered. However, as a result of the technology available in the early 1970s, CMOS circuitry, with its lower power-usage requirements, had predominated. Innovations followed, and two alternatives emerged, although CMOS remained the standard technology. CMOS-on-sapphire, developed by RCA, permitted smaller, faster circuits that had lower power requirements and could operate at higher frequencies.[1] TI improved the standard bipolar circuitry and developed a new technique—integrated injection logic (I^2L)—that had power requirements as low as CMOS-on-sapphire and performed better on frequency response. In addition, I^2L was compatible with the high-current, bipolar circuits needed to power the displays in digital watches.

By the end of 1975, the price for a CMOS IC for an LED watch was approaching $6.50. Forecasts called for the same parts to be selling for half that by 1978 and perhaps as low as $1 by the 1980s. Comparable prices for the simpler analog circuits were $1.25 in 1976, and corresponding price reductions were anticipated.

Displays. The greatest uncertainty was in the area of display technology. The LED technology was well developed because of its use in calculators. However, it did not allow for continuous display, a feature most

---

[1] Frost and Sullivan report, *The Electronic Watch Industry* (New York, 1975).

industry experts felt desirable. LCDs, first used in 1972, did offer this feature but had other drawbacks. While most of the early reliability and readability problems had been overcome, this type of display required background light to be readable.

LCD prices had been unstable because expected demand had not materialized. Prices declined from $13 in 1973 to $10 in 1974 to as low as $5 in 1975. With increases in volumes, LCD prices were predicted to fall to $3 in 1976 and to the 50 to 25 cents range by the 1980s.

LED displays were a more mature product. An LED display panel that sold for $10 in 1973 had an average selling price of $5 in 1975 and was predicted to be $4 in 1976 and $1 to 50 cents in the 1980s.[2]

Quartz Crystals.   Crystal manufacture was different from conventional electronics, and there were relatively few suppliers. In 1975, these included:

American Microsystems*	Sentry Manufacturing
CTS Knight	Statek
Bulova	Litronix*
Motorola	Omega*
Reeves-Hoffman	

* These firms also manufactured electronic watches.

The major source of cost improvement in crystals was expected to result from the development of smaller crystals that operated at higher frequencies. This would require better frequency (i.e., higher speed) response from the ICs. Expectations were for a change from 32 KHz to up to 4 MHz (4,000,000 cycles per second). In 1974, a 4 MHz crystal cost about $2 (one half the cost of a 32 KHz crystal) and was expected to fall to 65–50 cents by the 1980s.[2]

Batteries.   Union Carbide, Ray-O-Vac, and Mallory were the major power-cell producers. Development of improved batteries was ongoing, but better performance was likely to be accompanied by higher prices. In 1976, the average selling price for a battery was 60 cents (in volume)—$1.20 for watches requiring two power cells. Relative to other components, price declines for batteries had been modest and were not expected to change.

TPD—THE ELECTRONIC WATCH EXPERIENCE

In 1974, as part of the corporate commitment to become involved in the manufacturing of consumer electronics, TI prepared to introduce a high-

[2] Ibid.

priced electronic watch. After several false starts, this $90-and-up line was launched in 1975. Sales were disappointing; by mid-1976, this line was being withdrawn. Meanwhile, the low-priced end of the market had continued to expand rapidly. In January 1976, TI revised its strategy by announcing a line of low-priced digital watches, the 500 series. The least expensive of this line retailed for $20 and wholesaled for slightly over $13. Part of the reason for this change was TI's realization that the $100-plus market was potentially only 6 percent of the dollar volume.

To achieve volume production and market leadership, Stewart Carrell, group vice president (Consumer Products Division), transferred Bob York, Peter Bradley, and a number of others, many of whom had been involved with calculators, to the Time Product Division (TPD).

When Peter Bradley was moved to Time Products and given responsibility for module production and watch assembly in February 1976, the "jewelry line" was being produced by a batch process, and the low-priced watch was not yet being produced in quantity. Although batch processing was considered for the low-priced line, Peter quickly dismissed it and began the design and construction of a continuous assembly line. As He explained:

> There was only a discussion . . . a little discussion of batch production. Then we got on with the only way we were aware of to build them cost effectively. You just don't do anything cost effectively in these volumes in a batch mode.

An assembly line for the electronic modules was already operating in Dallas, and space for final assembly of the case and the components and packaging of the product was available in Lubbock (300 miles from Dallas) at the same plant that assembled calculators. To achieve corporate goals, Peter and his staff had to start with an empty manufacturing area in February and be in full operation by April—from planning to quantity production in 45 days.

TPD—ORGANIZATION

As part of Consumer Products under the direction of Stewart Carrell, TPD was growing rapidly. Bob York, TPD general manager, expressed his philosophy as "stretching the people in my organization" to achieve maximum performance. There was complete agreement that this had been done, at least for operations during the past few months.

Peter Bradley understood his task and that of his organization as "concentrating on the day-to-day operating decisions." It was up to the division general manager "to concentrate on the future."

The organization of TPD operations (Exhibit 3) was straightforward. Peter had brought "a lot of key people, good solid senior people, who'd rally around a challenge" with him to TPD. Many of these, including Alan

EXHIBIT 3
TPD Organization Chart

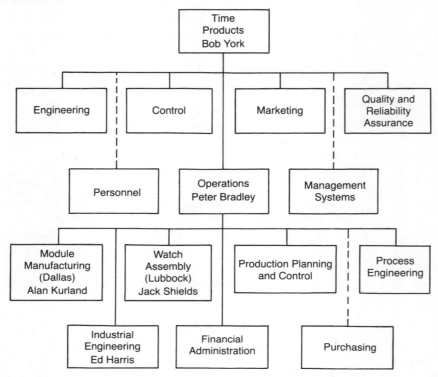

Kurland and Jack Shields, had calculator manufacturing experience. Peter had been with TI for 10 years, having joined the company upon graduating from Stanford with an M.S. in industrial engineering.

Production planning and control was responsible for day-to-day production scheduling to meet the overall plan and to assist in making sure raw materials were available. However, everyone in operations was very concerned about output and the meeting of commitments. Other staff support included process engineering, which physically designed the production process, managed any new or improved tooling of the line, and assured that the fabrication process would result in an acceptable product. Naturally enough, industrial engineering was also heavily involved in these activities. In addition to Ed Harris, who was responsible for industrial engineering and facilities management, TPD had Fred Harper, an industrial engineer on loan from the Calculator Division. Purchasing had a dotted-line relationship to Peter because this activity was centralized for the Consumer Products Division.

Quality and reliability assurance (QRA) reported directly to Bob York but worked closely with operations. Line operators performed 100 percent inspections, and their output was sampled by QRA. If rejects exceeded specified levels at any of the checkpoints, the line would be slowed or stopped until the problem was corrected. If a problem was developing, line supervisors usually knew about it and took early corrective action. Line stoppages due to QRA problems had been common during start-up but now were infrequent. Finished goods inventory was also sampled and tested.

MANAGEMENT SYSTEMS

Organization charts failed to portray the unique management processes and programs within TI. The objectives, strategy, and tactics program provided a clear statement of expectations and of means to achieve them at each level of the company. It was clear throughout the company that once a manager accepted responsibility for agreed-upon goals, that it was then performance that counted. This generally required help from other TI groups who were also trying to meet their own performance objectives. Peter Bradley had met with TI's president, Fred Bucy, twice since February to review performance and discuss plans for the future. There were also meetings twice a week with Bob York: a staff meeting on Mondays to discuss overall TPD problems and plan solutions; and on Wednesdays, a specific review of operations.

At TI, managers were expected to wear two hats: first, as operating managers they had to be concerned with day-to-day operating results; and second, as managers of strategic activity, they had to be concerned with longer term results. On day-to-day operations, managers like Peter Bradley were measured relative to their planned operating profit. On the strategic side, managers were measured on how effectively they met strategic goals.

The people and asset effectiveness (P&AE) program, a required activity throughout TI, was an integral part of the company's management philosophy. This program involved all personnel; its objective was to involve everyone in solving the problems of each particular unit. Although the organization of this program was left to line managers, P&AE typically involved meetings for all personnel on one afternoon a week to work in various-sized teams on specific problems identified by management or workers. The teams were usually composed of several operators who were directly involved with the problems plus additional members from other areas and perhaps a member of management. An attempt was made to develop an egalitarian atmosphere for teamwork. In addition, the personnel of the entire operating unit (e.g., TPD assembly at Lubbock) would meet once each month to review past performance and to discuss expectations for the future and the impact this would have for that unit. This might be broad enough to involve a review of leading economic indicators and their predicted impact on that particular TI product line.

TI was not unionized. A profit sharing program tied to overall corporate profits was used. Line operators usually realized 2–5 percent of their earnings from this incentive program, although the figure had been as high as 15 percent.

TPD's LOW-COST DIGITAL WATCH

TI's experience with the jewelry line had demonstrated the importance of a "clean," easily assembled watch module in keeping yields high throughout the process. TI's unique watch module had the IC chip bonded to a lead frame that was then molded to become the substrate for the entire module. This substrate served as switch contacts, battery contacts, display interconnects, and crystal and capacitor contacts (Exhibit 4). This eliminated

EXHIBIT 4
Electronic Watch Module Assembly

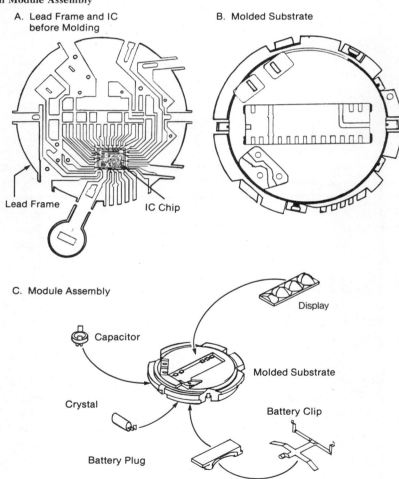

A. Lead Frame and IC before Molding

Lead Frame   IC Chip

B. Molded Substrate

C. Module Assembly

Capacitor

Crystal

Battery Plug

Display

Molded Substrate

Battery Clip

many interconnects and greatly simplified fabrication of the module. Chips and substrates were assembled and then molded in TI's plant in Sherman, Texas.

The molded substrate was sent to Dallas, where the module assembly line under Alan Kurland's direction fabricated the finished modules. This involved the addition of the LED display, the tuning capacitor, the quartz crystal, and the back (battery) plug (Exhibit 5). The battery clip was installed later in Lubbock. Finally the module was tuned to keep the correct time (within five seconds per month). During module assembly, five visual inspections or functional tests were performed at various points along the line. LED displays came from a TI plant in Taiwan; tuning capacitors and quartz crystals were supplied by outside vendors.

EXHIBIT 5
Watch Assembly

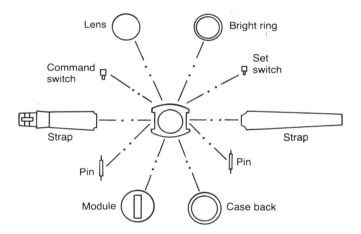

For the low-priced plastic line, TI injection-molded its own lenses, bezels, and back covers at Lubbock. It was then necessary to ion-plate a thin layer of copper to the inside of the plastic components to make the plastic cases static resistant—a property inherent in metal cases. Metal cases and straps, as well as straps for the plastic models, were purchased. So too were smaller components—switches, battery clips, and pins.

CONTINUOUS WATCH ASSEMBLY—LUBBOCK

Assembly facilities at Lubbock were new and incorporated some unique aspects in their design. Discrete units of 40,000 square feet were attached at intervals to a 1,200-foot-long spine that ran the length of the facility (Exhibit 6). Other innovations included a light, open atmosphere and a carpeted floor throughout the manufacturing areas.

EXHIBIT 6
Lubbock Production Facilities

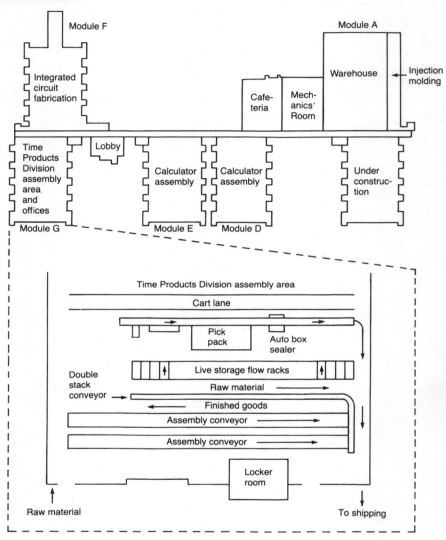

Line Design.   Once the decision had been made to use an assembly line for watch production, implementation required the combined efforts of the process engineer and his people, of tooling and test equipment people, of Fred Harper from industrial engineering, and of Jack Shields, the watch manufacturing manager. This group conceived the production-line flow as in Exhibit 7.

EXHIBIT 7
Assembly Production-
Line Flow

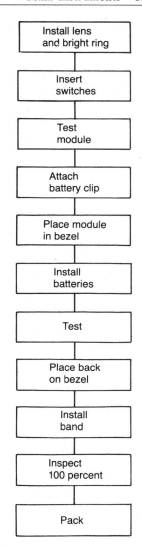

As the first step in setting up the line, the tooling and test equipment people in conjunction with the process engineer went through the first iteration of line design. The major criterion for the tooling and test equipment people was "having adequate machine capacity to meet peak monthly demand." Marketing supplied information on peak monthly requirements; from these data, output of finished watches on a two-shift basis was calculated and converted to hourly throughput. Thus the capacity required for a balanced line to meet peak annual demand was determined. Next, the time for each operation was estimated. (Actual results were very close to these estimates.)

Peter Bradley explained operations' philosophy as to tooling the line:

> There is a lot of technology wrapped up in the line, although it looks very simple. We had a lot to learn. So rather than commit to an expensive piece of gear before we understood the process parameters, we tried to start off with a very practical approach.

He expanded on this:

> If there is any overriding philosophy, it is to take the simple approach because that's what I think is the key to manufacturing. Don't try to do anything too exotic until you've proven the process.

Most of the equipment used on the line was designed and fabricated in-house. New or improved tooling was constantly being added when its advantages were clear. (A six- to nine-month payback was maximum.) All tooling costs were expenses.

While the assembly line was being designed, its effect on the work force was considered, and attempts were made to eliminate or avoid jobs that might create long-term industrial hazards to the individual, require specialized skills, or create other problems.

Line Configuration. After tooling developed a tentative line design, Jack Shields and Fred Harper arrived at the final layout for the production area (Exhibit 6). Initially, the area was to have two identical assembly conveyors, each 120 feet long. Each assembly line was tooled to produce both low-cost metal and plastic watches, although at any given time it produced one or the other. Workers sat on stools on both sides of the conveyor. Each worker would pick up a watch on the line, perform all the tasks required for the assigned operation, and then place the watch back on the line. For any operation that took longer than the standard cycle time, more than one worker would be assigned to that operation. On such multiple assignments, each worker would still complete the work on one watch but, depending on the length of time required, would only work on every second or third watch.

There were marks on the conveyor belt every 10 inches. When a watch was placed on every mark, there would be over 100 watches on the line at a given point in time. Since this was considerably more than the number of workers on the line, it provided a one- or two-watch buffer between each operator so that if a preceding operator occasionally took longer than expected, it wouldn't idle the following worker as long as the worker causing the delay caught up within the next couple of watches. When the conveyor was run at normal speed, as was the case in June 1976, a completed watch came off the line every 21 seconds.

Modules shipped from the Dallas plant were prepared and placed on the line near the head of the belt; additional raw materials were added at the operation where they were required. One material handler supplied raw materials to all lines. Since all watches used the same basic module, different colors of watches could be produced at the same time as long as those attaching the bands and coding the finished units matched the components appropriately.

The process of assembly had changed considerably since the line had started in February. Many adjustments to increase efficiency were implemented by Fred Harper, although the idea might have come from a line supervisor or a worker. Changes were also made to accommodate tooling improvements. (Line operation and flow in early June is shown in Exhibit 8.)

EXHIBIT 8
Assembly Flow, Time Estimates, and Personnel Requirements for Final Assembly (TI-500 series watch)

Operation Number	Description	Estimated Time per Operation (direct labor seconds)	People per Operation (June 1976)	People* per Operation (balanced line)
1†	Prepare module (bend tab)................	20	2	1
2	Functional test—module (light-up display and cycle through functions)........	21 (avg.)	2	1
3	Frequency test—module...................	21 (avg.)	1	1
4†	Scrape novalac off the switch contacts	20	1	1
5†	Clip one post from module (TI-502 only)	18	1	1
6	Apply static resistant tape on module........	14	1	1
7	Remove tape tab cover	16	1	1
8‡	Heat-stake lens to bezel	21	21	1
9†	Inspect bezel and deburr at switch..........	41	3	2
10†	Clean switch holes (air nozzle)..............	11	1	—
11	Install and press set switch in bezel and clean	18	1	1

* Based on seconds per operation and desired production capacity.

† Nonstandard operations: Certain tasks had not originally been anticipated but had been added to overcome a problem that emerged when production started up. All told, there were five of these nonstandard operations.

Operation 1: It was necessary to bend a tab on the module to prevent it from grounding out on the case. This problem would be eliminated in any subsequent module redesigns, but this was not expected to happen for some time.

Operation 4: When the back plug was installed during module assembly, the epoxy glue used to cement it in place quite often covered the switch contacts. This problem was so common that a decision had been made to clean all incoming modules. There was no obvious solution to this problem.

Operation 5: A post on the module was used to align the module and the bezel. The model 502 bezel molds were made without the appropriate indentation; therefore, the post on the module had to be removed before being installed into these bezels.

Operations 9 and 10: Holes for the switches were drilled after the bezels were made. These two nonstandard operations were necessary to ensure a good seat for the switches. A new method of molding was already being used on one of the presses, where the holes were made as part of the injection-molding process. When all the presses were using this method, switch holes would no longer have to be deburred and cleaned.

‡ Machine time for this operation was 14.5 seconds; it took 3 seconds to load and 3 to unload.

Source: Prepared by Fred Harper from estimates derived from observation, experimentation, and experience.

EXHIBIT 8 (*concluded*)

Operation Number	Description	Estimated Time per Operation (direct labor seconds)	People per Operation (June 1976)	People* per Operation (balanced line)
12	Install and press command switch in bezel and clean	18	1	1
13	Check switch travel	12	1	1
14	Clean inside bezel using air nozzle...........	12	1	1
15	Install module in bezel	21	2	1
16	Install battery clip on module	20	2	1
17	Heat-stake battery clip on module	15	1	1
18	Install two batteries in module	21	2	1
19	Switch check (light up)	10	1 ⎫	
20	Date-code inside of watch back..............	10	⎬	2
21	Place O-ring on flange on watch back........	14	1 ⎭	
22	Install back on watch.......................	15	1	1
23	Functional text—watch	21 (avg.)	2	1
24	Install band on watch.......................	42	3	2
25	Cosmetic inspection and clean...............	17 (avg.)	1	1
26	Final test	35	2	2
27	Quality control	—	—	—
28	Place watch on cuff and buckle band	36	2	2
29	Place watch and cuff in display box...........	19	1	1
30	Apply label on display box base.............⎫	14	1	1
31	Place cover in display box base ....⎭			
32	Place owner's manual inside sleeve over display box and place box in tub	30	2	2
	Total assembly-line operators..........		43	33
	Line rover		—	1
	Material handler....................		1	1
	Troubleshoot and repair		4	3
			48	38

Each conveyor line had a supervisor whose desk was at the head of the belt. The line supervisor was responsible for the smooth flow of production on that line. Troubleshooting and repairing were generally done on line. Watches that failed specific tests were shunted off for repair and returned to the belt as soon as the repair was complete. Most failures were of a predictable nature; for example, if a watch failed operation 19, switch check, it was usually because the module and bezel were misaligned—an easily corrected problem.

Nonstandard Operations. Certain tasks had not originally been anticipated but had been added to overcome a problem that emerged when production started up. All told, there were five of these nonstandard operations (Exhibit 8).

ADVANTAGES OF LINE ASSEMBLY

Various members of the operations department spoke of the advantages of line over batch processing. These included less materials handling, less cosmetic product damage since material was not collected in tubs, lower work in process inventories, and faster quality-control and production-rate feedback. This last advantage was particularly valuable, since good throughput was compared against objective at different points on the line three times per shift, and negative deviations were quickly dealt with.

There were problems however. The most frequently mentioned was the regimentation of the line and concomitant loss of flexibility. Operators who took unscheduled breaks had to be covered. The need for constant, smooth flow of raw materials for the line complicated the management task, especially for first-line supervisors.

Unsanctioned buffer inventories were occasionally accumulated between operations. This practice was discouraged by Jack Shields who recognized it as counter to an efficient line operation. It was the adjustment of mentality from batch to line that was identified by many as the critical change necessary. Fortunately this was minimized at Lubbock because most workers and several of the line supervisors did not have previous experience with batch processes.

EXHIBIT 9
Texas Instruments Plastic Watch Cost Data (June 1976)

Manufacturing selling price		$13.50
Module cost*	$4.85	
Assembly labor†	0.80	
QRA‡ labor	0.03	
Assembly component parts	1.40	
Other	0.20	
	7.28	
Assembly overhead	0.10	
Contribution		6.12

* This cost is below the market price of module components shown in the text of the case because of TI's use of marginal costs in computing internal contribution.

† Based on 48 people producing 1 watch every 21 seconds [48 × $2.85 per hour × 21 seconds per watch ÷ (60 seconds × 60 minutes)].

‡ Quality and reliability assurance.

COST STRUCTURE

In mid-1976, labor rates at Lubbock were $2.85 per hour for line operators. These rates were regularly reviewed to keep them competitive or slightly above wage rates for the surrounding areas. Two thirds of the labor content of the watch was added after completion of the module; this was expected to decline to 60 percent (Exhibit 9).

OPERATIONAL CONSIDERATIONS

Peter realized that he had recently been involved in a lot of "fire-fighting," especially in trying to assure an adequate supply of raw materials. He knew, however, that he was expected to reduce costs over time according to a learning curve that was the result of "a lot of specific actions." He wondered what specific actions he or his operations people should be taking, especially in watch assembly where he felt the next 60 days were critical. Forecasted sales and peak monthly requirements had increased substantially since the line was designed. He was satisfied with the way the watch assembly line was running and felt that it had definite advantages over batch processing; nonetheless, it was accepted TI practice to step back periodically and review an operational method. Now appeared to be a good time for Peter Bradley and his managers to carry out such a review.

CASE 6

Max-Able Medical Clinic (A)

Harry D. Eugene, M.D., felt a growing sense of concern for the Automated Multitest Laboratory (AML) project as he reread the memorandum from his close associate Dr. George Johnson, a radiologist in the Max-Able radiology department (Exhibit 13). As head of the medical systems technology department he had worked closely during the past year with Drs. George Johnson in radiology, Roy Burns in internal medicine, and members of the executive committee at Max-Able, such as Dr. Long, to develop plans for an innovative automated multiphasic testing laboratory at the Max-Able Clinic. He reminded himself that he must take concerns such as those expressed in the memo into account as he prepared the final proposal for the project to the executive committee.

The Max-Able Medical Clinic was a private, multispecialty group-practice clinic. It was located in a relatively affluent urban area in the Southeast, where it had spacious modern facilities and laboratories. It was organized as a partnership with more than 130 affiliated physicians.[1] (See Exhibit 1.) Individual salaries and participation in earnings were closely proportional to the revenue each physician generated. Revenue from patient charges at Max-Able was generated from three sources: physician visits, tests and other procedures performed by the attending physician during the visit, and procedures ordered by the attending physician. These categories accounted respectively for 37 percent, 42 percent, and 21 percent of the revenue overall, but they varied from 70 percent, 7 percent, and

---

[1] In typical usage the term *multispecialty group practice* refers to an affiliated group of physicians who largely practice in the medical specialties. They typically treat patients with acute, difficult to diagnose, or complex health problems, whom they attract by referral from a primary care physician or by reputation. In contrast, the primary care physician (including general practitioners, internists in general practice, family practitioners, and pediatricians) typically treat the full range of health problems they encounter and assume much of the responsibility for preventative medicine and education.

23 percent for general practice in internal medicine, to 10 percent, 85 percent, and 5 percent for radiologists (X ray). All major specialties and subspecialties were represented in the clinic, and almost all the clinic's physicians also held appointments as "clinical" faculty at a nearby well-known university school of medicine. Max-Able was one of the early models of "group practice" and had a national reputation for its innovations in community health care and health program organization.

Consequently, it was not surprising that when a firm in the health services industry—AML International—had developed an automated health testing service characterized by modular design and a "carousel" configuration of patient flow, it had brought the design to Max-Able for consideration.

Dr. Eugene was currently facing the problem of deciding whether to proceed, what tests to include in the automated laboratory (lab), how the tests would be scheduled in a process flow, proper design of test sequences, pricing, and how to handle possible resistance among the clinic's physicians.

EXHIBIT 1
The Max-Able Medical Clinic Staff

Executive board:
  6 M.D.s

Internal medicine:
  Cardiology—4 M.D.s
  Chest diseases—6 M.D.s
  Endocrine and
    metabolic diseases—5 M.D.s
  Gastroenterology—3 M.D.s
  General medicine—5 M.D.s
  Hematology and oncology—2 M.D.s
  Infectious disease
    and immunology—1 M.D.
  Nuclear medicine—1 M.D.
  Peripheral vascular diseases—1 M.D.
  Renal diseases—1 M.D.
  Rheumatology—2 M.D.s

Allergy—2 M.D.s

Neurology—3 M.D.s

Dermatology—2 M.D.s

Pediatrics—7 M.D.s

Pediatric cardiology—1 M.D.

General practice—7 M.D.s

Psychiatry and clinical psychology—
  3 M.D.s, 2 Ph.D.s

General surgery—3 M.D.s

Administration:
  5 administrators

General and thoracic surgery—1 M.D.

General and vascular surgery—2 M.D.s

Plastic and reconstructive—2 M.D.s

Neurosurgery—1 M.D.

Orthopedic surgery—6 M.D.s

Orthopedic surgery and athletic
  medicine—1 M.D.

Urology—3 M.D.s

Ophthalmology and optometry—
  7 M.D.s

Otolaryngology—3 M.D.s

Obstetrics/gynecology—6 M.D.s

Anesthesiology—5 M.D.s

Environmental medicine—2 M.D.s

Environmental medicine/industrial
  surgery—1 M.D.

University Health Service—9 M.D.s

Radiology—7 M.D.s

Laboratory medicine—1 M.D.

Pathology—1 M.D.

Medical electronics—1 M.D.

Medical systems—1 M.D.

BACKGROUND ON AUTOMATED
MULTIPHASIC LABORATORIES

With the recent focus on the nation's health care delivery system, automated multiphasic laboratories were being heralded as an important breakthrough. The basic idea underlying the automated health testing concept was that a battery of critical medical tests could be administered to patients receiving medical checkups through the use of a special facility employing advanced technology and operated by medical technicians rather than physicians. In this way, a comprehensive sequence of carefully designed, standardized tests whose quality was carefully controlled could be effectively administered to a large number of patients at low costs and without the use of scarce and costly physicians' time. Such a facility promised to provide better quality information for diagnosing the health status of patients and the early detection of diseases than was typically available for the traditional health checkup.

In traditional medical practice a checkup involved an initial visit to a physician, typically a general practitioner or internist (practicing general medicine). In the course of the visit the physician would write up a lengthy medical history, examine the patient and perform a number of routine tests depending upon the patient's history, condition, symptoms, the equipment available in the office, and the physician's customary procedures. The patient might then be sent for further tests, laboratory procedures, X rays, etc., often in other locations, and, following the receipt of results, scheduled for another visit with the physician. If medical difficulties could not be diagnosed by this physician or if special procedures were required, then the patient might be referred to a specialist such as a cardiologist for heat diseases or a surgeon in any one of several specializations.

As planned, the multiphasic testing laboratory would be used at Max-Able to shortcut many of these time-consuming steps and improve the effectiveness with which physician and patient used their time. The patient would visit the multiphasic laboratory at his own convenience before the initial visit to the physician and results would be available before the initial physician visit. In this way, the physician would have a strong information base even at the initial visit and could make the best use of his time and knowledge in exploring particulars and making judgments rather than on the mechanics of testing procedures. The patient would be assured of a thorough and comprehensive checkup at a low cost and with a minimum waste of time in making repeat visits. Dr. Eugene thought the new laboratory would prove useful in several ways: in providing important diagnostic data for patients that came for general checkups, as a source of baseline data on patients with specific medical problems that came to the specialists at Max-Able; as a service to nonaffiliated physicians in the community that might wish to have such a good workup on their patients, and it might provide a resource for Max-Able physicians who wished to innovate in establishing new programs, like executive health checkup programs, etc.

Multiphasic health testing laboratories had been introduced several years earlier and successfully used in several major institutions. They were currently being introduced in many others. Pioneering work had been carried out, among other places, at Kaiser Permanente in California and the Mayo Clinic in Minnesota. Kaiser was world famous for the success which it, as a private institution, had achieved in providing a rather complete program of health care to several million persons in California at a reasonable predetermined annual charge. Because it provided complete health services at a fixed annual charge and was highly integrated, Kaiser had the incentives to seek the health improvement as well as labor-saving benefits of a multiphasic testing concept. It would experience the direct economic consequence of any improvement in its patients' health condition (or deterioration) that influenced the rate with which costly acute hospital facilities were utilized. It was therefore not surprising that Kaiser had been an innovator in this type of program. The Mayo Clinic, renowned for specialty care and not heavily involved in prepaid comprehensive care, had strong governance and instituted the multiphasic concept as a matter of policy.

In some of the early applications the multiphasic testing laboratory concept was used to screen patients, i.e., to separate the "worried well" from the sick and thereby determine which should receive the immediate and serious attention of a physician. Critics sometimes compared such facilities with military induction physicals where service is impersonal and patients are denied privacy, being required to dress and undress at several stations during the test sequence. There was also concern with use of multiphasic automated tests to screen patients, since it might lead to the denial of appropriate medical care.

The multiphasic lab, as proposed for Max-Able, differed in important respects from some of the earlier approaches. It would complement rather than replace the initial physician-patient contact. Furthermore, it would emphasize personalized services with many patient amenities.

It was technically feasible to include many tests in the lab, but the mix of tests would largely determine the potential demand. Most tests under consideration were costly. Dr. Eugene realized that the facility would have to offer profitable operations before the directors of the clinic would approve its implementation, yet the price for the battery of tests would greatly affect the usage of the facility. He also knew that gaining the support of the physicians before the lab was implemented was especially important in a group practice. Poor acceptance by physicians and their patients would not only cause problems at Max-Able but would also delay the widespread application of the concept elsewhere. AML International was anxious that the system be accepted at Max-Able because recovery of its development costs required broad adoption of the AML design in many practices. Failure of the design at Max-Able would mean an almost certain end to potential sales.

PROPOSED LABORATORY DESIGN

The modular "carousel" design proposed by AML International promised to offer all the benefits of previous automated testing labs at Kaiser and Mayo:

More information for the physician's use in diagnosis.

No need for the physican to perform the tests himself.

Less need for the physician to refer the patient to a laboratory for general tests and for the patient to schedule another visit to the doctor.

A sophisticated base of medical data for comparative analysis of long-term health trends.

Use of paramedical and nonmedical personnel to staff the AML.

Substantial decrease in medical costs and improvement in quality of testing.

Early diagnosis of certain diseases at a stage when they are most responsive to therapy.

The new design offered two additional benefits:

Convenience—no long waits, travel between test areas, or multiple dressing and undressing.

A personal touch—one technician assigned to a patient for the whole sequence of tests.

The general layout of the laboratory as proposed is presented in Exhibit 2. The entire sequence of patient movement through the facility would consist of five stages of activity: (1) pretest arrangements, (2) medical history and patient preparation, (3) initial stationary tests, (4) carousel tests, and (5) final stationary tests. Tests for all stages except the carousel had been tentatively decided.

PRETEST ARRANGEMENTS

Patient processing at the facility would begin when an appointment was made with the laboratory. Only patients referred by a physician could make an appointment, although for self-initiated patients the facility might suggest the names of several physicians to sponsor the tests. The patient would then be assigned an appointment time and asked to fast for five hours beforehand. Except in the case of rush appointments, the patient would be sent a questionnaire to be completed before the appointment. Upon arrival at the lab, the patient would give the questionnaire to the laboratory appointment secretary, who would assign a number to the patient to be used for test identification. The information from the questionnaire would be fed through an on-line terminal into a computerized patient record.

EXHIBIT 2
Facility Design

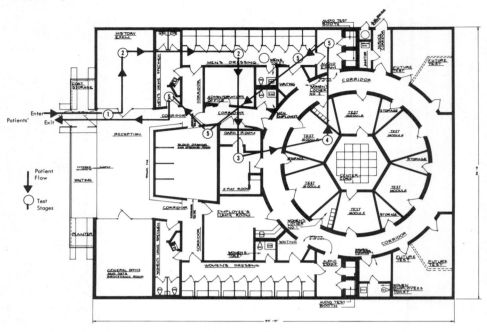

MEDICAL HISTORY AND PATIENT PREPARATION

The patient would then be instructed in the use of a computerized medical history terminal consisting of a back-projected filmed questionnaire and simple answering device. The patient would be presented a sequence of questions with several logical branches. If, for instance, the patient answered a question indicating a prior known medical condition, the terminal would branch to present a special questionnaire section to explore this condition. These answers would also be automatically fed into the patient's stored computer record.

Upon completion of the history portion of the exam, a patient would be given a large amount of glucose and shown to the males' or females' dressing area, where disposable garments would be issued for wearing during the tests. (The patient flow can be visualized from the layout in Exhibit 2 where major testing activity groups are indicated by numbers in circles.)

INITIAL STATIONARY TESTS

The next stage of tests would involve those performed in stationary rooms in the facility before the patient entered the carousel. A technician would be assigned to the patient and stay with the same patient throughout this and the next test stage.

The first test in the initial stationary stage would consist of an X ray. This would be followed by a digitally displayed measurement of the patient's height and weight. The X-ray test required a shielded X-ray room. After these procedures the patient would be led into one of the modules of the carousel, accompanied by the AML technician for the next stage of testing.

CAROUSEL TESTS

The carousel consisted of a "core" room which provided space for a large amount of test equipment, with six patient testing rooms, "modules," in a circle around it (Exhibit 2). The wall of the core, which was the inner wall of each module, turned to present the connections for various tests to each module. The patient would stay in his assigned module throughout this stage of the testing. Although the carousel could accommodate up to six modules, not every module had to be operable and furnished. Also, the carousel could be operated, if necessary, without having patients in all operable modules. For instance, only three modules might be equipped to handle patients. On any given cycle all three modules might not be full, but each module with a patient would still face, in turn, each side of the central core which paced the test sequence. Large expensive equipment would be located in the core of the carousel (Exhibit 2), while equipment for other tests would be located in or on the wall of each module. Only the central wall rotates with respect to the modules according to the sequence of test operations.

The technician would perform the appropriate tests or connect electrical leads to the core through input jacks located in the exposed section of the core wall. In fact, if a test were being given which did not require connection to the central core, the rotation of the wall merely served to pace the technician. An interlock device would prevent the carousel wall from rotating until all modules had been disconnected from the core. For instance, failure to get an adequate reading from equipment located in the core would prevent rotation until the core technician signaled that the test had been completed and the patient had been disconnected. Communication on the test's status between the technician in the module and the core technician would be permitted by windows in the core wall facing the module. Testing in other modules would be able to proceed even in the event of one delayed module if connection to the central core were not required at that point in the test sequence. While patients could be loaded into the carousel either sequentially or simultaneously, it was felt that having all the patients that would be tested at one time enter their assigned modules simultaneously provided the easiest organization with only minimal bottlenecks or waiting. Consequently, given morning startup and evening shutdown constraints, about seven hours of operation of the carousel was considered maximum for each of the five days per week the AML would be open.

FINAL STATIONARY TESTS

After the sequence of tests in the module, the patient would be directed to an audiometer room for a hearing test. Two audiometers each could be located next to the males' and females' dressing areas. After completing the hearing test, the patient would be directed by the AML technician to return to the dressing room and then to proceed to the blood drawing and specimen room. After two hours since the administering of the glucose "load" prior to testing, the blood sample and the urine specimen would be taken and the examination would be over. One-way doors would prevent the patient from returning to the carousel or test areas.

PLANNING FOR THE LABORATORY

The staffing plans for the laboratory were to have it headed by a registered nurse. The number of supporting personnel would largely be a function of the number of active modules per day, i.e., the number of filled modules per cycle around the core, the number of scheduled cycles to fulfill demand, and the general technology of the facility. A computer operator would be required to update the automated records and complete the medical history records in a batch mode using as input the results of the AML tests. The proposed AML staffing requirements, job specifications, and salary requirements are presented in Exhibits 3 and 4.

PROPOSED TESTS

The medical planning committee for the lab had decided that the X ray, height and weight test, audiometer hearing test, and blood and urine tests should be included in any test sequence. However, the number of duplicate units of each type of test equipment and the complete testing sequence were as yet undetermined. Dr. Eugene realized that each test was expensive and consequently was concerned that the total cost might exceed the level acceptable to a large number of patients. A certain test might also add too much time to the cycle of the carousel, thereby limiting the number of patients that could be handled in a working day.

The committee, including Dr. Eugene and representatives from many departments at Max-Able, had examined a number of technically feasible and medically proven tests and had found that the quality of each testing procedure was acceptable:

> *Spirometry* —a test of lung capacity that required the patient to exhale through a mouthpiece into a device measuring the volume and pres-

EXHIBIT 3
Staffing Requirements and Costs

Personnel requirements:

Assuming one or two test sequences per half hour:

Supervising nurse..........	1
Technicians:	
Front desk..............	1
Test sequence...........	1 per operative module
Core equipment operator..............	1
Computer operator.......	⅓ part time

Job descriptions:

Supervising nurse—responsible for directing, supervising, and counseling staff members of the AML. Must arrange for EKGs and X rays to be sent to a cardiologist and radiologists for reading and interpretation and then returned to the AML to be forwarded to the referring physician. Responsible for the purchase of laboratory supplies and the detection of any malfunction in equipment.

Technician—under the general supervision of the supervising nurse, administers a battery of medical tests to patients and performs clerical duties. Must be able to record test measurements and operate testing equipment.

Computer operator—must be able to operate a small computer in batchmode to complete the medical records with the results of the AML tests.

Suggested wage structure:

Supervising nurse......	$12,000 average wage
AML technician.......	6,100 average wage
Computer operator.....	3,600 part-time cost

EXHIBIT 4
General Costs per Annum

1.	Office supplies................	$ 350
2.	Utilities.....................	1,500
3.	Maintenance and repair.........	1,800
4.	Telephone...................	850
5.	Insurance and miscellaneous....	1,100
6.	Taxes.......................	1,850
	Total....................	7,450

sure of the exhalation. Results contribute to the diagnosis of heart disease and lung diseases such as emphysema.

Mamography—a test for cancer of the breasts, an appropriate testing procedure only for females in the mid 40s to early 50s.

Electrocardiography (EKG)—a test for heart disorder or weakness performed with the patient connected electrically to a device measuring the electrical impulses of the heart. Results had to be interpreted by a trained cardiologist.

Vision —a test for corrected vision (reflecting mirrors would provide the standard distance for the test within the confines of the module).

Ocular tension (tonometry) —a test for the indications of glaucoma (a serious eye disease usually occurring in late middle age or later) per-

EXHIBIT 5
Death Risk Profiles with Modifying Condition (specifies probabillity of death within 10 years by four principal causes for each age sex group in percentage terms)

	Male Age 20–24	Female Age 20–24	Male Age 40–44	Female Age 40–44
*†‡ Motor-vehicle accidents	0.58%	0.12%	0.28%	0.10%
With seat belts 75–100% of time	0.46	0.09	0.23	0.08
Heavy social drinking—definite excess	2.90	0.60	1.42	0.51
*†‡ Suicide	0.13	0.04	0.26	0.09
† Chronic rheumatic heart disease	0.02	0.03	0.17	0.13
†§ Vascular lesions affecting central nervous system (hemorrhage)........................	—	0.02	0.22	0.20
* Homicide	0.06	0.02	—	—
* Accidents, drowning.............................	0.04	—	—	—
†§ Arteriosclerotic heart disease	0.03	—	1.88	0.30
One or more packs cigarettes per day	0.04	—	2.81	0.62
Cigarettes plus 75% overweight and high cholesterol level	0.23	—	10.56	2.34
With success in prescribed exercise, weight reduction, stopped smoking	0.02	—	1.26	0.33
‡ Cirrhosis of liver	—	—	0.22	0.13
With heavy social drinking—definite excess.......	—	—	1.11	0.66
§ Cancer of breast	n.a.	—	n.a.	0.35
If mother or sister had C.B.	n.a.	—	n.a.	0.70
With regular self-exam and mammogram	n.a.	—	n.a.	0.17
§ Cancer of cervix.................................	n.a.	—	n.a.	0.14
Jewish.......................................	n.a.	—	n.a.	0.01
Low socioeconomic status with teenage marriage or sex relations	n.a.	—	n.a.	0.60
With three negative Pap smear tests in last five years............................	n.a.	—	n.a.	0.01
Overall probability of death from all causes in %...............................	1.58	0.60	5.56	3.02

No entry indicates cause was not included in top 14 causes of death for group in question.

* Four principal causes of death for white males 20–24 years of age.
† Four principal causes of death for white males 40–44 years of age.
‡ Four principal causes of death for white females 20–24 years of age.
§ Four principal causes of death for white females 40–44 years of age.
n.a. = Not available.
All probabilites are approximations.
Source: Based upon data in Robbins and Hall, *How to Practice Prospective Medicine*, Methodist Hospital of Indiana, 1970.

formed by placing a rubber probe against the surface of the eye. To facilitate the test, the eye must be anesthetized; consequently, the test must be performed after the general vision test, and the patient must be observed for at least 20 minutes afterwards until adequate vision is regained.

Blood pressure —a test for blood pressure performed by a device measuring the Doppler effect associated with the changes in pressure.

Pap smear —a test for cancer of the cervix performed on most adult women.

This menu of tests was developed for possible inclusion in the lab on the basis of medical importance, quality of automated equipment, and the precedents established in earlier automated test labs. The 10-year death risk profiles given in Exhibit 5 show some of the respects in which test applicability varies with conditions in the population segment being served. All tests had been included in existing automated labs previously established for screening. For instance, mamography was included in the Kaiser testing facility. The Pap smear test for cervical cancer (an inexpensive and effective test, especially in particularly susceptible socioeconomic categories including many of Max-Able's patients) was often included, too. This test required professional training, however, because the setup was similar to a general gynecological examination. Several committee members wondered if many physicians would feel that the Pap smear should be an integral part of the doctor-patient relationship. Even though the test might uncover some incidence of the disease, he questioned whether it should be included in the module in the face of such possibly adverse reaction.

As part of the AML International proposal, variable and fixed costs as well as the duration of each test under consideration were provided. The medical planning committee had updated these figures and thought they represented the costs that should be used in reaching a decision (Exhibits 6 and 7.)

EXHIBIT 6
Capital Costs and Test Duration

Test and Necessary Equipment	*Cost**	*Duration*
1. History documentation: 5–6 terminals and computer	$80,000	15–45 minutes
2. Chest X ray: Odelca camera and darkroom facilities	22,220	2 minutes
3. Height and weight: load cell, linear potentiometer, and digital readout	4,200	1 minute
4. Audiometer: Rudmose Model ARJ-4A	1,800 per set	5 minutes
5. Blood sample and urine collection	1,200 per station	5 minutes

EXHIBIT 6 (*concluded*)

Test and Necessary Equipment	Cost*	Duration
6. Spirometer: Electro-Med Model 780 and Pulmo-digicomp Model 1000	8,180	2–3 minutes
7. Electrocardiograph: Hewlett-Packard 1513A (three-channel recorder)	4,600	15 seconds to 5 minutes
8. Ocular tension: MacKay-Marg Electronic Tonometer	2,000 per module	5 minutes
9. Vision: American Optical Project-O-Chart.	275 + $500 per module	3–5 minutes
10. Blood pressure: Godart Model 151-CC	3,600	4 minutes
11. Mamography: several types available	25,000 per module	9–11 minutes
12. Pap smear: no capital equipment necessary		2 minutes
13. Miscellaneous (dressing, rotation, instruction)		10 minutes
14. General module equipment.	1,000 per module	

* Represents total test equipment capital cost for up to six modules except where cost per module is specified.

EXHIBIT 7
Variable Costs of the AML

Expendable Supplies per Patient	Cost per Item	Subtotal
1. Appointment procedures:		
a. Appointment brochure	$0.06	
b. Confidential medical information form	0.02	
c. AML letter-size envelope.	0.02	
d. Stamp (postage)	0.08	
e. AML appointment scheduling chart.	0.02	
	0.20	$0.20
2. Computer processing:		
a. Storage envelope	0.05	
b. Labels (identification)	0.07	
c. Labels (EKG)	0.01	
d. Computer paper.	0.08	
e. AML medical report folders	0.10	
f. Cardboard storage boxes	0.01	
g. Computer ribbons	0.01	
	0.33	0.53

EXHIBIT 7 (*continued*)

	Expendable Supplies per Patient	*Cost per Item*	*Subtotal*
3.	Main desk:		
	a. Glucose drink (100 gm. carbonated cola).........	0.25	
	b. Cups for glucose	0.02	
	c. Disposable thermometer tip	0.04	
	d. Exit brochures	0.05	
		0.36	0.89
4.	Laboratory:		
	a. Urine specimen cups........................	0.05	
	b. Urine specimen cup lids.....................	0.05	
	c. Bili-Labstix...............................	0.12	
	d. Testuria..................................	0.28	
	e. Prepacked.................................	0.02	
	f. Vacutainers (two tops, holder, and needle).......	0.40	
	g. Serum tubes...............................	0.04	
	h. Alcohol wipe..............................	0.01	
	j. Band-Aid.................................	0.01	
	k. Wood applicators..........................	0.01	
	l. Glass beads...............................	0.02	
	m. Dispo pipets..............................	0.01	
		1.02	1.91
5.	Dressing booth:		
	a. Gown.....................................	0.25	
	b. Slippers...................................	0.06	
	c. Plastic bag................................	0.02	
		0.33	2.24
6.	X-ray department		
	a. Chest X-ray film...........................	0.83	
	b. Envelope..................................	0.05	
	c. Developing chemicals.......................	0.02	
	d. Radiological interpretation....................	1.00	(by contract with radiologists)
		1.90	4.14
7.	Test modules:		
	a. Tonometry:		
	(1) Ophthaine..............................	0.02	
	(2) Tissues.................................	0.01	
	(3) Tonotips	0.10	
	(4) Wetting agent	0.01	
	(5) Recording paper	0.05	
		0.19	4.33

EXHIBIT 7 (*concluded*)

Expendable Supplies per Patient	Cost per Item	Subtotal
b. EKG:		
(1) Electrolyte cream	0.02	
(2) Alcohol wipes...........................	0.02	
(3) Tissue	0.01	
(4) Cardiological interpretation................	1.00	(by contract with cardiologists)
(5) Interpretation—abnormal EKGs $20 (25% occurrence)........................	5.00	
	6.05	10.38
c. Blood pressure: No supplies.		
d. Vision: Visual field pattern card	0.01	10.39
e. Spirometry: Spirotubes.................................	0.05	10.44
f. Mamography.................................	9.50	19.94
g. Pap smear	4.00	23.94
8. Miscellaneous:		
a. Paper head protectors	0.04	
b. Paper towels	0.02	
c. Tissues	0.01	
d. Soap	0.01	
e. Technical supplies	0.21	
	0.29	24.23

PROCESS UTILIZATION

One of the most difficult problems in designing the lab was determining its potential utilization. Dr. Eugene was able to find little published data that might help him in reaching a conclusion.

The committee approached the problem of obtaining data in several different ways. He believed that ultimate demand would be based on several factors:

1. The number of patients coming to Max-Able for a checkup or for general health care, not for follow-up or "routine" visits.
2. The applicability of the lab for any specialty. Many patients seeing a physician or specialist might not need the sequence since they have a well-defined health problem or because the general tests might not be as thorough or exact as special tests performed in the laboratory.
3. Age and sex of patients.
4. The price of the sequence.

It was felt that demand could be estimated from data on these factors.

Two statistical samples were taken, one that represented all Max-Able patients during a typical "composite week" and the second was a study of new patients only. Fortunately Max-Able used a computer-based billing system; these records contained the patient's name and information about the attending doctor and his services—his name, specialty, charges, and some of the laboratory procedures performed during the visit or subsequently ordered. Using these sources, Dr. Eugene randomly drew a day's history for each day of the week to make up a composite week at Max-Able that was free of seasonal variations. From this composite week he determined the number of eligible patients by types of diagnosis and laboratory procedures. Patients for whom the lab tests were completely inapplicable, such as those returning for follow-up visits, were excluded. Exhibit 8 gives the number of visits to Max-Able by eligible patients during this composite week by selected medical specialty and a subjective estimate of the percentage of eligible patients for whose diagnostic and treatment regime the lab tests might be applicable.

EXHIBIT 8
Weekly Composite Study

Visits by Specialty	Total Visits	Men	Women	Percentage for Whom AML Was Applicable
Internists	1,357	556	801	75
General practice	531	232	299	75
Environmental medicine	118	39	79	10
Obstetrics/gynecology	487	—	487	5
Subtotal...................	2,493	827	1,666	
Other specialties	4,983	2,413	2,570	1
Total	7,476	3,240	4,236	

The 7,476 visits in the composite week were further examined to determine visits that were equivalent to a comprehensive initial physical examination or regular annual checkup but not necessarily as comprehensive as the lab. Approximately 10 percent, or 781, of the visits fell in this category. Exhibit 9 gives the age and sex distribution of these patients.

The best judgment suggested that the highest potential utilization of the lab would come from the groups of patients who were properly most concerned about their health, those over, say, 40 years old. Even though a doctor might prefer that all patients have a comprehensive test sequence like the lab's, the basic good health of young people and the cost of the lab sequence might induce the doctor to omit such a sequence for lower age groups and rely instead on detection during the normal office visit.

EXHIBIT 9
General Physical Examinations by Sex and Age (from the composite week sample)

Age Group	Males		Females		Total	
	Number	Percent	Number	Percent	Number	Percent
Infants (0–11 months)	35	8.5	24	6.5	59	7.6
Children (1–12 years)	45	10.9	28	7.7	73	9.3
Teens (13–19 years)	22	5.3	25	6.8	47	6.0
Twenties (20–29 years)	35	8.5	39	10.6	74	9.5
Thirties (30–39 years)	55	13.3	44	12.0	99	12.7
Matured (40–49 years)	98	23.7 ⎫	56	15.2 ⎫	154	19.8
Middle aged (50–69 years)	100	24.2 ⎬ 53.6	103	28.0 ⎬ 56.5	203	26.0
Elderly (70 years plus)	23	5.7 ⎭	49	13.3 ⎭	72	9.2
Total	413	100.1	368	100.1	781	100.1

To obtain further data, the treatment patterns of new patients at Max-Able were examined. Of the 1,685 new patients seen during a month's time, 14 percent, or 235, were considered candidates for the lab.

Further analysis was performed to obtain the distribution of current total testing fees for these 235 patients at Max-Able. Undoubtedly, the price of the lab facility would be compared by both patients and physicians to fees for similar tests performed by existing laboratory facilities, either at Max-Able or elsewhere. Since Max-Able physicians would not be constrained to refer patients to the lab even if it were built, the price would have a great effect on demand. The present fees for laboratory testing are summarized in Exhibit 10.

EXHIBIT 10
Actual Laboratory Costs for Sample of Initial Patients

Billing	Number of Patients out of 235	Billing	Cumulative Frequency Percent
$0–$9	55	Over 0	100
$10–$19	12	Over $9	77
$20–$29	58	Over $19	72
$30–$34	9	Over $29	47
$35–$39	10	Over $34	43
$40–$49	43	Over $39	39
$50–$59	31	Over $49	21
$60 or over.	17	Over $59	7

Current Testing Charges
(through existing MAMC laboratories)

EKG (without interpretation)	$17.50
Spirometer	10.00
X ray	12.00
Blood and urine tests	25.00
History (done by physician).	7.00
Visual test (done by optometrist or ophthalmologist).	3.00
Audiometer	10.00
Mamography	10.00
Pap smear.	5.00
	99.50

Each test under consideration for the lab would have a different usefulness to a physician depending on his specialty. The committee ranked each test's usefulness for each specialty from "very useful" (an integral part of most diagnoses) to "generally useful" (related only to the physician's concern for the overall health of his patient; see Exhibit 11).

EXHIBIT 11
Usefulness of Tests by Medical Specialty

	Internists: General Medicine, Gastroenterology, Cardiologists, Subspecialties	General Practice	Environmental Medicine	Obstetrics/ Gynecology	Other Specialties	Radiologists
History	Very useful	Very useful	Very useful	Very useful	All tests generally useful for diagnosis, but tests often too broad in scope, or doctor has complete medical record when he sees patient (i.e. patient has been referred, so tests have already been performed).	
Chest X ray	Very useful	Very useful	Very useful	Generally useful		Only X rays appropriate; 50% of work done on chest X rays for routine physicals.
Height and weight	Very useful	Very useful	Very useful	Very useful		
Blood and urine	Very useful	Very useful	Very useful	Very useful		
Audiometry	Generally useful	Generally useful	Very useful	Generally useful		
Spirometry	Very useful	Very useful	Very useful	Generally useful		
EKG	Very useful	Very useful	Very useful	Generally useful		
Blood pressure	Very useful	Very useful	Very useful	Generally useful		
Vision	Desirable for patient	Desirable for patient	Generally useful	Generally useful		
Tonometry	Very useful	Very useful	Generally useful	Generally useful		
Pap smear	Very useful	Very useful	Generally useful	Very useful		
Mamography	Very useful	Very useful	Generally useful	Very useful		
Applicability factor (for patients over 40)	75%	75%	10%	5%	1%	—

Dr. Eugene initially felt that the maximum potential demand might be quickly approximated as the 1,068 patients per week that were represented by an adjusted sum of the composite week group plus the new-patient potential. These adjustments involved weighing the composite week demand by patient age percentages and the applicability factor for each specialty. Based on these calculations (presented in Exhibit 12), Dr. Eugene revised his estimate of the maximum potential demand upward to almost 1,100 patients per week. Finally, this demand was adjusted for each price range that might be charged by multiplying the cumulative percentage of all laboratory procedures that cost more than a given price for the new lab. For instance, only 7 percent of new patients were currently charged more than $60 for laboratory tests by existing laboratories. Consequently, Dr.

EXHIBIT 12
Total Weighted Potential Demand

A. Weighting by patient age percentages over 40 (weekly demand from composite study [Exhibit 8] weighted by percent of patients over 40 [Exhibit 9]):

Male = 53.6% over 40   Female = 56.5% over 40

	Male		*Female*		*Total*
Internists	556 × 53.6% =	300	801 × 56.5% =	450	750
General practice	232 × 53.6% =	124	299 × 56.5% =	170	294
Environmental medicine	39 × 53.6% =	21	79 × 56.5% =	44	65
Obstetrics/gynecology	0 × 53.6% =	0	487 × 56.5% =	275	275
Specialties (other)	2,413 × 53.6% = 1,300		2,570 × 56.5% = 1,460		2,760

B. Weighted by specialty applicability factor (from specialty applicability factor [Exhibit 11]):

Internists . . . .   750 × 75% = 562
General practice . . . .   294 × 75% = 222
Environmental medicine . . . .   65 × 10% =   7
Obstetrics/gynecology . . . .   275 ×   5% = 14
Specialties (other) . . . . 2,760 ×   1% = 28
                                                            ———
                                                            833

Total potential weighted demand = 833 + 235 new patients = 1,068 patients per week or 55,536 per year for a 52-week year.

C. Weighted by price:

Cumulative Percent

If AML costs over $29 . . . . . 47% × 55,536 = 26,000
If AML costs over $34 . . . . . 43% × 55,536 = 23,800
If AML costs over $39 . . . . . 39% × 55,536 = 21,600
If AML costs over $49 . . . . . 21% × 55,536 = 11,600
If AML costs over $59 . . . . . 7% × 55,536 = 3,900

Eugene assumed that only 7 percent of the total weighted potential demand would desire the AML tests at a cost of $60 in lieu of Max's regular laboratory tests (even though they may not have been as comprehensive as the new lab sequence).

THE REPORT TO THE EXECUTIVE COMMITTEE

As he prepared to draw up final recommendations for the automated lab, Dr. Eugene reviewed the basis for his interest in the project and the origin of resistance to the project within Max-Able. The impressive stack of reports on his desk from the Public Health Service and elsewhere provided convincing evidence that such a lab, if properly implemented and supported, both could and had improved the rate of condition finding in diagnosing patients, helped to reduce morbidity in the population of patients that were processed, and reduced the cost of health care.

He felt that it was important to draw up a final plan specifying the exact tests that would be included, the number of units of test equipment that should be purchased, the patient flow through the facility, and a pricing recommendation. The recommendations should be so carefully thought out that potential opponents would find no basis for criticism in these specifics.

At the same time Dr. Eugene recognized some very real sources of resistance to aspects of the new project. There was very little doubt but that the tests would be of high quality, but in many instances they would present established physicians with new and unfamiliar sources of evidence upon which to base their diagnosis. These would represent documentary evidence that the busy, established physician would have to interpret fully if he used the facility at all. Otherwise he would be exposed to the risk of a malpractice suit in the event that a medical problem was overlooked.

There were physicians who claimed that a standardized battery of tests were inappropriate in the first place since patients differed enormously in the conditions that warranted exploration. This line of reasoning led to the argument that the new concept would actually raise health costs since it induced unnecessary testing.[2]

Finally, while results from the lab report would undoubtedly save a great deal of time during the patient's visit, it might also result in a reduction of physician fees for tests that would otherwise have been done in the office. Since each physician's fees were ultimately related to the procedures he performed, the introduction of the lab into the group practice might redistribute fees among physicians and between physicians and the lab. For instance, both the electrocardiograph and X-ray tests would be interpreted by specialists before being sent to the physician who referred the patient.

---

[2] It would not be unusual for the results from a particular test to be far outside a normal range for a particular patient when he was otherwise apparently healthy. This anomaly might result from prior diet, emotional conditions, drugs taken, or unexplained reasons, but involve considerable retesting to ensure that medical problems were not the source of the test result.

Although Dr. Eugene had negotiated a low $1 interpretation fee, these might run normally from $5 to $25.

Dr. Eugene was sensitive to the large investment that AML International had made for technical, architectural, and system development and realized that if the AML facility were built, Max-Able would have to invest over $250,000 in land and another $500,000 in the building. All the partners of Max-Able would be very concerned with the lab's economic viability, because Max-Able expected to obtain a reasonable net contribution on any investment.

In large part, the executive board of Max-Able would decide the general feasibility of the facility on its merits as a potential investment. Since the project had the strong support of Dr. Long, an eminent national figure in medicine as well as at Max-Able, Dr. Eugene felt confident that a sound proposal would be accepted, provided that affiliated physicians would not be required to use it for their patients. Given the type of resistance that was evident in Dr. Johnson's memo (Exhibit 13), he still wondered if there was other action he should take.

EXHIBIT 13
Resistance to AML

MEMO

To: Harold D. Eugene, M.D.

From: George P. Johnson, M.D.

Re: Automated Multitest Laboratory

If a vote were held in the X-ray department on the acceptance of an AML, I calculate that it would lose, 4 to 2. Some of the department members are disturbed that there was not more research into the value, patient acceptability, and cost of such an endeavor. Furthermore, there is a genuine desire to practice episodic medicine rather than encourage mass surveys of essentially well patients. There are some reservations against entering into a project with a commercial company (AML International). The department as a whole would prefer to exclude chest films from the AML and retain the present system of having the individual physician request the films and interpretation from us as indicated.

Lowell Steel Corporation

Big Product Ranges

The Lowell Steel Corporation, a major producer of steel in the United States, was located in a small town on the Shenango River about 16 miles from Youngstown, Ohio. The company and its subsidiaries manufactured and sold hot- and cold-rolled carbon steel strip, stainless and alloy steel strip, steel sheets, carbon and alloy seamless tubing, galvanized and other coated products, and certain miscellaneous items.

In 1955, the company began an extensive program of expansion and integration. The program was designed to (1) enlarge the company's steel ingot producing capacity and (2) secure manufacturing subsidiaries which could further process steel the company had been selling as hot-rolled strip and thereby enable the company to "take its products to market at higher levels of price." In April 1956, management was considering possible directions of further expansion. In addition, they were trying to decide whether to increase the operating rate by 10 percent.

MANUFACTURING FACILITIES

The Lowell Works had blast furnaces, steelmaking, and rolling-mill facilities on a single site (Exhibit 1). The two 800-ton blast furnaces had rated annual capacities over 250,000 tons of hot metal each, for a total annual capacity at the Lowell Works in excess of 500,000 tons of hot metal. Fourteen open-hearth furnaces could produce a million tons of steel ingots in a year. A 36-inch blooming mill, 24-inch bar mill, and 18-inch bar mill reduced the ingots to billets, blooms, and slabs for further processing at Lowell, or shipment to a subsidiary mill or a customer. All of these facilities had been constructed before 1940.

At the end of March 1956, the two blast furnaces at the Lowell Works were being operated as close to capacity as was possible and together were

No slabbing Mill Listed?

EXHIBIT 1
Photograph of Lowell Works (blast furnaces and open-hearth shop are in the background)

producing from 45,000 to 46,000 tons of pig iron per month. This metal was charged hot to the open-hearth furnaces. The company was operating 10 open hearths, each of which had an output of about 7,000 tons of steel ingots per month. The hot metal and scrap charge to the open-hearth furnace was made up of about 58 percent pig iron and 42 percent scrap metal. Each furnace was tapped every 10 to 11 hours and produced slightly over 100 tons per heat.

The company had found that the optimum ratio of molten iron in the metal charge for the open-hearth furnace was somewhere between 62 percent and 65 percent; a higher proportion of molten iron resulted in certain process difficulties, and a lower proportion increased the time per heat because of the larger amount of cold scrap which had to be melted. Under normal circumstances, the furnaces were never operated with less than 50 percent or more than 70 percent molten iron in the charge. Above 70 percent, the furnace reaction became so violent that it was somewhat uncontrollable. Below 50 percent, the furnace reaction removed too much of the carbon from the metal, and it became necessary to go to the cost and trouble of adding carbon to the melt. Moreover with more than 50 percent cold scrap in the charge, the melting times became excessively long.[1]

The Lowell Company's sales of ingots and semifinished steel products (plates, slabs, and bars) averaged approximately 17,000 tons per month in the spring of 1956. Of this amount, just over 7,100 tons were sold as ingots and almost 9,900 tons were sold as semifinished steel. In addition, semifinished steel was sold to a subsidiary, Perkins Tube and Steel Company.

---

[1] For 1 ton of steel output, 1.12 tons of hot metal and scrap input were needed, regardless of percentage scrap.

(See discussion below.) Most of the company's semifinished steel output, however, was converted to hot-rolled strip at the Lowell Works. In 1956, the company was operating four hot-strip mills. The continuous mill was used for strip ranging between 5 inches and 22 inches in width, the 9-inch mill for strip between 1 inch and 2¼ inches in width, and the 10-inch mill for strip between 2 inches and 5¼ inches in width.

More than half of the hot strip was further processed on the company's cold-finishing equipment at Lowell or in subsidiary plants. About 11,500 tons per month were being cold rolled at the Lowell Works, and another 9,000 tons transferred to subsidiaries. The remaining strip (18,700 tons per month) was sold to customers in many different industries for fabrication into a very wide range of end products.

SUBSIDIARIES

The activities carried on by the several subsidiary companies may be summarized as follows:

The Perkins Tube and Steel Company operated a tube plant in Detroit and a cold-rolling mill in Dearborn. The tube plant secured about 20 percent of its requirements of semifinished steel rounds from the Lowell Works and purchased the remainder on the open market.[2] Requirements from all sources in early 1956 averaged 7,500 tons per month. The Lowell Works did not have sufficient equipment to produce all of the different sizes and types of rounds required in the tube plant. Additional equipment was to be installed for rolling rounds, but it was anticipated that the tube plant would always buy some of its steel from other companies. The output of the tube plant was sold primarily to the automobile and oil industries.

The cold-rolling plant in Dearborn secured all of its requirements of hot-rolled strip from the Lowell Works. Monthly shipments to Dearborn were averaging 5,000 tons of hot-rolled strip in early 1956. About 80 percent to 90 percent of the output of this plant was sold to customers in the automobile industry and the remainder to miscellaneous steel stamping companies.

The Maynard Steel Corporation operated cold-reducing and cold-finishing mills in Cleveland. The requirements of hot-rolled strip 4,000 tons per month were secured from the Lowell Works. The finished products of the company were sold to a large number of relatively small customers in all sections of the country. The most important item in the company's line was box strapping.

MANUFACTURING COSTS

The Lowell Steel Corporation was not a "low-cost producer of tonnage steel" in the same sense as were the larger concerns in the industry. The

---

[2] These rounds did not go through the hot-strip mill.

company's production operations in 1956 were integrated to a greater degree than were those of the other specialized, small independent steel producers. It did not, however, own sources of raw materials, ore mines, ore boats, loading docks, or railroads; ownership of these properties was quite common among the United States Steel Corporation, the Bethlehem Steel Corporation, the Republic Steel Corporation, and other large producers. In some instances, the Lowell Steel Corporation purchased its raw materials from the larger concerns (or their subsidiaries) and used their transportation facilities to assemble the materials at its plants. Moreover, the equipment in its plants was smaller in size and operated at slower speeds than the equipment maintained by some of the big steel companies. Illustrative manufacturing costs for the winter of 1956 are presented in Exhibit 2.

EXHIBIT 2
Manufacturing Costs—March 1956

Blast Furnace Operations
(materials charged to furnace 2 during March)

	Tons	Cost per Ton	Total Cost
Iron ore............................	39,683	$ 9.04	$ 358,734
Scrap, dust, cinder, miscellaneous	5,547		35,167
Limestone...........................	9,445	2.80	26,446
Coke	23,096	19.53	451,065
Subtotal.........................			871,412
Labor and other direct operating costs (not including depreciation)			142,592
Total cost			1,014,004
Tons of hot metal produced			22,971
Net cost per ton of hot metal			44.14

Open Hearths
(cost per ton of ingots, based on 10 furnaces producing 70,000 tons per month)

Metals Charged	Tons Charged per Ingot Ton Produced	Cost per Ton of Charge	Cost per Ton Ingots Produced
Hot metal from blast furnace.....	0.650	$44.14	$28.69
Steel scrap	0.470	48.00	22.56
Ore and miscellaneous metals	0.060		1.74
Subtotal....................			52.99
Cost above metal (labor, operating expenses, molds, fluxes, etc., excluding depreciation)................			19.78
Net cost per ton of ingots........			72.77

EXHIBIT 2 (*concluded*)

Blooming Billet and Bar Mills
(cost per ton of slabs produced)

Gross metal input (84.7% yield):
1.18 ingot tons × $72.77 per ton.............................	$85.87
Scrap credit (13.7% salvaged, at $48 per ton)*	(7.76)
Net metal cost...	78.11
Cost above metal...	7.24
Net cost of slabs	85.35

Continuous Hot Rolling Mill
(cost per ton of hot-rolled strip)

Gross metal input (93.6% yield from slabs):
1/.936 tons × $85.35	$ 91.20
Scrap credit (6% salvaged at $48 per ton)†	(3.08)
Net metal cost...	88.12
Cost above metal...	14.43
Net cost of hot-rolled strip	102.55

* 13.7 percent of input is salvaged; 1.18 × 0.137 × $48.
† 6 percent of input is salvaged; 1.07 × 0.06 × $48.

As a result of these circumstances, the Lowell Steel Corporation operated at somewhat of a cost disadvantage with respect to the big steel producers on large tonnage orders for standard grades of steel. The company was in a favorable position to compete, however, for small-volume orders on certain specialty items. It was thus necessary for the company to "discriminate" in its selling activities; that is, to seek out customers whose particular requirements were such that the company could capitalize on the flexibility of its small plant, the capabilities of the particular equipment it operated, and the "know-how" it had acquired over a great many years for handling certain special grades of steel.

For example, a customer might wish to buy hot-rolled strip 18¼ inches in width and 0.090 inches in thickness. The Lowell Steel Corporation could roll such steel in its continuous hot mill at a rate of perhaps 500 tons per 8-hour shift. A big producer with large equipment, however, would probably be able to roll the same steel in 37-inch or 54-inch widths at a rate of perhaps 1,000 to 2,000 tons per 8-hour shift. The large widths could then be quickly slit to the desired dimension of 18¼ inches. In a situation of this type the conversion costs of the big producer would unquestionably be lower than those of the Lowell Steel Corporation.

The Lowell Steel Corporation was in a favorable position to compete, however, if the customer wished to buy in a quantity which was too small to justify the large producer in setting up his mills. The company was also in a favorable position if the customer insisted on having "mill" rather than "sheared" edges on the steel, because then the big producer could handle the order only by running it in single thickness with his equipment operating at less than full capacity.[3] Similarly, if the customer wished a very high carbon steel or unusually close tolerances on the gauge, the Lowell Steel Corporation might be in a favorable position to handle the order, because high carbon steels were difficult to roll in wide widths and the problems in controlling tolerances tended to increase as the width of the strip increased.

Circumstances analogous to those noted for hot strip existed in the case of the many other different grades and finishes of steel which the company sold. As a result, it was the policy of the company to seek out customers and markets where the manufacturing requirements were such that it would enjoy a competitive advantage or at least compete on equal terms with the larger producers. Conversely, the company made no attempt to solicit business in such markets as automobile sheet steel where the contracts were let for very large tonnages of standard grades and finishes.

During early 1956, steel prices were such that the Lowell Steel Corporation could have met competitive prices and secured a fair rate of return in almost any market. In the long run, however, the executives believed that the company's interests would best be served by developing those markets which the large producers were not too well equipped to serve. As a result of its sales policies, the company had established a position as one of the most important producers in the field of special and coated steels. It was a major producer of high carbon steel and ranked as perhaps the largest producer of cutlery and cooperage steels in the United States.

SITUATION IN APRIL 1956

The steel market was strong in early 1956, and the Lowell Company benefited from the high operating rate and firm product prices. In early April, management was considering whether to authorize the start-up of open-hearth furnace 11, which would add 7,000 ingot tons to monthly output. Steel scrap prices had recently risen to $50 per ton in the Shenango Valley, and many observers were expecting a further rise of 5 percent to 10 percent in the next 30 days. The management was certain that any additional production could readily be sold in ingot form for further processing by other mills at or near the prevailing market price of $80 per ton. The market for semifinished steel seemed strong, and it seemed likely that existing customers would be interested in additional tonnage during the summer. The Lowell Company was presently realizing an average revenue of $95 per ton on semifinished steel sales. The most attractive market was for hot-rolled sheet and strip. Sales revenues averaged $140 per ton of strip,

---

[3] A "mill" edge was the edge resulting from normal hot-rolling operations; a "sheared" edge was the edge left after shearing operations.

but the sales manager was uncertain whether additional volume for these products could be generated within the next few months.

A furnace that is ready for start-up must be heated for about 24 hours before the first steelmaking heat can begin. Three heats are usually required to reach the normal cycle. Cost of the light-up is $2,200, of which one half is for fuel. Once a furnace has been started up, it is kept in operation for a campaign of 450 heats. This campaign is divided into two parts. After approximately 250 heats, the furnace roof must be rebuilt. This entails shutting the furnace down and relining the roof with refractory materials. The furnace is fired up again and run for another 200 heats. It is then shut down and completely rebuilt—end walls, sides, and roof. The floor is not rebuilt; it is patched after every heat and will last about 20 years. The checker chamber (where air going to the furnace is heated) is cleaned of soot and its top layer of bricks is replaced. To rebuild the roof on a 100-ton furnace after 250 heats takes 5 days around the clock, from gas off to light-up, and costs $60,000. The cost of completely rebuilding a furnace is $150,000 and takes 9–10 days.

Furnace 11 at the Lowell Works had been completely rebuilt and was ready for start-up in early April. The Lowell Company's practice was to amortize the costs of rebuilding a furnace by a per ton charge against all ingots subsequently produced in that furnace. This charge was included in the "cost above metal" for the open hearths.

An Example of Input-Output Analysis: The Production of Gypment

The old adage "you only get out what you put in" can be usefully applied in the analysis of certain types of production processes. The following discussion of the production of the fictitious product "gypment" illustrates the basic ideas of input-output analysis.

Gypment is a fine grey powder. When mixed with water it binds together other minerals (sand, gravel, stone) to form a useful building material known as "gypcrete." The production of gypment begins in the quarry where large pieces of rock are dug out of the ground and crushed to the size of golf balls. In the kiln department, the rock is mixed with purchased limestone, ground into a fine powder, and fed into a large rotating kiln. The raw material is heated to 1500°C. (2700°F). The heat burns off certain elements in the form of gases, leaving a substance called "clinker," small grey pellets about 2 cm in diameter. The clinker is either sold to other

EXHIBIT 1
Gypment Production Data by Department

	Input		Output	
Department	Material	Amount (tons)	Material	Amount (tons)
Kiln:	Limestone	56,742	Clinker	38,421
	Rock	45,894		
Grinding:	Clinker*	26,305	Gypment	25,639
	Gypsum	946		

Note: The difference in weight between inputs and outputs is accounted for by waste (dust, gases, and the like).
* 12,116 tons of clinker were sold to other gypment producers.

gypment producers or mixed with gypsum and ground (in the *grinding department*) into an extremely fine powder.

Exhibit 1 presents production data from a typical gypment manufacturer. The process has been divided into two departments. Clinker, the output of the kiln department, is an input into the grinding department. To meet the demands of the market for a given amount of gypment production, the firm must secure the appropriate amounts of gypsum, limestone, and other inputs. One way to summarize the relationship between outputs and inputs is to calculate *unit input requirements* —the amount of a given input required to produce one ton of a given output. To calculate the amount of limestone required to produce one ton of clinker, for example, we divide total input of limestone by the total output of clinker:

$$\frac{\text{Tons of limestone}}{\text{Tons of clinker}} = \frac{56,742}{38,421} = 1.4768$$

A similar procedure for rock input yields the following:

$$\frac{\text{Tons of rock}}{\text{Tons of clinker}} = \frac{45,894}{38,421} = 1.1945$$

The result of these calculations provides a concise summary of the relationship between inputs and outputs. The limestone coefficient indicates that each ton of clinker requires 1.4768 tons of limestone as input. The relationship between inputs and outputs is presented in Exhibit 2.

The unit input requirements can be used in analyzing potential changes in the production process. If we assume (perhaps as a first approximation) or if we know (because of technical considerations) that the amount of input needed to produce a unit of output does not vary with the level of output, the input requirements can be treated as technical constants. In such a situation the input coefficients can be used in evaluating any changes in the process, small or large.

For example, the company may wish to know how much limestone will be needed to raise gypment production to 37,000 tons from the present level of 25,639 tons. The calculation proceeds in two steps. We first determine the amount of additional clinker required. From Exhibit 2 we know that each ton of gypment requires 1.0260 tons of clinker. To calculate the extra clinker needed, we multiply the desired increase in gypment—11,361 tons (37,000 tons − 25,639 tons)—by 1.0260, the clinker input coefficient. The result is 11,656 tons of clinker.

Additional clinker:

$$(37,000 \text{ tons} - 25,639 \text{ tons}) \times 1.026 = 11,656 \text{ tons}$$

In effect, the procedure starts with the amount of additional output needed, and uses the requirements coefficient to translate output into input.

In the second step of the calculation we treat the additional clinker (11,656 tons) as the output and calculate the amount of limestone required

EXHIBIT 2
Input Requirements Coefficients for Gypment Production

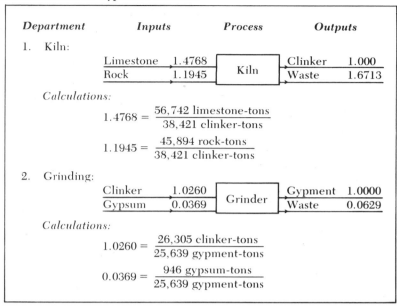

Department	Inputs		Process	Outputs	
1. Kiln:					
	Limestone	1.4768	Kiln	Clinker	1.000
	Rock	1.1945		Waste	1.6713

Calculations:

$$1.4768 = \frac{56,742 \text{ limestone-tons}}{38,421 \text{ clinker-tons}}$$

$$1.1945 = \frac{45,894 \text{ rock-tons}}{38,421 \text{ clinker-tons}}$$

Department	Inputs		Process	Outputs	
2. Grinding:					
	Clinker	1.0260	Grinder	Gypment	1.0000
	Gypsum	0.0369		Waste	0.0629

Calculations:

$$1.0260 = \frac{26,305 \text{ clinker-tons}}{25,639 \text{ gypment-tons}}$$

$$0.0369 = \frac{946 \text{ gypsum-tons}}{25,639 \text{ gypment-tons}}$$

as input into the kiln. From our earlier calculation we know that each ton of clinker requires 1.4768 tons of limestone. Multiplying desired output of clinker (11,656 tons) by the limestone coefficient (1.4768) will yield the desired amount of limestone:

Additional limestone:

11,656 tons × 1.4768 = 17,216 tons

It is important to note that the calculation assumes that the level of outside clinker sales would remain at 12,116 tons.

The limestone example illustrates an essential rule in input-output analysis: *keep the units of measurement straight.* Our objective is to relate limestone to gypment. We began with the final product, gypment, and translated the desired additional gypment production into required clinker. We then treated the clinker as an output and translated the additional clinker into the amount of limestone required. Although we proceeded in two steps, one calculation is sufficient. Collapsing the two calculations into one illustrates the importance of units of measurement:

Gypment to limestone:

$$[(37,000 - 25,639) \times 1.0260] \times 1.4768 = 17,216$$

$$\left[(\text{Gypment-tons}) \times \frac{\text{Clinker-tons}}{\text{Gypment-tons}}\right] \times \frac{\text{Limestone-tons}}{\text{Clinker-tons}} = \text{Limestone-tons}$$

The terms in brackets represent the first step in the two-step procedure—translating gypment into clinker. Note that the coefficient expresses tons of clinker per ton of gypment; in the multiplication, the tons of gypment cancel out leaving tons of clinker. The clinker can now be treated as an output and multiplied by the limestone input coefficient (1.4768) to yield tons of limestone. Again, the output units (clinker-tons) cancel out, leaving the units of input as desired. Since clinker is an intermediate product, it appears as an output and an input. In processes with several intermediate products, keeping the units straight can be helpful in avoiding errors.

Thus far we have related outputs to inputs in physical terms. In situations where the firm needs information about the costs of current operations, the input-output relations can be expressed in dollar terms. Exhibit 3 presents input prices and illustrates how the unit input requirements coefficients can be used to calculate the costs of production. In the case of clinker production, for example, limestone costs $9.50 per ton. With each ton of clinker requiring 1.4768 tons of limestone, the limestone component of clinker cost is:

$$1.4768 \times \$9.50 = \$14.03$$

$$\frac{\text{Limestone-tons}}{\text{Clinker-tons}} \times \frac{\text{Dollars}}{\text{Limestone-tons}} = \frac{\text{Dollars}}{\text{Clinker-tons}}$$

A similar calculation yields the rock component of clinker costs. The table adds a third element of cost—other direct operating costs per ton of clinker produced, which includes primarily the costs of energy and labor. Adding each component yields the cost per ton of clinker:

$$\$14.03 + \$6.21 + \$15.00 = \$35.24$$

In the grinding department clinker is treated as an input, and the cost per ton calculated above ($35.24) appears as an input price. As before, multiplying the input prices by the unit input coefficients yields the input's component in the cost of output. Thus, clinker accounts for $36.16 of the cost of a ton of gypment (1.0260 × $35.24), while the gypsum cost per ton of gypment is 74 cents (0.0369 × $20). With other direct costs amounting to $6 per ton, the cost per ton of gypment is $42.90.

The input-output framework gives the firm a way of relating input prices to the cost of output. Application of input-output analysis can be useful in assessing the effects of changes in the market for inputs. Consider the previous example in which the firm sought to raise gypment production from 25,639 to 37,000 tons. We found that such a change would require 17,216 tons of limestone. Suppose now that the firm discovers that the additional limestone cannot be purchased at $9.50 per ton but instead will cost $12 per ton. What effect will the new limestone price (which applies only to new limestone purchases) have on the cost of the additional tons of gypment?

The question can be answered in two equivalent ways. We could enter the new limestone price in Exhibit 3 and carry out all of the calculations as before. The result could then be compared to the original gypment cost to determine the impact of the limestone price increase. But if the price of limestone is the only thing which has changed (as we shall assume) then the same answer can be obtained by working with the change in the limestone price directly. Exhibit 4 illustrates the two calculations. Method I uses the procedures outlined in Exhibit 3 and leads to the conclusion that raising the limestone price from \$9.50 to \$12 per ton would raise the cost of gypment by \$3.78 per ton. Method II arrives at the same answer using only the change in input prices (any difference is due to round off error). An increase of \$2.50 per ton of limestone increases the cost of clinker by \$3.69:

$$1.4768 \times \$2.50 = \$3.69$$

This increase in the cost of clinker appears as a change in input price in the grinding department, and it leads to a change in the cost per ton of gypment of \$3.79:

$$1.0260 \times \$3.69 = \$3.79$$

Method II gives the same answer as method I because the price of limestone is the only thing that changes. Under method I factors which do not change (e.g. price of rock, other costs) enter in the same way in both the old and the new gypsum cost. When the one is subtracted from the other (\$46.68 − \$42.90 = \$3.78), things which do not change cancel out, leaving the effect of the new limestone price.

EXHIBIT 3
Calculation of the Cost of Gypment

Department	Cost per Ton of Input	Unit Input Requirements	Cost per Ton of Output
1. Kiln:			
Limestone.............	\$ 9.50	1.4768	\$14.03
Rock...................	5.20	1.1945	6.21
Other direct costs			
per ton of output*	—	—	15.00
Direct cost per ton of			
clinker	—	—	35.24
2. Grinding:			
Clinker.................	35.24	1.0260	36.16
Gypsum................	20.00	0.0369	0.74
Other direct costs			
per ton of output	—	—	6.00
Direct cost per ton			
of gypment	—	—	42.90

* Includes labor, energy, and the like.

EXHIBIT 4
Impact of a Change in Limestone Price

Method I	Input Price	Unit Input Requirement	Cost per Ton
Kiln:			
Limestone..............	$12.00	1.4768	$17.72
Rock...................	5.20	1.1945	6.21
Other costs.............	—	—	15.00
Cost per ton of clinker			38.93
Grinding:			
Clinker	38.93	1.0260	39.94
Gypsum	20.00	0.0369	0.74
Other costs.............	—	—	6.00
Cost per ton of gypment			46.68

Net impact per ton of gypment: $46.68 − $42.90 = $3.78.

Method II	Change in Input Price	Unit Input Requirement	Change in Cost Per Ton of Output
Kiln:			
Limestone..............	$2.50	1.4768	$3.69
Grinding:			
Clinker	3.69	1.2060	3.79

Net impact per ton of gypment: $3.79.

A final example illustrates the versatility of input-output analysis. Suppose the gypment firm is in the process of negotiating the price for a large shipment of limestone. The limestone is needed for a special contract. In order to maintain its contribution margin the firm must produce the gypment at a cost of $41 per ton. Assuming other costs remain the same, what is the limestone price which will yield a gypment cost of $41 per ton? The analysis proceeds in two steps. We first determine the required clinker cost, and we then find the corresponding price of limestone.

With other costs unchanged, we know that a gypment cost of $41.00 per ton requires a clinker component of $34.26:

$$\$41.00 - \$6.00 - 0.74 = \$34.26$$

We now need to know the clinker input price which would yield a clinker component in the cost of gypment of $34.26. The relationship between the input price of clinker and the clinker component of gypment cost was developed in Exhibit 3. If we let $P_{clinker}$ represent the unknown price of clinker input, the relationship is:

$$P_{clinker} \times 1.0260 = \$34.26$$

Dividing both sides of this equation by 1.0260, we find:

$$P_{\text{clinker}} = \frac{\$34.26}{1.0260} = \$33.39$$

The required clinker input price is \$33.39, which (again with other costs unchanged) implies that the limestone component of clinker cost must be \$12.18:

$$\$33.39 - \$15.00 - \$6.21 = \$12.18$$

To find the limestone price which corresponds to a limestone component in clinker cost of \$12.18, we divide by the unit input coefficient as before:

$$P_{\text{limestone}} = \frac{\$12.18}{1.4768} = \$8.25$$

Thus the firm must negotiate a limestone price of \$8.25 per ton if contribution margins are to be maintained.

Note that once again, keeping track of the units of measurement can be quite helpful. In this example we began with a price of gypment and worked back through the process to find the corresponding price of clinker, and then the price of limestone. In both steps we began with a price (or cost) expressed in dollars per ton of output, while the unknown price was in terms of dollars per ton of input. Our solution was to divide the known output price (or cost) by the unit input coefficient.

CASE 8

National Cranberry Cooperative

On February 14, 1971, Hugo Schaeffer, vice president of operations at the National Cranberry Cooperative (NCC), called his assistant, Mel O'Brien, into his office.

Mel, I spent all day yesterday reviewing last fall's process fruit operations at Receiving Plant No. 1 (RP1) with Will Walliston, the superintendent, and talking with the coop members (growers) in that area. It's obvious to me that we haven't solved our problems at that plant yet. Even though we spent $75,000 last winter for a fifth Kiwanee dumper at RP1, our overtime costs were still out of control this fall, and the growers are still upset that their trucks and drivers had to spend so much time waiting to unload process fruit into the receiving plant. I can't blame them for being upset. They are the owners of this cooperative, and they resent having to lease trucks and hire drivers to get the berries out of the field and then watch them stand idle waiting to unload.

Will Walliston thinks that the way to avoid these problems next fall is to buy and install two new dryers ($25,000 each), and to convert our dry berry holding bins so that they can be used to store either water-harvested or dry berries ($5,000 per bin). I want you to go out there and take a hard look at that operation and find out what we need to do to improve operations before the 1971 crop comes in. We're going to have to move quickly if we are going to order new dryers since the equipment and installation lead times are in excess of six months. By the way, the growers in that region indicated that they plan on about the same size crop this year as last. But, it looks like the percentage of water-harvested berries this year will increase to 70 percent of total process fruit from last year's 58 percent.

NCC AND THE CRANBERRY INDUSTRY

NCC was an organization formed and owned by growers of cranberries for the processing and marketing of their berries. In recent years, 99 percent of all sales of cranberries had been made by the various cooperatives that are active in the cranberry industry. NCC was one of the larger cooperatives and had operations in all the principal growing areas of North America: Massachusetts, New Jersey, Wisconsin, Washington, Oregon, British Columbia, and Nova Scotia. Exhibit 1 contains industry data for U.S. production and sales of cranberries.

Some significant trends are observable in the data of Exhibit 1. Probably the most important of these trends is the growing surplus of cranberries produced over those utilized. This surplus was serious enough by 1968 for the growers to resort to the Agriculture Marketing Agreement Act of 1937. Under this act growers can regulate and control the size of an agricultural crop if the federal government and more than two thirds of the growers by number and tonnage agree to a plan for restriction. In 1968, this act was used to create the Cranberry Marketing Order of 1968, which stipulated that no new acreage was to be developed over the next six years and that each grower would have a maximum allotment at the end of six years that would be equal to the average of his best two years from 1968 through 1973. Eighty-seven percent of all growers voted in favor of the order, making it binding on all cranberry growers.

In 1970, the growers resorted to the Agriculture Marketing Agreement Act once again. Under the Cranberry Marketing Order of 1970, the growers and the government agreed that 10 percent of the 1970 crop should be "set aside." The "set aside" berries (berries that are either destroyed or used in a way that will not influence the market price) amounted to more than 200,000 barrels. (A barrel of cranberries weighs 100 pounds.) Handlers physically set aside 10 percent of the berries before harvesting under the supervision of a committee of growers and representatives of the Department of Agriculture.

Another important trend was the increasing mechanization of cranberry harvesting. Water harvesting, in particular, was developing rapidly in the vicinity of RP1. Under traditional dry harvesting, berries were handpicked from the bushes. In water harvesting, the bogs were flooded, the berries were mechanically shaken from the bushes, and the berries then were collected easily since they floated to the surface of the water. Water harvesting could result in yields up to 20 percent greater than those obtained via dry harvesting, but it did cause some damage and it did shorten the time that harvested fruit could be held prior to either its use or freezing for long-term storage. Water harvesting had developed at a remarkable rate in some areas. RP1 received 25,000 barrels of water-harvested fruit in 1968, 125,000 barrels in 1969, and 350,000 barrels in 1970.

Water harvesting was not the preferred harvesting method for fruit that was to be sold fresh since fresh fruit must be undamaged and have as long a shelf life as possible. It was also necessary to ship fruit that was to be sold fresh to receiving plants in "field boxes" that contained about one third barrel of berries rather than in bulk (trucks holding up to 400 barrels) in

EXHIBIT 1

U.S.* Cranberry Crop (acreage harvested, yield per acre, production/utilization, season average price, five-year averages and annual)

Crop Year	Acreage Harvested (acres)	Yield per Acre (barrels)	Production/Utilization†			Average Price (all uses)‡ ($ per barrel)
			Production (barrels)	Fresh Sales (barrels)	Processed (barrels)	
Five-year average:						
1935–39	26,022	23.7	615,100	466,844	148,256	11.06
1940–44	25,434	24.9	634,300	380,965	253,335	15.50
1945–49	26,205	31.3	822,580	381,320	436,060	17.15
1950–54	24,842	39.8	983,660	439,170	532,070	11.71
1955–59	21,448	51.2	1,096,160	427,520	543,860	9.79
1960–64	20,778	62.6	1,300,120	468,340	755,760	10.90
1965–69	20,988	73.7	1,546,120	327,980	1,169,360	15.88
Annual:						
1965	20,640	69.6	1,436,800	389,600	1,033,200	15.50
1966	20,760	77.0	1,598,600	328,000	1,249,600	15.60
1967	21,220	66.2	1,404,300	278,300	1,034,900	15.50
1968	21,135	69.4	1,467,800	301,900	1,111,200	16.50
1969	21,185	86.1	1,823,100	342,100	1,417,900	16.30
1970§	21,445	95.1	2,038,600	367,000	1,418,600	12.90

* Five states: Massachusetts, New Jersey, Oregon, Washington, and Wisconsin.

† Differences between production and utilization (fresh sales and processed) represent economic abandonment.

‡ Beginning in 1949, the series represents equivalent returns at first receiving station, fresh and processing combined. Years prior to 1949 represent season average prices received by growers for all methods of sale, fresh and processing combined.

§ Preliminary figures for 1970.

Source: Annual reports of Crop Reporting Board, Statistical Reporting Service, USDA.

order to avoid damage. Fresh fruit was inspected berry by berry prior to packaging. Altogether, fresh fruit production remained a very labor-intensive process.

RECEIVING PLANT NO. 1 (RP1)

RP1 received both fresh fruit and process fruit during a season that usually started early in September and was effectively finished by early December (Exhibit 2). The fresh fruit operation was completely separate from the process fruit operation and took the fruit from receiving through

EXHIBIT 2
Daily Deliveries of Berries (both fresh and process) to RP1

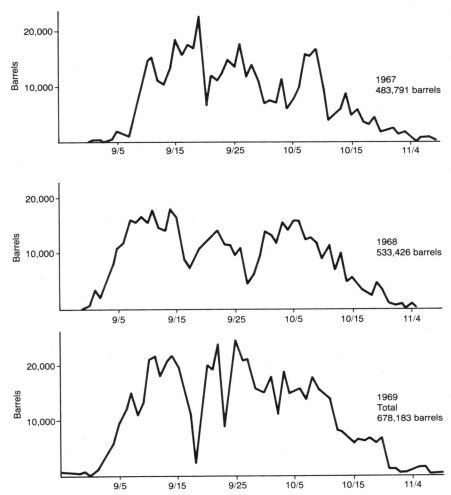

packaging. This operation involved more than 400 workers during the peak of the season. Most of the workers were women who inspected berries as they moved by on teflon-coated conveyors. Packaged fresh fruit was shipped from RP1 directly to market by truck. No problems had been experienced in fresh fruit processing in the past.

Handling of process fruit at RP1 was highly mechanized. The process could be classified into several operations: receiving and testing, dumping, temporary holding, destoning,[1] dechaffing,[2] drying, separation, and bulking and bagging. The objective of the total process was to gather bulk berries and prepare them for storage and processing into frozen fresh berries, sauce, and juice.

PROCESS FRUIT RECEIVING

Bulk trucks carrying process berries arrived at RP1 loaded with anywhere from 20 to 400 barrels. These trucks arrived randomly throughout the day as shown in Exhibit 3. The average truck delivery was 75 barrels. When the trucks arrived at RP1, they were weighed and the gross weight and the tare (empty) weight were recorded. Prior to unloading, a sample of about 30 pounds of fruit was taken from the truck. Later this sample would be run through a small version of the cleaning and drying process used in the plant. By comparing the before and after weight of this sample, it was possible to estimate the percentage of the truck's net weight made up of clean, dry berries. At the same time, another sample was taken to determine the percentage of unusable berries (poor, smaller, and "frosted" berries) in the truck. The grower was credited for the estimated weight of the clean, dry, usable berries. In 1970, on the average, the growers were credited for 94 percent of the scale weight of dry deliveries and 85 percent of the scale weight of wet deliveries.

At the time the truck was weighed, the truckload of berries was graded according to color. Using color pictures as a guide, the chief berry receiver classified the berries as 1, 2A, 2B, or 3, from poorest color (no. 1) to best (no. 3). There was a premium of 50 cents per barrel paid for no. 3 berries since color was considered to be a very important attribute of both juice products and whole sauce. Whenever there was any question about whether or not a truckload was 2B or 3 berries, the chief berry receiver usually chose no. 3. In 1970, the 50-cent premium was paid on about 450,000 barrels of berries. However, when these berries were used, it was found only about half of them were no. 3s.

---

[1] Destoning was the separation of foreign materials (such as small stones) which might be mixed in with the berries.

[2] Dechaffing was the removal of stems, leaves, etc., which might still be attached to the berries.

In order to improve this yield, Mr. Schaeffer was considering the installation of a light meter system for color grading. This system was projected to cost $10,000 and require a full-time skilled operator at the same pay grade as the chief berry receiver.

TEMPORARY HOLDING

After a truckload of process berries had been weighed, sampled, and color graded, the truck moved to one of the five Kiwanee dumpers. The trucks were backed onto the dumper platforms which then tilted until the contents of the truck dumped onto one of five rapidly moving belt conveyors. Each of the five conveyors took the berries to the second (upper) level of the plant and deposited them on other conveyors which were capable of running the berries into any one of 27 temporary holding bins. Bins 1–24 held 250 barrels of berries each. Bins 25, 26, and 27 held 400 barrels each. All of the conveyors were controlled from a central control panel. Since the person running the control panel could not see all of the conveyors, others working in the plant were relied on to help him or her by shouting necessary information up to the control room.

It usually took from 5 to 10 minutes to back a truck onto a Kiwanee dumper, empty its contents, and leave the platform. However, at times some trucks had to wait up to three hours before they could empty their contents. These waits occurred when holding bins became full and there was no place in the receiving plant to temporarily store berries before further operations.

The holding bins emptied onto conveyors on the first (lower) level of the plant. Once the bins were opened (a manual operation), the berries flowed onto the conveyors and started their way through the destoning, dechaffing, drying (for water-harvested berries only), milling (quality grading), and either bulk loading or bagging operations. The rate at which berries flowed from the holding bins was determined by the degree to which sliding doors on the bottom of the bins were opened.

DESTONING, DECHAFFING, AND DRYING

Holding bins 25–27 were for wet (water-harvested) berries only. Holding bins 17–24 could be used for either wet or dry berries. Wet berries from these bins were taken directly to one of the three dechaffing units (destoning was unnecessary with water-harvested berries) that could process up to 1,500 barrels per hour each. After dechaffing, these wet berries were taken to one of the three drying units where they were dried at rates up to 200 barrels per hour per dryer for berries that were to be loaded into bulk trucks, and approximately 150 barrels per hour per dryer for berries that were to be bagged. Wet berries that were to be bagged had to be drier than bulked

EXHIBIT 3
Log of All Deliveries for September 23, 1970

Time*	Color	Wet or Dry	Weight (pounds)	Time	Color	Wet or Dry	Weight (pounds)	Time	Color	Wet or Dry	Weight (pounds)	Time	Color	Wet or Dry	Weight (pounds)
411	3	D	33,940	594	3	W	13,500	897	3	D	11,240	1,140	3	D	9,020
413	3	D	9,980	597	3	W	11,560	900	3	W	7,160	1,140	3	D	9,020
416	3	D	10,020	599	3	D	18,340	904	3	D	17,600	1,140	3	W	8,240
428	1	D	12,200	601	3	D	20,340	916	3	D	8,780	1,140	2	D	7,660
439	3	D	8,980	604	3	D	9,600	922	3	D	3,660	1,140	3	D	3,960
445	3	D	7,520	609	3	W	13,020	924	3	W	14,840	1,140	2	W	4,100
446	3	D	4,140	625	2	D	2,680	937	3	W	9,160	1,140	3	D	11,860
448	3	D	11,730	630	2	W	11,460	942	3	W	15,960	1,140	3	D	11,460
451	2	D	6,580	633	3	D	3,600	945	3	D	1,280	1,140	2	W	11,840
456	3	D	1,480	634	2	W	7,280	947	3	D	10,300	1,140	3	D	1,980
459	3	W	12,660	636	3	W	9,840	949	2	W	11,540	1,140	3	D	10,480
460	3	D	31,640	638	3	W	12,700	954	3	W	12,580	1,140	2	D	11,600
462	3	W	11,920	640	3	W	28,780	957	3	D	11,040				
463	3	D	2,060	645	2	D	18,000	959	3	D	7,740				
468	3	D	6,020	648	3	D	8,240	961	3	W	12,500				
471	3	W	12,640	650	3	W	13,820	962	3	D	7,000				
472	3	D	3,940	651	2	W	11,280	968	3	D	7,340				
477	3	D	6,060	655	3	D	1,280	969	3	D	4,260				
480	3	D	4,660	660	3	D	500	975	3	D	1,660				
482	3	D	1,880	663	2	D	29,560	977	3	D	4,980				
485	3	D	7,260	664	2	D	9,720	980	3	W	12,640				
495	3	D	4,860	665	3	W	8,800	982	3	D	6,420				
498	2	D	3,160	666	3	W	24,640	984	3	D	11,200				
499	2	D	3,320	671	3	D	1,880	996	3	D	11,920				
500	3	D	17,280	673	2	W	12,760	1,000	3	W	12,320				
508	3	D	3,360	674	3	D	9,980	1,005	3	W	8,860				
511	3	D	10,420	677	3	W	12,980	1,008	2	W	7,140				
512	2	D	5,780	678	2	D	7,860	1,010	3	D	7,180				
513	3	W	5,500	681	3	W	11,480	1,011	2	D	11,220				

Totals for September 23

Total pounds	1,834,020
Wet	768,600
Dry	1,065,420
Color 1	34,460
Color 2	401,080
Color 3	1,398,480
Total number of trucks...........	243

No.			Amount	No.			Amount	No.			Amount
515	3	D	8,880	684	3	D	12,680	1,012	2	D	6,840
519	3	D	17,880	698	2	D	5,640	1,022	3	D	9,600
522	3	D	1,580	780	3	D	2,220	1,040	3	D	11,100
524	3	W	6,440	790	2	W	11,500	1,043	3	W	11,080
527	3	W	7,860	791	3	W	9,460	1,046	1	W	11,020
528	3	W	33,720	793	3	W	12,660	1,047	1	W	11,240
533	2	W	11,340	809	2	W	5,620	1,050	3	D	35,060
534	3	D	6,480	811	2	D	2,540	1,051	3	W	31,580
535	3	D	5,280	817	3	D	11,760	1,056	3	D	7,420
538	3	D	11,640	818	2	D	7,720	1,061	3	D	4,500
543	2	W	11,180	823	2	W	7,080	1,064	2	D	5,700
551	3	D	2,900	825	2	W	20,400	1,068	3	D	4,940
560	3	D	3,580	838	3	D	12,200	1,073	2	D	2,420
565	3	D	8,400	841	2	D	7,420	1,079	3	D	9,440
567	3	D	3,920	842	2	W	3,140	1,081	2	D	11,620
570	3	D	1,200	843	3	D	13,740	1,082	3	D	8,360
572	3	D	3,480	845	3	D	2,840	1,084	3	D	10,500
577	3	D	3,680	846	3	D	15,240	1,085	3	D	3,240
580	3	W	8,440	848	2	D	11,540	1,090	3	W	10,280
581	3	D	8,500	850	3	W	31,460	1,091	3	D	8,140
584	2	D	7,560	865	3	W	9,300	1,092	2	W	2,440
586	3	D	4,540	862	1	D	4,580	1,095	3	D	13,720
587	2	D	6,040	874	3	W	11,280	1,101	3	W	13,180
588	2	D	3,360	876	2	W	12,720	1,111	3	W	13,420
591	3	D	2,820	877	2	D	14,140	1,116	3	D	7,400
				878	3	D	26,700	1,126	3	D	7,260
				879	3	W	11,280	1,127	3	D	6,240
				882	3	D	12,800	1,129	2	W	13,120
				887	2	D	7,980	1,132	3	D	8,340
				895	3	D	8,900	1,134	3	D	6,160

* The time recorded is *minutes from (after)* 12 A.M. That is, the recorded time of 411 is equivalent to 6:51 A.M.

berries since the bags tended to absorb moisture and would stick together when frozen.

Holding bins 1–16 were for dry berries only. Berries from these bins were routed through one of three destoning units which could process up to 1,500 barrels of berries per hour before going through the dechaffing units. Frequently, both wet and dry berries were processed at the same time through the system. The wet berries would be processed through the part of the system that included the dryers, while the dry berries were processed through different machines.

MILLING (QUALITY GRADING)

After destoning, dechaffing, and drying (when necessary), berries were transported to one of three large "take-away conveyors" that moved berries from the first level of the receiving building to the third level of the adjoining separator building. Here these same conveyors were called feed conveyors (Exhibit 4) as they were now feeding berries into the jumbo separators. There were nine jumbo separators along each of the three feed conveyors. The jumbo separators identified three classes of berries: first-quality berries, *potential* second-quality berries, and unacceptable berries. The separation

EXHIBIT 4
Separator Building—Elevation View

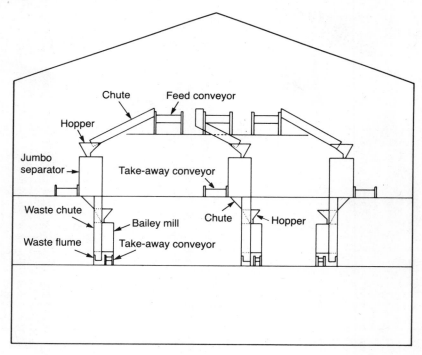

process was a simple one that was based on the fact that "good" cranberries will bounce higher than "poor" cranberries. (See Exhibit 5 for an explanation of the separation process.) The first-quality berries went directly onto one of three take-away conveyors on the second level and were transported to the shipping area. The unacceptable berries fell through waste chutes into water-filled waste flumes on the first level and were floated off to the disposal area. The potential second-quality berries fell into the Bailey mills on the second level of the building. The Bailey mills separated the stream of incoming berries into second-quality berries and unacceptable berries. The Bailey mills operated on the same principle as the jumbo separators. Over the years, the percentage of second-quality berries had consistently been close to 12 percent.

EXHIBIT 5
Separator Operation

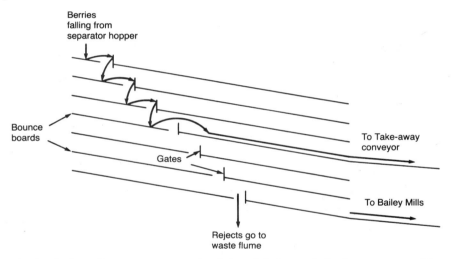

The sketch above illustrates a cross-sectional view of the heart of a jumbo separator and the path a particular first-quality berry might take through the separator. The separator operation was based on the fact that "good" cranberries are more resilient than "poor" cranberries and thus the good berries will bounce higher than the poor berries. Berries that failed to bounce over any of the seven gates in a jumbo separator were considered rejects. Berries that bounced over any of the first four gates were considered first-quality berries. Berries that jumped over gates 5, 6, or 7 went to the Bailey mills where they would be classified as either second-quality berries or rejects. The Bailey mills are essentially the same as the jumbo separators, but somewhat smaller.

The gates in the separators could be raised or lowered to control the fraction of berries that were classified first-quality berries. When it was known that berries coming into the separators were high-quality berries, then the gates were lowered to speed up the separation process. Two women working in the separator area took three cup samples every 15 minutes from each separator to determine the actual quality of the berries that were bouncing over the first four gates. If the quality was not up to first-quality standards, the gates were raised to reduce the fraction of berries that would be classified first quality. Raising the gates did, however, slow down the separation process.

Each of the three separator lines could process up to 450 barrels per hour, but the rate of processing declined as the percentage of bad fruit increased. It was estimated that the average effective capacity was probably slightly less than 400 barrels per hour for each line.

BULKING AND BAGGING

Six conveyors carried berries from the separator building into the shipping building: three from the jumbo separators and three from the Bailey mills. Each of those six conveyors could feed berries onto any one of the three main flexible conveyors in the shipping area. Each of the three conveyors in the shipping area could be moved to feed berries into any one of four bagging stations, any one of four bulk bin stations, or any one of two bulk truck stations. The berries left RP1 in bulk trucks for shipment directly to the finish processing plant, in bins for storage at freezers with bulk storage capability or for storage in freezers which could handle only bagged berries. These frozen berries were then held for year-round usage by one of the NCC processing plants. Some processing plants could receive only bagged berries, while others could receive either bulk or bagged berries.

A maximum of 8,000 barrels could be bagged (60 pounds of berries per bag) in a 12-hour period. To attain this output, three five-person teams ran three of the bagging machines and stacked bags was in trucks. A fourth bagging machine was kept as a spare in case there was a jam or a breakdown of one of the three operating machines. A study had shown that it cost about 5 cents more in direct labor per barrel for bagging than for bulk loading, and the cost of bags was 12 cents each. In 1970, four commercial freezers were under contract with NCC to accept bagged fruit according to the rate and capacity schedules shown in Exhibit 6. Trucks were under contract with NCC to haul berries to the freezers at the freight rates also shown in Exhibit 6. They were available 24 hours per day, and there was rarely a holdup for want of a truck. Freezers were generally open 24 hours per day, 7 days per week.

Exhibit 6 also shows the rate and capacity schedules for those freezers that were equipped to handle bulk berries. Included are NCC's own freezer and the local NCC processing plant which converted the bulk berries to finished products. The local processing plant utilized an average of 700 barrels daily from bulk bins that could be filled at the rate of about 200 barrels per hour at each of the four bin stations. Berries could be loaded directly into bulk trucks at two stations each capable of loading up to 1,000 barrels per hour. One person ran both stations. There was normally about a 10-minute delay between the time when one truck was filled and the time when another truck was in position ready for filling. This is one instance where the station operator had to shout up the line that the flow of berries coming to one of his or her stations should be slowed or stopped. Others relayed the information to the control room.

EXHIBIT 6
Freezer Rates and Capacities (1970)

		Freight ($ per barrel)	Initial* ($ per barrel)	Continuing ($ per barrel month)	Total Capacity (barrels)
I.	Bulk berries:				
	Frostway†.................	$0.25	$0.81	$0.22	280,000
	Inland....................	0.30	0.76	0.23	25,000
	NCC freezer..............	0.23	—	—	30,000
	NCC process..............	0.23	—	—	—
	Total....................				335,000
II.	Bagged berries:				
	Farmers..................	0.29	0.76	0.23	75,000
	Northern (5½-day week).....	0.29	0.80	0.22	‡
	American (6-day week)......	0.60	0.75	0.22	‡
	Freeze-Rite (6-day week)....	0.70	1.24	0.34	‡
	Total....................				‡

* Initial cost included in and out handling cost and freezing cost.
† The contract with Frostway included a guarantee that at least 280,000 barrels would be put in the Frostway freezer. For every barrel less than 280,000, NCC would pay a penalty of 81 cents.
‡ Total capacity was not a constraining factor.

MANNING

During the harvest season (September 1 to December 15), the process fruit side of RP1 was operated seven days a week with either a 27-person work force or a 53-person work force, depending on the relative volume of berry receipts (Exhibit 7). When the volume of berry receipts was expected to be low, the plant operated with six people in receiving (two 3-person teams operating one Kiwanee dumper each); 10 people in the milling area (one 5-person team per feed conveyor); 8 people in shipping (one 5-person team on a bagging station, 1 person operating the two bulk stations, and 2 people together operating a bulk bin station); 1 person supervising the destoning, dechaffing, and drying operations; and 2 people (1 on each of two shifts) in the control room. Exhibit 8 shows the planned daily manning schedule for the low-volume periods which were anticipated before the 1970 harvest season began.

During the peak of the season, the 53 people who operated the process fruit side of RP1 were assigned as follows: 15 people in receiving (five 3-person teams, each assigned to one dumper); 15 people in milling (three 5-person teams, each assigned to one of the feed conveyors); 20 people in shipping (three 5-person teams each assigned to one bagging station, 1 person operating the two bulk stations, and two 2-person teams each assigned to one bulk bin station); 1 person supervising the destoning, de-

120

EXHIBIT 7
1970 Deliveries of Process Berries

Day	Scale Weight Total Deliveries (barrels)	Percent Delivered Wet	Percent Color 1	Percent Color 2	Percent Color 3
9/1–9/19	44,176	54	6	72	22
9/20	16,014	31	0	44	56
9/21	17,024	39	0	35	65
9/22	16,550	39	0	22	78
9/23	18,340	42	0	22	78
9/24	18,879	41	0	21	79
9/25	18,257	36	0	14	86
9/26	17,905	45	0	10	90
9/27	16,281	42	0	18	82
9/28	13,343	38	0	15	85
9/29	18,717	43	1	11	88
9/30	18,063	59	1	9	90
10/1	18,018	69	1	11	88
10/2	15,195	60	2	18	80
10/3	15,816	60	3	12	85
10/4	16,536	57	5	21	74
10/5	17,304	55	2	26	72
10/6	14,793	46	7	32	61
10/7	13,862	61	3	39	58
10/8	11,786	56	0	36	64
10/9	14,913	54	0	33	67
10/10–12/10	238,413	75	0	22	78
9/1–12/10	610,040	58	1	25	74

chaffing, and drying operations; and 2 people (1 on each of two shifts) in the control room. Exhibit 9 shows the planned daily manning schedule for the high-volume periods anticipated at receiving station no. 1 before the 1970 harvest season began.

There were 27 employees at RP1 who were employed for the entire year; all others were hired for the season only. The 27 nonseasonal employees were all members of the Teamsters Union, as were 15 seasonal workers. Seasonal workers could work only between the dates of August 15 and December 25 by agreement with the union. Most seasonal workers were employed via a state employment agency that set up operations in a trailer adjacent to the plant each fall. The employment agency helped in placing seasonal workers in the receiving plant and in harvesting jobs with the local growers. The pay rate for seasonal workers in the process fruit section was $2.25 per hour. Many of the seasonal workers worked 12 to 16 hours per day, 7 days a week. They were paid the overtime rate of 1½ times their

EXHIBIT 8
Twenty-seven-Person Schedule (September 1 to September 19 and October 11 to December 15)

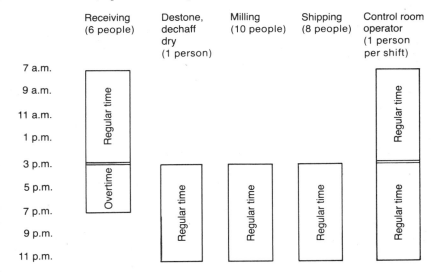

EXHIBIT 9
Fifty-three-Person Schedule (September 20 to October 10)

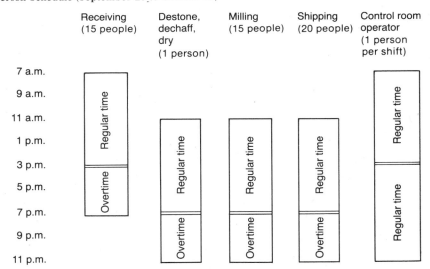

straight-time rate for anything over 40 hours per week. The straight-time pay rate for the full-year employees averaged $3.75 per hour.

The amount of overtime used in a day or week depended on how effectively workers could be scheduled. If it were known, for instance, that the plant would have to run beyond the normal 11 P.M. shutdown time, then it would be desirable to have some people report for work at 6 P.M. or later, but it was not always possible to find people who would do this. There was also the problem of absenteeism, which caused Will Walliston to carry more people on the payroll than he really needed. He had to have "20 on the payroll in order to be reasonably sure I'll have 15 on hand." Higher than expected absenteeism, of course, often resulted in overtime for those who were there. For the 1970 season, the process fruit operation at RP1 utilized about 22,000 labor-hours of straight-time direct labor and about 12,000 labor-hours of overtime.

When it was necessary to work beyond 11 P.M. a crew of only eight or nine people was required to run the holding bins empty and do bulk loading. Although dry fruit could be held in the bins overnight, it was considered undesirable to hold wet fruit in the bins any longer than necessary, so wet fruit was always run out before shutting down. The plant never ran more than 22 hours a day since at least 2 hours were required for cleaning and maintenance work. Downtime due to unscheduled maintenance was very small: "We ran 350,000 barrels through the wet system in 1970 and we were down a total of less than eight hours."

CASE 9

Arrow Diagramming Exercise

A major firm in the field of industrial machinery fabrication is planning to launch a massive campaign to push the sale of a recently developed item of industrial hardware. You are asked to prepare the arrow diagram from which schedules for the campaign preparation can be developed. You have available the information listed in the following paragraphs. The number in parentheses following the description of each activity indicates the estimated time required for its accomplishment.

In general, the project may be broken down into three major categories:

1. The training of sales personnel.
2. Consultation with and training of marketing personnel.
3. Preparation of the necessary advertising and instruction material for the campaign.

SALES

In order to save time on the sales side, it has been decided to prepare phase 1 of the training program for sales personnel (8) at the same time that the sales managers are selecting the sales personnel who are to be trained (2).

Both the above activities will therefore begin at the start of the project. Following their selection, the chosen sales personnel must be relieved of their responsibilities in their areas and sent to the company's training center in the home office (4).

Obviously it would be foolish for the salespeople to arrive before phase 1 of the training program is ready for them. When phase 1 of the program is prepared, the selected sales personnel will be trained in this part of the program (10). While they are being trained in phase 1 of the program, phase 2 will be prepared (9).

As soon as the salespeople have completed the first phase of their training and phase 2 of the program has been completed and approved, sales training in the second phase can commence.[1] The second part of the program will take (12).

At the conclusion of the two major phases of their training, the sales personnel will be issued "Customers' Instruction Manuals" on the new machine and will spend a short time at the home office becoming familiar with them (5).

When the salespeople are familiar with the manuals, they will return to their respective territories ready to begin their effort simultaneously with the national advertising campaign. Getting back to their territories should take (1).

MARKETING

I. Personnel

The first step in the project for the marketing side will be the determination of the general marketing approach (10). When this has been arranged, the necessary marketing personnel will be selected (4) and brought into the home office (2).

Following the determination of the general marketing approach, and while the marketing trainees are being selected and brought in, specific training plans for the marketing personnel will be consolidated (2).

After these plans are consolidated, a familiarization course for these personnel will be designed (8).

When personnel and course are ready, the training of marketing personnel will proceed. It is estimated to take (8).

II. Advertising

Immediately after the general marketing approach has been determined, advertising plans must be consolidated ["firmed up" in the jargon of the trade (6)].

When this consolidation is complete, a paper is to be prepared (6) and printed in a professional journal (8).

Also immediately following the consolidation of advertising plans, national advertising must be prepared (10), approved (4), and distributed to the proper media (2).

Not until the *marketing* people are trained, the professional paper published, and the advertising distributed will the national advertising be released and carried by the media involved. The release and preparation to carry the national advertising will take about (2).

---

[1] Approval cannot be given until the general marketing approach (see marketing section) has been determined.

It is not planned to proceed further with the national advertising campaign until the newly trained sales personnel have returned to their territories.

III.   Printing

As soon as the advertising plans are consolidated (the first step under the advertising section above), a general brochure will be drafted and approved (4).

Following the approval of the brochure, a layout must be designed (5) and the brochure printed (3).

As soon as the brochure is approved, a "Customers' Instruction Manual" will be prepared (3). The "Customers' Instruction Manual" in its turn must be approved (1) and printed (2).

Copies of the instruction manual alone will be sent to the training center (1) where it will be utilized in completing the training of the salesmen.

As soon as both the brochure and manual are printed, they will be packaged together and delivered to marketing for general distribution. The packaging and delivery together should take about (8).

Actual implementation of the campaign (which may be regarded as the termination of this project) cannot begin until the sales personnel are back in their territories, the national advertising campaign released, and the proper brochures and manuals have been received by marketing.

Required:

Prepare the arrow diagram for this project and select the critical path or paths. You will probably show from 30 to 35 activities.

CASE 10

Space Constructors, Inc.

In 1961, Space Constructors, Inc. (SCI), had received a fixed-price contract to construct a missile launching site for the National Bureau of Aeronautics (NBA). By the fall of 1962, work was nearly complete on the main launch site; however, it was apparent that work on a special remote control building would have to be finished earlier than originally planned if the contract was to be completed on time.

Mr. James Alison, field construction supervisor for SCI, had arranged a meeting with Mr. Henry Phillips, SCI's project engineer to restudy the arrow diagram of their critical path schedule for the construction of the remote control building in an effort to determine the shortest possible time in which the job could be done without spending more money than necessary.

The critical path method, sometimes referred to as "the latest and most powerful management technique for planning, scheduling, and controlling large projects," is intended to provide improved project planning and scheduling and a diagrammed display of all project activities.[1] On the typical diagram, arrows of any convenient length are drawn to represent a single pertinent project element or activity. These arrows, indicating time progression only, terminate at arrow junctions (or "nodes") indicated by circles signifying the beginning or termination of activities. Arrows *originating* at a junction indicate activities that can begin only after all activities (arrows) terminating at that junction have been completed. When combined with a cost table, the diagram indicates the possibility and cost of speeding up a given activity. The sequence of consecutive activities requiring the longest time to complete before the end of the project is known as the "critical path" for that project. The path is considered "critical"

---

[1] *General Electric Bulletin 198.*

because any delay in the particular sequence will delay the completion of the entire project.

Mr. Alison had the original arrow diagram for the remote control building project (Exhibit 1) in his office. It was, of course, considerably simpler than similar diagrams developed for the control of the entire missile site construction job.

Using the data provided by the cost table for this project (Exhibit 2), it was apparent to Mr. Alison that the critical path for this project followed the sequence of activities A–D–G and would require 12 weeks. The original project cost was estimated at $61,000. Mr. Alison could also see that the sequence of activities along one path, C–E–G, could lag as much as four

EXHIBIT 1
Critical Path Diagram for Remote Control Building Project

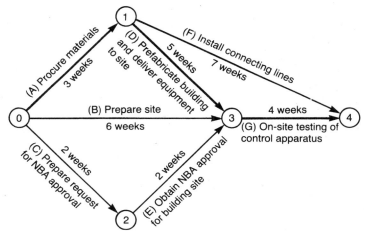

Heavy arrows indicate critical path.

EXHIBIT 2
Cost Table for Remote Control Building Project

Activity	Normal Weeks	Normal Dollars	Crash* Weeks	Crash* Dollars	Cost Slope, Dollars per Week
A	3	$ 5,000	2	$ 10,000	$5,000†
B	6	14,000	4	26,000	6,000
C	2	2,500	1	5,000	2,500
D	5	10,000	3	18,000	4,000
E	2	8,000	2	8,000	—
F	7	11,500	5	17,500	3,000
G	4	10,000	2	24,000	7,000
Total		61,000		108,500	

* Crash weeks shown represent the minimum possible time for the given activity.
† This is the cost of gaining one week over the normal time by use of "crash" methods.

weeks behind schedule without affecting the planned time for the completion of the project. This available slack time was known as "float."

Although a computer was necessary for the rapid solution of critical path problems in larger projects, Mr. Phillips had manually worked out a schedule for this project which indicated that the job could be completed in nine weeks at a total cost of $77,000. The additional cost of $16,000 was largely attributable to the cost of extra shift operations necessitated by a "crash" program. It will be noticed that in his revised schedule (Exhibit 3), three paths had become critical to the completion of the project as rescheduled.

EXHIBIT 3
Revised—Program Schedule for Remote Control Building Project

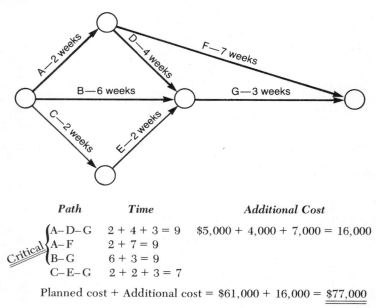

Path	Time	Additional Cost
Critical { A–D–G	2 + 4 + 3 = 9	$5,000 + 4,000 + 7,000 = 16,000
A–F	2 + 7 = 9	
B–G	6 + 3 = 9	
C–E–G	2 + 2 + 3 = 7	

Planned cost + Additional cost = $61,000 + 16,000 = $77,000

In their conference, Mr. Alison and Mr. Phillips concluded that a further speedup of the job was both necessary and possible.

Required:

1. Reduce total project duration as much as possible without unnecessary additional costs. Indicate the new critical path or paths. Show how much slack time or "float" remains in the noncritical paths.
2. Assume that the situation proves to be less urgent than it seems to Messrs. Alison and Phillips. Revise the schedule in order to complete the job within 10 weeks. Indicate the new cost and critical path or paths.

3. Suppose SCI were proceeding on the 10-week schedule and it became obvious that it would take not 2 but 5 weeks to prepare the necessary data for the request for NBA approval and that this step alone would now cost $7,000. What steps would you take to keep on schedule? What would be your new critical path or paths? What would happen to project costs?

4. Assume the project is planned to be completed in six weeks. If there is a penalty cost of $10,000 per week for every week the project is late, what action would you take?

CASE 11

PLANETS II PLAnning and NETwork Simulation II MANUAL

PLANETS is a project management exercise which simulates the progress of a development project currently scheduled for completion in six months. Successful completion of the project requires careful planning and scheduling of a variety of interrelated activities under severe time and cost constraints. The educational objectives of the exercise include:

Introduction to the nature and significance of time/cost trade-offs for the achievement of project objectives.

Familiarization with the problem of planning under time constraints.

Development of skill at working with a network representation of a project.

Experience in the use of a computer simulation model for testing alternative management decisions in an uncertain environment.

Approximately three players will be assigned to each project management team. Although several teams play simultaneously, an individual team's decisions do not affect any other team's performance. However, since the objective is successful completion of the project—that is, completion at minimum cost—there is a definite element of competition between teams. Final time and cost results for a team's performance can be readily compared with other teams' results.

THE PLANETS PROJECT

PLANETS is based on a sequence of design, testing, and plant setup activities for a large component of an electronic system. The project has been broken down into 43 activities; these activities and their interrelationships are described in Appendix A. Each activity is identified by an "activity code" consisting of its starting and ending events. For instance, activity A–B starts at event A and ends at event B.

A network representation of the 43 activities which comprise the PLAN-ETS project is shown in Exhibit 1. The network uses an "activities on arrows" notation; that is, each arrow represents a time-consuming activity. The nodes represent events—start and/or completion of activity. A basic network rule requires that *all* activities coming into a node must be complete before any activity leaving the node can begin.

The structure of the network shown in Exhibit 1 will remain unchanged throughout the exercise. This differs from normal practice in which networks are often changed substantially as the project progresses; such changes can be an important method of shortening critical paths.

Each of the 43 individual activities shown on the PLANETS network must be completed to complete the development project, and these must be completed in a sequence which does not violate the precedence relationships shown in the network diagram. As in real life, the activities which make up the total project do not have a single, fixed duration but can vary with the amount of resources management expends. The primary task for a project management team is to decide on the activity times (durations) to be scheduled for each activity, taking into account costs and project completion time implications. In addition to management's plan there are factors beyond the control of management that can influence the length of an activity. During the project, occurrences such as strikes or acts of nature may cause some activities to be delayed beyond their planned duration. On the other hand, "fortune" may smile and result in an earlier than planned completion of some activity.

The PLANETS network shows the original plan for the project. The times *above* the arrows represent the time originally planned (in days) in each activity. The times *below* each arrow represent the upper and lower limits between which the project management team may vary the planned duration of each activity. For example, activity H–K (the mechanical breadboard) is scheduled to take 16 days at the start of the exercise; this time can be rescheduled by player decision to any integer duration from 11 to 16 days.

$$\begin{array}{c} 16 \\ \text{\large(H)} \longrightarrow \text{\large(K)} \\ 11\text{--}16 \end{array}$$

Original plan at start = 16 days
Minimum possible duration = 11 days
Maximum possible duration = 16 days

The original planned activity duration decisions which have already been made have resulted in an expected completion time for the project, as well as a total cost for completing the project. The expected completion time is obtained by adding up the total time to complete the activities along the critical path in the network. The critical path here is path A–B–E–G–K–P–S–Y–Z, which totals *123* days. The project is assumed

EXHIBIT 1
PLANETS Network

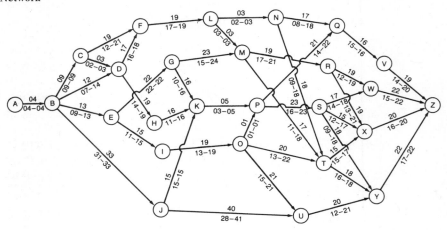

to start on July 1; therefore, the expected project completion date at the start of the exercise is December 24, 123 working days after the project starts. Note that no work is planned for *weekends or holidays.*

Total project cost is made up of the sum of the *delay cost* (described below) and the planned *task costs* for each of the 43 tasks. These task costs are derived from Exhibit 4 which shows, for each activity, the cost associated with each possible planned duration. As shown in Exhibit 3, the total task cost for the original set of durations (the initial plan in Exhibit 1) is $382,022.

Player decisions will establish new planned duration times for some activities and will therefore change both the planned completion time of the project and its total cost. Decreasing activity duration times will increase costs. The maximum task cost, $433,007, for the project would result if all activities were planned at their shortest duration. Minimum task cost, $378,954, on the other hand, results when all activities have their longest duration. The difference between these two costs, $54,053, is the amount of resources that can be influenced by the management team's decisions.

The simulation begins on July 1. The *expected* completion date, based on the plan in Exhibit 1, is December 24. A new target completion date has been established for December 2. This is 16 working days earlier than originally planned. If the project is *not* complete by December 2, a *$500 penalty will be imposed for each day of overrun.* The expected delay cost for the current plan is therefore $8,000. Shortening the entire project to bring the final event to completion by December 2 may be accomplished by the expenditure of resources where necessary to shorten various activities throughout the network. The way money is spent—for overtime, for additional workers, for extra machinery and the like—is not specified in this exercise. The assumption is made that manpower and resources are available to accomplish activities within any planned duration which does not fall outside the limits in Exhibit 1. Each project management team is thus responsible for planning activity durations, so that the project is completed *at the lowest possible total cost,* where total cost is the sum of task costs *and* delay costs.

During this exercise the management team must submit six decisions. After a decision has been submitted, the computer will simulate the passage of 20 working days and will provide management with a list of all activities completed in that time period. In addition, the computer will provide an explanation of any delays or early finishes that may have caused an activity to take a different amount of time than was planned by the project team. Before any decision, the management team can change the planned duration for any activity that has *not* been completed. Obviously, the duration of a completed activity can no longer be altered by management decision.

Because of the large number of activities and complexity of the planning task the computer can be used to help in your analysis. At any time before a decision is submitted, management can ask for a trial run. The computer will provide a list of all tasks and their current planned duration along with the amount of slack in that task. A sample of this printout is shown in Exhibit 2. More detailed instructions on this and other computer options will be provided by your instructor.

STARTING INFORMATION

Each project management team will begin play with the same information and proceed independently to the objective end event. Group starting information will include the following items found in the exhibits.

1. A master network showing the starting position and limits on activity duration times (Exhibit 1).
2. A computer printout of a trial simulation run under the starting conditions. This printout shows the starting and ending events for each activity, planned project duration, and slack in days (Exhibit 2).
3. A full computer printout of the starting position (Exhibit 3).
4. Cost data for each activity in the network (Exhibit 4).

THE COMPUTER PRINTOUT

The computer printout in Exhibit 3 shows the starting position for the project and identifies:

1. Starting and ending events for each activity.
2. Planned activity duration.
3. Actual date of activity completion (these dates will be entered by the computer as activities are completed during the simulation).

EXHIBIT 2
Trial Run—Complete
Report (starting decisions)

CPM REPORT 7–1–69

TSK	DUR	SLK
W–B	4	–16
B–E	13	–16
E–G	22	–16
G–K	16	–16
K–P	5	–16
P–S	23	–16
S–Y	18	–16
Y–Z	22	–16
G–M	23	–15
M–R	19	–15
R–W	19	–15
S–W	17	–15
W–Z	22	–15
B–J	33	–13
J–K	15	–13
R–X	19	–13
X–Z	20	–13
B–C	9	–12
B–D	12	–12
C–D	3	–12
D–H	19	–12
H–K	16	–12
J–U	40	–12
M–T	17	–12
T–Y	18	–12
U–Y	20	–12
S–X	15	–11
P–Q	21	– 9
Q–V	16	– 9
V–Z	19	– 9
D–F	17	– 8
E–I	15	– 8
F–L	19	– 8
I–O	19	– 8
L–M	3	– 8
O–P	1	– 8
C–F	19	– 7
0–U	21	– 7
T–X	15	– 7
L–N	3	– 6
N–T	18	– 6
O–T	20	– 4
N–Q	17	– 0

PROJ FINISH   12–24–69
DELAY COST   8000
TASK COST   382022
TOTAL COST   390022

EXHIBIT 3
Actual Run Report
Format

CPM REPORT   7–1–69

TASK	DUR	ACTUAL FINISH	EXPECT FINISH	LATEST FINISH	SLACK
A–B	4		7– 8	6–13	−16
B–E	13		7–25	7– 2	−16
E–G	22		8–26	8– 4	−16
G–K	16		9–18	8–26	−16
K–P	5		9–25	9– 3	−16
P–S	23		10–28	10– 6	−16
S–Y	18		11–21	10–30	−16
Y–Z	22		12–24	12– 2	−16
G–M	23		9–29	9– 8	−15
M–R	19		10–24	10– 3	−15
R–W	19		11–20	10–30	−15
S–W	17		11–20	10–30	−15
W–Z	22		12–23	12– 2	−15
B–J	33		8–22	8– 5	−13
J–K	15		9–15	8–26	−13
R–X	19		11–20	11– 3	−13
X–Z	20		12–19	12– 2	−13
B–C	9		7–21	7– 2	−12
B–D	12		7–24	7– 8	−12
C–D	3		7–24	7– 8	−12
D–H	19		8–20	8– 4	−12
H–K	16		9–12	8–26	−12
J–U	40		10–20	10– 2	−12
M–T	17		10–22	10– 6	−12
T–Y	18		11–17	10–30	−12
U–Y	20		11–17	10–30	−12
S–X	15		11–18	11– 3	−11
P–Q	21		10–24	10–13	− 9
Q–V	16		11–17	11– 4	− 9
V–Z	19		12–15	12– 2	− 9
D–F	17		8–18	8– 6	− 8
E–I	15		8–15	8– 5	− 8
F–L	19		9–15	9– 3	− 8
I–O	19		9–12	9– 2	− 8
L–M	3		9–18	9– 8	− 8
O–P	1		9–15	9– 3	− 8
C–F	19		8–15	8– 6	− 7
O–U	21		10–13	10– 2	− 7
T–X	15		11–12	11– 3	− 7
L–N	3		9–18	9–10	− 6
N–T	18		10–14	10– 6	− 6
O–T	20		10–10	10– 6	− 4
N–Q	17		10–13	10–13	0

PROJ FINISH   12–24–69
DELAY COST   8000
TASK COST   382022
TOTAL COST   390022

4. Expected date or earliest date that an activity can be expected to be completed.
5. Latest date that an activity can be completed without missing the scheduled completion date for the project.
6. Slack in days showing the extent to which an activity is ahead of or behind schedule.

The computer printout used in PLANETS is a *slack sort*. In this type of report, the most critical activities are printed at the top of the list. Since the most critical activities of a network comprise the critical path, the first entries on the PLANETS printout along a path from event A to Z identify the critical (longest) path for this project. Subsequent entries on the printout show subcritical paths in the order of their criticality. When an activity has negative slack the entry will be preceded by a minus sign. (Note in Exhibit 3 that the minimum slack is minus 16 days. This can be explained by the fact that the initial expected project completion date, December 24, is 16 working days behind the scheduled completion date of December 2.)

PLANETS COST DATA

Cost data in Exhibit 4 shows the change in cost associated with a change in planned activity duration. Cost data is furnished for all changes that are permitted between the upper and lower time limits for each activity. Time changes that are not within the limits will be rejected by the computer.

PRELIMINARY ANALYSIS

Each project management team should study the starting position date, considering alternative courses of action for meeting the required project completion date approximately six months away. While a complete analysis of the network is not essential at this point, the group should at least identify critical and subcritical paths, and consider carefully activities that are likely to be completed during the first 20-day report period. Remember once a decision is made, activities completed during that period cannot be changed.

EXHIBIT 4

The following are differential and/or absolute cost matrixes for each of the 43 project activities.

Determine the change in cost for change in an activity duration by referring to the *differential* cost matrix for that activity. Determine the total cost for an activity set at a particular time by referring to that activity's *total cost* list (at the far right of the differential cost matrix).

For example, activity B–D is currently planned to take 12 days. This has added $3,450 to the total cost of the project. If you wish to reduce this activity to 10 days, the differential cost would be $150. The total cost activity for B–D for 10 days would thus be $3,450 + $150 = $3,600. Once the project plan for activity B–D is fixed at 10 days you may wish to make another change. For example, increasing this time to 14 days. The differential cost is −$258 which would make the total cost $3,000 − $258 = $3,342.

Activity A–B:

Days	Total Cost
4	$1,000

Activity B–C:

Days	Total Cost
9	$500

Activity B–D differential cost matrix:

From (days) \ To (days)	7	8	9	10	11	12	13	14	Total Cost
7	0	−160	−285	−385	−467	−535	−593	−643	3,985
8	160	0	−125	−225	−307	−375	−433	−483	3,825
9	285	125	0	−100	−182	−250	−308	−358	3,700
10	385	225	100	0	−82	−150	−208	−258	3,600
11	467	307	182	82	0	−68	−126	−176	3,518
12	535	375	250	150	68	0	−58	−108	3,450
13	593	433	308	208	126	58	0	−50	3,392
14	643	483	358	258	176	108	50	0	3,342

EXHIBIT 4 (continued)

Activity B–E differential cost matrix:

From (days) \ To (days)	9	10	11	12	13	Total Cost
9	0	−133	−243	−333	−410	3,033
10	133	0	−110	−200	−277	2,900
11	243	110	0	−90	−167	2,790
12	333	200	90	0	−77	2,700
13	410	277	167	77	0	2,623

Activity B–J differential cost matrix:

From (days) \ To (days)	31	32	33	Total Cost
31	0	−282	−548	19,032
32	282	0	−266	18,750
33	548	266	0	18,484

Activity C–D differential cost matrix:

From (days) \ To (days)	2	3	Total Cost
2	0	−167	650
3	167	0	483

Activity C–F differential cost matrix:

From (days) \ To (days)	12	13	14	15	16	17	18	19	20	21	Total Cost
12	0	-77	-143	-200	-250	-294	-333	-368	-399	-428	4,000
13	77	0	-66	-123	-173	-217	-256	-291	-322	-351	3,923
14	143	66	0	-57	-107	-151	-190	-225	-256	-285	3,857
15	200	123	57	0	-50	-94	-133	-168	-199	-228	3,800
16	250	173	107	50	0	-44	-83	-118	-149	-178	3,750
17	294	217	151	94	44	0	-39	-74	-105	-134	3,706
18	333	256	190	133	83	39	0	-35	-66	-95	3,666
19	368	291	225	168	118	74	35	0	-31	-60	3,631
20	399	322	256	199	149	105	66	31	0	-29	3,600
21	428	351	285	228	178	134	95	60	29	0	3,571

Activity D–F differential cost matrix:

From (days) \ To (days)	16	17	18	Total Cost
16	0	-74	-139	3,750
17	74	0	-65	3,676
18	139	65	0	3,611

Activity D–H differential cost matrix:

From (days) \ To (days)	14	15	16	17	18	19	Total Cost
14	0	-119	-223	-315	-387	-460	8,785
15	119	0	-104	-196	-278	-351	8,666
16	223	104	0	-92	-174	-247	8,562
17	315	196	92	0	-82	-155	8,470
18	387	278	174	82	0	-73	8,388
19	460	351	247	155	73	0	8,315

EXHIBIT 4 (*continued*)

Activity E–G:

Days	Total Cost
22	$750

Activity E–I differential cost matrix:

From (days) \ To (days)	11	12	13	14	15	Total Cost
11	0	−3,788	−6,993	−9,740	−12,121	50,454
12	3,788	0	−3,205	−5,952	−8,333	46,666
13	6,993	3,205	0	−2,747	−5,128	43,461
14	9,740	5,952	2,747	0	−2,381	40,714
15	12,121	8,333	5,128	2,381	0	38,333

Activity F–L differential cost matrix:

From (days) \ To (days)	17	18	19	Total Cost
17	0	−327	−619	10,382
18	327	0	−292	10,055
19	619	292	0	9,763

Activity G–K differential cost matrix:

From (days) \ To (days)	10	11	12	13	14	15	16	Total Cost
10	0	−910	−1,667	−2,308	−2,858	−3,334	−3,750	20,000
11	910	0	−757	−1,398	−1,948	−2,424	−2,840	19,090
12	1,667	757	0	−641	−1,191	−1,667	−2,083	18,333
13	2,308	1,398	641	0	−550	−1,026	−1,442	17,692
14	2,858	1,948	1,191	550	0	−476	−892	17,142
15	3,334	2,424	1,667	1,026	476	0	−416	16,666
16	3,750	2,840	2,083	1,442	892	416	0	16,250

Activity G–M differential cost matrix:

From (days) \ To (days)	15	16	17	18	19	20	21	22	23	24	Total Cost
15	0	−1,041	−1,961	−2,778	−3,509	−4,166	−4,762	−5,303	−5,797	−6,250	19,666
16	1,041	0	−920	−1,737	−2,468	−3,125	−3,721	−4,262	−4,756	−5,209	18,625
17	1,961	920	0	−817	−1,548	−2,205	−2,801	−3,342	−3,836	−4,289	17,705
18	2,778	1,737	817	0	−731	−1,388	−1,984	−2,525	−3,019	−3,472	16,888
19	3,509	2,468	1,548	731	0	−657	−1,253	−1,794	−2,288	−2,741	16,157
20	4,166	3,125	2,205	1,388	657	0	−596	−1,137	−1,631	−2,084	15,500
21	4,762	3,721	2,801	1,984	1,253	596	0	−541	−1,035	−1,488	14,904
22	5,303	4,262	3,342	2,525	1,794	1,137	541	0	−494	−947	14,363
23	5,797	4,756	3,836	3,019	2,288	1,631	1,035	494	0	−453	13,869
24	6,250	5,209	4,289	3,472	2,741	2,084	1,488	947	453	0	13,416

EXHIBIT 4 (*continued*)

Activity H–K differential cost matrix:

From (days) \ To (days)	11	12	13	14	15	16	Total Cost
11	0	-189	-349	-487	-606	-710	7,772
12	189	0	-160	-298	-417	-521	7,583
13	349	160	0	-138	-257	-361	7,423
14	487	298	138	0	-119	-223	7,285
15	606	417	257	119	0	-104	7,116
16	710	521	361	223	104	0	7,062

Activity I–O differential cost matrix:

From (days) \ To (days)	13	14	15	16	17	18	19	Total Cost
13	0	-1,373	-2,564	-3,605	-4,525	-5,342	-6,073	31,730
14	1,373	0	-1,191	-2,232	-3,152	-3,969	-4,700	30,357
15	2,564	1,191	0	-1,041	-1,961	-2,778	3,509	29,166
16	3,605	2,232	1,041	0	-920	-1,737	-2,468	28,125
17	4,525	3,125	1,961	920	0	-817	-1,548	27,205
18	5,342	3,969	2,778	1,737	817	0	-731	26,388
19	6,073	4,700	3,509	2,468	1,548	731	0	25,657

Activity J–K:

Days	Total Cost
15..........	$3,750

Activity J–U differential cost matrix:

From (days)	To (days) 28	29	30	31	32	33	34	35	36	37	38	39	40	41	Total Cost
28	0	−863	−1,667	−2,420	−3,125	−3,788	−4,412	−5,000	−5,556	−6,082	−6,579	−7,052	−7,500	−7,927	35,000
29	863	0	−804	−1,557	−2,262	−2,925	−3,549	−4,137	−4,693	−5,219	−5,716	−6,189	−6,637	−7,064	34,137
30	1,667	804	−0	−753	−1,458	−2,121	−2,745	−3,333	−3,889	−4,415	−4,912	−5,385	−5,833	−6,260	33,333
31	2,420	1,557	753	0	−705	−1,368	−1,992	−2,580	−3,136	−3,662	−4,159	−4,632	−5,080	−5,507	32,580
32	3,125	2,262	1,458	705	0	−663	−1,287	−1,875	−2,431	−2,957	−3,454	−3,927	−4,375	−4,802	31,875
33	3,788	2,925	2,121	1,368	663	0	−624	−1,212	−1,768	−2,294	−2,791	−3,264	−3,712	−4,139	31,212
34	4,412	3,549	2,745	1,992	1,287	624	0	−588	−1,144	−1,670	−2,167	−2,640	−3,088	−3,515	30,588
35	5,000	4,137	3,333	2,580	1,875	1,212	588	0	−556	−1,082	−1,579	−2,052	−2,500	−2,927	30,000
36	5,556	4,693	3,889	3,136	2,431	1,768	1,144	556	0	−526	−1,023	−1,496	−1,944	−2,371	29,444
37	6,082	5,219	4,415	3,662	2,957	2,294	1,670	1,082	526	0	−497	−970	−1,418	−1,845	28,918
38	6,579	5,716	4,912	4,159	3,454	2,791	2,167	1,579	1,023	497	0	−473	−921	−1,348	28,421
39	7,052	6,189	5,385	4,632	3,927	3,264	2,640	2,052	1,496	970	473	0	−448	−875	27,948
40	7,500	6,637	5,883	5,080	4,375	3,712	3,088	2,500	1,944	1,418	921	448	0	−427	27,500
41	7,927	7,064	6,260	5,507	4,802	4,139	3,515	2,927	2,371	1,845	1,348	875	427	0	27,073

Activity K–P differential cost matrix:

From (days)	To 3	4	5	Total Cost
3	0	−166	−266	966
4	166	0	−100	800
5	266	100	0	700

Activity L–M:

Days	Total Cost
3	$2,000

EXHIBIT 4 (*continued*)

Activity L–N differential cost matrix:

From (*days*) \ To (*days*)	2	3	Total Cost
2	0	-167	650
3	167	0	483

Activity M–R differential cost matrix:

From (*days*) \ To (*days*)	17	18	19	20	21	Total Cost
17	0	-78	-148	-211	-269	6,411
18	78	0	-70	-133	-191	6,333
19	148	70	0	-63	-121	6,263
20	211	133	63	0	-58	6,200
21	269	191	121	58	0	6,142

Activity M–T differential cost matrix:

From (*days*) \ To (*days*)	11	12	13	14	15	16	17	18	Total Cost
11	0	-159	-294	-409	-509	-597	-674	-743	4,909
12	159	0	-135	-250	-350	-438	-515	-584	4,705
13	294	135	0	-115	-215	-303	-380	-449	4,615
14	409	250	115	0	-100	-188	-265	-334	4,500
15	509	350	215	100	0	-88	-165	-234	4,400
16	597	438	303	188	88	0	-77	-146	4,312
17	674	515	380	265	165	77	0	-69	4,235
18	743	584	449	334	234	146	69	0	4,166

Activity N–Q differential cost matrix:

From (days) / To (days)	8	9	10	11	12	13	14	15	16	17	18	Total Cost
8	0	−334	−600	−819	−1,000	−1,154	−1,286	−1,400	−1,500	−1,589	−1,667	8,000
9	334	0	−266	−485	−666	−820	−952	−1,066	−1,166	−1,255	−1,333	7,666
10	600	266	0	−219	−400	−554	−686	−800	−900	−989	−1,067	7,400
11	819	485	219	0	−181	−335	−467	−581	−681	−770	−848	7,181
12	1,000	666	400	181	0	−154	−286	−400	−500	−589	−667	7,000
13	1,154	820	554	335	154	0	−132	−246	−346	−435	−513	6,846
14	1,286	952	686	467	286	132	0	−114	−214	−303	−381	6,714
15	1,400	1,066	800	581	400	246	114	0	−100	−189	−267	6,600
16	1,500	1,166	900	681	500	346	214	100	0	−89	−167	6,500
17	1,589	1,255	989	770	589	435	303	189	89	0	−78	6,411
18	1,667	1,333	1,067	848	667	513	381	267	167	78	0	6,333

Activity N–T differential cost matrix:

From (days) / To (days)	9	10	11	12	13	14	15	16	17	18	Total Cost
9	0	−244	−444	−611	−752	−873	−978	−1,069	−1,150	−1,222	12,444
10	244	0	−200	−367	−508	−629	−734	−825	−906	−978	12,200
11	444	200	0	−167	−308	−429	−534	−625	−706	−778	12,000
12	611	367	167	0	−141	−262	−367	−458	−539	−611	11,833
13	752	508	308	141	0	−121	−226	−317	−398	−470	11,692
14	873	629	429	262	121	0	−105	−196	−277	−349	11,571
15	978	734	534	367	226	105	0	−91	−172	−244	11,466
16	1,069	825	625	458	317	196	91	0	−81	−153	11,375
17	1,150	906	706	539	398	277	172	81	0	−72	11,294
18	1,222	978	778	611	470	349	244	153	72	0	11,222

EXHIBIT 4 (continued)

Activity O–P:

Days	Total Cost
1	150

Activity O–T differential cost matrix:

From (days) \ To (days)	13	14	15	16	17	18	19	20	21	22	Total Cost
13	0	−127	−236	−332	−417	−492	−559	−619	−674	−724	9,269
14	127	0	−109	−205	−290	−365	−432	−492	−547	−597	9,142
15	236	109	0	−96	−181	−256	−323	−383	−438	−488	9,033
16	332	205	96	0	−85	−160	−227	−287	−342	−392	8,937
17	417	290	181	85	0	−75	−142	−202	−257	−307	8,852
18	492	365	256	160	75	0	−67	−127	−182	−232	8,777
19	559	432	323	227	142	67	0	−60	−115	−165	8,710
20	619	492	383	287	202	127	60	0	−55	−105	8,650
21	674	547	438	342	257	182	115	55	0	−50	8,595
22	724	597	488	392	307	232	165	105	50	0	8,545

Activity O–U differential cost matrix:

From (days) \ To (days)	15	16	17	18	19	20	21	Total Cost
15	0	−79	−149	−211	−266	−316	−362	7,266
16	79	0	−70	−132	−187	−237	−283	7,187
17	149	70	0	−62	−117	−167	−213	7,117
18	211	132	62	0	−55	−105	−151	7,055
19	266	187	117	55	0	−50	−96	7,000
20	316	237	167	105	50	0	−46	6,950
21	362	283	213	151	96	46	0	6,904

Activity P–Q differential cost matrix:

From (days) \ To (days)	14	15	16	17	18	19	20	21	22	Total Cost
14	0	−71	−134	−189	−238	−282	−321	−357	−390	7,571
15	71	0	−63	−118	−167	−211	−250	−286	−319	7,500
16	134	63	0	−55	−104	−148	−187	−223	−256	7,437
17	189	118	55	0	−49	−93	−132	−168	−201	7,382
18	238	167	104	49	0	−44	−83	−119	−152	7,333
19	282	211	148	93	44	0	−39	−75	−108	7,289
20	321	250	187	132	83	39	0	−36	−69	7,250
21	357	286	223	168	119	75	36	0	−33	7,214
22	390	319	256	201	152	108	69	33	0	7,181

Activity P–S differential cost matrix:

From (days) \ To (days)	16	17	18	19	20	21	22	23	Total Cost
16	0	−111	−209	−297	−375	−447	−512	−571	10,875
17	111	0	−98	−186	−264	−336	−401	−460	10,764
18	209	98	0	−88	−166	−238	−303	−362	10,666
19	297	186	88	0	−78	−150	−215	−274	10,578
20	375	264	166	78	0	−72	−137	−196	10,500
21	447	336	238	150	72	0	−65	−124	10,428
22	512	401	303	215	137	65	0	−59	10,363
23	571	460	362	274	196	124	59	0	10,304

Activity Q–V differential cost matrix:

From (days) \ To (days)	15	16	Total Cost
15	0	−75	9,200
16	75	0	9,125

EXHIBIT 4 (continued)

Activity R–W differential cost matrix:

From (days) \ To (days)	12	13	14	15	16	17	18	19	Total Cost
12	0	−224	−416	−583	−729	−858	−972	−1,074	12,916
13	224	0	−192	−359	−505	−634	−748	−850	12,692
14	416	192	0	−167	−313	−442	−556	−658	12,500
15	583	359	167	0	−146	−275	−389	−491	12,333
16	729	505	313	146	0	−129	−243	−345	12,187
17	858	634	442	275	129	0	−114	−216	12,058
18	972	748	556	389	243	114	0	−102	11,944
19	1,074	850	658	491	345	216	102	0	11,842

Activity R–X differential cost matrix:

From (days) \ To (days)	13	14	15	16	17	18	19	20	21	Total Cost
13	0	−76	−143	−201	−253	−299	−340	−376	−410	6,576
14	76	0	−67	−125	−177	−223	−264	−300	−334	6,500
15	143	67	0	−58	−110	−156	−197	−233	−267	6,433
16	201	125	58	0	−52	−98	−139	−175	−209	6,375
17	253	177	110	52	0	−46	−87	−123	−157	6,323
18	299	223	156	98	46	0	−41	−77	−111	6,277
19	340	264	197	139	87	41	0	−36	−70	6,236
20	376	300	233	175	123	77	36	0	−34	6,200
21	410	334	267	209	157	111	70	34	0	6,166

Activity S–W differential cost matrix:

From (days) \ To (days)	14	15	16	17	18	Total Cost
14	0	−109	−205	−290	−365	13,642
15	109	0	−96	−181	−256	13,533
16	205	96	0	−85	−160	13,437
17	290	181	85	0	−75	13,352
18	365	256	160	75	0	13,277

Activity S–X differential cost matrix:

From (days) \ To (days)	12	13	14	15	16	17	Total Cost
12	0	−109	−202	−283	−354	−416	9,916
13	109	0	−93	−174	−245	−307	9,807
14	202	93	0	−81	−152	−214	9,714
15	283	174	81	0	−71	−133	9,633
16	354	245	152	71	0	−62	9,562
17	416	307	214	133	62	0	9,500

Activity S–Y differential cost matrix:

From (days) \ To (days)	9	10	11	12	13	14	15	16	17	18	Total Cost
9	0	−144	−263	−361	−444	−516	−578	−632	−680	−722	7,444
10	144	0	−119	−217	−300	−372	−434	−488	−536	−578	7,300
11	263	119	0	−98	−181	−253	−315	−369	−417	−459	7,181
12	361	217	98	0	−83	−155	−217	−271	−319	−361	7,083
13	444	300	181	83	0	−72	−134	−188	−236	−278	7,000
14	516	372	253	155	72	0	−62	−116	−164	−206	6,928
15	578	434	315	217	134	62	0	−54	−102	−144	6,866
16	632	488	369	271	188	116	54	0	−48	−90	6,812
17	680	536	417	319	236	164	102	48	0	−42	6,764
18	722	578	459	361	278	206	144	90	42	0	6,722

EXHIBIT 4 (*continued*)

Activity T–X differential cost matrix:

From (days) \ To	15	16	17	Total Cost
15	0	−625	−1,177	25,000
16	625	0	−552	24,375
17	1,177	552	0	23,823

Activity T–Y differential cost matrix:

From (days) \ To	16	17	18	Total Cost
16	0	−92	−174	7,562
17	92	0	−82	7,470
18	174	82	0	7,388

Activity U–Y differential cost matrix:

From (days) \ To	12	13	14	15	16	17	18	19	20	21	Total Cost
12	0	−160	−298	−417	−521	−613	−695	−768	−833	−893	9,083
13	160	0	−138	−257	−361	−453	−535	−608	−673	−733	8,923
14	298	138	0	−119	−223	−315	−397	−470	−535	−595	8,785
15	417	257	119	0	−104	−196	−278	−351	−416	−476	8,666
16	521	361	223	104	0	−92	−174	−247	−312	−372	8,562
17	613	453	315	196	92	0	−82	−155	−220	−280	8,470
18	695	535	397	278	174	82	0	−73	−138	−198	8,388
19	768	608	470	351	247	155	73	0	−65	−125	8,315
20	833	673	535	416	312	220	138	65	0	−60	8,250
21	893	733	595	476	372	280	198	125	60	0	8,190

Activity V–Z differential cost matrix:

From (days) \ To (days)	14	15	16	17	18	19	20	Total Cost
14	0	-62	-116	-164	-206	-244	-278	3,928
15	62	0	-54	-102	-144	-182	-216	3,866
16	116	54	0	-48	-90	-128	-162	3,812
17	164	102	48	0	-42	-80	-114	3,764
18	206	144	90	42	0	-38	-72	3,722
19	244	182	128	80	38	0	-34	3,684
20	278	216	162	114	72	34	0	3,650

Activity W–Z differential cost matrix:

From (days) \ To (days)	15	16	17	18	19	20	21	22	Total Cost
15	0	-208	-392	-556	-702	-833	-953	-1,061	9,333
16	208	0	-184	-348	-494	-625	-745	-853	9,125
17	392	184	0	-164	-310	-441	-561	-669	8,941
18	556	348	164	0	-146	-277	-397	-505	8,777
19	702	494	310	146	0	-131	-251	-359	8,631
20	833	625	441	277	131	0	-120	-228	8,500
21	953	745	561	397	251	120	0	-108	8,380
22	1,061	853	669	505	359	228	108	0	8,272

Activity X–Z differential cost matrix:

From (days) \ To (days)	16	17	18	19	20	Total Cost
16	0	-129	-243	-347	-439	16,187
17	129	0	-114	-218	-310	16,058
18	243	114	0	-104	-196	15,944
19	347	218	104	0	-92	15,842
20	439	310	196	92	0	15,750

EXHIBIT 4 (concluded)

Activity Y–Z differential cost matrix:

From (days) \ To (days)	17	18	19	20	21	22	Total Cost
17	0	-82	-155	-220	-280	-334	7,470
18	82	0	-73	-138	-198	-252	7,388
19	155	73	0	-65	-125	-179	7,315
20	220	138	65	0	-60	-114	7,250
21	280	198	125	60	0	-54	7,190
22	334	252	179	114	54	0	7,136

APPENDIX A: PLANETS II

The first activity establishes the project organization and identifies and locates the technical staff who will be drawn from other project teams, as well as from the corporate R&D staff:

A–B   Organization and staffing.

When the organizational activities are complete and the technical staff has been assembled, four major activity sequences can begin.

1. Recruitment and orientation of hourly employees who, when trained, will process and inspect purchased equipment and then receive further technical training:

B–C   Employee recruiting.
C–F   Orientation training.
F–L   Equipment processing and delivery.
L–N   Inspection and report.
N–T   Technical equipment orientation.

2. Process design and layout for inspection equipment. The layout must wait on completion of a report which includes a list of hourly employees and their skill classifications:

B–D   Design study.
C–D   Report preparation.
D–F   Layout design.

3. Design, procurement, testing, and installation of power and safety equipment:

B–E   Power source study.
E–G   Power equipment procurement.
G–M   Install power equipment.
G–K   Testing (can be concurrent with installation [G–M]).
M–R   Install safety equipment (must be preceded by setup [L–M]).
R–W   Trial run—power and safety equipment.
R–X   Machinery adjustment (can be concurrent with trial run [R–W]).

4. Design, programming, and testing of computer software for the project; these activities are performed by data processing personnel and do not require project personnel:

B–J   ADP systems design.
J–U   Simulation testing.
J–K   Control application testing (can be concurrent with simulation testing [J–U]).

When the purchased equipment has been processed, some hourly employees will be free to set up the jigs and fixtures required for the installation of the safety equipment (M–R). After the setup and after installation of the power equipment (G–M), the customer must inspect the facilities:

L–M   Setup.
M–T   Customer inspection.

Completion of the power source study (B–E) also triggers the start of following sequence:

E–I   Site modification.
I–O   Preliminary model design.
O–T   Design translation.
O–P   Report preparation (can be concurrent with design translation [O–T]).
O–U   Theoretical testing (can be concurrent with report preparation [O–P]).
U–Y   Concurrent testing (theoretical testing [O–U] and simulation testing [J–U] must be complete).

Methods work can begin as soon as the process design study (B–D) is finished; a mechanical breadboard can begin when the methods study is through:

D–H   Methods study.
H–K   Mechanical breadboard.

When the breadboard is built (H–K) and both the power equipment (G–K) and the control application software (J–K) have been tested, a test report can be prepared, trial runs can be made with the breadboard, and technical literature can be developed for the customer:

K–P   Report preparation.
P–S   Trial run—breadboard components.
P–Q   Literature development (can be concurrent with trial run [P–S]).

Completion of the inspection report on purchased equipment allows the start of a three-activity sequence involving the writing, review, and distribution of a specification study:

N–Q   Specification study.
Q–V   Review and approval.
V–Z   Printing and distribution.

After trial run of the breadboard components (P–S), these activity sequences can start:

1. Preliminary production of customer's production prototype, including inspection:

   S–W   Preliminary model production.
   W–Z   Inspect and adjust customer prototype (trial run of power and safety equipment [R–W] must precede [W–Z]).

2. Adaptation and adjustment of components for volume production:

   S–X   Component adaptation.

3. Layout and design of control reports.

   S–Y   Control report design.

The completion of activities N–T, M–T, and O–T unblocks fabrication of a preliminary model and stress-testing development:

   T–X   Preliminary model fabrication.
   T–Y   Stress-testing development.

Now the last two activities—preliminary production run and final simulation—can begin and the project can be completed:

   X–Z   Preliminary production (must be preceded by [T–X], [S–X], and [R–X].
   Y–Z   Systems simulation (must be preceded by [U–Y], [T–Y], and [S–Y]).

CASE 12

McDonald's Corporation

The bell rings and the "Vehicle" button lights up. "Welcome to McDonald's! May I take your order please?" Among the sounds of a growling muffler and a blaring radio, a male voice responds, "Yes. Twobigmacsaquarterwithcheesetwolargefries . . . alargecokeandalargerootbeer." My fingers search desperately for the correct buttons on the order register as I struggle to remember and decipher the order. "Would you like some dessert with dinner?" "No thanks, that's it." Torn between the urge to look up into the microphone and the necessity of looking down at the register display, I fumble with the "Speak" switch, read back the order at a snail's pace, get confirmation, and read off the total. "That'll be $5.72. Please drive around to the window." Oh yes, I'm supposed to pour drinks. I reach awkwardly for the drink cups, scoop up too much ice and have to dump the extra out, read each label on the drink machine until I see "Coke," and press the "Large" button. The bell has already rung again. "Welcome to McDonald's!"

After an hour, I can reach for the right register key most of the time and know, for example, that root beer caps should be creased to differentiate them from Coke caps on orders that contain both. As I was relieved by Sandy, I watched her start to pour two drinks before the order was completed ("God gave you two hands. Use them!" the store manager had said). She upgraded "fries" to large fries and read the whole order back in a flash. She capped the drinks, put them on the assembly counter, helped Betsy check another order, and "Welcome to McDonald's!"

(Casewriter's experience at the Hillybourne McDonald's Drive-Thru window from 5:30 to 6:30 P.M.)

The McDonald's production process, from frozen meat patties coming in the rear door to hot meals going out the front, was geared to providing a uniformly high-quality, quickly served meal in clean and pleasant surroundings. This case describes that process.

THE MCDONALD'S CORPORATION

> After World War II, Richard and Maurice McDonald were having trouble staffing their San Bernardino, California, carhop restaurant; there was the usual parade of drunks and drifters. "We said," Dick McDonald recalls, "let's get rid of it all. Out went dishes, glasses, and silverware. Out went service, the dishwashers, and the long menu. We decided to serve just hamburgers, drinks, and french fries on paper plates. Everything prepared in advance, everything uniform. All geared to heavy volume in a short amount of time."[1]

Ray Kroc, then 52 and a milk-shake machine salesman, found the McDonald brothers in 1954. "I was amazed," Kroc remembered, "this little drive-in having people standing in line. The volume was incredible." Kroc proposed a deal with the brothers to sell franchises, was accepted, and the spectacular story of the Golden Arches had begun.

McDonald's has dominated the hamburger fast-food industry, with a 1979 market share of 35 percent, dwarfing Burger King's 11 percent and Wendy's 8 percent. "It's not that we're so smart," said Chairman Fred Turner. "It's that this business takes a lot of attention to detail." That attention has fueled an average annual revenues growth through the 70s of 29 percent in systemwide sales, 26 percent in corporate revenues. This growth has resulted from increasing the number of units (at an average annual rate of 15 percent), extending store hours with breakfast, increasing check size with an expanding menu, and adding new services such as the Drive-Thru window. By June 1980, there were 5,951 McDonald's restaurants worldwide, with 4,998 in the United States. Of these, 1,292 were company owned and operated (McOpCo stores), and the remainder licensee operated (with the real estate leased from McDonald's at one third of the sites). In 1979, systemwide sales totaled $5.4 billion while corporate revenues were $1.9 billion and net income was $189 million (77 percent and 17 percent, respectively, from company-owned store operations). The average annual sales of restaurants open 13 months or more reached $1 million, with 57 restaurants exceeding $2 million and one exceeding $3 million. New restaurants cost an average of $722,000. Systemwide advertising expenditures totaled $261 million.

Corporate headquarters were located in Oak Brook, Illinois. Within the United States, operations were divided into 5 zones and, further, into 24 regions. "Each region is an individual profit center (and) is headed by a regional manager. Among the regional staff are the field consultants, who serve as the direct link between the corporation and its franchised restaurants and who work with licensees to assist them in operating their restau-

---

[1] *Forbes*, January 15, 1973.

rants in accordance with McDonald's tradition of Q.S.C.&V., our motto for Quality, Service, Cleanliness, and Value, . . . and area supervisors, our employees who assist the managers of company-owned stores in the operations area, . . . and real estate, marketing, construction, purchasing, training, personnel, and accounting specialists." [A McDonald's executive]

THE HILLYBOURNE STORE[2]

Hillybourne was a New England college town with a population of about 30,000. The McDonald's store was located on heavily commercialized Maple Street, about 1 mile south of an interstate highway intersection and ½ mile north of the town center. It sat between a Kentucky Fried Chicken restaurant and a gas station, and across the street from a shopping plaza. Towards the interstate, Maple Street was lined with several restaurants including a Burger King, several car dealers and gas stations, and a dozen small businesses. The central business district, adjacent to the college, contained public buildings, theaters, department stores, banks, and several restaurants.

The Hillybourne McDonald's (a McOpCo store) was open from 7 A.M. to 12 midnight, 363 days a year. Daily volume peaked at lunch (with 15 percent of daily sales between noon and 1 P.M.), while weekly volume peaked on Friday (with 18 percent of weekly sales). The store's annual volume totaled about $1.1 million in 1980. The average customer's check was $2.24 in June 1980. The store had 61 parking places and 106 dining seats inside. Further details are presented in Exhibit 1 (menu and product mix), Exhibit 2 (weekly and daily distribution of sales), and Exhibit 3 (June 1980 operating results). (Exhibits occur at end of case.)

Each McDonald's store was unique in the demand pattern that it faced, the local labor pool from which it drew, and the decor of its dining room. (There were, however, certain corporate standards and policies in areas that ranged from landscaping to not installing a public telephone in or immediately around a restaurant.) Thus, the Hillybourne store had a sharp peak from noon to 1 P.M., while another store might have three steady hours over lunch; the Hillybourne store employed mostly high school and college students, while another store might employ older women; and the Hillybourne store dining room featured a central, "ski-lodge" fireplace, while another store might feature an airplane with seating arranged along the fuselage.

The store manager, Ted Leone, had been raised in Maine and was an avid sportsman. He had worked at McDonald's for two years during college and had joined the company as a management trainee upon his graduation in 1973. In the spring of 1980, with two years' experience as a store manager, Leone had been assigned to the Hillybourne store. He noted:

---

[2] Hillybourne is a disguised location.

We have a good mix of business—a lot from the Interstate so Friday and Sunday nights are busy, a good coffee trade in the morning as people go to work, a sharp peak at noon as workers and shoppers come for lunch, and a lot of kids on school holidays. In my last store, the town had a strong family structure—kids said "Yes sir, No sir," and they all went to college. I often knew their parents, brothers, and sisters. We built a real team. I haven't been here in Hillybourne long enough to build these community ties.

AN OVERVIEW OF STORE OPERATIONS

Customer Service

Customers entered the Hillybourne store lobby through doors on either side of the building. Figure 1 shows the food flow of the Hillybourne store. The long service counter had five cash registers ("windows") spaced along it and the lighted menu board above it.

"May I help someone?" With a smile, the counter person greeted the customer and accepted the order. S/he typically used a suggestive sell-up to add a missing item such as dessert or to upgrade a regular size to large. S/he punched the order into the register, which had a labeled key and lighted display for each item, and used this display as a visual record for confirming, assembling, and checking the order. (Thus, if a hamburger was ordered, the "HAMB" key was pressed and a "1" would light up beside it.)

The order was assembled by collecting the food from the appropriate machines and bins in the sequence below.

Cold drinks: Machine-portioned soft drinks were poured and capped (7–12 seconds); employee-portioned shakes were poured and capped (5–7 seconds); milk was picked from an iced tray.

Hot drinks: Employees poured coffee and tea, and a machine dispensed hot chocolate. All took about five seconds to pour and cap.

Sandwiches: Boxed and wrapped sandwiches were selected from warming bin.

Dessert: Pies and cookies were selected from racks; ice cream desserts were poured from spout (8–20 seconds).

Fries: Bags of fries were selected from the fry bin (or bagged during slow periods).

FIGURE 1
The Food Flow

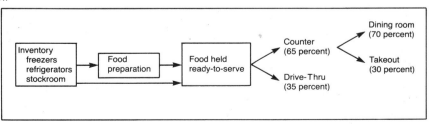

When the order had been assembled and bagged or placed on a tray, the customer was asked for payment and given change. The transaction ended with a "Thank you, come again!"

As volume increased, more windows were opened and one or more "backers" were assigned. A backer, or expediter, helped to put orders together and was often able to start on this before the customer had finished giving an order. Working behind the counter demanded teamwork and cooperation for, as Leone noted, "Five to eight people can also spend their time tripping over each other and mixing the orders up." The Hillybourne store strove to meet a standard of keeping a customer waiting less than 1 minute in line and less than 30 seconds at the counter. (These standards, 50 percent faster than corporate standards, were applicable to stores in the Hillybourne area.) During the first six months of 1980, the total line and counter time at the Hillybourne store had averaged 2 minutes and 3 seconds (as measured by the area supervisor during inspection visits—see Exhibit 4 for the store visitation report form).

At the Drive-Thru window, the order was taken as described in the case introduction. In the Hillybourne region, only one check was allowed per car. As each order was completed, it was recorded on a TV screen in the Drive-Thru work area (and on a second screen over the sandwich bin). The list on the screen became the visual record used to assemble the order (as described above) and, when each car reached the "pad" outside the window, to request payment. As at the counter, presentation of the order and a "Thank you, come again!" completed the transaction.

As Drive-Thru business increased, the three tasks (order taking, order assembly, and cash receipt/order presentation) were divided among two and then three people, with a backer also available to help. Again, teamwork was important. Area standards allowed 30 seconds on the pad per car.

Special orders, such as "a plain hamburg" or "a filet without tartar sauce," called "grills," were noted on a slip of paper by the order-taker and handed to the grill workers. Since a "grill" always entailed a wait (until the next batch of that sandwich came up), the counter customer was asked to step aside (with his or her order stored in the register for retrieval when the order was ready); and the Drive-Thru customer was asked to pull up to a special parking space to wait (when ready, the order was hand-carried out to the car by an employee). These procedures were also followed when a regular sandwich was not ready.

Sandwich Production

The Hillybourne McDonald's menu listed six standard sandwiches which were produced from three preportioned frozen products, as shown in Figure 2.[3] Sandwiches were prepared in batches upon order from a person "up

---

[3] During the summer of 1980, the area was considering the introduction of the McChicken and Chopped Beefsteak sandwiches. It was anticipated that the chicken filet would be fried

FIGURE 2
McDonald's Sandwiches

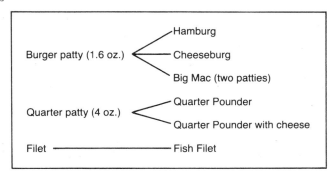

FIGURE 3
Sandwich Preparation

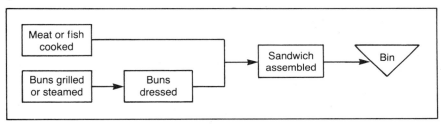

front" as shown in Figure 3. The specific composition of each sandwich and a diagram of the building pattern is presented as Exhibit 5, and a detailed flow for the hamburger and cheeseburger, as Exhibit 6.

"Six burgers and three Macs, please." "Thank you." The grill person took 12 patties from the small freezer by the grill and laid them quickly onto the grill in 2 side-by-side rows of 6. The grill held up to 8 rows of 6 patties, although individual batches did not exceed 12 and one grill person generally did not have more than 24 cooking at one time. Quarters were cooked on a separate, higher temperature grill that held up to 4 rows of 5 patties each, with batches not exceeding 10. Each patty was seared (pressed hard into the grill with a flat-surfaced implement [see Figure 4]), turned individually, and pulled (removed) in pairs at standard times signaled by a light and buzzer system, as detailed in Figure 5. After the patties were removed, the grill had to be scraped clean with a heavy scraper which took about 15 seconds.

Meat sandwich buns were carmelized on their inside surfaces by placing them in contact with extremely hot platens for 55 seconds (Figure 6). The Hillybourne store had two burger, one Mac, and one Quarter bun carmelizers. For a given batch, half the bun was carmelized first, and while it

in a fryer adjacent to the current fish station and that the chopped beefsteak portion would be grilled on a third grill to be located beside the Quarter grill.

FIGURE 4
Searing Implement

FIGURE 5
Elapsed Cooking Time

	Burgers	Quarters
Start	0 Sec.	0 Sec.
Sear	20	20
Turn	60	150
Pull	100	270 (4½ min.)

FIGURE 6
Diagram of Bun Carmelizing Process

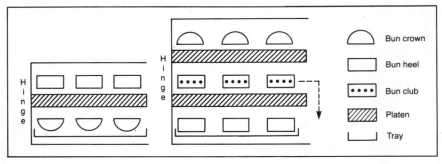

was being dressed, the other half was carmelized. Handling was minimized by placing the first halves on a tray upon which they remained through dressing and assembly and by moving the second halves on a smooth paddle onto and from which the entire batch was slid at once. Batch sizes were set by the size of the trays: 12 burgers, 6 Macs, and 10 Quarters.

The sandwich dressings were applied at the dressing table. Mustard, ketchup, and Mac Sauce were dispensed in premeasured amounts from containers with the pull of a lever, while pickles, onions, lettuce, and cheese were applied by hand. The fraction of the batch that were to be cheeseburgers was determined by a person up front in response to the call "Cheese on six burgers, please," from a grill team member. "Three, please." "Thank you." And three burgers in the batch received a slice of cheese. When the sandwiches were dressed, the tray was moved to the grill and hooked on its edge. The patties were removed from the grill and placed on the buns in pairs, the final bun halves were slid on top (as a unit), and the completed sandwiches were placed on top of the bin. "Burgers up, wrap please."

"Four filets please." "Thank you." The frozen fish filet portions were placed in a basket that held up to 10 portions and deep-fat fried for 3½ minutes in one of two vats. As with burgers, a light and buzzer system signaled the completion of cooking. Filet buns were steamed for 90 seconds in one of two steamers, each of which held up to six complete buns at a time. The crowns were dressed with a premeasured amount of tartar sauce and a piece of cheese, the filet was positioned, the heel was added to complete the sandwich, and the tray was passed up front: "Filet up, wrap please." "Thank you."

"Grill" orders, noted on a slip of paper by the counter or Drive-Thru worker and handed back to the grill workers, were always filled "on the first tray" of that product, even if that meant discarding a bun (Figure 7). The slip was tucked under the bun crown (heel for a Big Mac) to identify it through dressing and wrapping.

FIGURE 7
"Grill" Slip for a Hamburg with No Onions

☑	K	M	⊖	Pi	DBL	¼ lb	CB	(HB)
☐	K	TS	CH	PL	FILET			
☐	S	L	O	Pi	CH	BIG MAC		

The grill area was operated by one person in slow times and up to five in busy periods as the task became segmented (burger grill, Quarter grill, buns, dressing, filet). Teamwork was important since the crew worked in a small space and could easily assist each other (for example, the filet station worker could turn around and help with the dressing).

Fry and Pie Production

Frozen french fries were placed in wire baskets and stored on a rack to thaw for up to two hours before use. The contents of a 6-pound box of fries (approximately 26 regular servings) were placed in four (busy periods) or six (slow periods) baskets. The potatoes were fried in one of three vats for 2 minutes, 5 seconds, with each basket shaken 20 seconds into the cooking time and removal signaled by a beeper. After being drained, the fries were emptied into a hopper warmed by heat lamps and stored for up to 7 minutes. Using a special scoop, a worker bagged fries to order in slow times and for storage on a heated, 20-serving carousel in busy periods. The fry station was handled by a grill person or floater when the volume was under $345 per hour and by a specifically assigned worker in busier hours.

The apple and cherry pies were fried in one of two vats for six minutes in batches of up to 10. When finished, they were boxed and held for up to 90 minutes in a warming rack up front (the discard time was written on the box). Pies were produced by the fish station operator.

The Bin

Acting as the interface between the production personnel in the back, who could not see the bin nor hear orders being given, and the workers at the counter and Drive-Thru, who could not see the production area, the employee "on the bin" managed the flow of products into the sandwich holding bin, calling for production as needed, wrapping the sandwiches as they were passed up, and keeping the bin stock organized and fresh. In order to ensure that the customer received only hot, fresh products, sandwiches were held for no longer than 10 minutes after wrapping before either sale or discard. This time was checked by placing plastic numerals with each batch as it came up: for example, a "6" meant to discard at half-past the current hour. During slow periods, counter people or a floating manger called orders back as needed to maintain minimal stocking. Above a $240 per hour sales pace (approximately), a bin person was specifically assigned. Lindy Boyd, who ran the bin at lunch, described her job:

> I've worked here for a couple of years now, and have a pretty good sense of when our peaks occur and how big they will be. But you always get the surprise, too, as happened today when two customers in a row each ordered five Big Macs and cleaned me out. I'll build up the bin before the peak starts, and try to run as smoothly as I can because I know it produces a lot of tension on the grill if I order 4 burgers one minute and 12 the next. We usually run Quarters on the turn, and can do that with burgers too—the old "less product more often" idea so we have more flexibility.[4] I've seen charts that tell how many of each sandwich to stock at each volume level but, in the end, I have to watch what is selling and observe the incoming traffic to judge how much to have in the bin.[5] I'd rather have too much than keep a customer waiting. It also makes a difference to me who's on the grill, and I'll stock higher with new people or a slow team there. I like this job—there's a lot of hustle.

Store Manager Leone noted that he could predict sales volume "pretty accurately":

> I'll go back and look at the past few week's data for the day of the week, note any special events, the time of year, and the weather—and I can usually be within $10–$20 for an hour. In theory, we stock the bin to about 50–75 percent of what we expect to sell in the next 10-minute period. In practice, we can judge pretty well by experience.

Breakfast

This case does not describe the breakfast operation in which eggs and pancakes were cooked on the grill and sausages and potatoes were fried. Breakfast items were sold from 7–10:30 A.M., and accounted for about 9 percent of sales.

---

[4] "On the turn"—a new batch was started when the previous batch was turned; "on the pull"—a new batch was started when the previous batch was removed.

[5] Lindy's rules of thumb for a $600–$700 hour were 20–24 hamburgs, 20–24 cheeseburgs, 9 Big Macs, 3–4 Quarters, 3–4 Quarters with cheese, and 6–7 filets.

Support Activities

Store opening and closing each took about an hour—to set up machines or clean them, to restock, to count change and check for cash shortages (and overages), and so forth. During the night, a custodial person thoroughly cleaned the store.

The Hillybourne store had three freezers: a large walk-in at the back of the lot, a medium-sized reach-in in the kitchen, and two small ones by the grill and fish station. Refrigerated items such as milk, eggs, dressings, and juice were stored in a walk-in refrigerator. Dry goods such as paperware were stored in the basement. The store received one delivery per week from local suppliers of milk and buns. All food arrived ready to use.

During slower periods, workers were assigned to move stock and to tackle various cleaning chores. In addition, workers periodically patrolled the parking lot, lobby, and restrooms to empty trash bags and to ensure that each area was clean.

The Crew

In June 1980, the Hillybourne store employed 45 hourly crew members. Hourly wages ranged between $3.10 and $3.50. All were young, most under 20, some 20–25, and a couple over 30, and most were women. The full-time day-crew members tended to be older, and to show significantly less turnover, than the part-timers. Leone noted:

> Ninety percent of the problems in dealing with kids comes from lack of communication, especially when they don't open up to the manager. I keep telling them, "you gotta care." They have to be involved, looking for problems whether it be the orange soda tank empty (you replace it), a customer waiting for a sandwich (you talk to him), or a mess on the floor (you clean it up). Thirty percent of this is training, but the rest is pride. I like to give the kids responsibility, to keep them busy. There is a lot of peer pressure among them, and I try to keep it positive, toward hustling, and not negative, toward loafing. I think managing is the ability to manipulate what you have, to look at people and see what they can do well. For example, is she a people person or a production type? And it's a matter of constantly, constantly training.

Crew selection, hiring, and scheduling were the direct responsibility of first assistant manager, Steve Sangree, although the store manager also interviewed most candidates. The store advertised for help through newspapers, on-site posters ("Smiling Faces Wanted"), and local high school and college job offices. Employees also referred friends. Sangree noted:

> Kids tend to be enthusiastic when they come for a job interview and will say they'll work any hours. I try to temper that and won't, for example, encourage them to work both Friday and Saturday nights because I'd like them to start with a sustainable pace that they'll maintain over the longer run.

I make up the schedule every Wednesday morning for the following Sunday through Saturday. The kids know they have to let me know by then if they have any conflicts or want some time off. At first, I limited the number who could take the weekend off, but now I hire others if I need hours. Then, when I have a surplus, I weed out the deadwood.

See Exhibit 7 for a summary of staffing levels.

McDonald's had introduced a new crew pay system in early 1980. Called the Crew Bonus System (CBS), the plan provided for crew members to receive minimum wage plus a three-times yearly (January, May, September) bonus check determined by multiplying actual hours worked during the bonus period by a bonus factor (cents per hour) keyed to performance and seniority (Figure 8). A crew member had to be active through the end of the period and had to begin work at least 16 calendar days prior to the end of the period to be eligible. Exceptions to this minimum base were threefold: (1) a "grandfather" clause that set pay rate at plan implementation as the base rate for people working then, (2) the assumption of additional responsibilities by a worker (such as the daily fry and shake yield calculations), or (3) special competitive pressures in a local market that demanded higher pay. All exceptions required operations manager approval.

FIGURE 8
Crew Bonus System (Bonus Factor) Chart (cents per hour)

Performance Rating	Years of Service									
	1st	2nd	3rd	4th	5th	6th	7th	8th	9th	10th
Outstanding	15	20	25	30	35	40	45	50	55	60
Excellent.............	10	15	20	25	30	35	40	45	50	55
Good	5	10	15	20	25	30	35	40	45	50
Needs improvement ...	0	0	0	0	0	0	0	0	0	0
Unsatisfactory.........	0	0	0	0	0	0	0	0	0	0

Performance appraisals were conducted at the end of each bonus period, with an abbreviated version held halfway through the period: "A person has to know where he or she stands in your eyes," Leone explained. The appraisal focused on a written assessment of the worker's versatility, availability, dependability, appearance, and overall performance that was discussed in a meeting between the manager and crew member and signed by both.

Employees punched a computerized time clock that relayed payroll information to Oak Brook. Workers had to be assigned for a minimum of three hours and were entitled to a half-hour unpaid break during a six- to eight-hour shift. The store had a crew break room in the basement which, Leone noted, "enables the kids to relax more and it keeps off-duty people out of sight—nothing is more frustrating to a waiting customer than to see a uniformed employee sitting down with a shake and not serving him." Crew members were given a food allowance, nominally 40 cents per hour worked, although Leone's policy was: "I'm not real tight about that—if they work hard, they deserve what they want." Employees also received uniforms.

Full-time (37½ or more hours per week) employees received medical, dental, and life insurance (80 percent company paid) after one month of service. After one year, part-time employees received one week of paid vacation while full-timers received two weeks. After 10 years, full-time employees received an 8-week paid "sabbatical."

Training was a constant process. Most training was done on the job, but a series of 15-minute videocassettes and an eight-section training course that Leone had developed were also used.[6] Managers felt that it took a new person two weeks to get up to speed in most areas and perhaps four on the grill. New employees first worked two shifts with experienced people and then were assigned to positions such as the fish station, the Drive-Thru order taking, or the counter during a slower period. While people tended to gravitate toward certain positions, Leone referred to everyone as "crew member" and encouraged them to learn several jobs.

Management

The Hillybourne store had five salaried McOpCo managers, a number set by the corporation based on store volume. In addition, Leone had hired two swing managers. Swings were generally college-aged men and women who had performed well as crew members and who were paid on an hourly basis, starting at $3.90. Managers were responsible for running the shift, often from a floater position from which they could observe and help where necessary, for various "extracurricular" activities such as scheduling and ordering, for customer relations, and for training. "We constantly, constantly train," Leone repeated.

McOpCo managers were hired and promoted by the area operation manager with the approval of the region's director of operations. Candidates interviewed at the store, supervisor, and area levels, and spent five days in an on-the-job-evaluation (OJE) working in a store. Approximately 40 percent of successful candidates had been swing managers. The McOpCo career path progressed from trainee through second assistant manager and first assistant manager to store manager. This was typically a two- to three-year process that included a basic, intermediate, and advanced operations course (the latter segment at Hamburger University), self-paced workbook study, and increasing responsibility. Managerial pay was straight salary and

[6] Sections included: lot and lobby; buns; grill; dress, pie, filet; fries; stocking; breakfast; windows and customer relations.

ranged from $12,500 to $27,500. Managers were evaluated quarterly on preestablished goals negotiated between a manager and his/her supervisor. Raises were granted annually and were closely tied to a manager's performance ranking (for example, "outstanding" meant a 12–14 percent raise). One supervisor explained:

EXHIBIT 1
Menu and Product Mix

Category	Description	Price	Percent of Sandwiches
Sandwiches	Big Mac......................	$1.13	18.8
	Quarter Pounder..............	1.03	5.9
	Quarter Pounder with cheese...	1.18	8.8
	Hamburg.....................	0.44	22.0
	Cheeseburg..................	0.52	21.7
	Happy Meal..................	1.47*	5.4
	Fish filet.....................	0.70	15.7
	Other........................	—	1.7
			100.0
Fries	Regular......................	0.42	32.1
	Large........................	0.57	25.1
			57.2
Beverages	Shakes[†]......................	0.60	19.8
	Soft drinks:[‡]		
	Regular....................	0.42	20.6
	Medium....................	0.47	18.2
	Large.....................	0.57	11.2
	Coffee.....................	0.33[§]	19.9
	Other......................	—	7.7
			97.4
Deserts	Pies........................	0.40	4.1
	Sundaes.....................	0.45	5.3
	Other.......................	—	1.9
			11.3
Breakfasts		—	—

Note: Data from Hillybourne store, June 1980:

Customers... 42,645
Number of sandwiches sold... 55,703

* A Happy Meal was packaged in a special box and included a hamburg or cheeseburg, a soft drink, fries, cookies, and a little surprise.
† Vanilla, strawberry, and chocolate shakes.
‡ Coke, orange, 7up, Tab, root beer.
§ Includes regular and large coffees.

The manager and I negotiate his or her (35 percent of our managers are women) goals for the next time period and those goals vary from manager to manager. Ultimately, it all boils down to people skills—how well do they train and motivate their people, for that is what will increase volume and keep costs down. I can feel a difference from store to store as I walk in, and much of that comes from the manager—the store reflects the manager.

EXHIBIT 2
Weekly and Daily
Distribution of Sales

A.   Distribution of sales throughout week:

Day	Percent of Week's Customer's
Sunday	14.0
Monday	12.3
Tuesday	12.4
Wednesday	13.2
Thursday	14.8
Friday	16.3
Saturday	16.8
	100.0

B.   Distribution of sales throughout day:

For Hour Ending at —	Percent of Day's Sales
8 A.M.	3.4
9	4.1
10	4.0
11	3.9
12	7.5
1 P.M.	14.9
2	9.1
3	5.0
4	3.5
5	5.5
6	9.1
7	8.4
8	5.6
9	5.3
10	4.6
11	3.4
12	2.5
	100.0

Note: Data from Hillybourne store, June 1980.

EXHIBIT 3
Hillybourne Store Operating
Results—June 1980

Line Item	Percent of Sales
Sales	100.0
Food	33.4
Paper	4.5
Gross profit	62.1
Controllable expenses:	
Hourly labor	17.6
Management labor	5.8
Payroll taxes	2.4
Utilities	2.8
Advertising and promotion	5.2
Other	3.1
	37.0*
Profit after controllable	25.1
Noncontrollable expenses:	
Rent	9.8
Other income depreciation	6.8
	16.6
Store operating income	8.5

* Sum rounded off.

EXHIBIT 4
Store Visitation Report*

Store_____ Completed by_____

Date_____Time_____Reviewed with_____ Person in Charge_____

Q.S.C. Grade_____Customers in Serving Line_____Customers in Dining Room_____

SERVICE	Points	Store Grade
1. Management in backup position, following proper procedures, expediting service.	3	
2. Service atmosphere--smiles, hustle, teamwork, neat appearance.	0 / 3 / 5	
3. Suggestive Sell--all crew following area policies and techniques. Describe how you placed your order and what type of suggestive sell technique was used on you.	0 / 3 / 6	
4. Greeting, order assembly, presentation, thank you, and asking for repeat business.	3	
5. Service accuracy--order accurately filled, change accurately made.	3	
6. Amount charged_____ Correct amount_____		
7. Service Speed:		
In line 1'30" - 2'00"	2	
In line 1'00" - 1'30"	6	
In line under 1'00"	8	
At counter 1'00"	6	
At counter 45"	8	
At counter 30"	12	
Sub-Total	40	

COMMENTS_____
_____
_____
_____
_____

QUALITY SECTION

BREAKFAST	Points	Store Grade
Egg McMuffin	12	
Scrambled Eggs	12	
Hotcakes	12	
Danish	6	
Coffee & Hot Choc.	6	
Juice	6	
Sub-Total	30	
TOTAL		

NOTE: Store not complying with holding procedures--subtract 5 points.

HAMBURGERS	Points	Store Grade
Quarter Cheese	10	
Quarter Ham	10	
Big Mac	10	
Filet	10	
Hamburger	10	
Cheese-burger	10	
Chicken Sandwich	10	
Steak Sandwich	10	
Fries	10	
Soft Drink Shakes	5	
Sundaes/ Desserts	5	
Sub-Total	30	
TOTAL		

COMMENTS_____
_____
_____
_____

*The Store Visitation Report was completed by a supervisor for each of his/her stores. The inspections were made on four unannounced visits per month (typically during breakfast, lunch, dinner, and on a weekend). Leone reported, "We usually score 80–85 (of 100), though sometimes we come out smelling like a rose with one in the 90s. The inspections are strict—a sandwich is either *hot* or it's 'cold,' for example."

EXHIBIT 4 (*concluded*)

CLEANLINESS, MERCHANDISING, OUTSIDE	Points	Store Grade
1. Neighborhood--free of litter. (1 block in each direction)	1	
2. All signage and flag--in good repair, clean, properly lighted according to conditions and properly displayed.	1	
3. Landscaping--free of litter and well maintained.	1	
4. Painted surfaces--in good condition and clean.	1	
5. Corral--clean, neat, and gate closed.	1	
6. Parking lot--free of litter, clean, seal & stripe in good condition, traffic pattern.	1	
7. Waste receptacles--clean, good repair and emptied as needed.	1	
8. Sidewalks--clean, sealed, and free of ice, snow, or hazardous conditions.	1	
9. Windows and doors--glass and all associated areas clean.	2	
Sub-Total	10	

COMMENTS_____
_____
_____
_____

CLEANLINESS, MERCHANDISING, INSIDE	Points	Store Grade
1. Lobby and dining room floors--chairs, tables, walls & decor--ceiling & airvents--lighting--trash bins.	9	
2. Rest rooms--clean and supplied with tissue, soap, and hand towels or dryer.	6	
3. Menu board and P.O.P.--presents unified theme, clean, and in good repair.	1	
4. Customer conveniences--napkin & straw available, dispensers and high chairs clean and in good repair, additional condiments available upon request, breakfast newspaper available.	2	
5. Stations & equipment--orderly and clean, stainless steel clean and bright.	1	
6. Service, production, and back room--floors, ceiling, walls, lights, airvents--clean, orderly, and in good repair.	1	
Sub-Total	20	

COMMENTS_____
_____
_____
_____

GENERAL OVERVIEW -- COMMENTS
_____
_____
_____
_____
_____
_____
_____
_____

EXHIBIT 5
Sandwich Composition

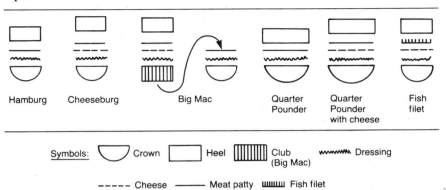

	Hamburg	Cheeseburg	Big Mac	Quarter Pounder	Quarter Pounder with cheese	Fish filet

Symbols: ⌣ Crown   ▭ Heel   ▥ Club (Big Mac)   〰 Dressing

‑ ‑ ‑ ‑ Cheese   —— Meat patty   ⊔⊔⊔ Fish filet

				Dressings				
Sandwich	Mustard	Ketchup	Mac Sauce	Tartar Sauce	Pickle	Onions	Lettuce	Cheese
Hamburg.......	x	x			x	x		
Cheeseburg.....	x	x			x	x		x
Big Mac........			x		x	x	x	x
Quarter........	x	x			x	x		
Quarter with cheese........	x	x			x	x		x
Fish filet.......				x				x

EXHIBIT 6
Production Process for Hamburgers and Cheeseburgers

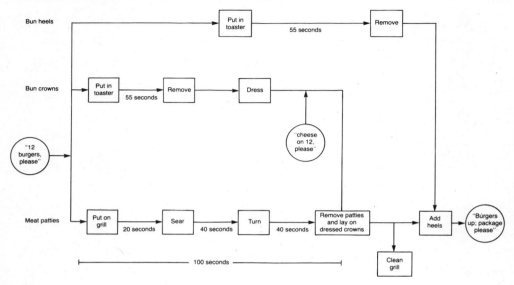

EXHIBIT 7
Staffing

	Percent of People	Grill	Windows	Drive-Thru	Bin	Fry	Floaters*	$ per Hour Volume Guidelines
Minimum to open:	4	1	1	1	—	—	1	$120
	5	1	1	1	—	—	2	150
	6	2	1	1	—	—	2	180
	7	2	2	1	—	—	2	210
	8	2	2	2	1	—	1	240
	9	2	2	2	1	—	2	275
	10	3	3	2	1	—	1	310
	11	3	3	2	1	1	1	345
	12	3	3	3	1	1	1	385
	13	4	3	3	1	1	1	425
	14	4	3	3	1	1	2	475
	15	4	4	3	1	1	2	525
	16	5	4	3	1	1	2	585
Fully staffed:	17	5	5	3	1	1	2	645

* Floaters "help the cause"; patrol lot, lobby, and restrooms; re-stock; cover on breaks.

CASE 13

Burger King Corporation

The first Burger King restaurant in Miami in the mid-50s featured a walk-up window, a very limited menu (burgers and shakes for 19 cents, sodas and fries for 10 cents), and "your food ready by the time you'd paid for it."[1] As one early manager recalls, "Our windows faced front so we could see customers driving in. With the limited menu, we pretty much knew what they'd order, and we'd have it ready." In the 1960s and 1970s, Burger King developed an assembly-line production process that delivered a fresh, hot, high-quality sandwich, yet that had the flexibility to customize that sandwich. One executive explained: "Market research showed us that our ability to give the customer what he wanted clearly differentiated us from McDonald's, so we capitalized on it." The jingle used in Burger King advertisements in the 1970s ran as follows:

Hold the pickles,
Hold the lettuce.
Special orders
Don't upset us.
All we ask is that you
Let us serve it your way.

More recently, however, *Fortune* noted:

Hold the jingle. The Burger King hamburger chain has abandoned that bouncy promise to build its sandwiches to suit the customer. Tailoring Whopper Sandwiches was manageable when relatively few fast-food fanciers were coming through the doors. But now so many are lining up, at least at peak

---

[1] "Burger King" and "Whopper" are registered trademarks of Burger King Corporation. The operational aspects of the Hillybourne restaurant are presented for case study purposes only and do not necessarily reflect current operating procedures of the Burger King restaurant system.

hours, that special orders are, well, upsetting. Burger King will still make it your way, if you insist, but isn't going to invite you to and rather hopes you won't.[2]

THE BURGER KING CORPORATION

Founded in 1954 by Jim McLamore and David Edgerton, Burger King Corporation had grown from one store in 1954 to 2,766 units, including 136 outside the United States in 1980. Milestones in the company's development included the invention by Edgerton of the continuous chain broiler, and creation by McLamore of the Whopper Sandwich, both in 1956; franchising agreements in 1959; the sale of Burger King Corporation to The Pillsbury Company in 1967; and the hiring of Donald Smith, then 36 and third-ranking executive at McDonald's, as chief executive in 1977. In fiscal 1980 (ending May 31, 1980), systemwide sales grew 26 percent to $1.84 billion, an 11 percent market share in the hamburger fast-food industry (led by McDonald's with a 35 percent share). Average annual sales for the 412 company-operated domestic units rose 13 percent to $747,000. Advertising and promotion expenses grew 35 percent to $88 million. At year-end, the corporation had a real estate interest in 804 of the 2,218 domestic franchised units. Average investment per store was estimated by industry experts at slightly over $500,000 per unit.

Also in 1980, Burger King headquarters were located in Miami, Florida. The company, a wholly owned subsidiary of The Pillsbury Company, was organized on a geographic basis with three divisions and, within them, a region, area, and district structure. On average, for example, five company-operated restaurants reported to a district manager. The corporate relationship with franchisee restaurants had evolved from a policing function to one that included significant consulting. Support services, such as personnel, training, and accounting, reported to the region level.

Burger King restaurants varied widely in size and design, reflecting locations that ranged from shopping malls to interstate highway intersections. Each store typically had a unique pattern of sales and a work force drawn from the local labor market.

THE HILLYBOURNE RESTAURANT[3]

Hillybourne was a New England college town with a population of about 30,000. The Burger King restaurant was located on heavily commercialized Maple Street, about ¼ mile south of an interstate highway intersection and 1¼ miles north of the town center. The modern, landscaped, brick and glass

---

[2] *Fortune*, June 16, 1980, p. 90.

[3] Hillybourne is a disguised location.

building sat between a diner and a manufacturing plant (with 200 employees), and across the street from a shopping plaza. Toward town, Maple Street was lined with several restaurants, including a McDonald's, half a dozen car dealers and gas stations, and a dozen small businesses. The central business district, adjacent to the college, contained public buildings, theaters, department stores, banks, and restaurants.

The Hillybourne Burger King restaurant, a company-owned unit, was open from 10 A.M. to 12 midnight 363 days a year.[4] The restaurant had a drive-thru window and dining room seating for 80 people. The parking area contained 70 car places and 5 bus places. Annual volume was about $700,000 with an average customer check of about $2.50. Sales typically peaked at noon during the day and on Friday during the week. Further details are presented as Exhibit 1 (menu and product mix), Exhibit 2 (daily and hourly distribution of sales), Exhibit 3 (June 1980 profit and loss statement), Exhibit 4 (restaurant visitation report), and Figure 1 (the food flow). (Exhibits occur at end of case.)

The restaurant manager, Frank DeMasi, had grown up in the Hillybourne area and had joined Burger King in 1971 after graduating from the state university. Married and the father of three children, DeMasi had been Hillybourne restaurant manager since 1974. Describing his restaurant business, he said:

> We have a predictable peak just after noon, when the plant workers come over for lunch. Friday and Sunday nights are often heavy with travelers and, on Friday, with families out shopping. But there are a lot of variables too, such as weather, the time of year, or a holiday. After being here a while, you get a sense of what to expect, but there are always surprises, too.

AN OVERVIEW OF RESTAURANT OPERATIONS

FIGURE 1
The Food Flow

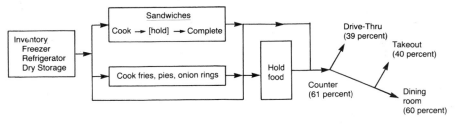

[4] During the summer of 1980, restaurants in the Hillybourne area were considering adding breakfast. It was anticipated that this meal would be served from 6 to 10 A.M. and feature biscuits, sausages, and eggs (scrambled on a grill whose bottom surface was heated by the oil in a frying vat).

Hamburger Preparation

The Burger King hamburger-based sandwiches consisted of a beef patty in one of two sizes (2 or 3.6 ounces), a bun, and several condiments (see Exhibit 5A for exact composition). The beef patties were cooked and the buns toasted as they passed through an infrared broiler while on a continuous chain. The broiler had two meat chains, each with an 80-second transit time (yielding 8 burgers per minute or 5.5 Whopper Sandwiches per minute per chain) and one bun chain that moved twice as fast (see Figure 2 for diagram). (Both sized patties were the same thickness and so cooked in the same length of broiler.) Since the chains traveled relatively slowly, a 2-foot loading space had been designed at the front end of the broiler so that the operator could "batch load" the chains with up to 12 burgers (8 Whopper Sandwiches). As the patties and buns reached the end of the broiler, they fell into separate pans from which they were taken and mated, Whopper patty with Whopper bun, and placed in the steam table for storage (up to 10 minutes). The broiler was typically run by one employee as a part or all of his/her assignment, although in very busy periods, a second person was assigned to "catch."

Sandwiches were finished on the board, a stainless steel table bounded at one end by the steam table and at the other by the chutes upon which finished sandwiches were placed (Figure 2). The board had a row of condiments down the middle, accessible to a worker on either side, and a shelf over the condiments upon which two microwave ovens sat, one facing each side, and upon which sandwich boxes were stored. Although a sandwich could be made on either side of the board, the Whoppers and doubles were typically made on the left side and the remainder on the right because DeMasi had found that this division worked well in his restaurant: "The Whopper side is a little light, but that person often has fries or specialty sandwiches, too. Some restaurants use a cheese and noncheese division." Sandwiches were held for 10 minutes after preparation, and if not sold

FIGURE 2
Broiler and Board

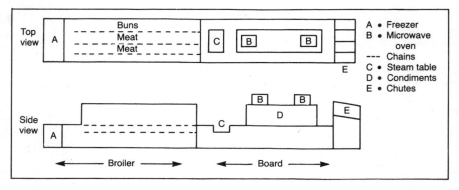

within that time, they were discarded. A clock with only the minute hand on it was used for the timing, with the digit at which the sandwich was to be discarded written on the wrapper/box.

To finish a cheeseburger, for example, a worker took a burger and bun from the steam table, pulled a cheeseburg wrapper from a dispenser, and set the sandwich on it with the crown (bun top) set to one side. Two pickles were placed on the center of the patty by hand, ketchup and mustard were dispensed in a spiral pattern from plastic squeeze bottles, and a slice of cheese was positioned. The worker replaced the crown, wrapped the sandwich, and placed it in the microwave oven for a 12-second timed cycle. When the buzzer sounded, he/she removed the sandwich, marked the appropriate symbols on the wrapper if a customer was "having it her way," noted discard time on the wrapper, and slid the completed sandwich in the cheeseburg chute (on the lower level if a standard sandwich, the upper level if special). See Exhibit 5B for examples of the special markings on the wrappers and boxes, and Exhibit 6 for a summary of the production process for a Whopper.

Elapsed time for steam table to chute was about 30 seconds for a burger or Whopper Sandwich. In busy periods, output was increased because workers used the microwave time to work on other sandwiches, and because many steps, such as reaching for a burger from the steam table, were as quickly done for two as for one ("you have two hands—use them!"). DeMasi estimated that his day crew could produce 200 burgers and 100 Whopper Sandwiches per hour.

Specialty Sandwich Preparation

Burger King specialty sandwiches were oblong (⬭), in contrast to the smaller, circular burgers. Specialty sandwich preparation followed the same general pattern as with burgers, but was done in a separate area. Frozen fish and chicken portions were fried for 4 and 3¼ minutes, respectively, in batches of up to 10 portions in a deep fat fryer with an automatic timer and buzzer (activated by pressing a button with a fish or chicken symbol on it). Cooked portions were held in a warmer, called the Henny Penny, for up to 30 minutes. The roast beef and ham portions, precooked and individually wrapped, were held at the specialty sandwich table and opened as a sandwich was made.

To make a fish sandwich, for example, the worker placed both halves of the bun in the top of the specialty bun toaster, from which the bun emerged in 20 seconds. He/she spread tartar sauce on heel and crown; sprinkled lettuce on the crown; placed the fish portion on the crown; mated the two halves; wrapped and sliced (⬭ with diagonal) the sandwich; placed it in a box, marked it for type, discard time, and any specials; and handed it to the board worker to slide into the appropriate chute. This procedure was similar for other specialty sandwiches, except that a roast beef portion was microwaved for 10 seconds before assembly. Elapsed time to produce a specialty sandwich was about 45 seconds although, as before, output could be increased. DeMasi estimated that a good worker could produce 150 specialty sandwiches per hour.

Fry Products

Six-pound bags of frozen french fries were emptied into wire baskets (six in slow times, four in busy periods) that were stored on a rack while the fries thawed for at least one, but not more than three hours. A six-pound bag contained 24 regular servings or 16 large servings of fries. Fries were cooked in one of four computer-controlled fry vats for just over two minutes. A flashing light and buzzer signaled the completion of the cooking cycle. The fries were briefly drained, emptied into the dump station, and salted. Individual servings were bagged with a special scoop, to order in a slow period, ahead in a busy one. Fries were held for seven minutes in the dump station and for two minutes when bagged.

Frozen apple pies were cooked for 6½ minutes in the same fryer used for chicken and fish, cooled for 10 minutes, boxed, and held on the chutes for up to two hours.

Frozen onion rings were blanched in the fryer for 2 minutes, then stored on a tray in a nearby freezer for up to 30 minutes. When an order was received, a serving was finished in the fryer for 30 seconds and put in one part of the dump station for immediate bagging service.

The Counter

Customers entered the front of the Hillybourne restaurant and faced the counter with the menu board above and behind it. The counter had three "drawers"—registers with labeled buttons for each item and microphones—spaced along it.

"May I help you?" After greeting the customer, the host/hostess accepted the order. S/he keyed each item into the register and called each sandwich into the microphone (connected to a loudspeaker in the production area). He or she would also call other "noteworthy" items such as onion rings or a large root beer to alert production personnel. Specials, such as a fish sandwich with extra tartar sauce, were marked on the printed register slip. Payment was requested, change given, and the slip placed on a tray ("for here") or on the counter ("to go"). The counter person assembled the order in a "drink, sandwich, fries" sequence so there would be a clockwise traffic flow around the service area. Shakes took about 6 seconds to pour and soft drinks from 5 seconds (small) to 15 seconds (large) to ice and pour (all operator-controlled operations). The drink machine, accessible from the front and rear, had two Coke, one root beer, one orange, and one 7up dispensers. Milk was picked up from a refrigerated tray, while coffee and tea were poured from pots. The register slip was used to check the order as it was given to the customer.

The Hillybourne restaurant service standards specified a three-minute, "door-to-door" target (total of time in line and at the counter). During a recent inspection, the restaurant had averaged four minutes, five seconds. If part of an order was delayed, the customer was asked to wait and another order was taken. Area guidelines, however, specified that no more than one customer be left on "hold" at any drawer.

The Drive-Thru

The Hillybourne restaurant had a designated drive-thru lane with the ordering station (menu board and speaker) at the rear of the building and the pickup window along the side, under a roof. "Welcome to Burger King! Can I help you?" As the order was received over the speaker, the order-taker keyed the items into the register and repeated the sandwich items over the internal microphone system. Specials were marked on the register slip, and the order confirmed and totaled. In order to match the meal with the customer, each order was numbered sequentially; that number was written on the register slip, and the dollar total was recorded next to that number on a ruled sheet used by the employee at the window to request payment in the correct sequence. The register slip was used to assemble the order and to match the order with the proper customer. While the restaurant preferred one check per car, multiple checks were allowed.

The drive-thru window was staffed with one to three people; indeed, during very slow times, a hand-held extension speaker enabled a worker to take an order on one of the counter registers, while in busy times, the three tasks of order taking, order assembly, and cash handling were separated.

Information Flow

Whopper, large fries . . . three burgers, ketchup only . . . two fish . . . Whopper, double cheese, large root beer . . . cheeseburg . . . two Junior . . . chicken . . . Whopper no onions . . . fish, large fries . . . Whopper Sandwiches . . .

During busy times, workers in the back heard a constant stream of sandwich orders over the speaker system, as illustrated above. Each worker had to extract the orders s/he was responsible for from this general flow. Special orders (*Whopper no onions*), which represented about 20 percent of the total, were made immediately, while the flow of orders for standard sandwiches helped the workers gauge the appropriate stocking levels for the chutes more accurately. In very slow times, a minimum supply of cooked burgers was kept in the steam table (fish and chicken in the Henny Penny), and all finished sandwiches were made strictly to order. As volume picked up, an increasing inventory of standard sandwiches was maintained in the chutes under heat lamps as specified on a "level" chart posted over the chutes. Levels, from I to IV, were signaled by a series of four red lights controlled by the manager: one light on meant level I and so forth (see Exhibit 7A for DeMasi's level chart). Workers on the board and at the specialty table could see the chutes and the level lights and were responsible for keeping the chutes stocked with standard sandwiches (as well as, of course, for making special sandwiches on order). The employee on the broiler was responsible for keeping the steam table appropriately stocked. This involved, according to DeMasi, "The ability to watch and sense the flow of product," although workers tended to see the position as the "pits" since it was hot and active.

Support Activities

The Hillybourne restaurant had two walk-in freezers and a walk-in refrigerator, as well as two small, open-top freezers near the broiler and fry vats. Dry items such as paperware were stored on high shelves around the production area. The restaurant received one delivery per week from Distron,® a Burger King subsidiary, and three to four deliveries per week from local suppliers of buns and milk. Most foods arrived at the restaurant ready to use or cook. One exception was tomatoes which were received whole and sliced every morning as a part of the opening procedure. The daily opening tasks typically took two hours, while closing took an hour and a half. During these times machines were set up or cleaned, supplies restocked, drawers prepared or their cash checked, and major cleaning done. Cleaning continued throughout the slower periods of the day in the kitchen, restroom, dining room, and parking lot areas of the restaurant.

Staffing

Staffing levels in the Hillybourne restaurant were set by Frank DeMasi based upon his projections of hourly sales and upon corporate standards for labor-hours per sales dollar. Using the "Sales and Labor Worksheet," DeMasi developed his projections and staffing needs on a day-by-day basis, working six days in advance (for example, on Tuesday he worked on the plan for the following Monday; thus the Monday pattern was freshly in mind when the Monday schedule was constructed). DeMasi noted:

> Our volume is surprisingly consistent, at least over an hour and certainly by day. I can often project a day, for example, within $25–$50, an hour within $10–$20. Once I have the sales projected, and hence know the labor-hours I'm allowed, I schedule my people, within the constraint that someone must work at least a 3-hour shift and that minors (under 18) can't work past 10 on school nights. In practice, I schedule some people pretty regularly—for example, Fran works 9–2 every weekday—while I use others where they'll fit or where their schedules let them fit. We tend to think of people as day or evening/weekend people rather than as counter or broiler people. In fact, I'll

use people in different jobs over time to give us more flexibility—quite in contrast to what is possible in some city restaurants that are unionized with workers classified by job. I also have flexibility with when I schedule breaks[5] (and, on the spot, with when people actually take them), and the kids will help me out sometimes by leaving early or staying late. On the other hand, someone is missing almost every day for one reason or another, and I almost have to plan on that.

As volume increased, broad jobs were broken down into narrower pieces. For example, under minimum staffing, one person ran fries, specialty sandwiches, and the left side of the board; under maximum staffing, these three components had been split into three separate jobs. In addition, expediting roles developed, both behind the counter (an expediter, if good, could practically have an order assembled by the time the customer had finished paying; but the corporation preferred adding another drawer to using an expediter) and in spots such as the drink station, at which a supply of popular drinks was kept ready (in a refrigerated tray, holding time 5 minutes) and more unusual ones, such as a large orange, poured when a call was heard or a counter person requested it in passing. The manager typically circulated, helping here and there to clear bottlenecks, trying to anticipate problems, reassigning people as volume changed, getting problems taken care of, and constantly watching how people were working ("Sandy, bag the fries the correct way, please.") See Exhibit 7B for a listing of job assignments as volume increased.

In June 1980, the Hillybourne restaurant employed 33 hourly workers, 15 of whom were minors. Hourly pay ranged from $3.10 (minimum wage) to $3.50, and hours worked in a week from 3 to 40. DeMasi noted:

> I've been at this restaurant store for six years now. Most of my workers are young, school and college age, and I've had several kids from the same family come work for me over the years. I do have several employees in their late 20s and am pleased now to have two older folks working at lunch—great workers, and I hope their being here will encourage others to apply.

DeMasi advertised for openings in local papers, used on-site signs, worked through school counselors, and, of course, encouraged referrals from employees. New workers spent about half an hour on paperwork with DeMasi, were given a detailed employee's handbook, taken on a thorough tour of the restaurant, and shown, over time, a series of 19 video cassette training films.[6] A new worker typically started during a slow period (such as 2–5 P.M.) on a cash drawer or the broiler and worked under the supervision of an experienced worker or the manager. "Some may be on their own by the second shift," DeMasi reported, "while others may take six or eight." Training was a continuous process, both formal and informal—for

---

[5] Employees who worked shifts of four to eight hours were entitled to half-hour unpaid breaks. These were usually spent sitting (and eating) at a booth in the dining room near the kitchen door.

[6] The 15-minute films were shown in the office.

example, "Susan, will you show John how to make Whopper Sandwiches now," was a frequently heard request in slower periods. DeMasi tried to introduce workers to all parts of the operation over time.

Workers began at minimum wage. Day-crew members and closers (generally the more serious workers) were eligible for a 10 cents raise after two weeks if they were particularly good. All were evaluated informally after 60 days (formally, if there were problems, to build a disciplinary record). In January and June, the manager conducted a formal crew member performance review, rating the employee upon job performance, attitude, dependability, and appearance. Raises were granted by the district office with the amount based upon seniority and grade (typically, 10–20 cents). "That raise is pretty mechanical," DeMasi noted. "In addition, I can recommend raises any time if I feel one is needed, but I have to convince my supervisor to sign off on it. I can usually take care of my good workers. And, you have to remember, nondollar benefits, such as flexibility with working hours or a Saturday off can mean a lot to many of these people."

Employee benefits included free uniforms, half-price meals, and paid holidays and vacations (with amounts based on hours worked). Full-time employees (more than 30 hours per week) received company-paid medical insurance, group life insurance, and a pension plan after six months of service.

Management

The Hillybourne restaurant operated with a three-person management team—DeMasi, First Assistant Manager (AM1) Natalie Banks, and Second Assistant Manager (AM2) Debbie Brown—who covered the 14 weekly shifts (8 A.M.–6 P.M., 4 P.M.–closing). The manager on duty was responsible for "good food, fast service, and a clean restaurant," with running the shift his or her prime focus ("paperwork is done after hours").

Managers were hired and promoted by the district manager (with input from the restaurant manager). New assistant managers worked in the restaurant for one week to learn the positions, spent 10 days in a regional training center to learn basic management and people-handling skills, and then worked two weeks on site to learn the paperwork routines, the opening and closing procedures, and so forth. The new AM2 was then "shift ready." New restaurant managers typically attended Burger King University in Miami after five to six months in their new position. Managers were paid straight salary with pay ranging from $11,500 to $26,000. Raises were based upon annual evaluations that graded managers on areas of performance such as profits, attitude, and ability to train and control people. Grades ranged, DeMasi noted, from "walks on water" to "look for another job." All managers were also evaluated quarterly in order to identify and prioritize areas of performance on which to work. District Manager Sandy Philbrick described restaurant management in this way:

I find that a crew will take on the image of the manager. So we look for an outgoing person who is good at getting things done through others, who can tell people exactly what he or she expects, who can train people and not just come down on them. To say, for example, "Waste is too high, reduce it," is useless. The good manager will figure out *why* it is high, and do the training necessary to reduce it. In fact, 90 percent of the job is training. Similarly, my job is to develop the managers in my restaurants.

EXHIBIT 1
Menu and Product Mix

Sandwiches	Price	Percent of Sandwiches
Burgers:		
Whopper	$1.25	14.5
Whopper with cheese	1.40	7.7
Whopper Jr.	0.72	9.0
Double cheeseburger	1.10	9.4
Cheeseburg	0.56	20.0
Hamburg	0.48	18.6
Other	—	4.0
Specialty:		
Roast beef	1.69	3.4
Chicken	1.59	6.2
Ham and cheese	1.49	2.5
Fish	1.25	4.7
		100.0
Fries:		
Regular	0.45	34.9
Large	0.60	20.9
Onion rings	0.65	9.3
		65.1
Beverages:		
Shakes*	0.60	15.5
Soft drinks†		
Small	0.42	17.0
Medium	0.49	19.9
Large	0.59	8.5
Other	—	15.7
		76.6
Desserts:		
Apple pie	0.40	2.7

Note: This data is from the Hillybourne restaurant, June 1980:

Volume $56,681
Customers 22,750
No. of sandwiches sold 34,227

* Vanilla, chocolate, strawberry.
† Coke (66 percent of soft drinks), root beer, orange, 7up.

186

EXHIBIT 2
Daily and Hourly Distribution of Sales

A. Distribution of sales throughout week (June 1980):

Day	Percent of Week's Sales
Sunday	12.8
Monday	11.9
Tuesday	11.4
Wednesday	12.5
Thursday	16.5
Friday	18.0
Saturday	16.9
	100.0

B. Distribution of sales throughout day (June 1980):

For Hour Ending at —	Percent of Day's Sales
11 A.M.	2.0
12	8.7
1 P.M.	17.9
2	10.7
3	6.3
4	4.3
5	6.5
6	10.4
7	9.9
8	7.0
9	5.5
10	4.3
11	3.1
12	3.4
	100.0

Note: Data from Hillybourne restaurant, June 1980.

EXHIBIT 3
Hillybourne Restaurant
Profit and Loss
Statement, June 1980

Line Item	Percent of Sales
Sales	100.0
Food	31.5
Waste	0.4
Condiments/shortening	1.1
Paper.....................	3.6
	36.5
Gross profit	63.5
Hourly wages..............	17.7
Salaries	6.0
Fringes	3.5
Other controllable expenses ..	3.2
	30.4
Controllable profit	33.0
Utilities..................	4.9
Sales promotion............	1.6
Rent.....................	9.0
Advertising and promotion ...	4.0
Other....................	3.0
	22.4
Restaurant operating profit	10.7

Column totals may not sum due to rounding.

EXHIBIT 4
Restaurant Visitation Report*

Restaurant Number _____ Address _____ _ _____ A.D.I. _____ _____

Date _____ Day _____ Time _____ Report By _____ _____

Title and Name of Person in Charge _____

Grade: I. _____ II. _____ III. _____ IV. _____ V. _____ Overall _____

INSTRUCTION FOR SCORING: Only fill in the areas applicable to your visit. Grading is on an all or nothing system, with a comment provided on all deficient areas. For the overall score, divide the actual points received by the total points possible.

I.	OUTSIDE APPEARANCE	
1.	SIGNS: In good repair, clean & properly lighted.	3
2.	LIGHTS: In good working order.	2
3.	LANDSCAPING: Well maintained & free of litter.	3
4.	DUMPSTER: Clean, neat, gate closed.	2
5.	PARKING LOT: Free of litter, clean, sealed & striped.	2
6.	WASTE RECEPTACLES: Clean, in good repair.	2
7.	SIDEWALK: Clean, free of ice, snow or trip hazards.	2
8.	WINDOWS & DOORS: Clean.	2

TOTAL POSSIBLE 18, SUB TOTAL _____
COMMENTS: _____
_____
_____

II.	DINING ROOM	
1.	DINING ROOM: Floors, seats, tables, walls, ceiling, vents, lights, decor, plants, clean & in good repair.	5
2.	REST ROOMS: Clean & fully supplied.	2
3.	MENU BOARD & P.O.P.: Clean & current.	2
4.	CUSTOMER CONVENIENCES: Napkin & straws available, high chairs & booster seats clean & in good repair.	2
5.	WASTE RECEPTACLES: Clean, in good repair, not overflowing.	2

TOTAL POSSIBLE 13, SUB TOTAL _____
COMMENTS: _____
_____
_____

III.	SERVICE	
1.	Adequate number of crew and management working for this period and are they located properly?	9
2.	Proper procedures being followed by cashiers. (greeting, thank-yous, attentive)	8
3.	SPEED OF SERVICE: Average of door to door times not in excess of three minutes.	6
4.	ATTITUDE: Courteous, smiles, enthusiastic, helpful, overall sense of urgency.	7

TOTAL POSSIBLE 30, SUB TOTAL _____
COMMENTS: _____
_____
_____

DOOR TO DOOR TIMES: _____
_____
_____

* The district manager completed at least one restaurant visitation report per month during a shift run by the store manager and by each assistant. DeMasi noted, "It is very hard to score well on the RVR because it is an all-or-nothing system. For example, I got a 49 score on the last one my boss did. But it is the improvement that he looks for."

EXHIBIT 4 (*concluded*)

V.   OTHER
1.   EMPLOYEE APPEARANCE: Uniforms clean,   5
free of wrinkles & stains, well and properly
groomed.
2.   STEAMER & SANDWICH CHUTE: Controls   10
being utilized.
3.   HOSTESS PROGRAM: Being used prop-   5
erly.
4.   DRIVE-THRU: Staffed properly,   8
flow of traffic moving smoothly, move
times within standards.
5.   KITCHEN APPEARANCE   5

MOVE TIMES: _____

_____

TOTAL POSSIBLE 33, SUB TOTAL_____
COMMENTS:_____

MANAGER B.O.A._____ %

EMPLOYEE B.O.A._____ %

IV.   QUALITY
1.   SANDWICHES: Hot, neat, proper   10
portions, proper handling in
steamer & in the chutes.
2.   FRIES: Hot, fresh, salted, flavorful,   10
neatly packaged, seven minute
holding time being observed.
3.   SOFT DRINKS: Proper amounts of ice,   8
carbonation good, temperature correct,
cup filled properly, clean, capped,
flavor & ratio correct.
4.   SHAKES: Proper viscosity, flavor good,   6
cup clean, & properly filled.
5.   COFFEE: Proper serving temperature,   5
good flavor & aroma, cup clean and
properly filled.
6.   ONION RINGS & PIES: Hot, fresh,   7
holding times being observed,
& neatly packaged.

TOTAL POSSIBLE 46, SUB TOTAL_____
COMMENTS:_____

OVERALL COMMENTS AND FOLLOWUP:_____

EXHIBIT 5A
Sandwich Composition

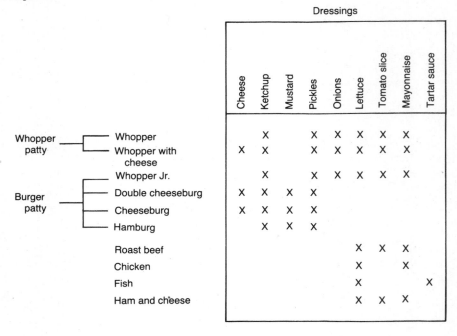

	Cheese	Ketchup	Mustard	Pickles	Onions	Lettuce	Tomato slice	Mayonnaise	Tartar sauce
Whopper patty — Whopper		X		X	X	X	X		
Whopper with cheese	X	X		X	X	X	X		
Whopper Jr.		X		X	X	X	X		
Burger patty — Double cheeseburg	X	X	X	X					
Cheeseburg	X	X	X	X					
Hamburg		X	X	X					
Roast beef						X	X	X	
Chicken						X		X	
Fish						X			X
Ham and cheese						X	X	X	

EXHIBIT 5B
Sandwich Wrapper/Box Markings

For burgers:

Markings on the wrapper (hamburgs, cheeseburgs) and box (Whopper, Whopper Jr.) conveyed two bits of information from the production people to the counter people:

1. The end of the 10-minute sandwich holding period, signaled with a digit corresponding to the clock minute hand reading at discard.
2. The customer's special instructions, such as "plain cheeseburg" or "Whopper no onion," if any, signaled by marking the appropriate condiment sign (the condiments were pictured on each wrapper/box) with one or more of the following symbols:

     ◯   Only   ✕   Extra   ——   None

Thus, in the examples below, (a) represents a regular cheeseburg that was to be held until 20 of the hour, and (b) represents a Whopper with extra ketchup and no onions that was to be held until 10 past the hour.

EXHIBIT 5B (*concluded*)

a.   *b.*

For specialty sandwiches:

The four types of specialty sandwiches were packaged in one box that had four symbols on it:

Ham
Roast beef   and   Fish
Cheese   Chicken

The markings on a specialty sandwich box included the holding time and special instructions, as with burgers, plus a mark to indicate the type of sandwich. In the example below, a worker has prepared a fish sandwich with tartar sauce only that can be held until half past the hour.

EXHIBIT 6
Burger Sandwich Preparation Process

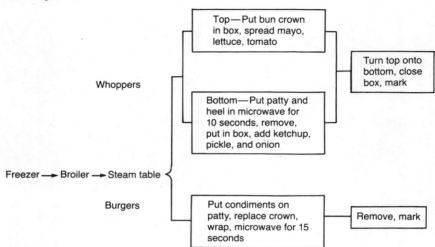

EXHIBIT 7A
DeMasi's Level Chart

Number of Sandwiches in:	"Opening"	<$100	Level 1 $100–$200	Level 2 $200–$300	Level 3 $300–$400	Level 4 >$400
Steamer:						
Whopper	0	1	2	3	5	6
Burger	0	4	6	9	10	10
Double burger	0	1	1	2	3	4
Chutes:						
Whopper	0	0	1	2	3	4
Whopper with cheese	0	0	0	0	1	1
Double cheese	0	0	1	1	1	2
Burger	0	0	2	3	4	5
Cheeseburger	0	0	2	3	4	5
Whopper Jr.	0	0	1	1	2	2
Whopper Jr. with cheese	0	0	0	0	0	0
Fish	0	0	0	1	2	3
Chicken	0	0	0	1	3	4
Roast beef	0	0	0	1	2	3
Ham and cheese	0	0	0	0	0	1

At hourly dollar volume:

Note: Chart within dotted lines was posted in store above chutes.

EXHIBIT 7B
Staffing Order

Work Station

No. of workers	Hourly volume* ($)	Counter	Counter	Counter	Drive-Thru	Drive-Thru	Drive-Thru	Broiler	Board, right	Board, left	Specialty sandwiches	Fries	Dining Room	Drinks/broiler	Expediter
4	$ 70														
5	110														
6	150														
7	190														
8	230														
9	270														
10	310														
11	350														
12	390														
13	430														
14	470														

Note: Each line represents one worker. The length of the line indicates the span of the task.
* Corporate guideline for this size of restaurant, with a drive-thru and with a dining room.

CASE 14

Master Operations Scheduling Game

BACKGROUND TO YOUR COMPANY OPERATIONS

Marketing Considerations

Your company manufactures a consumer product which is purchased for resale by numerous wholesale and retail establishments. The market for your product is highly competitive and subject to both cyclical and seasonal fluctuations. The timing and extent of seasonal peaks are influenced by weather conditions and thus can be forecast with only moderate accuracy. Although the annual sales forecast made each November has been, on the average, within plus or minus 10 percent of total actual sales, there had been years in which the forecast total varied from the actual results by as much as plus or minus 20 percent. Moreover, the forecast of sales for any of the four 13-week "operating periods" into which the year is divided is sometimes in error by as much as plus or minus 33 percent of the results actually obtained.

These forecasting inaccuracies are tempered somewhat by the fact that certain customers usually negotiate purchase contracts for at least a portion of their requirements 60 to 120 days in advance of the shipping date. As a result, in most years anywhere from 10–30 percent of the shipping requirements for a given operations period are "booked" sometime during the second operating period ahead of the period in which delivery has to be made. An additional 20–60 percent are booked one period ahead. In total, therefore, "advanced commitment sales" already on the books at the start of a period rarely represent less than 30 percent—and sometimes amount to as much as 90 percent—of the shipments that the factory will be called to make out of current production or finished goods inventory during the period.

The remaining delivery commitments, known as "single-period sales"—that is, sales that are booked and shipped during the same operating period—sometimes involve as little as three weeks' leadtime. Since such sales frequently represent supplemental orders placed by important customers, your company makes every effort to meet even the tightest delivery deadline, as do its major competitors.

Customers rarely cancel an order once it has been booked. On the other hand, since the product is bulky and therefore costly to handle and store, customers are unwilling to accept delivery much in advance of the date requested. Therefore, if factory production runs ahead of the actual shipping requirements during a given operating period, your company has to carry the excess units as finished goods inventory.

Advertising and Sales Promotion Efforts: Basic Programs and Special Supplementary Campaigns

Within your company and the industry there is agreement that industrywide sales for any operating period are more decisively influenced by weather conditions than any other single factor. Moreover, research studies have indicated that "brand loyalty" is significant to only about half of the customers who regularly purchased this product. Therefore, even though weather plays a major role in determining when and in what quantities retail customers buy such items, the choice between competing brands can be considerably influenced by advertising and other sales promotional techniques such as price discounts, premium offers, and contests.

In common with all major companies in the industry, prior to the start of each calendar year your company commits itself to a carefully planned basic advertising and sales promotion program for the ensuing year. This entails the commitment of a specific amount of money. The exact amount usually is a predetermined percentage of the sales revenues forecast for the coming year.

Experience has convinced your organization's top management that under certain circumstances it is profitable to augment this basic program with supplemental advertising and sales promotion campaigns (SASP) during all, or part, of particular operating periods. To assess the advisability of launching such campaigns, the following "rules of thumb" have proven useful:

For any of these supplemental campaigns to yield results during a given operating period, it is essential that commitments be made no later than the start of the period. Nor is it possible, except at prohibitive cost, to abandon a campaign once it has been undertaken. Furthermore, experience indicates that even if the extra expenditures are increased substantially beyond $50,000, sales are not likely to exceed 130 percent of the level they will reach with only the basic program.

In commenting upon this phase of operations, one of your senior executives has stated, "It is imperative that a decision regarding a SASP campaign

Type of Supplemental Advertising and Sales Promotion Campaign	Extra Costs per Period Incurred from Supplemental Campaign	Approximate Percentage Increase in Sales for the Period That Can Probably Be Achieved over the Sales That Would Result from the Basic Program Alone
Type X (modest step-up in efforts)	$10,000	10
Type Y (major step-up in efforts)	20,000	20
Type Z (maximum step-up in efforts)	50,000	30

be based on a painstaking analysis of the total situation. I refer not only to the status quo then surrounding the company but also the probable future course of events, the plans being launched by the other sectors of the business, and so on. This can be tricky. It is a nightmare to find yourselves committed to a 'maximum effort' type Z campaign during a period in which actual sales are so favorable that the factory is unable to meet even the demand that would have been generated by the basic program. On the other hand, not to have launched an SASP campaign during a period in which sales fall seriously short of the factory output appears, by hindsight, to be inexcusably poor management. But by digging and analyzing, it is possible to assess if a supplemental campaign is likely to be helpful."

Factory Output Capabilities and Direct Labor Costs

As noted previously, your company divides the calendar year into four consecutive operating periods of 13 weeks each. The range of factory output capabilities per period and the average direct labor cost per unit under each of the three factory operating conditions that management believes to be feasible are as follows:

Factory Operating Conditions	Output Capabilities per Operating Period*	Average Direct Labor Cost per Unit
Single shift without overtime...........	60,000 units or less	$5
Single shift with overtime...........	61,000 to 80,000 units	$5 for first 60,000 units, $7.50 per unit thereafter
Two shifts.............	61,000 to 110,000 units	$5 for first 60,000 units, $5.50 per unit thereafter

* Note: For planning and scheduling purposes, factory output is always expressed in multiples of thousands of units.

Scheduling and Planning Factory Activity

Until recently, your company's policy has been to increase or to decrease the rate of factory output frequently. This has been accomplished by hiring or laying off workers, increasing or decreasing overtime, changing the number of shifts, and so on, whenever sales fluctuations seemed to warrant it. After careful study, however, your board of directors has become convinced that the costs and inefficiencies associated with such frequent changes are excessive, and that with careful planning a more stable, and hence more profitable, pattern of operations could be achieved. Instructions have been given, therefore, to your operating management that until further notice it is to adhere to a policy decision that the level of factory operations can be changed no more than four times per calendar year, and that such changes can only occur at the start of an operating period. Once the level of factory activity has been determined for a given period, it cannot be changed until the start of the next period.

In commenting on this new policy, your board chairman has stated, "Granting that forecasting is difficult in our industry, we feel that it still is not unreasonable to expect our operating management to do a sufficiently sound job of planning to be able to live with their decisions for at least a three-month period."

Extra Costs Arising from Scheduling or Forecasting Problems

Simultaneously with announcing the new policy regarding the number and frequency of changes in factory output rate, your company's directors announced their intention to employ the results of a recently completed cost analysis. This study had been undertaken by representatives of the sales, production, finance, and accounting departments to provide information on the extra costs incurred whenever problems of scheduling or forecasting caused your company to adopt any of the following three types of action:

1. *Making changes in the rate of factory operations* —that is, the extra costs incurred from having to recruit, hire, and train additional employees, or from having to lay off present employees; from having to place rush orders for additional materials; from increases in state unemployment taxes arising from an irregular employment record; and so on.

2. *Carrying finished goods inventories* —that is, the extra costs incurred from the physical movement and storage of finished products; the cost of insurance, the risk of theft, damage, deterioration, or obsolescence, or all of these; the cost of the capital tied up in such inventories; and so on.

3. *Defaulting on a delivery promise made to a customer* —that is, extra costs arising from the use of airfreight to expedite delivery on a delayed order; losses arising from a customer's refusal to accept late delivery; estimates, based on past experience, of the risk that such nondeliveries will result in legal action or in the loss of future sales from the customer in question or from other customers who learn of the situation; and so on.

The results of the study were as follows:

1. Extra costs incurred from changes in the rate of factory output: $2 per unit of change, regardless of whether the change is upward or downward.
2. Extra costs, in addition to those cited above, from changes in the number of shifts employed in the factory:
   a. Going from one shift to two shifts: $7,000.
   b. Going from two shifts to one shift: $3,000.
3. Extra costs from overtime or second-shift premiums:
   a. *Overtime:* $2.50 per unit for each unit of factory output in excess of 60,000 units per period.
   b. *Second shift:* 50 cents per unit for each unit of factory output in excess of 60,000 units per period.
   (Note: Single shift plus overtime can be used only up to a maximum factory output rate of 80,000 units per period. To obtain an output rate in excess of 80,000 units requires the use of a second shift. To obtain an output rate between 61,000 and 80,000 units, operating management can choose either single shift plus overtime or two-shift operations.)
4. Extra costs of missed delivery promises: $6 per unit per period.
5. Extra costs of carrying finished goods inventory: $1 per unit per period (to be applied to the average size of the inventory, that is, one half of the sum of the beginning inventory for the period plus the closing inventory).

Special Internal Controls

One of the top management's objectives in obtaining such cost information was to establish a special system of internal controls which would help the directors make a continuing assessment of the performance of operating management. Therefore, in addition to the conventional profit and loss statement, the directors also now require that at the close of each operating period operating management complete and submit the form shown in Exhibit 1.

These internal controls are based upon the conviction that on the average, each unit shipped from the factory generates a potential contribution of $3. That is to say, if operations are at maximum efficiency, your company can meet all variable costs arising from the production of the unit in question and still have $3 of the selling price available as a contribution toward its fixed costs, taxes, and profits. This potential contribution is reduced, however, by any extra costs incurred during the period.

Use of this concept requires that the following computations be made for each operating period:

1. Number of units actually shipped × $3 = Potential contribution for the period.
2. Extra costs incurred during period = Cost of any supplementary advertising or sales promotion campaign plus any extra costs arising from scheduling or forecasting problems.
3. Net operating contribution for period = Potential contribution minus extra costs incurred.

An Example of the System at Work: The First Operating Period of the Current Year

During the final week of the year just concluded, your factory was operating at an output rate of 71,000 units per period, that is, the rate that had been set at the start of the period. This had been accomplished through use of single shift plus overtime. All orders calling for shipments during the fourth period have now been received, and it has been determined that after meeting these your company will end the current year with a finished goods inventory of 10,000 units.

The sales forecast for the following year, prepared by the sales department in November, is as follows:

Period	Delivery Requirements Forecast (units)	
1	70,000	84
2	82,000	98,4
3	125,000	
4	59,000	76.7
Total ...	336,000	

By late December, your company's operating management also knew that 44,000 units of advance sales commitments calling for delivery during period 1 of the coming year were already on the books. Of this total, 18,000 units had been booked during period 3 of the year just concluding and 26,000 units during period 4. An additional 28,000 units of advance commitments had been booked in period 4 for delivery during period 2 of the coming year.

EXHIBIT 1
Net Operating Contribution Calculation Sheet (to be turned in after each period)

Management # _____   Period #_1_   Year #_1_

I. **ACTIVITIES DURING THIS PERIOD** (circle appropriate phrases & fill-in blanks)

    (a) Factory Operations (circle one): Single Shift without Overtime   or   (Single Shift with Overtime)   or   Two Shift.

    (b) Factory Rate this period _62,000_ units;   Rate prior Period _71,000_ units; Change in Rate therefore equals _9,000_ units.

    (c) Supplementary Advertising & Sales Promotion Campaign (circle one): None or (Type X ($10,000))   or   Type Y ($20,000)   or   Type Z ($50,000).

II. **SHIPPING REQUIREMENTS THIS PERIOD** (units)

Delivery Deficits from prior Periods _nil_
+ Advance Commitment Sales booked
  for delivery this Period.......... _44,000_
+ Single Period Sales, this Period _32,000_
equals TOTAL SHIPPING REQUIREMENTS _76,000_

III. **SHIPPING CAPABILITIES THIS PERIOD** (units)

Starting Finished Goods Inventory............. _10,000_
+ Factory Output Rate this Period........ _62,000_
equals TOTAL SHIPPING CAPABILITIES....... _72,000_

IV. **SHIPMENTS MADE DURING THIS PERIOD** (i.e. the total shown in either item II or item III above, whichever is the _lower_)........... _72,000_ units

V. If item II above is _greater_ than item III, the difference equals a **DELIVERY DEFICIT** of........................ _4,000_ units

VI. If item II above is _less_ than item III, the difference equals a **ENDING FINISHED GOODS INVENTORY OF** .... _nil_ units

VII. **POTENTIAL OPERATING CONTRIBUTION FOR THIS PERIOD**
    Shipments made this period (item IV above) _72,000_ units x $3.........$ _216,000_.

VIII. **EXTRA COSTS AND EXPENSES INCURRED THIS PERIOD**

    (a) Supplementary Advertising (see item I-c above).............. $ _10,000_

    (b) Change in Factory Rate (item I-b above x $2) .... $ _18,000_.
        _9,000_

    (c) Change in # of Factory Shifts (changing from 1 to 2 costs $7,000; from 2 to 1 costs $3,000) .... $ _nil_

    (d) Overtime or 2nd Shift Premiums (Overtime costs $2.50 per unit for all units in excess of 60,000; 2nd Shift costs $.50 per unit for all units in excess of 60,000............ $ _5,000_.
        2,000 units X $2.50

    (e) Inventory Carrying Costs i.e. (Starting Inventory + Ending Inventory) x ½ x $1 .... $ _5,000_.
        _(10,000+0)_

    (f) Missed Delivery Promises (item V above x $6.00)............. $ _24,000_
        _4,000_

        TOTAL EXTRA COSTS & EXPENSES INCURRED...................... $ _62,000_.

IX. **NET OPERATING CONTRIBUTION FOR PERIOD** (item VII minus item VIII..........$ _154,000_

  + Cumulative Operating Contribution from prior Periods.................$ _____

  equals NEW CUMULATIVE NET OPERATING CONTRIBUTION.....................$ _____

****

YOUR COMPANY'S DECISIONS REGARDING NEXT OPERATING PERIOD (fill-in blanks)

  Factory Operations:_____ : Factory Rate_____ units

    Supplementary Advertising_____

After studying these facts, your company's operating management decided that during period 1 of the new year the factory would be operated on a single-shift-plus-overtime basis at an output rate of 62,000 units; that is to say, a reduction of 9,000 units would be made in the rate maintained during the fourth period of the year then concluding. In addition, it was decided that a "type X" supplementary advertising and sales promotion campaign would be launched during period 1 in an effort to stimulate sales by about 10 percent.

During actual operations in period 1, the following sales results were achieved:

Period in Which Shipment Called for	Amount of Orders Booked (units)
1 (Single-period sales)	32,000
2.	40,000
3.	28,000

As a result of these developments, total delivery requirements for period 1 turned out to be 76,000 units: the 44,000 units of advanced commitment sales booked prior to the start of period 1, plus the 32,000 units of single-period sales booked during period 1. However, your company was able to ship only 72,000 units of this total: the 62,000 units that were produced by the factory during period 1, plus the 10,000 units which were available in the form of finished goods inventory at the start of the period.[1]

Therefore, your company will enter period 2 with a shipping deficit of 4,000 units in overdue orders which will have to be met at the earliest possible date out of period 2 factory output.

Under your company's internal control system, period 1 operations resulted in a net operating contribution of $154,000, computed as shown in Exhibit 1.

Now, operating management must make various decisions regarding operations during period 2. It knows positively that as early as possible in period 2 your company must ship the 4,000 units of delayed deliveries, that is, the shipping deficit incurred in period 1. It knows also that during period 2 the factory will have to ship an additional 68,000 units to satisfy advanced sales commitments booked for period 2: the 28,000 units booked during period 4 of the previous year plus the 40,000 units booked during period 1 of the current year. Before deciding upon the rate at which to operate the

---

[1] In most instances, orders shipped from the factory during the last few days of a period are not received by the customer until early in the following period. This brief lag is not considered important within the industry, however, and all shipments leaving the factory during a particular period are assumed to be applicable to the shipment requirements of the period.

factory during period 2, your management will also have to reach a conclusion regarding the additional shipping requirements that are likely to arise from single-period sales that will be booked during period 2. Attention will have to be given to the possibility that the factory should begin building up its inventory position in anticipation of shipping requirements in period 3. Decisions on these points will be based, of course, on a careful analysis of the sales forecasts and the sales trends that seem to be developing, as reflected in sales to date for the year.

An Unexpected Development

Several hours prior to the time they were to meet to reach final decisions regarding period 2 operations, the entire operating management of your company was "pirated en masse" by a desperate competitor who tripled their salaries and offered them lavish stock options.

In light of this crisis, you have accepted an assignment to join a newly formed management group which will assume full responsibility for the company's operating decisions. You and your new associates have agreed to meet as soon as possible to decide upon the organizational techniques and procedures you will employ in meeting your new responsibilities. In recognition of the difficulty of your situation, the directors have given you and your associates complete latitude regarding who, among you, will assume what executive positions.

While congratulating you on your new responsibilities, one of the directors offers you a few words of advice:

> Look, the secret of success in our company—like any other—is organizing an effective management team. In a technical sense, there are only three things that *have* to be done: (1) before the start of each period you have to decide upon the rate at which the factory is going to be run during the ensuing 13 weeks; (2) you have to decide whether or not to employ a supplemental advertising and sales promotion campaign during the forthcoming period and, if so, which one; and (3) you have to compute the net operating contribution for the period just ended, and submit this figure to the directors. Clearly it's imperative that you assign specific responsibility for each of these steps.
>
> But these formal requirements represent only part of the story. Sound decisions regarding the factory rate and the desirability of a supplemental advertising campaign can only grow out of careful analysis of various known facts, and a resourceful prediction regarding certain unknowns. There are data, and trends, and other evidence that helpfully can be brought to bear on both of these matters. The trick is to organize for the analytical job that is required. The task is too complex—and the time pressure too great—for any one man to do alone. And the situation is undergoing too rapid a rate of change to permit operating management to rely merely on intuition, or on the hope that the disorganized efforts of able men will somehow yield wise results. Instead, each manager must assume some portion of the total job, and all of these individual efforts must then be blended into an effective whole.

I urge you and your colleagues to start by making a careful analysis of our company, the market it serves, the relationship between the various costs it encounters, and so on. Then reach agreement regarding the precise information and data that you need to compile to sharpen your judgment regarding the various decisions you know you will be having to make. For example, might there be some way to highlight the constantly changing relationship between sales forecasts and actual sales results? Might there be some way to assure that before committing the factory to a given output rate for the next period, you examine the costs under several different output rates? Is there some device that will assure that the plans of the factory, and of the sales department, are carefully coordinated? And so on.

Once you decide the analytical approaches you want to employ, pin down responsibility for executing them. And decide in advance just how you plan to go about making final decisions. Is the president alone going to have the "final say," with all of the other managers acting as staff advisors to him? Or are decisions to be divided up functionally, with a sales manager deciding matters relating to sales, a production manager deciding factory matters, and so on? Or should the management group act as a committee, reaching decisions via majority vote? Or would some still different organizational approach be better suited to management's needs?

Well, best of luck. We're up against some tough competitors. But the other directors and I expect you to run circles around them.

CASE 15

Walton Instruments—Manufacturing

John Manley, manufacturing vice president for the Walton Instruments Company, smiled and stood up. "That's about all the background information that would make sense to you at this point, Dave," he said. "Before you try to absorb any more, you ought to get out and look at what's going on." He waited while Dave Rostow put the papers that they had been discussing into a semblance of order and led the way briskly down the corridor.

COMPANY BACKGROUND

Walton Instruments had been formed in 1966 when four engineers from a nearby aerospace company joined forces and struck out on their own. The company's stated purpose at its inception was the "development and mass production of precision electronic measuring and test equipment," but by 1980 it had branched out into a variety of other fields, primarily medical electronics. Company income statements and balance sheets for 1979 are shown in Exhibits 1 and 2.

The company's president, Robert Jacobson, had described the circumstances surrounding the founding of the company as follows.

> One of the major problems that we (my former employer, that is) encountered in the development of a new piece of electronics apparatus was the lack of commercial testing equipment having the necessary convenience and precision. Laboratory test equipment was fine in the design stage, of course, but it wasn't adequate for use in the actual production of the device. It required too high a skill level and cost too much. So I found myself spending more and more time designing test equipment to be used in the production phase of products that were still being designed. I enjoyed this work and got to be rather good at it, I think, and eventually I was put in charge of a group of three other engineers whose major function was this kind of design work. As we did more and more of it, we began to think about the possibility of doing it commercially.

205

EXHIBIT 1

WALTON INSTRUMENTS
Income Statements
Years Ending December 31, 1978, and December 31, 1979
($000)

	1979	1978
Net sales	$7,260	$5,734
Cost of goods sold:		
Direct labor	812	592
Materials	2,950	2,102
Manufacturing overhead	858	700
	4,620	3,394
Gross profit	2,640	2,340
General administrative	386	304
Marketing	930	776
Research and development	1,164	946
	2,480	2,026
Profit before taxes	160	314
Provision for income taxes	66	144
Net profit	$ 94	$ 170

The problem—lack of high-quality test equipment—was a common one, as we learned in conversations with colleagues at various conferences. After about a year of informally surveying the market, we decided to give it a go.

Our first couple of years we relied for most of our business on our old company, which commissioned us to do about the same thing we had been doing for salary before. We rented the top floor of an old, run-down warehouse near the river and designed and produced everything there. As our business grew, we divided up the management along functional lines. John Manley was put in charge of all production operations (see Exhibit 3), and Ray Carter was made sales manager. Up until that time we had relied for sales mostly on word of mouth and personal contacts with our friends in other companies. But until we got our manufacturing organization geared up we really couldn't afford too much sales volume.

Our financing was really about the easiest problem we faced, primarily because we had that built-in business with my former employer. We used that in getting bank financing for working capital, tossed in some of our own savings leveraged with personal loans, and when we started expanding in earnest, we got some help from a venture capital company. We went public in 1975, which, looking back, was a pretty good time to do it!

In 1972, when sales first passed the million dollar mark, the company exercised its option to lease the remaining three floors of the warehouse and put $100,000 of its own money into renovation over the next five years. The

EXHIBIT 2

WALTON INSTRUMENTS
Balance Sheets
As of December 31, 1978, and December 31, 1979
($000)

	December 31, 1979	December 31, 1978
Assets		
Current assets:		
Cash.........................	$ 12	$ 106
Accounts receivable..............	1,292	998
Inventory......................	2,094	1,436
Other..........................	38	48
Total current assets............	3,436	2,588
Net fixed assets...................	468	452
Total assets........................	$3,914	$3,040
Liabilities		
Current liabilities:		
Notes payable..................	$1,054	$ 704
Account payable................	944	596
Accruals.......................	352	280
Total current liabilities..........	$2,350	$1,580
Long-term debt.....................	406	406
Capital stock and surplus............	300	300
Earned surplus....................	848	754
Net worth...................	$1,148	$1,054
Total liabilities.....................	$3,914	$3,040

EXHIBIT 3
Manufacturing Organization (April 30, 1980)

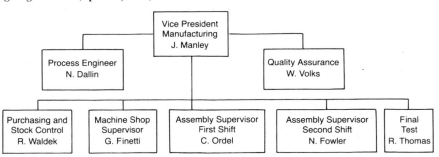

first floor was now used for the receiving and shipping departments, a machine shop, and parts and finished goods inventories. The machine shop, which was devoted primarily to the preparation of chassis and some of the simpler cabinet components, consisted of a stamping press, a punch press, four drill presses, and assorted cleaning and finishing equipment. This shop had previously been an independent company, located three blocks away, which Walton had called upon to do most of its chassis and cabinet work. In 1972, when Walton accounted for over 75 percent of this company's business, the owner announced that he was retiring. Rather than locate and train another job shop to do the same work, Jacobson had decided to buy him out and move his shop onto Walton's premises. The former owner of the job shop was put on a retainer and spent about half his time after the transition managing its operation until 1976, when ill health gradually cut down on his activities. It was now a department whose head, the former job shop supervisor, reported directly to the manufacturing vice president.

In early 1980, Jacobson visited a well-known business school to speak about his company and its prospects, and particularly about its growing involvement in the field of "medical electronics." A highly fragmented field, medical electronics included everything from electroencephalographs to automatic laboratory analyzers. Walton Instruments, however, was confining its effort to what it did best: automatic (patient) monitoring equipment that digitalized input information and prepared it for a variety of end uses. Of the four products in this field that they were currently marketing, three were for exclusive use in operating or delivery rooms. David Rostow, a first-year business school student, approached Jacobson after his speech and inquired about the possibility of a summer job with his company. He explained that as an undergraduate he had prepared to enter medical school but had finally decided that the growing demands and complexity of health services would require a more organized and businesslike approach, and massive infusions of new technology. Jacobson took his name, and two weeks later Rostow received a letter from John Manley (Exhibit 4).

THE MACHINE SHOP

Rostow followed Manley down the stairs to the first floor (Manley explained over his shoulder that the elevator was too slow and usually loaded with equipment). As they walked through the machine shop, Manley stopped by a drill press where one of the workmen was drilling holes in a chassis that had been formed out of sheet metal by the stamp press. The holes would be used for mounting various parts to the chassis during assembly. Rostow noticed that a pile of completed chassis lay beside the drill press, and as he watched, the operator finished the piece he was working on, added it to the pile of completed chassis on the handcart beside his bench, and wheeled them away.

EXHIBIT 4
Letter to Mr. David Rostow, March 18, 1970

Dear Mr. Rostow:

Mr. Robert Jacobson has described his meeting with you earlier this month and your interest in obtaining a summer position with our company. We certainly feel that this possibility should be explored further, since we are convinced of the usefulness of having an outside person of your qualifications look at our operations from an objective point of view. Your resume was most impressive.

You mentioned, I believe, being particularly interested in working with the marketing side of our organization. Frankly, this isn't where our current problems lie: we are selling all we can make, and it is very clear that the only way we can sell more is by increasing capacity and/or being able to promise quicker delivery—without sacrificing our reputation for quality.

We are currently in an exciting phase of our development, making the transition from a rather small, "handcrafting" company to one that increasingly competes with some of the largest, most sophisticated companies in the world. In recognition of the importance of this, I have instituted two studies: cost control and production control. Both must come to grips with the fact that we are now dealing with about a hundred different product-model types and several thousand parts in a rapidly changing, high technology business. We need an accounting system that will provide us with the information necessary to make informed decisions, and a production/inventory system that will get our products to our customers at a competitive cost and in a reasonable amount of time. The two men responsible for these studies report directly to myself and Mr. Jacobson.

I would like you to participate in both these studies. I think you can make a real contribution to our company. Please let me know whether such an assignment would be attractive to you.

John S. Manley
Vice President,
Manufacturing

"Is that all he makes at one time?" he asked. Manley nodded. "He doesn't make very many for several reasons. First, we make almost 30 different kinds of equipment now, and most of them have two or three models. With that many models we just can't afford to run too long at any one time with just one of them. We have to keep our inventories in balance so that if the need arises, assembly can schedule a special run. Second, even though the majority of our designs are "fixed," most of the newer ones, particularly in the medical field, are still getting engineering changes fairly frequently. Often this means moving some of the components around on the chassis, so the old hole configuration isn't applicable any more. Rather than try to make do with the old chassis that are still in stock; we just toss them out and use only the chassis drilled to the new specifications. Finally, these lot sizes turn out to be the 'optimal' ones as calculated by the standard square root formula."

He went on to explain that the previous owner of the job shop, before being bought out, had instituted the economic lot size concept. Walton Instruments, not wanting to meddle with what appeared to be a smoothly running operation, had gone along with his suggested lot sizes for various categories of items until the previously mentioned pressures for smaller lot sizes had caused them to look into the calculations. They found that the previous owner had been using a 5 percent interest rate on capital tied up in inventory. "That might have been applicable in the late 50s," said Manley, "but not now. We bumped it up to what seemed to us a more reasonable figure in light of today's market—12 percent. I've got memos on each of these sizes, as well as on the order quantities we use for purchased com-

EXHIBIT 5
Manufacturing Memo 131 (February 10, 1980)

		Unit:	H17
Subject: Revised lot size		Model:	C
		Part:	Chassis

Monthly usage		15
Set-up cost (at $6 per hour):		
Stamp press.	(0.3 hours)	$1.80
Drill press	(0.4 hours)	2.40
Finishing	(0.1 hours)	0.60
		$4.80
Running time per piece (at $6 per hour):		
Stamp press.	(0.05 hours)	0.30
Drill press	(0.5 hours)	3.00
Finishing	(0.4 hours)	2.40
		5.70
Raw material: Steel blank		5.00

Interest rate: 12 percent per annum + 5 percent handling and storage.

Lot size: $\sqrt{\dfrac{2SD}{iC}}$ 30

Plus allowance for rejections (5%)		+2
Less obsolesence factor (20%)		−6
Lot size		26

ponents back in my office. The Standards Manual has a note on EOQ which one of our young industrial engineers wrote up. Though he developed it for finished goods inventory, we use it for all products with some minor adjustments. I'll show them to you if you're interested." (See Exhibits 5 and 6.)

"Frankly, we'd hoped that this decision to reduce lot sizes would help to reduce inventories; you probably noticed that our parts inventory looks like a rat's nest—it's really chock full. Unfortunately the reduced lot sizes have not reduced inventories so far; if anything, inventories have gotten worse, and we don't know why. Maybe you can make that one of your projects."

EXHIBIT 6
Manufacturing Memo 217 (May 15, 1980)

Subject: Revised lot size	Part: Power Transformer T-7
	Uses: Items H10, 11, 15, 17 (all models)

Monthly usage   85

Order cost:
   Comment: 1979 cost of operating order
     department was \$33,630 for 4,213 orders
     processed) . . . .   \$ 8.20

Purchase cost \$62.50

Interest rate: 12 percent per annum plus 5
  percent handling and storage.

Lot size: $\sqrt{\dfrac{2SD}{iC}}$ 39

    Less obsolescence factor (10%) . . . . -4

      Order size . . . . $\underline{\underline{35}}$

ASSEMBLY

On the next floor they stopped and watched one of the two assembly lines bolting components onto the chassis and wiring them according to detailed, color-coded specifications. The assembly line essentially consisted of a long table with 10 work stations spaced about every 6 feet. Each worker was responsible for a specific series of operations (which had been arranged so that the work load for each worker was roughly the same); and after the series was completed for a given chassis, it was shoved down the table to the next station. Manley explained that there were no explicit checks for proper assembly along the line, this being handled by final test after the chassis was completely assembled. Workers often noticed misplaced wires in the course of their operations, however, and corrected them on their own initiative. "Morale is high," Manley said, "they work together as a team."

"Do they use the economic lot size concept in scheduling production here?" asked Rostow. "No. For one thing, this isn't a machine shop like down below," replied Manley. "There isn't the element of setup costs that you have to balance out. Also, we're more hooked into the consumer side of the picture here. Chuck Ordel, the first shift assembly supervisor, makes his own decisions about what to produce and when, given his analysis of sales forecasts, committed orders, and finished goods. Then he goes out and makes sure he has everything he needs. In this sense, he plays quite an independent role. The supervisors of the two shifts coordinate their activities quite well. However, the workers in each shift have been known to complain about the work habits of the workers in the previous shift."

"How does Ordel decide how many to make at one time?" "Well, one important consideration is how many he thinks are going to be needed. Another revolves around the availability of the required components. Another has to do with the fact that it takes a little while for a line to get up to speed. Every time you change models the rate slows down until people get back in the groove. Look over here," he pointed at the wall where a large chart showed the model number being produced, the number started and completed each day, and the cumulative number produced up to the evening before (see Exhibit 7 for an example of this chart). "It levels out after three or four days, so you want to go at least that long." He went on to explain, in reply to Rostow's question, that when a new model was introduced the end people on the line didn't just wait around until the flow got to them; the model change would be instituted at the first station while the other stations were finishing up the last items of the old model run.

"Finally," Manley concluded, "he has to weigh all this against the necessity for keeping the finished goods inventory from getting too imbalanced." As they climbed the stairs to the final test department, Manley remarked that by the time a unit had been assembled it contained more than $1,000 worth of labor and materials on the average.

On one end of the hall, there was a separate section for special products, consisting of four separate work tables. Each of these tables was occupied by one person with a kit of parts and detailed assembly instructions. The products being assembled were special one-of-a-kind customer orders, and each worker assembled the entire product. "Are the workers at those four tables more skilled?" Rostow inquired. "No, there is no difference in seniority or grade between the workers at the assembly line or at the special products section. In fact, with the high morale and team spirit we have, there is a constant interchange of workers between these two sections."

PRODUCT TESTING

They walked briefly through the testing area on the third floor. Each finished item was checked for a variety of performance characteristics, and if problems were located, they were traced down and corrected; each unit

EXHIBIT 7
We're Keeping Things Moving at Walton

Item: H17   1970 Run 2
Model: C
Work
  Stations: 8

Date	Shift	Lead Station Hours at Job	Number Units Begun at Lead Station	Number Units Completed
3/13/70	1	6	3	—
	2	8	4	—
3/16/70	1	8	6	4
	2	8	5	3
3/17/70	1	8	7	6
	2	8	6	5
3/18/70	1	8	8	8
	2	6	5	7
3/19/70	1	—	—	9
	2	—	—	2
			44	44

Efficiency Summary
(standard hours 8:)

Job Quarter*	Number of Units	Assembly Hours	Efficiency
1	11	160	55%
2	11	130	68
3	11	1C5	84
4	11	92	96
	44	487	

*That is, first 25 percent of assembly lot, second 25 percent, etc.

was made the sole responsibility of a single person. All of the persons in this department were highly skilled technicians. There were five technicians assigned to the first shift and four on the second shift. "They're the most important persons in the shop," said Manley with obvious pride. "We encourage each one to be a perfectionist. Their name goes on each delivered unit, so they want to make sure it works. Most of them make more than $1,500 a month, almost twice what the assembly people make."

This drive for perfection sometimes led to problems, Manley admitted as they walked up the stairs to his office. If the technicians had problems with a particular model because of close tolerances, the work piled up behind them. "We've had weeks when almost nothing got through, but usually the backlog is only on the order of three or four weeks."

"Is it getting better?" asked Rostow. Manley shook his head. "No," he said, a bit grimly, "it's not getting better. If anything, it's getting worse. As a matter of fact, recently Bob Thomas, the final test supervisor, has had a number of complaints on excessive work loads. The inspection group feels that the quality of the assembly work has been slipping and a lot of time is spent on fault diagnosis and error correction. The time spent on rework is fairly small, though."

Rostow interjected, "In that case can't you inspect the parts and sub-assemblies at specific points on the assembly line?"

"No, it is not as simple as that. Some of the problems are due to design. Over half of the items we produce have either design changes or are new products. Even if the assemblies were perfect we still have to go through all of the fault diagnosis in case there are design errors, and correct for them. This can be done only after the entire assembly is completed."

"Both Ordel and Fowler, our assembly supervisors, would be the first to admit that errors do get introduced in assembly. However, they insist that many of the problems brought up by inspection in our weekly review meetings are in fact design errors."

"Have you made any detailed study on where quality problems arise?" "I'm not sure whether we have done a study as detailed as you suggest. That might be something you might want to do this summer. We have done some studies on an ad hoc basis, and I could give you a recent memo that I received (Exhibit 8). In preparing the report Bob Thomas indicated to me

EXHIBIT 8
Manufacturing Memo 226 (May 21, 1970)

Subject: Quality problems in assembly

Special products section:

Twenty-six products produced between April 15, 1970, and May 15, 1970.

	Defectives		Error Free	Number of Products
	Design Error	Assembly Error		
Standard Design	1	1	8	10
New Design	14	2*	2	16
Totals	15	3	10	

* Both the products with assembly errors also had design errors.

EXHIBIT 8 (*concluded*)

Assembly line:

Two lots were examined in detail: the time to test, diagnose, and correct errors on each unit was obtained for each unit in the lot. It was found that these times declined dramatically as the number of units tested increased. Typically, the first device tested would take twice as long as the 10th device tested. The following table is a compilation of the times taken for different operations and are average times for the lot.

1. Product H17—model C, lot 70-2: Of the 42 units produced, 19 had assembly errors.

   The average time spent to test error-free devices . . . . 0.6 hr.
   The average time to test and diagnose devices with errors . . . . 4.5 hrs.
   Time to correct for errors . . . . 1.0 hr.

	1st Unit	10th Unit	19th Unit	Average
Test devices without assembly errors	1.0 hr.	0.6 hr.	0.3 hr.	0.6 hr.
Test and diagnose devices with errors	8.0	4.0	2.0	4.5
Error correction	1.8	1.0	0.5	1.0

2. Product P27—model B, lot 70-1: Of the 22 units produced, 10 units had assembly errors.

   The average time to test error-free devices was 5 hours.
   The average time to test and diagnose devices with errors was 5.1 hours.

	1st Unit	10th Unit	Average
Test devices without assembly errors	1.0 hr.	0.6 hr.	0.75 hr.
Test and diagnose devices with errors	7.2	3.6	5.1
Error correction	2.0	1.2	1.5

All the units were tested by one worker.

that they have been swamped by the pressures to meet deadlines and that a special effort was made to inspect the lot soon after it was assembled."

"If they are overworked, have you considered adding more people?" "Yes, we have. There are five persons assigned to the first shift and four on the second. We intend adding two people on the first shift and one on the second. The problem is that skilled technicians are hard to find. We have been looking for the last three months and have not found any."

Chaircraft Corporation

Frank, I don't want you to feel badly about the remarks that were directed at you and some of your people during yesterday's executive committee meeting, but I don't want you to forget about them either. Several members of the executive committee, myself included, feel that our manufacturing operations are simply not keeping pace with our sales growth and that our declining profit situation is caused in large part by conditions in manufacturing that are almost out of control. We've spent an awful lot of time during the past two years getting our field sales force reorganized and trained. Now that the results of that effort are really beginning to pay off, it appears that we haven't spent enough time looking at manufacturing problems.

The speaker was Richard Acton, president of Chaircraft Corporation. He was talking with Frank Johnson, the company's manufacturing manager.

The Chaircraft Corporation, which was located in a small southern community, manufactured an extensive line of upholstered chairs, platform rockers, and recliners. Sales were nationwide to 10,000 dealers through company salesmen. Sales volume for 1968 was $20 million, and a sales growth rate of 10 percent to 20 percent annually had been projected by Mr. Acton. Approximately 700 factory workers were employed. Mr. Johnson was responsible for all manufacturing operations as well as production control, inventory control, and shipping.

"My interpretation of the figures you gave us yesterday indicates that frame shop labor costs are going up despite the new equipment you added this year. Your labor and overhead variances are almost double last year's figures and material variance is up, too.

"Charlie Gibson (a region manager who supervised several salesmen) bent my ear for an hour last week in New York about quality complaints from dealers—and your figures show a 20 percent increase in rework costs this year over last.

"What really bothers me though, Frank, is the $6,000 increase in shipping costs for finished goods. We shouldn't spend a penny on shipping finished goods, but we're now spending over $10,000 per year on it."

"I'll admit we've got some problems, Dick, but I was pretty sore about the manner in which some of our problems were blown all out of proportion yesterday," Mr. Johnson replied. "Our biggest difficulties are in the frame parts and assembly areas, and I'm going to look into these areas carefully during the next few months. It may be that the computer can help."[1]

"Good, Frank," Mr. Acton responded. "I'll be in Chicago all next week, but I'll check with you again as soon as I get back a week from Monday."

THE MANUFACTURING PROCESS

The Chaircraft company was an integrated manufacturer, converting raw lumber, cotton, cloth fabric, and other materials into upholstered chairs. An upholstered chair is an assembly of three major elements: the frame (an assembly of a dozen or more wooden parts); upholstery materials (primarily springs and cotton, foam rubber, or foam plastic); and a cover fabric. The company produced seven lines, or general types, of upholstered chairs on as many assembly lines; the other manufacturing activities of the company supplied the required components to the assembly lines.

Lumber Purchase and Storage

Chaircraft frames were produced from solid southern hardwood lumber of varying species. Lumber was purchased by an independent commission broker. The company purchased three principal grades: first grade, number one common, and number two common. Five thicknesses were used: 1 inch, 1¼ inches, 2 inches, 2½ inches, and 3 inches. About three quarters of the lumber used was 1 inch or 1¼-inches thick. The cost of lumber was about 15 cents per board foot.[2]

Lumber was stacked upon receipt to form loads of a single grade and thickness. A load was a stack of boards forming a cube roughly 12 feet in each dimension and containing about 10,000 board feet. As the boards were stacked, each layer was separated from adjacent layers by slats which created spaces through which air could circulate during the drying process. Typically, the equivalent of six months' requirements of undried lumber was stored outdoors.

Lumber Drying

Operations connected with lumber drying occupied a rectangular area roughly 350 feet long and 100 feet in width, with one end abutting the

---

[1] Chaircraft owned a small second-generation computer which was programmed to run payrolls, billing, accounts receivable records, and other conventional accounting applications. These programs required only a portion of the computer's capacity.

[2] A "board foot" is the amount of lumber equal to 12 by 12 by 1 inches.

factory. The lumber loads were moved through this area on wheeled platforms which rode on steel tracks. The area was divided across its length into three sections of about equal size with the company's three dry kilns (ovens, each 100 feet long) occupying the center section (Exhibit 1). The section farthest from the factory was used as pre-dry storage. Here the loads from the inventory of undried lumber were lined up awaiting entry to one of the kilns. A full "charge" for each kiln was assembled before the kiln became available in order to minimize time spent in "recharging" an empty kiln. Drying time in the kilns varied considerably with species, grade, and moisture content of the lumber and with the season of the year. Exact drying time, therefore, could not be predicted. Average drying time for a charge was about one week.

EXHIBIT 1
Diagram of Plant Area

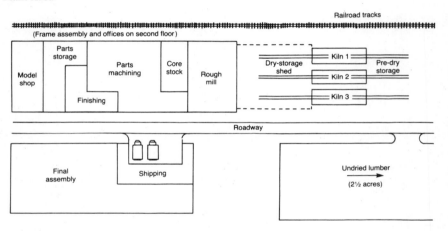

Subsequent to kiln drying, the lumber moved into the third section—a covered dry-storage area. Both the pre-dry and the dry-storage areas had a capacity of about 300,000 board feet; an amount roughly equal to the total charge capacity of the three kilns. The size of the dry-storage area was limited by the location of the kilns, the factory wall, and by property lines. The cost of extra handling prohibited the use of other areas for storing dried lumber.

Maximum use of the kilns depended upon availability of space in the dry-storage area to receive the dried lumber promptly upon completion of the drying cycle. But a rapid and orderly use of dried lumber to free storage space was dependent upon the degree to which the mix of sizes, species, and grades available in the dried lumber storage corresponded with factory requirements at the moment.

Parts Manufacture

After being removed from storage, the dried lumber was processed through the frame shop to produce frame parts. The frame shop had two departments: the rough mill department which cut the incoming lumber into "core stock," and the parts machining department which processed the core stock to produce finished frame parts which went into parts inventory.

In December 1968, the frame shop employed 54 workers on the day shift and 32 on the night shift. A full crew of 17 worked each shift in the rough mill, while there was only a partial second shift in parts machining. Both shifts worked five 10-hour days a week.

Rough Mill Department

In the rough mill, lumber was brought in a full load at a time and processed on a conveyorized production line operated by a team of nine workers. Boards in a given load varied in quality, width, and length, but were of approximately the same thickness. Along the production line, boards were cut to one of three standard lengths, planed, and jointed.[3] After these operations, the boards were sorted on carts according to length. Boards were produced in 70 standard length/thickness specifications.

Lumber from the conveyor line was then cut to width on a ripsaw to form core stock. A piece of core stock was a finished oblong board of predetermined dimensions which had been set by adding a standard allowance (e.g., ⅜ inch) to each dimension of the intended finished part. The ripsaw was operated by a four-person team. The saw was set to cut to a few selected widths. The cut pieces had to be sorted as follows: boards of desired width onto handling carts according to size; oversize boards returned to the operator on the "feed" side of the saw for another pass; undersize pieces set aside to be moved to another department where they would be glued up into larger boards; and scrap pieces onto a special conveyor for removal. The ripsaw operation called for special skills because of the rapid pace and the sorting decisions to be made. The rough mill manufactured core stock in approximately 250 specifications.

Parts Machining Department

In the parts machining department, core stock was shaped to form finished parts ready for assembly into frames. Most of the 500 parts produced were of relatively simple shapes. For "straight stock" (parts which were essentially rectangular in shape, usually containing dowels or dowel holes), the machining operations were simple. Principal operations were a double-

---

[3] The planing operation smoothed the top and bottom surfaces of the board and determined its thickness. The jointing operation smoothed the sides of the board.

end cutoff to finished length, rip to finished width, and any necessary boring. Parts with more complex shapes were formed on band saws or shapers. The few parts which would be visible in the finished chair were sanded after machining.

Material moved through the parts machining shop in lots, each lot traveling on one cart and containing pieces for one part specification. Each machine was tended by a specific operator who was paid a piece rate and who was also responsible for moving material to the workplace and for performing any required setup on the equipment to be used. When an operator completed work on a lot, he informed the department foreman and was assigned another job.

During 1968, the company had purchased two automatic machines. Shaped parts now could be produced on an automatic shaper at a much higher rate than on the band saw or hand shaper. The new machine required more than an hour to set up, however, whereas the manually controlled machines required at most a few minutes of setup time. A high-speed transfer machine combined the cutoff, boring, and dowel insertion operations for straight stock. With one operator this new machine operated at a rate faster than the previous method which required three operators using three machines.

Parts Storage

After the last machining operation, four stock handlers moved the completed pieces to bins in the frame parts storeroom. About 500 different parts were required to build the 50 different "frame styles" which made up the seven product lines. A few of the parts were used in more than one line.

Parts Withdrawal and Frame Assembly

Frames were assembled to meet the schedule of the final (upholstery) assembly line. A small buffer stock of assembled frames was used to "uncouple," or separate, the assembly of frames from the final line. Each assembler built complete chair frames, customarily in lots of 25 frames (lots often included two or more chair styles). Space limitations prevented locating more than the parts requirements for 25 chair frames near one assembler. The frame parts were wheeled on carts to the assembly operators by six "stock pickers." The pickers, working from lot tickets which listed the frame styles and the quantity of each style to comprise a lot of 25, called on their memory to determine what parts to remove from the stockroom shelves.

PRODUCTION CONTROL SYSTEM

The control of frame parts manufacturing was tied closely to the company's final assembly and shipment plans. The rate of production varied

EXHIBIT 2
Chair Orders Received, Production, and Shipments by Months (1965 through 1968)

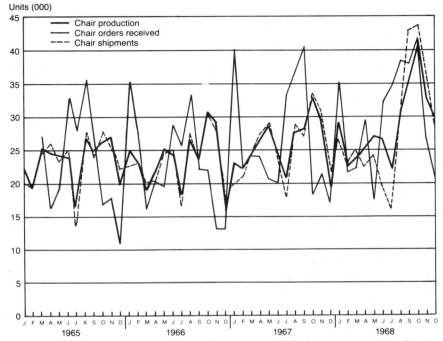

Note: This is a graphic presentation of the figures given in Exhibit 4.

seasonally and was matched to customer delivery needs (see Exhibits 2 through 5). In general, chairs were shipped within two days after completion of final assembly. A long-standing company policy against carrying finished goods inventories had been modified only twice during the last 10 years. At these times Chaircraft had built an inventory of no more than 10,000 chairs in a few popular standard items.[4] In both cases the entire inventory had been sold by the end of the year at regular prices.

The production rate was set by the manufacturing manager who specified the daily production goal, in units, for each of the seven final upholstery assembly lines. Production rates for all contributing departments were then set to match this rate.

Customer orders specified delivery in a given month, and upon receipt, orders were added to that month's backlog for each line. When the backlog for a given month reached the available capacity for the month (on the basis of the planned production rate for that month), a decision had to be made

---

[4] To cover its 50 different styles of frames, Chaircraft offered over 500 different fabric pattern/color combinations and other choices such as springs or foam rubber upholstery. As a result of these options, the variety in the final product numbered several thousand.

EXHIBIT 3
Production Activity by Months (July 1966 through December 1968)

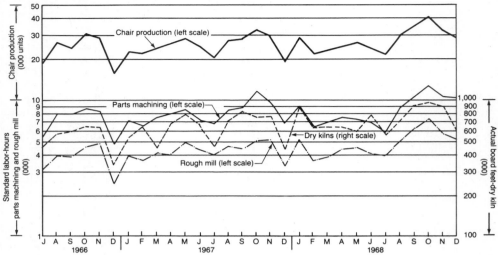

Note: This is a graphic presentation of the figures given in Exhibits 4 and 5.

either to increase the production rate (a common event) or to stop booking orders for that month. A report of orders received, backlog, and available capacity for each of the next three months was prepared daily. Orders to be shipped during a given month were normally on hand by the 15th of the prior month. Only exceptional orders were processed for shipment in less than three weeks.

The monthly production schedule was broken down into daily production schedules dependent upon shipping load plans, i.e., lists identifying each chair to be shipped in a given load on a given date. This conformance to shipping load plans reflected the magnitude of freight costs. Customers normally paid full freight costs on all shipments of their orders. To hold down their freight costs, customers expected that items ordered together would be shipped together and expected also that their shipments would be pooled[5] with others destined for the same geographical area. If some chairs on an order were not ready for shipment on the scheduled date, these were shipped separately at the Chaircraft company's expense. To satisfy customers' delivery expectations and to avoid freight charges to the company itself, the Chaircraft company shipped complete orders by pool cars and trucks and emphasized planned production to meet such shipments.

---

[5] Shipments occupying part of a truck or rail freight car cost considerably more than would the same shipment "pooled" or combined with other shipments to fill a "pool" car.

EXHIBIT 4
Source Data for Exhibit 2 (units 000's)

	1965			1966			1967			1968		
	Orders Received	Chairs Produced	Chairs Shipped	Orders Received	Chairs Produced	Chairs Shipped	Orders Received	Chairs Produced	Chairs Shipped	Orders Received	Chairs Produced	Chairs Shipped
January.....	n.a.	21.9	19.7	35.1	24.8	22.5	39.9	22.9	19.9	35.1	29.2	26.6
February ...	n.a.	18.8	19.3	27.4	23.0	22.9	21.9	22.0	21.0	21.7	22.6	22.8
March.......	26.8	25.0	24.2	15.9	18.8	19.9	23.9	24.1	24.3	22.3	23.7	25.1
April........	16.0	24.2	25.8	20.2	21.4	20.4	23.8	26.6	27.3	29.3	25.4	22.7
May.........	18.3	23.8	23.1	19.4	25.1	24.3	20.6	28.4	28.9	17.4	27.1	24.3
June	32.7	23.7	25.0	28.6	24.1	25.0	19.9	24.8	24.8	32.2	24.1	19.3
July.........	27.7	16.3	13.7	25.3	18.3	16.6	33.2	20.7	17.8	34.4	21.9	16.2
August	35.4	26.8	27.3	33.2	26.3	27.3	36.9	27.6	28.8	38.3	30.6	30.6
September..	26.8	24.6	23.7	21.9	24.0	23.4	40.3	28.2	27.2	37.9	35.7	43.1
October	16.6	26.2	27.7	21.8	30.6	30.7	18.1	33.1	33.6	41.8	41.1	43.8
November ..	17.7	26.8	25.1	12.8	28.8	27.8	21.5	29.3	30.5	26.6	32.9	36.8
December ..	10.5	19.8	22.2	12.9	15.7	18.0	16.9	19.3	21.9	20.0	29.0	28.0
Total	n.a.	277.9	276.8	274.5	280.9	278.8	316.9	307.0	306.0	357.1	343.3	339.3

n.a. Not available.

EXHIBIT 5
Production Activity

	Dry Kilns (actual board feet)	Rough Mill (standard labor-hours)	Parts Machining (standard labor-hours)
1966:			
July	467,200	3,064	5,432
August	571,000	3,911	7,897
September	599,900	3,835	7,957
October	646,500	4,596	8,620
November	624,400	4,857	8,347
December	339,600	2,467	4,741
	3,248,600	22,730	42,994
1967:			
January	532,600	3,959	7,107
February	650,700	3,680	6,549
March	456,000	4,139	7,459
April	685,800	4,058	8,074
May	793,800	4,973	8,601
June	670,300	4,331	7,235
July	463,700	4,026	6,828
August	718,500	4,625	8,682
September	732,000	4,440	8,907
October	768,000	5,197	11,709
November	775,600	5,208	9,615
December	448,500	3,294	6,802
	7,695,500	51,930	97,568
1968:			
January	897,400	5,181	9,171
February	649,500	3,632	6,462
March	657,300	3,870	6,974
April	645,200	4,409	7,619
May	609,800	4,520	7,387
June	795,500	4,093	6,918
July	579,300	3,966	5,879
August	723,700	5,043	8,990
September	928,600	6,327	10,746
October	981,300	7,360	12,863
November	917,700	5,793	10,798
December	610,500	5,092	10,471
	8,995,800	59,286	104,278

The translation of customers' orders into shipping load plans was the responsibility of the traffic control clerk. She planned each day's shipping loads three weeks in advance of the shipping date. Then, each Friday morning she turned over to the production control section the planned shipping loads for the five days ending on a Thursday three weeks hence. (See planning time cycle below.).

Planning time cycle

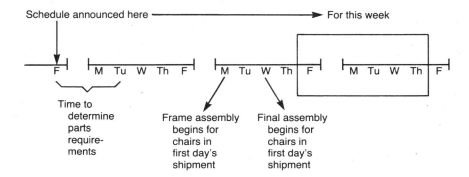

The production control section, consisting of a manager and three clerks, used the shipping plans to determine the corresponding frame parts requirements. This was done with the use of the standard parts list for the frames to be built. After parts requirements for a week were accumulated, these figures were compared with frame inventory balances.

Although shipping plans, by day, were established three weeks in advance, the "lead time" at which parts requirements were determined in advance of assembly was reduced considerably by these factors:

The shipping plans were accumulated each week until Friday. This achieved a "batching" of requirements but cut lead time.

Final (upholstery) assembly began two days before the planned shipping date and frame assembly two days before that.[6] This reduced lead time by nearly a week.

Production clerks were occupied from Friday until Tuesday in determining parts requirements and in comparing parts requirements with availabilities.

---

[6] The required time for a chair to move through final assembly and through frame assembly was considerably less than two days—just a matter of hours. The extra time was used as a buffer and was represented physically by completed frames awaiting the final assembly line and completed chairs awaiting shipment.

The net effect was that the actual requirements of parts to be assembled in any week were not known until Tuesday of the preceding week.

To compensate for the limited advance notice of known parts requirements, the production control manager forecast parts requirements each week for one week beyond the two weeks' requirements known. This one-week forecast was, in general, an extrapolation of a simple "visual" average of recent weeks' actual requirements.

In determining what parts to order from the frame shop, the production control manager used the following formula: Parts needed equals the requirements for three weeks (as established above) less the current book inventory and less any quantity currently on order and not received into inventory. If this calculation showed a parts shortage, an order was placed on the shop equal to the standard order quantity (or a multiple of the standard quantity) established for each part. Each standard order quantity was set at 80 percent of the number of pieces of that part that would fit on one of the carts used to move work in the frame shop.

Every Tuesday the production control department issued the week's frame parts orders to the frame shop foreman. These orders were represented by standard order tickets which specified the quantity ordered, the core stock to be used, and the standard routing through the parts machining department. Several hundred order tickets were issued each week. Once the core stock had been cut for a given part, the order ticket was placed on the cart and remained with the parts in process. The order ticket was returned to the production control department after the parts were stored in the frame parts storeroom.

The frame shop supervisor was given complete control in scheduling each order through his shop, subject to one restriction: all parts ordered were expected to be produced and in stock within two weeks of the date of issuance of the order. The supervisor tried to schedule orders to balance the load on various machines and operators in the shop. The schedule was dependent also upon the availability of the proper species and quality of lumber in the rough mill. To keep a balance between the mix of lumber being dried and the requirements of the frame parts schedule, the frame shop supervisor maintained an informal liaison with the dry-kiln supervisor. Of the actual orders handled in the frame shop during 1968, 70 percent were completed within one week of issue, and 90 percent were completed before the two-week deadline.

If all went well, on any Monday the parts inventory would assure the requirements for that week's frame assemblies. The production control manager pointed out, however, that achieving this result depended upon:

1. The book inventory being correct.
2. No serious underrun on orders outstanding.
3. Accurate forecasting for one week beyond known requirements.
4. Completion of parts within the two-week time.

THE MANUFACTURING MANAGER'S VIEW

Following his conversation with Mr. Acton, Mr. Johnson reflected on the comments which had been made during the executive committee meeting. He felt that the company's production control system for frame parts could be improved and his attention was drawn to three areas—parts ordering, machine loading, and control of the rate of production.

Parts Ordering

PROBLEM

REASONS

Excessive inventories frequently accumulated for some frame parts while other parts were unavailable when needed. This problem was attributed to several factors: the frame shop supervisor's discretion in scheduling parts for production; lack of central control of overruns and underruns on parts orders; and clerical errors in reporting receipts and withdrawals from stock. The stockroom typically reported from one to three items out of stock daily. Where the production control records indicated inventories of several hundred units, the discrepancy was attributed to failure to record withdrawals or was simply unexplained.

The book inventory record was maintained by the production control department. A new book balance was calculated weekly for each part by adding actual parts production and subtracting standard parts withdrawals. Standard withdrawal figures were arrived at by combining the count of frames actually assembled each week with the list of standard parts for each frame design. If assemblers used nonstandard parts or if they used more than the standard quantity due to spoilage, such use usually went unrecorded. In some instances, assemblers, anxious to increase piece-rate earnings, had found that substituting one part for another speeded assembly. The stock pickers were supposed to report extra withdrawals and to choose only standard parts, but this was difficult to enforce.

Some of the difficulties in parts ordering were related to the job of handling production control information. A standard two-day clerical delay existed between the time shipping load plans for a given week were accumulated and the time corresponding parts requirements could be compared with the record of inventory levels. Standard figures for withdrawals of parts per week were used instead of detailed reports of actual withdrawals to conserve time spent in clerical work.

An out-of-stock condition for frame parts caused difficulty because it greatly increased the chance of missing a shipping load schedule. A lot of the missing parts could be rushed through the shop, but this required special expediting attention by supervisors. Frequently they spent time determining why the stock records and actual stock conditions disagreed. They spent time, also, directing the "special handling" of needed parts through the shop and rescheduling parts orders that were displaced. In some instances extra setups were required when rush orders interrupted the machining of a lot already started.

Machine Loading

The shop supervisors were given discretion as to what machine to use for each parts order. Mr. Johnson felt this resulted in more machine time being spent than necessary. He believed the loading of some important machines should be centralized in the hands of the production control group. Steps had just been taken to plan loads for the automatic shaper. A production control clerk designated which jobs were to be done on the shaper following two rules. First, the clerk had been instructed to keep this machine fully loaded; and, second, if the available work exceeded the capacity of the machine, the clerk was to select the long-run jobs in order to realize the best return from the higher setup cost of this machine. In the absence of central loading, the mix of parts ordered in a given week frequently overtaxed the time available on one group of machines while leaving other machines and their operators idle.

Rules like this can kill you!

Trying to eliminate idle time?

The chief engineer felt, however, that more data was needed before effective machine load planning could be pursued generally on a centralized basis. Machine loads, he thought, should be scheduled by actual rather than standard times. Hence, it would be necessary to have data on setup times by machine and performance ratios (actual to standard) prepared separately for setups and machining times. Present average output was 125 percent of standard, but performance at individual work stations varied widely.

Production Rate

The seasonal character of sales combined with the Chaircraft scheduling practice led to substantial fluctuations in employment and hours of work. Peak production in the fall of 1968 had strained the dry-kiln capacity, although both the rough mill and parts machining departments could have increased appreciably their volume of work without significant expenditures for additional equipment.[7] Kilns had a replacement value of $27,000. No space existed for adding a kiln adjacent to the factory.

Mr. Johnson preferred to operate the plant on a 45-hour week. He set 36 hours as a minimum workweek and said that this could not be held for more than a month without a great loss in productive efficiency. Similarly, when the workweek went above 45 hours, efficiency began to fall. It would be difficult, he believed, to get workers to work more than 50 hours weekly. The average hourly base rate in the frame shop was $2.90, with time and one half paid above 40 hours per week. None of the attempts by an international union to organize the Chaircraft workers had been successful.

---

[7] Throughout 1968 and the immediately preceding years, Chaircraft had the use of two 100-foot kilns and one 50-foot kiln. In Decmeber 1968, work was completed to lengthen the 50-foot kiln, giving the company three 100-foot kilns, thus expanding dry-kiln capacity by 20 percent.

In August 1968, a full second shift had been hired for the rough mill and a partial shift added to break bottlenecks in parts machining. The personnel manager said it was difficult to get skilled operators for the night shift. The cost of hiring was high, and the quality and tenure of second-shift operators tended to be low. The personnel manager also indicated his belief that by January 1969 it would be necessary to cut back the work force again to match sales demand.

Training costs in the frame shop were high, although no exact figures could be obtained. It was known that 10 of the workers hired for the rough mill at the beginning of August 1968 began work at 50 percent of standard. Their production reached 80 percent on November 1, and 100 percent by the first week of December. Similarly, boring machine operators hired in August started at 65 percent of standard and reached 80 percent by late September and 100 percent in October. New employees were paid the full hourly rate until they reached 100 percent productivity and received a bonus above that level.

A STATISTICAL STUDY

In early December 1968, Mr. Johnson had ordered a study of frame parts usage and production. A random sample of 50 of the 500 frame parts was chosen for study and records covering a period of 22 weeks from July through November 1968 were examined to calculate usage, inventory, and production data on the parts comprising the sample. The parts included in the sample accounted for 7.75 percent of lumber consumed and 4.5 percent of standard frame shop labor-hours during the 22-week period. On the basis of usage, standard costs, and an assumed inventory carrying cost of 25 percent, an economic order quantity was computed for each part. This was compared with the company's existing standard order quantity (which was equivalent to 80 percent of the number of pieces held on one cart). For the parts covered in this study, the average standard time allowance per lot for setup was 0.46 hours, and the range of allowances was 0.27 to 1.76 hours. The standard cost rate for direct labor and variable overhead in the frame shop was $4 per hour.

The results of this study indicated that the typical lot size for frame part production was much smaller than the EOQ amount. In fact, for the sample of parts examined, the EOQ calculations suggested that only 608 setups would be required annually, whereas existing procedures would result in 1,504 setups for these parts annually.

CASE 17

Granger Transmission (A)

In early 1974, concern about the increasing requirements for working capital and the increase in the number of late deliveries was building at Granger Transmission. Expressions of this concern were most often directed toward Jim Tillich, vice president of materials management.

Tillich, a veteran of 18 years of experience in the company had previously held positions as foreman, engineer, supervisor, plant manager, and materials manager after having received an MBA from a well-known eastern business school. His response to these concerns about inventory turnover and missed deliveries is summed up in the following quote:

> We're living through hell!
>
> We call a forging company where we have had an order on the books for two years that's supposed to be delivered in March and say—how's it look? The guy on the other end says, "How the hell do I know? I haven't even had an acknowledgment from the steel mill on the order I placed for the steel that goes into your order." Then, he calls you back after calling the steel mill and says it doesn't look like March, it looks like August.
>
> Now, that order for forgings may be necessary to complete the assembly of maybe 200 orders that we have promised to deliver to our customers in June and July.
>
> We've got the same situation on ball bearings where order lead times are 101 weeks and on foundry castings where lead times are 99 weeks. Even little things, like cotter pins, must be ordered a year in advance.
>
> At the same time, we get over 100 requests each day to change the delivery dates on our customers' orders, most of them requests for early deliveries. Since our average product has over 200 parts, that means up to 20,000 part schedule changes each day, if we agree to the change, and that's getting rare. Is it any wonder that our delivery performance doesn't look so hot? (See Exhibit 1.)

EXHIBIT 1
Delivery Performance

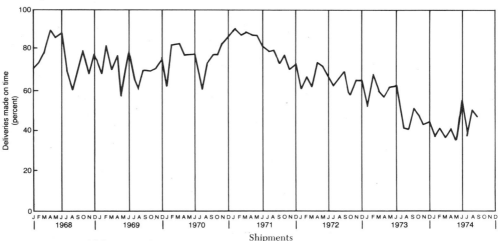

Note: Percent of deliveries made on time $= \dfrac{\text{Shipments}}{\text{Past-due orders} + \text{Shipments}}$

Source: Company files.

As for inventory turnover, well, we're not a retail grocer. That's for sure. But our domestic inventories turn almost three times a year, and that's not bad for our kind of business. You can see that when you compare our inventory performance against that of companies with similarly complex operations, although I really believe that none is as complex as ours. You see, in a job shop operation you need in-process inventory out your ears to keep loads balanced from machine center to machine center. Whenever our turnover gets over three, we have severe problems. We become very inefficient and sporadic, productivity goes down, and the number of missed deliveries goes up.

COMPANY BACKGROUND

Granger Transmission Company was a multinational producer and marketer of small-volume, heavy-duty transmissions for use in extractive industrial, marine, and construction equipment. Although founded as an independent firm, the company was acquired in 1935 by a large heavy equipment manufacturer. It has been operated as an independent subsidiary since that time.

Granger Transmission's products were designed to customer specifications and produced in small lots. The price of these products ranged from several hundred dollars to over $10,000 per unit. Sales of over $93 million in fiscal 1974 represented a 20 percent increase in sales over 1973. One third of the sales of Granger Transmission were to the parent company, another one third to three other large OEM manufacturers, and the balance to numerous smaller accounts. It was estimated that 90 percent of the customers of Granger Transmission accounted for 10 percent of the total volume. Approximately two thirds of all sales were manufactured in the company's domestic facilities.

The product line was divided into eight basic categories of assembled transmissions and clutches. An additional category of products was comprised of spare parts, which accounted for about 30 percent of the company's total dollar volume. The eight categories of assembled products were classified by function and in no way implied that the products in each line were standardized. Each product was assembled to customer order and specification. About 50 percent of the orders used some standard components and subassemblies, however. Demand for these components could thus be anticipated, and they could be produced before an actual order was received for an assembly that used them.

Granger Transmission competed largely on the basis of being able to offer high-quality, highly engineered special-purpose products. In the words of John Bonhoeffer, president of the firm, "Our products are the result of a total systems engineering approach whether they are sold as an individual component or part of an integrated transmission package. We have the capability to design and manufacture a complete driveline from the engine to the wheels. Our engineers work closely with customers in new product development, and extensive use is made of our multimillion dollar research and testing facility."

In addition to quality and engineering excellence, however, customers also expected other things of the company. A recent experience with a major account highlighted these factors.

> We've had four due date changes from one of our good customers for the same order in the last two weeks. They beat on us to stay flexible and to be able to react to these changes, but if we deliver two weeks early, they return the goods. If we're one week late, their assembly line shuts down. For the last year or so, demand has been very strong. With the materials shortage situation that means that we're telling our customers *when they can have* our products rather than them telling us when they want them. We're not very popular with some of our customers anymore.

MANUFACTURING

Granger Transmission's domestic manufacturing facilities were concentrated in two plants about 90 miles apart in central Ohio. The largest plant complex was at Dayton. The smaller plant at Columbus had a similar layout and produced the same products. About two thirds of the productive floor space in the Dayton plant was devoted to a general-purpose machine shop. Parts and components were finished and fabricated here from bar stock, castings, and forgings. About 75 percent of purchased materials cost was for completed parts and components purchased from outside vendors. The balance of materials cost was for raw materials (bar stock, etc.) which was processed through the machine shop to make parts.

The machine shop was composed of about 320 different machine centers, where general-purpose equipment was used to perform specific operations, such as boring, grinding, heat treating, and turning. The typical part traveled through 10 to 15 of these machine centers as it was being fabricated. When a part reached a particular machine center, the machine operator first set up the machine so that it would work the part according to specifications. The operator stayed with the machine while it was running.

Company reports indicated that the capacity of the machine shop was used in the following way: setup time, 22 percent; run time, 52 percent; and miscellaneous indirect labor activities (including material handling, getting tools, etc.), 26 percent. The number of parts which were worked on together in a batch (the lot size) was determined by the production control department. They used their judgment in setting these lot sizes. Frequently, the lot size was determined by the lot size used to obtain the raw material from which the part was made. Thus, if a semifinished part was purchased in lots of 100 because this was the "minimum buy," or because 100 qualified the company for a quantity discount, the size of the lots put into the machine shop for finishing the part was also 100.

Part production in the machine shop typically took a substantial amount of time, averaging about 16 weeks in process. The exact amount of time depended upon the priority of the item (how badly it was needed), the number and type of operations to be performed on it, and the lot size. For instance, part 203149A had an average usage of 1,000 pieces per month. If the lot size was maintained at the current level of 1,000 (one setup per month), the standard time to process it through the machine shop was 72 days, including 12 days to move the part from machine center to machine center. Lots of 2,000 pieces, on the other hand, would require a standard time of 110 days to process from bar stock to finished parts. If the part was urgently needed, however, it could be fabricated in 15 days by hand carrying it through the shop and breaking setups on machines where other parts were being manufactured. Such rush jobs were avoided if possible because of their disruptive effect on the shop and the consequent losses of productivity. Sometimes, rush jobs were subcontracted instead. On balance, though, subcontracting was kept to a minimum because of the additional expense involved and because there was difficulty in getting subcontractors to meet Granger's quality standards.

The other one third of productive floor space in the Dayton plant was devoted to assembly and testing. The typical product was hand-assembled in a stationary location from about 200 parts and components. As many as 20 or 30 different products were being assembled at any one time. The average time to complete the assembly of one product was about two days. However, the demand for any one product was very small. For example, one of Granger's big sellers was one type of special clutch for oil well drilling rigs. They produced and sold about 200 per year.

In addition to productive floor space, about one half of the total floor space was used for inventory storage (including space for work in process). There was a storage area for raw materials which was used to produce parts in the machine shop. In early 1974, the value of this inventory in the Dayton plant was $700,000. There was also a storage area for finished parts which separated the machine shop from the assembly area. This inventory ($8.5 million) was comprised of finished parts for use in assembly which were obtained both from the machine shop (about one third of the total number of parts) and from outside vendors. The last storage area was for finished assemblies waiting for shipment. The total value of this inventory in Dayton was $300,000. Included in the inventory value of these finished products was the total cost of purchased materials (about 40 percent), the value added by direct labor (20 percent), and factory overhead (40 percent). Of the total labor and overhead, 60 percent was attributable to the machine shop and 40 percent to the assembly operation. An additional inventory of $5.6 million was on the machine shop floor as in-process inventory. In May of 1974, about $5 million of the inventory in the Dayton plant was destined for use in orders which were already past due. The total annual cost of goods sold approximated $45.3 million.

Through 1974, most of Granger Transmission's operations in both the fabrication and assembly areas were worked three shifts per day, for six or seven days each week.

PLANNING AND CONTROL

Domestic planning and control activities were the responsibility of Bill Buber, materials manager. He supervised both the production control department, the purchasing department, and with the head of industrial engineering, was responsible for determining and justifying capital expenditures to top management. Purchasing was centralized for domestic operations and was operated with eight buyers, eight assistant buyers, a purchasing agent, and his assistant. The production control department was composed of eight product planners who worked closely with marketing in determining when orders for the eight basic product lines would be scheduled and in monitoring their progress. In addition, production schedules and stock chasers were located at the manufacturing locations to release and control specific parts orders. The stores control group, which disbursed, received, and recorded inventory transactions, was also a part of production control.

Domestic production planning and control activities at Granger Transmission revolved around computerized materials requirements planning and shop floor control systems installed in 1964 and 1969, respectively. The materials requirements planning system depended on data maintained in two computer files, and on requirements inputs, to operate. The bill of materials file contained product structure data, i.e., a list of which parts went into which subassemblies, and which subassemblies went into which final products. The file was analogous to a recipe book in a kitchen in that given the quantity of final products to be produced, say, 10 three-egg omelets, a complete list of input components could be derived, e.g., 30 eggs, 2 pounds of cheese, 2 pounds of bacon, 4 teaspoons of salt, etc. Engineering had the responsibility for maintaining an accurate bill of materials for each product or part they designed.

The other computer data file was an inventory file. This file contained current (updated daily) information on each of the company's 60,000 part, materials, subassemblies, and products. This information included on-hand balances, open purchase or shop orders, lead times, order quantities, safety stocks, unit costs, etc. Many people provided information for this file: purchasing provided lead time and order quantity data, stores control recorded inventory transactions, accounting provided costs, and production control provided expected lead times for fabrication.

Purchasing obtained lead time data from the company's suppliers. Lead times for fabricating parts were constructed by adding together (1) the sum of the standard setup times for each of the machines in the shop that the part would be processed on; (2) the sum of the standard unit run times for the part on each machine times the number of parts in a batch; (3) the sum of the standard times for moving the lot of parts from machine center to machine center, the standards allowed one day for each move; and (4) the sum of the queue times for each machine center the lot of parts would be processed through. The expected queue time for each machine center was the anticipated length of time a lot of parts waited once it got to a machine center to be processed. Typically, the expected queue time was three times the sum of the standard setup and run times for a lot at each machine center.

Given the data in these two files, the planning of materials requirements was a straightforward operation. For example, a production planner might accept an order for five model X transmissions for delivery in week 356 (using a numbered week calendar). The requirements and consequently the orders for all the parts that went into this product could be determined by exploding from the bill of materials file and offsetting lead times and quantities obtained from the inventory file. Exhibit 2 shows two of the exception report sheets which might be generated as a result of this process. The first is for a plate (A-3773) that goes into this transmission, as well as many other models. This status report indicates that 115 of these parts are required in week 355. Thus, 110 parts will be needed for other products or for spare parts in addition to the five parts needed for the model X_s. These are scheduled for completion in week 355 since the lead time to assemble the five transmissions is one week. The requirements can then be compared with scheduled receipts for orders already made, and projected on hand balances to indicate when orders should be planned. For example, the

EXHIBIT 2
Material Status Report

MATERIAL STATUS - PRODUCTION SCHEDULE

PART NUMBER	NAME	FORECAST QUANTITY	USED LAST YEAR	USED TO DATE	USED THIS PERIOD	YEAR TO DATE SCRAP	SAFETY STOCK	LEAD TIME	S.O.Q.	SM CONS	REQ FREQ	SPECIAL INSTRUCTIONS	MORGUE QUANTITY	MATERIAL COST	MODEL USED ON	LABOR COST	CRITICAL PART NUMBER	QUANTITY	PRINT DATE
A 3773	FLT PLT	36	2727	1672	102	2		4		15	2	A-R.O.-	415		CL6		#A 3773		01/23/71

On hand: 117 / 134 | Morgue: 255

																			TOTALS
REQUIREMENTS	343	344	345	346	347	348	349	350	351	352	353	354	355	356	357	358	359		941
SCHED RECEIPTS	24	8		2	15	612		14	267	148	6		115						636
AVAILABLE	134	127	119	112	76	652	616	580	313	165	129	93	22	58	94	130-	166-		1640
PLANNED ORDERS							36	36	36	36	36	36	36	36	36	36	100		100

REQUIREMENTS	360	361	362	363	364	365	366	367	368	369	370	371	372	373	374	375	376	377	
SCHED RECEIPTS	58	5			100						3		100	100				100	
AVAILABLE	224-	260-	296-	332-	432-	468-	504-	540-	576-	612-	648-	684-	720-	820-	856-	892-	928-	1028-	
PLANNED ORDERS	36	36	36	36	36	36	36	36	88	36	36	36	100	36	36	36	36	36	

REQUIREMENTS	378	379	380	381	382	383	384	385	386	387	388	389	390	391	392	393	394		TOTALS
SCHED RECEIPTS																			
AVAILABLE	1064-	1100-	1136-	1172-	1208-	1244-	1280-	1316-	1352-	1388-	1424-	1460-	1496-	1532-	1568-	1604-	1640-		1820
PLANNED ORDERS	36	36	36	36	36	36	36	36	36	36	36	36	36	36	36	36	36		188

FORM 158 REV. 10/68

MATERIAL STATUS - PRODUCTION SCHEDULE

PART NUMBER	NAME	FORECAST QUANTITY	USED LAST YEAR	USED TO DATE	USED THIS PERIOD	YEAR TO DATE SCRAP	SAFETY STOCK	LEAD TIME	S.O.Q.	SM CONS	REQ FREQ	SPECIAL INSTRUCTIONS	MORGUE QUANTITY	MATERIAL COST	MODEL USED ON	LABOR COST	CRITICAL PART NUMBER	QUANTITY	PRINT DATE
#A 3774	BH FLT PLT		3049	2269			6		500			A-PUR.-			CL6		#A 3774		01/23/71

On hand: 500 | 1 D

REQUIREMENTS	343	344	345	346	347	348	349	350	351	352	353	354	355	356	357	358	359		TOTALS
SCHED RECEIPTS					36			22	36	36	36	36	58	36	36	36	100		1820
AVAILABLE	500							22-		94-	130-	166-	224-	260-	296-	332-	432-		1820-
PLANNED ORDERS							500					500							188

REQUIREMENTS	360	361	362	363	364	365	366	367	368	369	370	371	372	373	374	375	376	377	
SCHED RECEIPTS	36	36	36	36	36	36	36	36	100	36	36	36	100	36	36	36	36	36	
AVAILABLE	468-	504-	540-	576-	612-	648-	684-	720-	820-	856-	892-	928-	1028-	1064-	1100-	1136-	1172-	1208-	
PLANNED ORDERS						500													

REQUIREMENTS	378	379	380	381	382	383	384	385	386	387	388	389	390	391	392	393	394		TOTALS
SCHED RECEIPTS	36	36	36	36	36	36	36	36	36	36	36	36	36	36	36	36	36		1820
AVAILABLE	1244-	1280-	1316-	1352-	1388-	1424-	1460-	1496-	1532-	1568-	1604-	1640-	1676-	1712-	1748-	1784-	1820-		1820-
PLANNED ORDERS	500																500		188

Source: Company files.

projected on hand balance here drops to -22 in week 355. Since the part has a shop lead time of four weeks, an order can be planned for week 350.

By referencing the bill of materials file, the planned orders for part A-3773 can be projected as the future requirements for the materials that go into it. For example, part A-3774 is purchased from an outside vendor whose lead time is currently six weeks. Here, the derived requirement for 22 part A-3774's in week 350 triggers an order for 500 pieces (the order quantity) in week 343, after offsetting the lead time of six weeks.

Requirements for parts came from several sources other than from exploding the requirements for higher level parts, subassemblies, and assemblies. For high usage parts, for example, a forecast of part usage derived with another computer program was also used. Part A-3773 again provides an example. Here, the forecast quantity is 36 units. This usage is subtracted from projected on hand balances but is not shown as a requirement so that firm orders and forecast orders are not confused. The reason for forecasting requirements is so that Granger would be able to promise delivery faster than they would if they only used firm orders for delivery in future periods. This was particularly important for items used as spare parts as well as in assembly, since the company wished to be able to respond immediately to customer needs for many of these products.

Another kind of forecast was used for a few final products (most were not forecasted). These were called management stock orders and were orders issued in anticipation of the receipt of an order from a good customer. Because of the high risk involved in committing the company to these, they originated from the highest levels of the company after preliminary negotiations with the customer. Safety stocks were yet another kind of requirement. These were set by marketing service and/or production control using the NRN (nice round number) method. They were used to protect against stockouts on important service parts and for parts which had high scrap rates or unreliable delivery problems. Safety stocks and management stock orders accounted for about $1 million of total domestic inventories in 1974.

All of the daily materials status reports issued by the materials requirements system were reviewed by Bill Buber before he passed them on for action by production control or purchasing. Essentially four kinds of action were indicated in these exception reports: order, cancel an order, reschedule an order, and expedite. Ordering was indicated whenever the planned on hand balance fell to a negative value over the lead time. Order cancellations for parts were generated whenever requirements were reduced because of order cancellations for assembled components, or when new parts were designed to replace an order. Order rescheduling was indicated whenever there was a delay in expected requirements. For example, when a customer moved the order due date out into the future. Expediting indicated that an order needed to be processed faster than the standard lead time because an order due date had been moved up or parts had been scrapped in the shop. Sometimes, orders for good customers were accepted with promised delivery dates that were less than the standard lead time into the future. This would trigger an expedite order if the appropriate parts were not already in stock.

Other exception and control reports issued by the system were the open purchase order buyer fail-safe report and the order acceptance report. The open purchase order buyer fail-safe report (Exhibit 3) was issued weekly to the purchasing department, and sometimes sent on to the appropriate vendor. This report listed all open purchase orders, the quantity ordered, and the due date. In addition, it listed a fail-safe week which indicated the latest date that a fail-safe quantity (also indicated) could arrive before threatening to make an order for an upstream part or assembly late. Thus, if buyers anticipated problems in getting a complete order on time, they could try to negotiate with vendors for at least the delivery of the fail-safe quantity by the fail-safe week.

The order acceptance report (Exhibit 4) was also issued weekly to the product planners, so that they could review the status or orders that had been accepted. This report indicated whether or not the delivery to a customer would have to be rescheduled for a later date. It also indicated the

EXHIBIT 3
Open Purchase Order Buyer Fail-Safe Report

02/05/71		OPEN P.O. BUYER FAIL-SAFE REPORT.	Dayton				WEEK – 343	
BUYER	VENDOR#	PART #	ORDER#	WEEK#	QTY.	FWEEK	FQTY.	CUT.
D	52487	# 9670A	791930	345	5	345	1	
D3	52487	# 9670B	819371	360	50			
D1	52487	# 9682	789410	344	50	338	19	
D1	52487	# 9700B	808601	347	35	347	31	
D3	52487	# 9753A	819380	352	100			
D3	52487	# 9791A	789561	345	25	348	25	
D3	52487	# 9791A	810201	351	65	351	1	
D1	52487	# 9813	810211	354	50			
D3	52487	# 9815B	788760	343	15			
D3	52487	# 9824	819390	350	25			
D3	52487	# 9825	793490	346	50	349	15	
D1	52487	# 9841	793730	345	50			
D3	52487	# 9870A	758611	347	50			
D1	52487	# 9957	810220	348	25			
D1	52487	# 201522	825880	352	1000			
D3	52487	# 203717A	822100	354	250			
D1	52487	# 205826	819330	349	100	349	38	
D3	52487	# 205896	826850	358	25			
D3	52487	# 205896L	825890	357	50			
D3	52487	# 206207	793770	348	200	346	108	
D1	52487	# 206331	791841	351	50	350	13	

Source: Company files.

most critical (most past-due) part or component that went into the product that was expected to be late. In most cases, the most critical part was the one which was going to make the entire order late. A late order was indicated whenever the standard lead time that remained to complete production and assembly of a part exceeded the time remaining until the order was due. The due date on all orders from Granger's customers had to be approved by the product planners before marketing could accept the order. Product planners could determine whether a due date was feasible by the standard lead times required to obtain the materials and components that went into the order on production video consoles which had access to the computer files. Most of Granger's best customers placed orders six to nine months in advance of their needs. Other customers often requested shorter lead times, but were often given longer ones than they required.

Granger's shop floor control system was an important adjunct to the materials requirements planning system. It was used to maintain the rela-

EXHIBIT 4
Order Acceptance Report

ORDER ACCEPTANCE REPORT							PAGE # 2	
CURRENT WEEK# 342- DATE OF RUN 01/25/71								
ORDER NUMBER	CUST. NUMBER	WEEK# REQUIRED	WEEK# ALLOCATED	PART NUMBER	QUANTITY	RESCH.	MOST CRIT. PART NUMB.	
28972C	0002	349	349	29965	5			
28972C	0002	353	353	29965	5			
28973C	0002	349	349	6875	5			
28974C	0002	357	357	A 6914	5			
28974C	0002	362	362	A 6914	5			
28974C	0002	366	366	A 6914	10			
28974C	0002	370	370	A 6914	5			
28975C	0002	353	355	33586	17	YES	2815 K	
28975C	0002	357	357	33586	25			
28975C	0002	362	362	33586	35			
28975C	0002	366	366	33586	35			
28975C	0002	370	370	33586	20			
28976C	0002	349	355	33591	1	YES	O 5499 E	
28976C	0002	353	355	33591	5	YES	O 5499 E	
28976C	0002	357	357	33591	15			
28976C	0002	362	362	33591	10			
28976C	0002	366	366	33591	15			
28976C	0002	370	370	33591	10			
28977C	0002	366	366	33593	10			
28978C	0002	353	355	33596	3	YES	OA 6070 F	
28978C	0002	362	362	33596	5			
28978C	0002	370	370	33596	5			
28979C	0002	353	357	33594	5	YES	M 2780	

Source: Company files.

tive priorities of the orders being processed by manufacturing. A key data file for this system was the routing file. It contained information on the sequence of manufacturing steps required to produce each part which Granger manufactured. When the materials requirements planning system released an order for the fabrication shop (which it would only do when all the materials required to produce the part were on hand or expected with some certainty), a computer program would print out a route sheet (Exhibit 5) and a packet of reporting cards for that order. The route sheet showed the sequence of operations, by work center, for producing the part along with other data such as the standard time to produce it, and directions. The reporting cards (one for each operation/work center) were standard computer cards with some prepunched data which would be sent to data processing whenever an operation was completed at the appropriate work center.

The data acquired from this reporting system was used in several ways. First, shop foremen would receive a daily schedule (Exhibit 6) listing all of the parts waiting for work at each work center and their priorities. These priorities were based on a "critical ratio," which was the ratio of the time remaining (in days) before the job was scheduled to be completed, to the standard hours (including queue time) of work remaining on the part. Thus,

EXHIBIT 5
Route Sheet

OPER. NO.	PART NUMBER	DESCRIPTION		PART NUMBER	WORK ORDER NO.
000-1	.A..3773..	FLOATING PLATE		A-3773	342 B 42
	ROUTING DATE	MADE FROM/SPEC. INSTRUCTIONS		QUANTITY 612	
000-2	05/26/70	#A-3773		LOAD OF	
	USED ON				
	CL6			LOAD QUANTITY	
	RANGE			VENDOR Brillion	
	50			HEAT NO.	

OPER. NO.	PLANT-DEPT. CENTER	s	HOURS/C	PIECES/HOUR	s	DESCRIPTION	PIECES GOOD	SCRAP	CLOCK NO.
010-0	1- 3-BH		1.25	40.0	X	TURN,FACE,BORE,CHAM & U.C.			
020-0	1- 3-HE		1.67	30.0	X	FACE TO LENGTH,CTBR & CHAM			
030-0	1- 3-J		.524	190.	X	BROACH TEETH			
040-0	1- 4-RW					WASH			
045-0	1- 3-FC		2.70	37.0	X	GRIND FRICTION SURFACE			
050-0	1- 6-EA		2.08	48.0	X	DRILL 24 HOLES			
060-0	1- 6-EA		1.20	83.0	X	DRILL FOUR HOLES			
070-0	1- 4-RW					WASH			
080-0	1-15-NB					INSPECT			

Source: Company files.

EXHIBIT 6
Daily Schedule

DATE 02/06/73			DAILY WORK CENTER JOB SCHEDULE			WEEK 446	DAY WEDNESDAY		
PLANT 03		DEPT 05	MACH.CTR. BH		SHIFTS WORKED 2.0		CAPACITY 110.9		
				-PRIORITY-		QTY QTY			
PART #	PART NAME	ORDER# OP#	OPER DESC	PO*	PI†	OF OP AT OP	HOURS	NEXT LOCATION	WORK REM.	TIME REM.

209335H	IMP WHL @	438C34 020	FIN	.436		142 142	11.1	0316NB	18.3	8.0
216140A	SPINNER	445C22 010	TURN	1.236		88 88	6.4	0305BQ	18.6	23.0
209308C	IMP WHL	445C67 020	FACE		.430	212 212	16.7	0316NB	18.5	8.0
A 4639A	CARRIER	445B45 010	TURN		2.675	54 54	5.4	**SAME**	8.5	23.0
A 4639A	CARRIER	445B45 02C	FACE		2.675	54	5.4	0305YE	6.3	23.0
B 1640A	RETAINER	441B22 010	FACE		4.106	108 108	7.3	0305EG	10.4	43.0

TOTAL HOURS IN THIS MACHINE CENTER   52.3

PARTS IN PREVIOUS WORK CENTER   PREVIOUS

208346	IMP WHL	443C31 010	TURN	.437		27 27	4.7	0316NBR	18.2	8.0
203587E	FW PILOT @	444C98 010	SEMI-TURN	.462		28 28	4.3	0316NBR	17.3	8.0
208346G	IMP WHL	446A09 010	TURN	.742		250 250	15.4	0316NBR	24.2	18.0
208346A	IMP WHL	446A07 010	TURN	.907		1234 1234	62.2	0316NBR	36.3	33.0
209335H	IMP WHL @	446A10 C10	TURN	1.388		141 141	11.1	0316NBR	20.1	28.0
B 5164	RETAINER	445C90 020	TURN		2.006	98 98	6.1	0305BQ	11.4	23.0
A 4639B	CARRIER	446B17 010	TURN		2.215	255 255	12.6	0316NBR	10.3	23.0
208457B	IMPELLER	444A44 C10	TURN		3.632	10 10	4.1	0316NBR	10.4	38.0
208346C	IMP WHL	446A08 010	TURN		4.105	50 50	5.8	0316NBR	20.2	83.0

TOTAL HOURS FOR THIS MACHINE CENTER IN PREVIOUS CENTERS   126.3

* PO = Priority for items for which firm customer orders existed.

† PI = Priority for items which were being made to forecast and which were not tied to specific customer orders (as yet).

Source: Company files.

an order with a low critical ratio (less than one) would probably be late, and should be processed first. Orders with high critical ratios (over one) were ahead of schedule, and not so critical. This report also indicated the parts which were at other work centers, which would go to this work center upon completion. This helped the shop foreman to schedule orders on his machines with some foresight.

In February of 1973, this report was a considerable source of agitation to Herb Hegel, a foreman for the gear manufacturing section of the Dayton plant, as he talked to the plant production controller on the phone.

> Hey, you guys are causing me a lot of problems. You aren't keeping me supplied with work down here. I've only got 50 hours of work for the BH work center, and damn little coming in from feeder work centers this week. What are we supposed to do when we run out of work? Sit on our hands?

Other reports generated by the shop floor control and reporting system were the daily location list (Exhibit 7) which showed the present and anticipated location of released orders. The long-range machine load report (Exhibit 8) projected the total hours of work at each machine center by forecasting both actual (orders already in the shop) and planned (unreleased) orders. Since Granger released orders as if they had "infinite capacity" in the shop, this report could be used to see where overtime, additional shifts, or machinery should be added for future business. In commenting on this report, Bill Buber said,

EXHIBIT 7
Location List

DATE 02/04/71 LOCATION LIST WK # 343 FRIDAY

PART #	PART NAME	W.O. #	OPER.	OPER DESC.	WORK CTR	QTY	P.O.	P.I.	COMP.
			030	WASH	1- 4-RW	1	7.750	7.750	344
			040	INSPECT	1-15-NB	1	9.073	9.073	345
.A..3771..	H&B PLT	342A95	020	TURN	1- 6-BC	35	1.412	.551	344
			050	FACE	1- 3-HE	35	1.578	.615	344
			060	FIN	1- 3-YB	35	1.721	.671	345
			075	CUT	1- 6-CRC	35	1.885	.735	346
			080	DRILL	1- 6-EA	35	2.410	.940	346
			090	FIN	1- 3-Y	35	2.742	1.070	347
			100	BROACH	1- 3-JA	35	3.213	1.254	347
			110	WASH	1- 4-RW	35	3.822	1.491	347
			120	DRILL	1- 3-IAA	35	4.180	1.631	348
			130	NUMBER	1- 3-Z	35	5.981	2.334	348
			140	DEBURR	1- 4-NB	35	7.018	2.738	348
			150	WASH	1- 4-RW	35	10.468	4.085	348
			160	INSPECT	1-15-NB	35	12.000	4.682	349
.A..3771A.	H&B PLT	342B43	020	TURN	1- 6-BC	20	99.999	1.506	344
			050	FACE	1- 3-HE	20	99.999	1.695	344
			060	FIN	1- 3-YB	20	99.999	1.859	345
			075	CUT	1- 6-CRC	20	99.999	2.051	346
			080	DRILL	1- 6-EA	20	99.999	2.567	346
			090	FIN	1- 3-Y	20	99.999	2.946	347
			100	BROACH	1- 3-JA	20	99.999	3.703	347
			110	WASH	1- 4-RW	20	99.999	4.532	347
			120	DRILL	1- 3-IAA	20	99.999	5.043	348
			130	NUMBER	1- 3-Z	20	99.999	7.909	348
			140	DEBURR	1- 4-NB	20	99.999	9.830	348
			150	WASH	1- 4-RW	20	99.999	15.870	348
			160	INSPECT	1-15-NB	20	99.999	19.680	349
.A..3773..	FLTPLT	342B42	010	TURN	1- 3-BH	612	1.436	1.236	344
			020	FACE	1- 3-HE	612	1.722	1.482	345
			030	BROACH	1- 3-J	612	2.034	1.752	346
			040	WASH	1- 4-RW	612	2.566	2.210	346
			045	GRIND	1- 3-FC	612	2.678	2.306	347
			050	DRILL	1- 6-EA	612	4.087	3.519	347
			060	DRILL	1- 6-EA	612	7.284	6.273	348
			070	WASH	1- 4-RW	612	9.000	7.750	348
			080	INSPECT	1-15-NB	612	10.536	9.073	348
.A..3774B.	H&B PLT	340B64	130	NUMBER	1- 3-Z	104	7.840	6.884	344
			140	DEBURR	1- 4-NB	104	9.742	8.554	344
			150	WASH	1- 4-RW	104	15.870	13.935	344
			160	INSPECT	1-15-NB	104	19.680	17.280	344

EXHIBIT 8

DATE 01/14/71 LONG RANGE MACHINE LOAD WEEK 339

PLANT 01 DEPT.# 03 MACH.CENTER BH CAPACITY 504.0

PERIOD	PLANNED	ACTUAL	TOTAL
339 TO 342	186.9	363.5	550.4
343 TO 346	386.3	.0	386.3
347 TO 350	620.4	.0	620.4
351 TO 354	794.9	.0	794.9
355 TO 358	662.5	.0	662.5
359 TO 362	622.7	.0	622.7
363 TO 366	622.2	.0	622.2
367 TO 370	627.0	.0	627.0
371 TO 374	637.0	.0	637.0
375 TO 378	627.4	.0	627.4
379 TO 382	626.5	.0	626.5
383 TO 386	639.3	.0	639.3
387 TO 390	633.5	.0	633.5

EXHIBIT 9

ONHAND WILL BE REDUCED BY 050% OF SAFETY STOCK.
LOOKING FOR LESS THAN 1.0 TURNS.
FIRST 12 PCNTHS CF CRDERS USEC.

PROD. CODE	PART NUMBER	ONHAND QTY.	100% SAFETY STOCK	SCHED. REC.	TOTAL AVAIL.	CRDERS 1ST 12	ORDERS 2ND 12	TURN OVER	STANCARC COST CF EXCESS IN DOLLARS LABOR	MATERIAL	BURDEN	PRODUCTION YTD.	PYTD.	SERVICE YTD.	PYTD.
08265	..212243..	1			1			.0		21	21		5		
08265	..213756..	4	5		4	3	3	.7		21		2	5		
08265	..213350..	3	5		3	3	1	1.0				21	5		
08265	..225270..	5			5	3	3	.6	7	25	2	17	5		
08265	..225279..	5			5	3	3	.6					5		
08265	..228350..	6			6	3	3	.5	48	142	15		20		
08265	.A..2495AU	12			12	12	12	1.0		10			20		
08265	.A..291GFV	100			100	12	12	.1	55	325	21				
	6=2200 SER.														
08280	..204552..	87	5		84	27		.3		25		21	6		
08280	..204552A.	90	5		87	27		.3		32		21	6		
08280	..204552B.	87	5		84	27		.3		54		21	6		
08280	..212710..	78			78	27		.3		150	80	17	16		
08280	..213660..	118	20		108	27		.2		152		21	9		
08280	..213660A.	121	20		111	27		.2		120		21	9		
08280	..213660AA	120	20		110	27		.2		149		21	9		
08280	..213671..	47			47	9		.1	121	266	76	5	6		
08280	..213673..	52			52	9		.1		485		7	2		
08280	..213688..	45	10		40	18		.4		5		10	12		
08280	..213702..	21			21	9		.4		342		7	2		
08280	..213718..	20			20	9		.4		425	80	7	2		
08280	..225185..	18			18	9		.5	71	89	64	7	3		
08280	..225186..	33			33	9		.2	195	144	95	7	3		
08280	..225187..	41			41	9		.2	216	191		5	6		
08280	..225214..	11		7	11	9		.8	11	11	3	7	2		
08280	..225221..	5			12	9		.7	40	68	33	7	2		
08280	..225237..	5		19	24	9		.3	56	50	29	5	6		
08280	..225243..	9			9	9		1.0				7	10		
08280	..225245..	1		18	14	5		.4	234	167	177	5	2		
08280	..228093M.	14			14	9		.6	80	66	66	7			
08280	..228130A.	26		15	26	10		.4	50	313	28	7	3		
08280	..228141..	7		9	22	9		.4	1258	3234	1451	7			
08280	..228102..	7			16	9		.5	609	1235	644	4	3		
08280	..228135A.	10			10	9	3	.9	10	20	5	10	3		
08280	.A..2669FB	68			68	13		.1		220		10	3		
08280	.M..19A5N	17			17	9		.5		25		7			
08280	.M..2007AG	700			700	171		.2		215		133	38		2
08280	.M..2032A	22			22			.0		33		2	1	3	
08280	.M..2051MP	15			15	18		.4	15	8	5	10	25		
08280	.M..2510C	44			44	27		.2		1		17	12		
08280	.M..2071F.	100			100	27		.2		122		24	14		
08280	.M..24A3A5	87			87	36		.0		22			34		
08280	.M..2602..	99			99			.0		16		5	6		
08280	.MA..351..	14			16	9				5		8	8		
08280	.MA..379AB	22			22	9		.4		37					

NOTE: Turnover is the ratio of the number of parts for which there are firm orders for delivery in the next twelve months, divided by the number of parts currently available in inventory (excluding safety stocks).

Note: Turnover is the ratio of the number of parts for which there are firm orders for delivery in the next twelve months, divided by the number of parts currently available in inventory (excluding safety stocks).

This report is losing its usefulness. For one thing, machine tools now have lead times far in excess of the time period spanned by this report, so it's not much good for telling us when to add capacity, except after the fact. We've tried to use it to reschedule orders, too (delay delivery to a customer to free up capacity). But, we just seem to succeed in causing bottlenecks at other work centers, or collossal underloads develop.

MAY 1974

Tillich: I don't know how we're going to do it. Bonhoeffer wants me to commit to a goal of an inventory turnover of 3½ for next year's plan, and four for the year after. I know that the capital crunch is hitting us, but I just don't think it's possible for us to do it in this kind of business.

Buber: Well, we've got the extended materials planning program working pretty well at the Arco Foundry.[1] If we can extend that to our other long lead time vendors, that might help some. Maybe that with some more fine tuning on our production planning system we'll get turnover up some. One thing I can do for sure is to review that list of items with turnovers of less than one that we got from accounting (Exhibit 9).

Tillich: I doubt if those things will give us anywhere near as much help as we need though, Bill. For one thing, we're running into a lot of vendors who don't want anything to do with extended materials planning. I think it helps them as much if not more than us, but they can't conceive of running a business without a fat order backlog behind them. As for the system, I don't know. Maybe it's time we started out with a fresh sheet of paper instead of just adding more band-aids and patches here and there. But I can't conceive of a better basic system than the one we've got. Sure, our performance doesn't look so hot, but without the system we'd really be in trouble. I think that we'll have to do something more drastic than fine tuning to get inventories down.

---

[1] *Extended materials planning* was the name of the program Granger was presenting to its vendors which had very long lead times. With it, the company would commit to buying a certain amount of the vendor's capacity each year, rather than placing individual orders for specific products one to two years in advance of when they would be needed. Since vendors usually didn't enter these orders into production until a month or so before the due date, Granger could enter its orders a month or two in advance of their needs once they had reserved the capacity. They applied this concept at the Arco Foundry by treating the portion of Arco's capacity committed to them as their own in the materials requirements planning system.

CASE 18

Corning Glass Works—Erwin Automotive Plant

One morning in late December of 1974, Mike Jensen, production planner for Corning's Erwin Automotive Plant, had been reviewing a recent article in *The Wall Street Journal*. The article had discussed the tremendous uncertainties facing the auto industry during the next two quarters and through the remainder of the 70s. Those uncertainties had resulted from a changing national environmental policy, a growing economic recession, and the continuing energy shortage. All three of the U.S. auto companies had announced major cutbacks in production during the fourth quarter of 1974, and there were indications that these would continue into the first and second quarters of 1975.

This outlook had not pleased Mike Jensen because the Erwin plant—less than a year old—was highly dependent on the fortunes of the auto industry. Erwin produced only one product, Corning's CELCOR™ brand ceramic substrate, which was used in the catalytic converters required on the exhaust systems of most 1975 cars sold in the United States. Due primarily to the rapidly changing demand for new cars—and thus for converters—the Erwin plant's employment level had jumped from zero in January 1974 to 1,500 in June and then had fallen back to 500 hourly workers by October. While Mike felt that there had been some unusual circumstances surrounding the start-up of the plant which had accentuated these extreme employment shifts, it was clear that he faced a difficult task in developing aggregate production plans for 1975 that both met corporate objectives and minimized employment fluctuations and layoffs.

As Mike contemplated his immediate task of preparing an aggregate plan for the 13 four-week periods of 1975, he wanted to be sure that he had the best information available concerning demand and that the decision rules he applied were those most appropriate to the situation. Additionally, he

246

wanted to identify opportunities for improving his planning, such as more appropriate performance measures for the plant, more favorable contract terms with the auto companies, or better procedures for generating and evaluating alternative plans.

CELCOR™ PRODUCT HISTORY

The CELCOR™ product was of a type referred to as a monolith. While General Motors (GM) had developed its own catalytic converter concept involving the use of alumina beads coated with platinum, the monolith approach used a ceramic substrate (made of a mix of light-colored clays) honeycombed with many different surfaces that could be coated with platinum. The most common substrate produced by Corning was about the size and shape of a large soup can, 6 inches long and 3½ inches in diameter. Oval and ellipitical shapes were also common and could be produced equally well with Corning's production processes. The base of the substrate looked much like a piece of graph paper with 200–300 cells (small squares or triangles) per square inch. These cells ran the length of the substrate allowing exhaust gases to enter one end and exit at the other (Exhibit 1). While the product could vary in length, base shape, cell pattern (e.g., triangular rather than square), pattern density, and ceramic materials, the production process was essentially the same in all cases. (In all, the Erwin plant produced 22 different types of substrates.)

The basic substrate produced at the Erwin Automotive Plant passed through two other manufacturing operations after it left Erwin and before it reached the auto assembly plant. The first of these was performed by a company which added the catalyst. This involved a dipping process whereby the catalyst—usually platinum—was applied to all the surfaces of the substrate. The catalyzer company then shipped the units to a "canner," where the substrate was enclosed in a metal can and where all welding and sealing necessary to make the complete tail pipe assembly was done. The tail pipe assemblies were then sent to the automotive plants for use in final assembly.

EXHIBIT 1
Typical CELCOR™ Ceramic Substrates

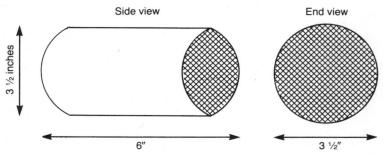

CELCOR™ had developed into a fully commercial product following a pattern typical of many of Corning's products. In 1971, a Corning development engineer had hit upon an idea for a product that would help the auto industry meet its 1975 emission control requirements. A technical team had been set up to develop an economical production process and to work with the auto industry in demonstrating the product's feasibility and Corning's ability to meet the requirements of individual auto companies.

Once Corning had been convinced that it possessed a usable product, it had begun negotiating with the major U.S. auto companies to obtain contracts for supplying a sufficient volume of substrates to justify building a new plant. That commitment had been realized in 1973, and construction of the plant at Erwin, New York, had started immediately. By January of 1974, the plant had been sufficiently completed to install production equipment; within two months, substrate production had begun. In April, the Erwin plant had shipped 50,000 substrates (production levels for the remainder of 1974 are shown in Exhibit 2).

Under the contract terms with the auto companies, Corning, the catalyzer, and the canner were each to keep two weeks of raw material inven-

EXHIBIT 2
Inventory, Production, and Shipments—Actuals for Last Six Months of 1974

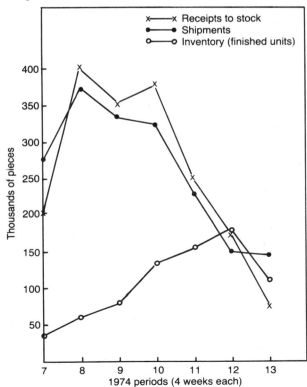

tory and two weeks of finished goods inventory on hand. This was required to minimize the chances of an automotive assembly plant having to close down due to a lack of finished tail pipe assemblies. Because of the substantial intermediate inventories and the pipeline throughput time of 13 weeks, the Erwin plant was subject to wide swings in demand.[1] As a practical matter, the auto companies with whom Corning had supply contracts—Ford, Chrysler, and Volkswagen—issued ship orders every couple of weeks which told Corning exactly how many substrates to ship in the coming period. Unfortunately, Corning's initial contracts with the auto companies had not anticipated the extent of shipping order fluctuations. In fact, the plant had realized only from recent experience that the auto companies tended to cut off shipments for several weeks at a time to draw down their own inventories when demand slumped.

Early 1974 had been a much more hectic period in the plant's development than anyone had anticipated. The auto companies had been extremely nervous about the EPA certification needed to sell 1975 model cars. This certification required most cars to be fitted with catalytic converters, so the auto companies had brought tremendous pressure on Corning to gear up quickly to preclude delay in final assembly of 1975 model cars (due to go on sale in September 1974). In addition, substantial initial production had been required simply to fill the catalytic converter pipeline. These start-up requirements and future potential had largely dictated the amount of production capacity installed at the outset.

An indication of the concern felt by the Erwin plant management had been the tension apparent at daily planning meetings held during the spring and summer of 1974. These meetings had involved the general manager of the automotive business, Bill Stroud, and three vice presidents from the corporation. On occasion, Tom MacAvoy, president of Corning Glass Works, had joined the meetings to keep abreast of the latest production progress (see organization chart, Exhibit 3). Ford and Chrysler had also sent their own people to the plant during that period to ensure getting their share of CELCOR™ production. Due to the pressures of that start-up period, little thought had been given to the plant's steady state production level. Rather, every effort had been concentrated on increasing the output of the plant and meeting customers' requirements as quickly as possible.

CELCOR™ MARKET

Corning's assessment of the substrate market had been extremely favorable from the outset. Even without GM as a customer, Corning had felt that it would be able to sell a substantial volume of substrates annually. The

---

[1] Pipeline throughput time for a unit was the time it took from when Corning shipped a given substrate until that substrate was part of a tail pipe assembly and ready to go onto a finished auto.

EXHIBIT 3
Organization Chart

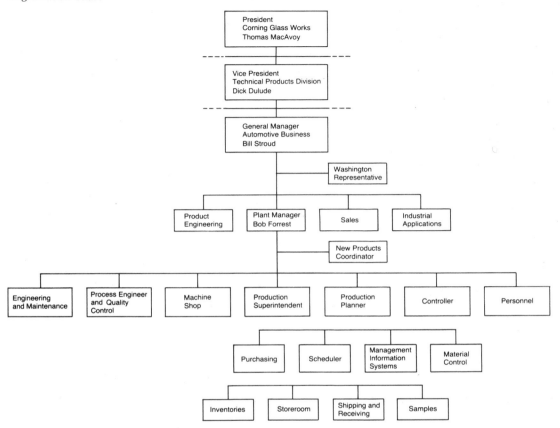

dollar volume had been expected to grow both as the number of units sold and as the unit price increased.[2] (Corning's competitors had used a different production process which Corning's engineers had felt would be more costly and difficult to control in the long run than its own.) There had been some chance that a delay or postponement of pollution standards for 1977 might enable other processes to be developed, but Corning had felt that the opportunities greatly outweighed that risk.

Corning had also felt that it commanded a competitive advantage in the substrate business due to its materials expertise and its innovative production process. The company's extensive background in ceramics had

---

[2] Management had felt that there was some chance that as pollution standards were tightened GM might have to go to a monolithic converter, in which case the Erwin plant would very likely become a supplier to GM. Tighter pollution standards would also require larger or more dense substrates, resulting in higher unit prices.

enabled it to identify the most appropriate mix of materials for making substrates, and its production and engineering skills had led to the design of manufacturing processes superior to those generally available. While the company in late 1974 did not have protective patents on all aspects of its substrate manufacturing, it was felt that its superior experience and knowledge as a company would make it extremely difficult for a competitor to copy the processes and materials mix and obtain the same results at comparable cost.

In late 1974, Corning had been investigating industrial uses of substrates with the hope of opening substantial new markets for CELCOR™. The most promising area appeared to be utilization of the honeycombed substrate in a large circular heat exchanger. Corning had been building such units with a slightly different production process, but there were indications that adaption of the CELCOR™ approach would provide substantial improvements and cost reductions in the product.

THE CELCOR™ PRODUCTION PROCESS

Production of the individual substrates was to tight specifications to ensure that the completed catalytic converter would have a life of 50,000 miles and use a minimum amount of platinum. Substrate porosity had to be closely controlled in manufacturing so the unit would not absorb excess platinum and cost considerably more than was necessary. The object from the auto company's point of view was to meet the standards but to minimize costs in so doing.

Substrate production at the Erwin plant was a three-step process. The initial step was the extrusion operation. In this phase ceramic materials were mixed, prepared, and extruded to obtain various lengths of substrate. These lengths were referred to as "green" logs and were placed in a green log inventory following inspection. The second step was the kiln operation. Green logs were batched and placed in one of the kilns where they remained for some number of days in order to be properly cured. Following firing they were referred to as "fired" logs and held in inventory for the next operation. The third step was the finishing operation where fired logs were cut into the appropriate lengths needed for the finished substrate, inspected, and packed in cartons for shipment to the catalyzer.

During the production operation workers had to keep close track of each individual kiln loading. Samples were taken from each lot and given an ID number and held for future reference. If at some time in the future an automotive company was forced to make a product recall, Corning could determine whether or not the defect was lot related.

A major management concern in the production of substrates at the Erwin Automotive Plant had been that of selection or yield. In the three-step production process, 100 percent inspections were carried out by quality control immediately following the first step of extrusion and then again towards the end of the finishing step. During plant start-up the yield at these points had been extremely low; but towards the latter part of 1974 they had improved substantially. Plant management had been confident that the yields could be further increased as direct labor personnel and management gained more experience in the production operations and control of the processes involved.

As a basis for monitoring the operation, plant management had established a standard cost system that assigned a full cost to each good unit produced. These costs included depreciation and overhead as well as direct material and labor. In December 1974, the standard cost of a good finished substrate had averaged $8.50. Of this cost about 10 percent represented depreciation charges, another 15 percent represented materials, direct hourly labor was 30 percent to 35 percent, and the balance represented contribution to overhead. (The high depreciation charges had been due to the substantial excess capacity at the plant.)

The weighted-average selling price per unit in late 1974 had been $8.90 per piece (prices had been predetermined by the terms of the contracts). While this had been a concern to plant management, their focus had been on managing gross margin and contribution margin since in the short run the plant did not have much control over the volume being shipped or the price per unit.

The average standard cost of a finished substrate held in inventory in late 1974 had been $9.80. This had exceeded the weighted-average cost of units shipped because a disproportionate amount of inventory had been in the slower moving items which tended to be more expensive and were run less frequently due to high setup costs.

The Erwin plant had maintained four basic inventories—raw materials, green logs, fired logs, and finished pieces. (The logs in a kiln were considered part of the green log inventory until firing was completed.) Historically, Corning's corporate policy had been to set a maximum dollar level for all its combined inventories and then to divide that up by plant. For example, in 1974 the Erwin Automotive Plant had been assigned a maximum inventory level of approximately $3 million. However, late in the year the corporation had been looking at the possibility of changing that criterion to one which measured inventory turnover. For a plant like Erwin, turnover would be measured by computing the standard cost of the units in the four inventories; this total would be divided into the total standard cost of budgeted sales for the year. If the company adopted this criterion for all its plants, which in December had appeared likely, corporate management would specify the desired number of inventory turns for Erwin. (Turns of 8–10 had been mentioned in some of the initial discussions with corporate management.)

PLANT OPERATING CONSTRAINTS AND
DECISION RULES[3]

In the first stage of production—extrusion—the Erwin plant had a number of separate production lines. Because of the high start-up costs associated with initiating production on any one line, the plant attempted either to run a given line for five days, 24 hours per day, or not at all. Operation of a single extrusion line required over 100 hourly workers and produced 1,000 to 2,000 green logs per 24-hour day. All of the extrusion lines were generally closed down at the end of the five-day week because of the high overtime costs of running on the weekend.

As green logs came off the extrusion lines they were 100 percent inspected. All good product was placed in large wire baskets and kept in inventory ready for firing. The plant had ample physical space, and even the peak 1974 inventory had not caused any storage problems. The plant tried to keep a minimum of 15,000 logs in green log inventory so that kiln firings would not be interrupted or have to be carried out with only a partial load.

The several identical kilns each had a batch capacity of 1,800 to 2,500 logs per firing, depending on the size and material mix of the product involved. Kiln firings were scheduled in a specific sequence due to technical requirements, energy costs, and energy availability. After firing, logs were placed in a fired log inventory and held for finishing. As with the green log inventory, a minimum of 15,000 fired logs was considered necessary in order to ensure a smooth production flow in finishing. Kiln operations continued seven days per week due to scheduling sequence requirements and needed 15 employees to monitor the kilns regardless of the number of firings per week.

The finishing process was scheduled by kiln lot in order to keep track of the ID number for each unit. Finishing capacity was measured in terms of the number of good units produced per line shift and completed units were referred to as receipts to stock (RTS) when they entered the finished goods inventory. The plant had several fully equipped finishing lines. Each could be run one, two, or three line shifts per day on a five-day week. Finishing output ranged from 1,500 to 2,300 good substrates per line shift. Approximately 30 people were required to operate a single line shift.

THE PLANT PRODUCTION PLANNER

Mike Jensen, Erwin's production planner, had joined the CELCOR™ operation in July 1974. Mike's previous experience had included running his own small manufacturing firm, working as a research engineer for a substantial oil firm, working as a staff assistant in a recreational firm, and

---

[3] Given the depressed state of the U.S. auto industry in late 1974, management has felt that the Erwin plant had ample equipment capacity for the next few years in all three of its production stages.

two years as an MBA student at the Harvard Business School. Since receiving his initial assignment as planner for the Erwin plant, Mike's responsibilities had evolved to their present scope and included the following tasks:

a. Development of an overall aggregate manufacturing plan for the 13 periods of 1975 and a detailed production schedule for the most immediate three periods (12 weeks).
b. Control of all plant inventories.
c. Development of improved inventory control procedures.
d. Interfacing with the CELCOR™ sales department in obtaining demand forecasts and meeting customer shipping requirements.
e. Management of samples production for the sales department.
f. Budget preparation and control.

In addition to these major areas of responsibility, Mike had recently been given responsibility for data processing at the plant level. As shown in the organization chart in Exhibit 3, Mike had four areas reporting to him—purchasing, materials control, MIS, and scheduling.

During the past six months, Mike had developed a number of decision rules to assist him in planning. His objective had been to improve the plans and schedules on an incremental basis as quickly as possible. He had anticipated that by early 1975 things would be running smoothly and that he could then take time to review those decision rules and determine how they could be better tuned or perhaps even replaced with a more useful set of rules. The existing set of rules which Mike intended to apply to his immediate task of preparing an aggregate plan for 1975 included the following:

1. *In-process inventories.*   Mike's experience had shown him that to keep production flowing smoothly and to avoid shutdowns or slowdowns caused by lack of product, a minimum of 15,000 green logs should be in inventory waiting for firing and a minimum of 15,000 fired logs needed to be in inventory waiting for finishing. The combined green and fired inventories needed to total 40,000 logs to provide sufficient flexibility so that kiln firings could be altered to balance the two in-process inventories.

2. *Kiln firings per week.*   The energy conservation and technical considerations necessitated a certain sequence of kiln firings and required that the kilns be operated seven days a week with an average of 2.3, 4.6, or 6.9 kiln firings per week. (These three rates of firings were based on experience and used for both planning and operating purposes. The firing rate had to be set at one of these three levels for any given week, but did not have to be held constant for an entire period and in fact there was no advantage to keeping firings per week at a constant level over time.)

3. *Product mix.*   Experience had shown that it was best not to mix the production of substrates requiring different combinations of ceramic

materials. Thus, even if more than one extrusion line were running, Mike would schedule all of the lines to produce products that used the same set of input materials. Similarly, in firing and finishing Mike tried to batch identical products to maximize production efficiency.

4. *Five-day plant operation.* Because of the high cost of overtime for weekend work, Mike tried to plan five-day workweeks for all operations but the kilns.

5. *Maintaining stability.* Any changes in the work force level or production output rates was disruptive and costly, so Mike tried to minimize the number of such changes.

EXISTING PLANNING PROCEDURES

As a first step in preparing an aggregate plan for 1975, Mike had decided to outline the procedures he had used recently for a somewhat shorter time horizon.

The starting point for Mike's aggregate plan was the shipments forecast that he and the sales department had developed. While they had developed a pessimistic and optimistic set of forecasts, Mike felt that as a first cut he would stick with the most likely set. (These shipment forecasts are shown in Exhibit 4.)

EXHIBIT 4
Sales Forecast for Calendar 1975* (by four-week periods)

	Optimistic	Realistic	Pessimistic (worst case)
1	160,000	150,000	130,000
2	165,000	145,000	120,000
3	190,000	145,000	115,000
4	245,000	170,000	140,000
5	300,000	210,000	150,000
6	340,000	230,000	150,000
7	360,000	225,000	155,000
8	375,000	230,000	160,000
9	340,000	225,000	165,000
10	315,000	215,000	150,000
11	305,000	210,000	160,000
12	300,000	215,000	165,000
13	275,000	230,000	160,000
Total substrate sales	3,670,000	2,600,000	1,920,000

* Based on marketing's estimates of demand from existing automotive customers for CELCOR™ substrates and on customers' estimates of seasonal factors affecting shipment rates. (Optimistic, realistic, and pessimistic forecasts assumed annual total auto sales of 9.0, 8.0, and 7.5 million cars, respectively.) The estimates considered auto assembly requirements only and did not include the status of pipeline inventories between Erwin and the assembly plants.

Following agreement on a most likely shipment forecast, Mike had reviewed the present level of operations. One of Mike's goals had been to maintain the status quo as long as possible because of the substantial disruption caused by changing the size of the work force and the level of plant output. Thus he would first project the receipts to stock (RTS) based on the existing level of operations and assuming shipments matched the forecast.

As a practical matter Mike used a form like Exhibit 5 in his aggregate planning. He selected the number of finishing line shifts for a period, used that and a weighted-average output of 2,000 good substrates per line shift to compute RTS for the period, and then used the shipments forecast and the previous ending inventory to determine that period's ending inventory. The procedure was repeated for each subsequent period, remembering that the number of finishing line shifts could be altered whenever ending inventory tended to get out of line.

EXHIBIT 5
Aggregate Planning Form, 1975—Inventory, Receipts to Stock, Shipments

1975 Period	Finishing Line Shifts *	Receipts to Stock †	Shipments ‡	Ending Inventory §
1	4	160,000	150,000	120,000
2	4	160,000	145,000	135,000
3			145,000	
4			170,000	
5			210,000	
6			230,000	
7			225,000	
8			230,000	
9			225,000	
10			215,000	
11			210,000	
12			215,000	
13			230,000	

* Beginning production level, period 1 = 4 line shifts per day in finishing.
† Based on weighted-average output of 2,000 good substrates per line shift.
‡ From sales department shipment forecast (Exhibit 4).
§ Beginning inventory, period 1 = 110,000.

With a tentative aggregate plan for finishing, Mike used a form like Exhibit 6 to develop a plan for extrusion. First he converted the RTS in Exhibit 5 to equivalent good logs using a factor of four good substrates per good green log. (This conversion factor included the appropriate yield factor for the finishing operation.) Next he selected the number of extrusion line days for a period, used that and a weighted-average output of 1,500 good green logs per line day as a standard to compute "green logs produced," and then used the "logs required" and the previous period's ending inventory to determine that period's "ending inventory."

EXHIBIT 6
Aggregate Planning Form, 1975—Extrusion Log Production, Total In-Process Inventory

Period	Extrusion (line days)*	Green Logs Produced†	Logs Required by Finishing‡	Total Ending Log Inventory§
1	1	30,000	40,000	50,000
2	1	30,000	40,000	40,000
3				
4				
5				
6				
7				
8				
9				
10				
11				
12				
13				

* Beginning production level, period 1 = 1 line day.
† Based on average-weighted output of 1,500 good green logs per line day.
‡ Computed from RTS in Exhibit 5 assuming four good substrates per green log.
§ Beginning log inventory, period 1 = 60,000. Includes both green and fired logs. This measure is used as a rough cut to determine green log production needs. It is further divided into green and fired log components to calculate kiln firings (Exhibit 7).

The four factors of no weekend work, no work force reductions, a minimum number of work force expansions, and minimum inventory were used in planning both finishing and extrusion operations. In evaluating his plans, Mike felt it less costly to vary the level of finishing operations than to vary extrusion operating levels because he could vary smaller units of capacity in finishing (line shifts) than in extrusion (line days) and the extrusion operation presented the more difficult quality control and yield problems.

With a complete plan for finishing and extrusion, Mike used a form like Exhibit 7 to plan kiln firings. This involved taking "green logs produced" from Exhibit 6, using starting inventories of green and fired logs and computing kiln firings and ending fired and green log inventories for each period. As a practical matter, Mike assumed that firings had to be some multiple of 2.3 per week, but not to exceed 27.6 per period, and he assumed an average batch size of 2,100 logs per firing.

Once a plan was completed for all 13 periods, it was evaluated using two rules of thumb. First, as a minimum the contract required that approximately half of the period's shipments be on hand at the beginning of the four-week period. Second, total inventories should be kept under 400,000 equivalent pieces. (Each log was considered equivalent to four good pieces.) If the plan violated these rules, then Mike would alter production levels to correct it. There was considerable judgment involved in deciding how much to alter the output rate of the two main departments and exactly

EXHIBIT 7
Aggregate Planning Form, 1975—Kiln Firings

Period	Green Logs Produced[a]	Fired Logs Required by Finishing[b]	Minimum Required Firings[c]	Actual Number of Firings[d]	Actual Number of Logs Fired[e]	Ending Green Log Inventory[f]	Ending Fired Log Inventory[g]
1	30,000	40,000	14.3	16.1	33,810	26,190	23,810
2	30,000	40,000	17.2	18.4	38,640	17,550	22,450
3							
4							
5							
6							
7							
8							
9							
10							
11							
12							
13							

[a] From Exhibit 6.

[b] From Exhibit 6.

[c] Based on an average of 2,100 logs per kiln firing. Minimum required kiln firings = (Fired logs required by finishing − Beginning fired log inventory + Minimum desired inventory level) ÷ 2,100 logs per firing. For period 1: (40,000 − 30,000 + 20,000) ÷ 2,100 = 14.3).

[d] Based on the rule that kiln firings may only occur in multiples of 2.3 per week with a maximum of 27.6 firings per period (see text). To cover period 1 minimum required firings (14.3), the kilns must be fired 16.1 times.

[e] Actual firings × 2,100 logs per firing.

[f] Beginning green log inventory for period 1 = 30,000. Ending green log inventory = Beginning green log inventory + Green log production − Actual logs fired. Minimum desired inventory level is 15,000 logs; minimum desired total inventory of green and fired logs is 40,000 logs. For period 1: 30,000 + 30,000 − 33,810 = 26,190.

[g] Beginning fired log inventory = 30,000. Ending fired log inventory = Beginning fired log inventory + Actual logs fired − Logs required by finishing. For period 1: 30,000 + 33,810 − 40,000 = 23,810. Minimum desired inventory level is 15,000 logs.

when to do it so that the new level of output could be maintained for as long as possible. While Mike might try half a dozen or more variations in the plan, he realized that he had no way of knowing how close his final plan was to the optimum.

TRADE-OFF CONSIDERATIONS

Mike had felt that each of the decision rules he used in planning involved certain trade-offs which always needed to be weighed carefully. He had summarized the major factors he examined when evaluating these trade-offs as follows:

1. *Maintenance of a five-day workweek.* The economics of overtime had made it unattractive to schedule extrusion or finishing operations for the weekend.
2. *Elimination of work force reductions.* The cost of layoffs had been very high for a number of reasons. First, all hourly workers at Corning had been represented by a single union and the labor contract had provided for bumping. This meant that if a finishing line shift were laid off, senior people on that shift were able to bump anyone else in a Corning area plant with less seniority. Thus, for each person laid off there would on average be two or three job changes, which caused disruptions at other Corning locations as well as at the Erwin plant. Second, motivation of employees remaining always had been extremely low after a layoff. With management continually urging increased production, after a layoff occurred hourly workers—fearing they would run out of work—tended to lower output per labor-hour. This made it extremely difficult to produce efficiently and continue to reduce costs through yield improvements.
3. *Minimization of expansions in production levels.* While hourly workers never complained about expansion of the level of output, it did cause considerable disruption. Shift supervisors had to learn to deal with a new group of people; different production standards and performance measures had to be established; and worker efficiency tended to decrease even if only temporarily.
4. *Minimization of inventory.* Erwin had to maintain adequate inventory to fulfill contract provisions and balance operations. However, the plant generally had kept inventories as small as possible since inventory was one of the factors by which Corning had evaluated the Erwin plant's performance.

The output of Mike's planning procedure was a set of documents like Exhibits 5, 6, and 7 which he gave to Plant Manager Bob Forrest, General Manager Bill Stroud, production supervisors, and sales personnel. Ending inventory figures went to the plant controller where they were converted into dollar amounts and compared with specified performance measures.

From the aggregate plan Mike had his scheduler prepare a detailed 12-week production schedule for each of the plant's 22 substrates.

The aggregate plan provided a helpful detailed guide for materials control and purchasing. It had not been uncommon for the basic ceramic materials and packaging materials to require a two- to three-period lead time in ordering. The aggregate plan allowed scheduling of rail car arrivals to balance production needs against the costs of early arrivals. In the initial months of the plant's operation bulk ceramic materials had often arrived far ahead of production needs and demurrage charges of $50 per day per rail car had run at a level of $20,000–$30,000 per period. (Storage facilities for these materials were limited.) Due partly to better aggregate plans and improvements in Mike's organization, demurrage had recently been brought under control and reduced to about $2,000 per period.

PRODUCTION PLANNING FOR 1975

Mike's immediate task had been preparation of an aggregate plan for the 13 periods in 1975. In preparing the plan, he wanted to consider closing the plant for two weeks vacation during the year if that would better meet his objectives. While at least one of those two weeks would need to occur in the summer so that employees would have part of their vacation when children were out of school, he felt that he could designate the other week almost any time during the year. For technical reasons, kilns had to continue to be operated during plant close-downs at the minimum of 2.3 firings per week, and could be operated up to the maximum rate of 6.9 per week if so desired.

In recent discussions with the department foreman of the extrusion operation, Mike had learned that the output of good green logs for the current period had been running 30–40 percent above standard due to workers producing at a faster rate than budgeted. (Yield at this point had not changed.) He had felt justified in assuming that this level could be maintained if doing so eliminated the need to lay off a shift in finishing. (There was sufficient group spirit in the plant that extrusion probably could maintain the high level of output if they knew the jobs of people in finishing depended on it.)

For the longer run, Mike had realized that there were several areas on which he might focus his attentions in order to improve his planning procedures and the production operations of the plant. These had included:

Development of more and better cost data. While Mike had felt that the information available to him in December had been adequate for planning, he had not had time during the hectic first nine months of plant operation to analyze the appropriateness of his cost inputs or to develop additional cost data.

Preparation of a computer model that would make it easier to evaluate alternative aggregate plans, to test alternative decision rules, and to perform sensitivity analyses on the impact of uncertain shipment forecasts and fluctuating production yields.

Development of improved forecasting procedures utilizing auto company sales data, information on inventories in the catalytic converter pipeline, and more formal forecasting techniques.

An evaluation of possible alternative contract terms with the auto companies that would provide greater stability for the Erwin plant.

An analysis of the relevant costs for the major trade-offs involved in the aggregate planning task and the conversion of the results into useful decision rules.

CASE 19

Cross River Products Company

In mid-November of 1975, Mr. George Spaulding, vice president of manufacturing at Cross River Products, was preparing production plans for the next several months. The aggregate planning task was not new to George or his production staff; however marketing was forecasting sales of 66,000 units in February of 1976 for the company's major product line, the umbroller, almost double the present rate of 35,000 per month. George had already identified options such as adding a second shift, staffing a secondary assembly line, utilizing overtime, and building some finished goods inventory. Before committing himself, he wanted to be sure that he had plans that could most efficiently handle this peak requirement and yet would not undo the progress in operations that he had been able to achieve over the past several months.

Complicating the problem of February's peak demand for umbrollers was the fact that one of the company's secondary products, a portable playcrib, was also showing a steady increase in demand. George was anxious to tie together the relevant planning considerations for both products by November 21. At that time he would sit down with the other members of top management to outline his plan and discuss its implications and justification.

CORPORATE BACKGROUND

Cross River Products had been formed in 1970 by two budding entrepreneurs not long out of a well-known eastern business school. Based on a product idea they had seen in Europe, Cross River began by producing the umbroller, a collapsible, lightweight stroller. Like many young companies, Cross River had difficulties attracting the capital required for expansion. In 1974, the founding management sold their interests and left for other endeavors, and a new management team including George Spaulding and his production people took over.

By late 1975, the umbroller product had captured almost a third of the U.S. and Canadian stroller market and two thirds of the collapsible, lightweight stroller market. In addition, the company had developed and was producing two other products—a portable, lightweight child's playcrib and a lightweight backpack for carrying a child.

In late 1975, the umbroller product accounted for a large portion of the company's sales. The portable playcrib had recently begun to attract attention among retailers, and Ron Klammer, the company's vice president of marketing, was predicting an increase in demand for that product. Sales of the backpack were only a small part of the company's volume in late 1975.

Manufacturing at Cross River Products was both a fabrication and an assembly operation. This was due to the nature of the products themselves. All three products required a small number of standard components, many of them requiring raw materials common to all the products. This enabled the company both to maintain small inventories (inventory turns were 20+ times per year in late 1975) and have access to a number of alternative sources of supply for the various components since no special tooling was required by suppliers.[1]

Marketing at Cross River Products was the responsibility of a vice president of marketing and a national sales manager. In addition, the company utilized the services of approximately 20 independent marketing representatives who carried Cross River Products as well as complementary products from other manufacturers. These reps called on various retail and wholesale accounts in their respective geographical areas, seeking orders for the company's products. The vice president of marketing and the national sales manager identified potential new accounts, sought major commitments from large retail chains, identified new marketing reps, and set corporate marketing policies.

PRODUCTS AND MARKETS

Ron Klammer and his marketing organization had successfully increased both the company's market share and its unit sales of the umbroller for the past three years. (See Exhibit 1 for actual umbroller sales.) Although Ron was aggressively trying to expand sales in both Europe and Canada, his forecasts for umbroller sales (Exhibit 1) indicated that U.S. demand would represent most of the 1976 sales. Ron anticipated that demand for the umbroller would follow a seasonal pattern as it had in the past with the peak occurring during the winter as retailers stocked up for spring sales.

The 20 independent marketing representatives sold the company's prod-

---

[1] Inventory turnover (turns) were calculated by dividing the annual cost of goods sold by the average inventory.

EXHIBIT 1
Monthly Umbroller Sales—Actual and Forecasts*

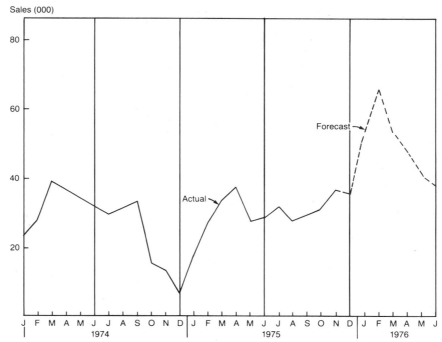

Total Monthly Umbroller Sales (Canadian portion)†

	1974	1975	1976
January	23,000	18,000 (3,000)	*53,000 (15,000)
February	27,500	27,000 (6,000)	*66,000 (13,000)
March	39,000	34,000 (7,000)	*54,000 (12,000)
April.	37,000	38,000 (8,000)	*49,000 (9,000)
May	35,000	28,000 (7,000)	*42,000 (9,000)
June	32,000	29,000 (6,000)	38,000 (8,000)
July	28,000	32,000 (7,000)	
August	29,500	28,000 (5,000)	
September . . .	33,500	30,000 (5,000)	
October.	16,000	32,000 (6,000)	
November. . . .	13,500	37,000 (7,000)	
December. . . .	7,000	*36,000 (8,000)†	
Totals. . . .	321,000	369,000	

* Forecast.
† The figure in parentheses represents the number of units going to Canada for completion of final assembly. For example, in December of 1975, it is anticipated that Rochester will ship 36,000 units, but of those, 8,000 will be shipped with seats, wheels, and frames not yet completely assembled. This assembly will then be completed in Canada. The firm has been sending units to Canada for final assembly since late 1974.

ucts to approximately 1,500 active accounts each year. Ron estimated that there were a total of 2,500–3,000 potential accounts in the United States and Canada for Cross River Products. Approximately 35 percent of U.S. sales went to discounters, an equal amount was sold through catalogs and showrooms, about 20 percent went to major retail chains, and the remaining 10 percent were sold in department stores. The umbroller retailed for $17–$28, depending on the model and the type of retail outlet involved. The average retail price was about $25. The wholesale price ranged from $12.50–$14.95, depending on the model.

Competition for Cross River's umbroller came from two sources: other manufacturers who imitated Cross River's design almost exactly and manufacturers who copied the general design and the folding principle, but who substituted heavier steel tubing for the aluminum support pieces. Cross River considered these steel strollers to be in a somewhat different market niche since they were heavier and consequently more difficult to carry. The company did not feel that the old-fashioned pram (buggy) with its substantial size, weight, and expense was competition for the umbroller.

The umbroller was available in three models: one with four shock absorbers, one with two shock absorbers, and one without shocks. Each of these models had seats made of one of four colors (yellow, yellow and blue hounds-tooth check, light blue, or pumpkin orange); each had rubber handles and fabric straps that were color coordinated with the seats. In spite of the variety of models and colors, each umbroller could be made with the same production operation and with only a minimum variation in labor input.

Although the company's portable playcrib and backpack had been on the market for over three years, there had been no major marketing effort for either product until mid-1975. At that time the sales organization began a

EXHIBIT 2
Monthly Playcrib Sales—Actuals and Forecasts*, 1974–1976 (June)

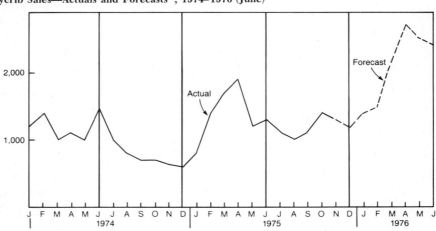

EXHIBIT 2 (*concluded*)

Playcribs

	1974	1975	1976
January	1,200	800	1,400*
February	1,400	1,400	1,500*
March	1,000	1,700	2,200*
April	1,100	1,900	2,700*
May	1,000	1,200	2,500*
June	1,500	1,300	2,400*
July	1,000	1,100	
August	800	1,000	
September	700	1,100	
October	700	1,400	
November	650	1,300	
December	600	1,200*	
Totals	11,650		

Backpacks

	1974	1975	1976
January	900	1,600	1,700*
February	1,700	2,300	2,500*
March	1,800	2,100	2,400*
April	1,500	2,400	2,400*
May	2,000	1,800	2,100*
June	1,400	1,700	1,800*
July	1,100	1,200	
August	1,100	900	
September	1,200	1,100	
October	900	1,000	
November	800	1,000	
December	600	1,200*	
	15,000		

Monthly Backpack Sales—Actuals and Forecasts*, 1974–1976 (June)

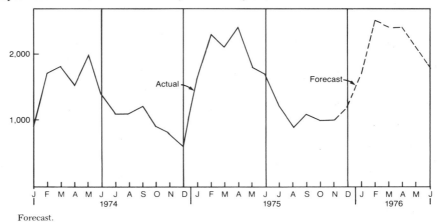

Forecast.

systematic push of the portable playcrib. The results were already beginning to appear as orders had been climbing substantially for each of the past several weeks. (See Exhibit 2 for actual sales and forecasts for these two products.)

MANUFACTURING OPERATIONS

The company's manufacturing activities were under the direction of George Spaulding. (See Exhibit 3 for an organization chart.) A graduate of the U.S. Naval Academy, George had several years as a naval officer and had worked many years in production management. It was George's philosophy that with good line management and firm leadership, production could be run efficiently and still respond to the important needs of marketing and finance. During his past year at Cross River, George had reduced product costs substantially (both in terms of labor and material content), improved delivery performance, and upgraded quality (as measured by number of returns and waste). While George was continuing his efforts in these areas, he saw a major part of his current task as running the production operation that he had now established and adapting it to meet changing marketing requirements.

The company's main production facility was located in an old factory building in Rochester, New York, and a satellite plant was maintained in Canada. The Canadian operation combined the completed seat assemblies, completed wheel assemblies, and completed frames manufactured in Rochester and packaged them for sale in Canada. (Completing the assembly in Canada allowed the units to be marked as "Product of Canada," which marketing felt was an important factor affecting Canadian sales.)

The company divided production into five main tasks: sewing, metal fabrication, plastic molding, subassembly, and final assembly. In the sewing operation, the workers cut the fabric and sewed it to form the seats and

EXHIBIT 3
Organization Chart, August 1975

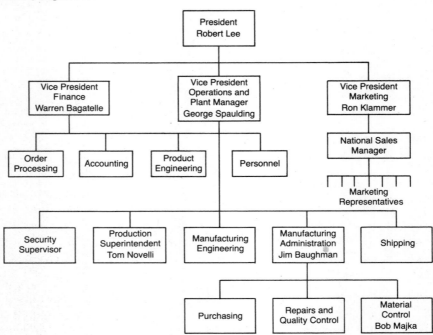

straps for strollers and backpacks and the bottom and side webbing for playcribs. In metal fabrication, the workers cut the aluminum tubing to prespecified lengths, punched holes, and formed required shapes. In plastic molding, parts for wheels and joints were injection molded. The subassembly operators assembled wheels and riveted together basic components prior to final assembly. For the umbroller product, a moving conveyor belt paced the final assembly production line. For the other two products, individual workers performed the full set of final assembly tasks on a batch basis. Until recently, George Spaulding had felt that the volume for these two products had been too low to justify an assembly line process for them.

The Rochester plant layout in late 1975 was as shown in Exhibit 4. The various processes were separated physically so that the noise from one task would not adversely affect the work in other areas.

Because of the company's umbroller volume, George had organized a conveyor-paced production line for its final assembly. This line (referred to as A line) had an output of approximately 2,000 units per day from a single shift. He had also set up a secondary conveyor-paced line (referred to as B line) that could produce 1,000 units per day of the umbroller product on a single-shift basis. In fabrication, sewing, plastic molding, and subassembly, individual workers repeated sets of tasks that might take anywhere from 15 to 60 seconds. Standards had been established for each task, and workers were expected to produce daily the number of units specified by the standard.

Due to the growing demand for playcribs, George had asked Jim Baughman, manufacturing administrator, to update plans that had been prepared several months ago for a conveyor-paced final assembly line for the playcrib. This line would have a single-shift capacity of 100–200 units per day, depending on the size of the work force operating the line. To date, both George and Jim felt that the volume of playcrib production did not justify paced-production assembly for that product.

THE WORK FORCE

With the exception of the workers in the sewing area, the plant's work force was unskilled and high turnover was a constant problem.[2] The founders of the company had made a point of hiring handicapped workers, and several of the most productive people in fabrication and assembly were deaf or mentally handicapped. In mid-1974, the textile workers' union had become the bargaining agent for virtually all of the hourly employees. Management considered this a positive factor since they could now deal with the workers as one group through the union.

Wage rates for the hourly workers ranged from $2.50 to $3.25 per hour on a straight-time basis and were competitive with alternative jobs available

---

[2] Turnover was presently averaging 1 percent per month for hourly employees.

EXHIBIT 4

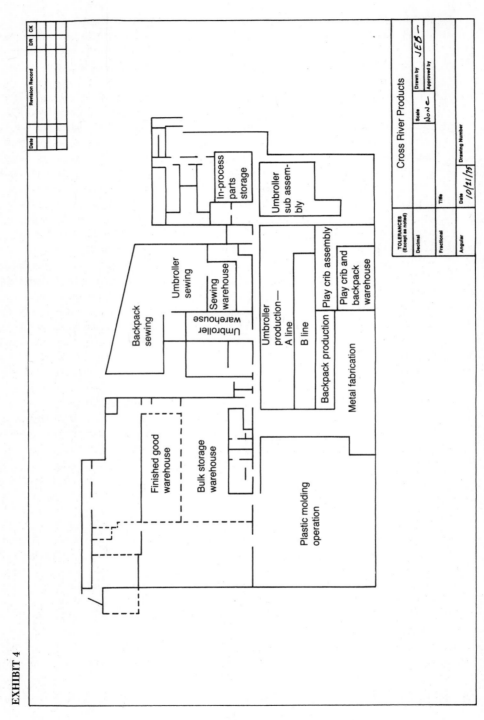

* Only outside lines are walls. Internal lines represent designated work areas as of October 1975.

to unskilled workers in the Rochester area. The actual pay rate for each individual was based strictly on seniority since all jobs were considered unskilled. Prior to signing the union contract, workers in the sewing area had been on an incentive, piece-rate basis; however, all workers were now paid on a day-rate basis. Because all jobs were considered unskilled, supervisors had complete discretion on the assignment of workers. They tended to assign tasks on the basis of personal work habits and general abilities, but no worker performed one job exclusively over more than a one- or two-week period. (The exceptions to this were in the sewing room and plastic molding where those actually operating the machines performed the same tasks on a permanent basis.)

Like many manufacturing operations employing low-skilled workers, Cross River suffered from high absenteeism, particularly on Mondays. Since workers were paid at the end of the shift on Friday, absenteeism was low on that day. The personnel department had recently initiated a program of making personal calls to missing workers on Monday mornings hoping to cut Monday's absenteeism from 8 percent to a more reasonable 3 percent or 4 percent. While labor was not particularly tight in the Rochester area, and while management had observed that most workers reached their full efficiency within one week of hiring,[3] it was difficult to find good workers. (The union contract allowed termination for just cause, which included layoffs required by declines in demand, with no required severance pay.).

On occasion in the past the company had operated a second shift. However, George Spaulding felt that a second shift spread existing production management too thin and required additional planning and control procedures to coordinate between shifts. Added to this were the higher direct labor rates—a 10 percent premium over straight time—and the fact that a second shift tended to be less productive than the first shift. Thus while George did not preclude the possibility, he considered other options to be less costly than this one.

Most workers were willing to work some overtime since they were paid time and a half for anything over 40 hours per week. However, George tended to plan production operations on the basis of straight time, using overtime only to complete the subassemblies or component parts needed for the following day's operations. (Actual overtime had averaged less than two hours per week per employee over the past several months.)

PRODUCTION AND MATERIAL CONTROL

One of George's first tasks in late 1974 had been to develop two important production guidelines: (1) since the umbroller was the company's main product, production should meet its requirements first and treat the

---

[3] The typical new hire worked at 75 percent normal efficiency during the first week on the job.

other products' requirements as secondary; and (2) since the major owners of the company wanted expansion to be based on internally generated funds and since the company already factored all its receivables, umbrollers should be built only to confirmed orders.[4] This second point necessitated an extremely flexible operation since variations in demand were handled principally by adjustments in production rates and not by a finished goods inventory.

Production and material control were under the direction of Jim Baughman, manufacturing administrator. Working for Jim was Bob Majka who handled the mechanics of material control. One of the goals Jim had given to Bob was to meet all delivery dates for confirmed orders. While Jim and marketing had never tried to determine explicitly the value of doing this, it was clear that lost sales would result if they missed very many delivery requests. Jim had also requested that Bob avoid early production both because of the financing requirements that would entail and because most retailers had limited warehouse space and thus were unwilling to accept early deliveries.

The company relied on aggregate planning to time the arrival of materials from suppliers so as to avoid stockouts of raw materials and yet maintain small inventories. Accounting provided Bob and his assistant with a list of total orders for each of the next 12–15 weeks. This list showed confirmed and unconfirmed orders by model and color for each week. Based on this order spread, which was updated each Friday and moved forward one week, Bob would issue ship orders to suppliers with whom Cross River had purchase contracts. About 50 percent of all orders were confirmed one week or less prior to their required shipping date, 25 percent were confirmed one to three weeks in advance, and the balance were confirmed more than three weeks in advance.

Since the company was purchasing standard raw materials from suppliers, it had been possible to establish two sources for most items and to set up open contracts that specified purchases of a minimum quantity over an extended period of time. Ship orders were then placed one to nine weeks in advance of requirements, depending on the lead time required by that supplier. Bob alternated his weekly purchases between the two sources. He determined the quantity to order by examining anticipated production for the week in question, existing stocks, units in transit, and expected production in the next few weeks. Since fabric material had to be ordered in mill run quantities, Bob issued make and ship orders for those only once or twice per month.

---

[4] Factoring of receivables simply amounted to borrowing working capital from a bank or other financing source using accounts receivable as collateral. In practice, each time an order was shipped, the company could borrow against that receivable, and then when it was paid, the money went directly to the factorer.

When Bob or other members of the management team became aware of pending fluctuations in umbroller volume, those became topics for discussion during the weekly planning and scheduling meeting. When the required work force changes appeared to be substantial, as they did for February 1976, the production management team spent considerable time gathering and analyzing information and evaluating a range of options.

To accommodate week-to-week variations in production mix and volume requirements, a scheduling system that operated on a one-week time horizon had been instituted. Each Wednesday, Bob Majka outlined the following week's umbroller production by spreading the confirmed orders according to delivery requirements and rules of thumb for minimizing production changeovers. After review and approval by George Spaulding, Jim Baughman, and others, this provided a daily production plan for final assembly which could be used to determine subassembly, component, and raw material requirements for the three days preceding final assembly. At this point raw material supplies were also checked to be sure they were adequate and to identify items that required expediting or rescheduling.

The next step in the scheduling procedure was the responsibility of Tom Novelli, production superintendent, who prepared a work plan for the week. While the total manpower did not vary widely from week to week, there were often major changes in the assignment of workers to various tasks and various products on a day-to-day basis in order to utilize available labor-hours in the best way possible. For example, since absenteeism was highest on Mondays, production for Canada was scheduled on that day since Canadian units required fewer people on final assembly.[5] Similarly, if Tom needed to complete an order on a particular day, he might assign extra people to components and subassembly in anticipation of that. This meant that fewer people would be making playcribs and backpacks on such days. To compensate for this, the plant tried to maintain a one- to two-week finished goods inventory on these two products so that orders could still be filled quickly.

As a final step in scheduling, a breakdown of the parts, components, and subassemblies was prepared to show the section supervisors the quantities that would be required as production shifted from one model and color of umbroller to another. It was Tom's responsibility to see that the proper parts of each order came together for assembly according to schedule. The actual transition between different colors and models was generally done without interruption as long as such changes did not occur more than two to three times per day.

---

[5] Rochester production for Canada required only 18 people on the final assembly line rather than the normal 26 people, since wheels and seats were not attached at that time. Rather, these components and the assembled frame were sent to Canada where assembly was completed and the units were packaged. Shipments to Canada were made on a daily basis in the company's own truck.

UMBROLLER PRODUCTION

Once the schedules had been set for all production operations for the week, section supervisors took responsibility for meeting those schedules. In sewing, this required that seats and straps be made for the umbrollers that would be in final assembly on the following day.

In metal fabrication, all bending and forming of the aluminum tubing was identical for all models, and thus it was the total output of these items as specified on the schedule that was important. However, as a part of this fabrication, the appropriate number of shaped handles had to be transferred to the plastic molding area for attachment of the colored plastic grips. These handles were then returned on a continuous basis and held for the following day's subassembly activities.

There were four distinct subassemblies prepared prior to final assembly—left and right side assemblies including wheels and two cross-piece assemblies. The subassembly operations produced one day in advance of final assembly. As the frame subassemblies were developed, they were passed from one station to another on gravity feed bars: upon completing a task, the worker would place the partially completed subassembly on the high end of a slanted metal bar and the piece would slide down about a 10-foot length where another worker would remove it and perform the next task. The bars each held 1,000 pieces and each worker was expected to empty the incoming bar for his station twice during the day.

In order to keep in-process inventories at a minimum, three full-time stock handlers were employed to move subassemblies and components to the next production phase as soon as they were ready.[6] These material handlers were also responsible for supplying the workers in their assigned area with the parts they required so that there would be no waiting.

After subassemblies were completed, they came together at the final production line. The main A line was paced by a moving conveyor and required 26 people for full production of 2,000 units per day. (Only 18 workers were required when frames were being assembled for shipment to Canada.) The tasks performed on the final assembly line included joining the frame subassemblies, attaching the foot strap, cleaning the aluminum (it became soiled with handling), attaching seats, final inspection, and packaging. Rejects from the final assembly operation ran about 5 percent. Two additional employees took these to a repair area and replaced defective parts and then returned them to the final packaging area.

The company had a second final assembly area, B line, available to handle peak requirements. This line was very similar to the main A line, but was set up to use only 15 workers and produce at a rate of 1,000 umbrollers per day. One additional employee was needed to repair the 5 percent defects from this line.

---

[6] In-process inventories seldom exceeded one to two days' worth of shipments.

CURRENT AGGREGATE PLANNING PROBLEMS

As George Spaulding met with his management team in mid-November to discuss production requirements for the next three months, he tried to summarize his own thinking:

"One of the first questions I raised with our marketing people was just how solid they think their projections (Exhibit 1) are for the next three months. I must say that they've pretty well convinced me that for the umbroller their forecasts, including the 66,000 units for delivery in February, look pretty sound. This is based on open orders we now have in hand, confirmed orders on the books, and anticipated orders. As always, we won't know the exact model and color on half of those units until one week in advance of the actual delivery date.

"On the backpacks, I also think the marketing estimates are fairly sound, since there's not much change predicted from what demand has been in the past. On the playcrib, however, there are some major uncertainties as to what demand will be. I think marketing's estimates (Exhibit 2) assume that they will continue to push that product as they have in the past few months, and that the effect of that will be cumulative as they realize the full impact of their recent playcrib promotions. Now there is the possibility of asking them to cut back their push of that product if we think there's just no way we can produce both it and the umbrollers. However, marketing wouldn't be very happy with that since they've been trying to get their reps and retailers excited about the Cross River playcrib for some time; and if we tell them to drop their push for a few months, they'll probably just have to start from scratch again at some time in the future.

"In terms of meeting estimated umbroller demand in February, it seems to me that there are several alternatives that we can choose from: use of B line for several weeks, overtime, addition of a second shift, and the building of some finished goods inventory. I should stress that we've used all of these at some time or another during the past year and have some feel for what each entails. I think I prefer the B line option because it's easy to control. However, it won't give us all the capacity that will be required. Overtime is a reasonable possibility, but it's expensive, and after a couple of weeks of it, both management and hourly workers begin to tire and efficiency starts to decline. The second shift option might work in a real bind, but to make it worthwhile we'd want to do it for several weeks, and even then I think it would add a lot of headaches to our planning and control systems. If we want to build more finished goods inventory, we're going to need some pretty strong arguments to get a bank to finance that. Given that we're already factoring our receivables, I imagine that financing might run 1½ percent per month if we could get it.

"My guess is that some combination of these possibilities would be best, keeping in mind that we'll have to add people to fabrication and subassemblies in order to keep a higher rate of final assembly busy. Since we've already got both A and B line in place and have some extra equipment in fabrication and subassembly, I don't think any additional capital investment would be required, unless this higher level of output becomes a longer term situation.

"As a basis for evaluating these options, I've asked Jim Baughman (head of manufacturing administration) to put together some production, labor,

EXHIBIT 5
Umbroller—Production, Costs, and Work Force

A. Standard and actual labor times per unit (fractions of hours):

	(A Line) Standard	Actual	(B Line) Standard
Sewing	0.071	0.073	0.071
Fabrication	0.051	0.047	0.051
Plastic molding	0.052	0.051	0.052
Subassembly	0.072	0.076	0.072
Final assembly	0.104	0.108*	0.120
Total	0.350	0.355	0.364

B. Umbroller work force—November 1975 (only A line in use in November):

Umbroller

Sewing	18
Fabrication	12
Plastic molding	13
Subassembly	19
Final assembly	26
	88

C. Production—November 1–4, 1975: 1970 units day for 10 days.

D. Standard unit cost structure (A line):

Average revenue		$13.70
Materials:		
Fabric	$1.247	
Metal	4.285	
Plastic	2.143	
Packaging	0.937	8.612
Labor 0.350 hours @ $3.40 per hour†		1.190
Total variable costs		9.802
Allocated factory overhead‡		2.380
Production cost		12.182
Contribution (before tax)		1.518

* Final assembly for units being shipped to Canada required only 0.073 per unit direct labor-hours on the assembly line at Rochester rather than the normal 0.108 hours per unit.
† This figure of $3.40 per hour represents average hourly wages, including fringe benefits and payroll taxes.
‡ Includes indirect hourly labor as well as production management personnel.

and cost figures for the umbroller. (These are shown in Exhibit 5.) We will probably want to delay adding to the work force as long as possible so that we'll have a better idea of confirmed orders before sticking our necks out, but I think it is important to prepare our plans now so that we can get them approved and not get caught in a squeeze at the last minute. I know marketing wouldn't be at all happy if we were more than one or two days late on February deliveries.

EXHIBIT 6
Playcrib and Backpack—Production, Costs, and Work Force

A. **Actual and standard labor times per unit (batch assembly):**

	Playcrib		*Backpack*	
	Standard	*Actual*	*Standard*	*Actual*
Sewing	0.237	0.243	0.066	0.068
Plastic molding	0.121	0.121	0.071	0.071
Fabrication.	0.179	0.176	0.069	0.069
Assembly	0.457*	0.470	0.232	0.244
Total	0.994	1.010	0.438	0.452

B. **Unit cost structure (batch assembly):**

	Playcrib		*Backpack*	
Average revenue (wholesale)		$26.28		$9.49
Materials	$15.478		$4.52	
Labor				
(standard x $3.40 per hour)	3.380		1.49	
Total variable cost	18.858		6.01	
Allocated factory overhead	6.760		2.98	
Production cost	25.618		8.99	
Contribution to corporate				
overhead and profits	0.662		0.50	

C. **Combined work force for playcribs and backpacks (November 1975):**

	Playcribs	*Backpacks*
Sewing	2	1
Plastic molding	1	1
Fabrication	1	1
Assembly	4	3
Total	8	6

D. **Production rates November 1–14, 1975:** playcribs, 60 per day; and backpacks, 100 per day.

E. **Finished goods inventory on November 14, 1975:** playcribs, 2,200; and backpacks, 2,750.

___

*If the paced assembly line were installed and run at 100–200 playcribs per day, this standard would be 0.297 hours per unit.

"As far as the playcrib production is concerned, if we are going to increase our production, it looks to me like there are basically two options. One is to just add more people and continue to make them in a batch operation as we presently do. As an alternative approach, I've had Jim update the design for a paced playcrib production line that could turn out 100–200 units per day. By going this route we would be able to substantially reduce the labor required per playcrib and thus improve our margins on that product.

"Jim has estimated that it might cost $1,000 in additional expense and take about 10 working days to get such a line set up. I think we also agree that the secret to realizing the benefits from such a paced playcrib line is continuity of production at a steady rate. Going to a paced playcrib line would affect our flexibility somewhat since we'd have to produce at least 100 per day on the days that line was in operation. Additionally, it would make it harder to draw from that pool of workers when we needed a few more people to work on the umbroller line. The figures that Jim has put together (Exhibit 6) are the ones that I think we should use in resolving this point.

"One of the things I think we should keep in mind as we prepare these plans is that we've improved our production operations substantially over the past several months and we don't want to take actions that would set us back to where we were in late 1974 as far as productivity and reliability are concerned. I'm most anxious to have each of you think about some of these issues and others that you see as being relevant so that we can finalize our production plans for December, January, and February early next week."[7]

---

[7] For purposes of planning, George felt he should assume four five-day work-weeks in December, January, and February.

CASE 20

The Swift River Box Company

Eric Wilson, controller and personnel manager of The Swift River Box Company of Newark, New Jersey, had just received the forecast of the company's 1978 work force requirements from Factory Manager Ed Kurtz. Swift River Box (SRB) manufactured high-quality metal display boxes for the precious jewelry industry—an industry with significant seasonality at the retail level. The company had dampened the effect of this seasonality by seeking good customers and encouraging them to order on an annual basis; however, the company did face two production peaks during the year. In 1975, Wilson had begun to use temporary workers (temps) to meet these peaks. Kurtz had frequently expressed his concern about the use of temps and spoke forcefully again as he gave his forecast to Wilson on November 2, 1977:

Kurtz: Twenty-three temps in August, 29 in September, and 49 in October! Eric, I think we're letting this get out of hand. The supervisors complain of lack of control; I'm worried that quality may slip; and we're both concerned about morale.

Wilson: I know, Ed, but look at the slowdown last spring; we handled most of the cutback just by reducing the number of temps. Providing long-term steady employment is important in this company, and the use of temps enables us to take a big step in this direction.

Kurtz: I still think we can find a better balance, Eric.

Forecast in hand, Wilson returned to his office. He was expected to develop a plan to meet SRB's projected work force requirements. "The first step is to determine the appropriate number of permanent employees," he thought. "But even that's not simple. For example, our turnover makes such a target quite elusive. And I do need to respond to Ed. I know temps are important to us, and for reasons that go well beyond meeting production peaks. He may have a good point, though."

THE COMPANY

Swift River Box (SRB) had been formed in 1950 when boyhood friends Ray Morvan and Dave Bourns purchased a small box manufacturer that was near bankruptcy. In 1950, the company had occupied 9,000 square feet; in 1977, the company owned a 53,000 square-foot two-story brick factory in Newark. Gross sales for 1976 were about $6 million, with a pretax margin of about 5 percent.

SRB boxes were used to display and protect quality jewelry products such as rings and necklaces. A finished box (Exhibit 1) consisted of a hinged, fabric-covered metal shell with a fabric-lined interior designed to hold a particular piece of jewelry. The customer's logo was frequently printed on the inside and/or outside of the box. SRB manufactured three basic box sizes—small (1.5 inches wide by 1.5 inches long by 1.5 inches high), medium (2.5 by 3.25 by 1.75 inches), and large (4 by 7 by 2 inches). Within each size, a wide variety of fabric types and colors were available. Unit prices ranged from 25 cents to $1.35 and depended upon size, material, interior design, and printing. Volume discounts were given.

EXHIBIT 1
Finished Box

The company emphasized "quality, reliability, and service at a reasonable price." Eric Wilson expanded on this:

> Some manufacturers may beat us on price, but we build high-quality boxes and deliver them on time. The cost of the box is but a fraction of the cost of the jewelry; manufacturers are thus willing to pay a little more for top-notch quality and appearance, and for timely delivery.

Ed Kurtz, who was the point of contact with many customers, spoke of his role:

> With my system, I know the status of each order. If a customer calls, I can confirm the delivery date immediately. And, just as important, I can forewarn the customer if I see a delivery problem developing. This gives our customers

confidence, and, I'm sure, contrasts with the response they get from most vendors.

SRB sold directly to jewelry manufacturers, frequently as a second source. The company had approximately 400 customers in 1977; over 70 percent had been with the company for several years. The top six customers accounted for 25 percent of sales, the top 20 for 50 percent, and the top 100 for 80 percent. Morvan and Kurtz directly handled sales in the Newark area—about 70 percent of the total. The remaining 30 percent were handled by six national sales representatives. Sales policies were strict: boxes were shipped upon receipt of payment to new or small customers, and not at all to delinquent customers. As a result, the company had experienced virtually no write-off of receivables. Prices for the year were set in April.

MANAGEMENT

The SRB management structure was lean and informal, with a hands-on style the norm (Exhibit 2). The owners, Ray Morvan and Dave Bourns, had been responsible for the growth, prosperity, and, indeed, character of the company. Morvan was an experienced manufacturing executive with a Wharton degree. Bourns, a toolmaker by trade, had designed most of the machines used in the production process. Financial results over the years supported the owners' belief that the machines and the company culture gave SRB a significant competitive advantage.

EXHIBIT 2
Organization Chart

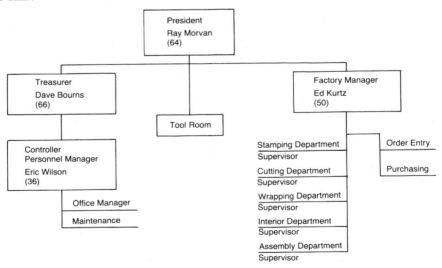

Note: Numbers in parentheses are ages.
Source: Company personnel.

EXHIBIT 3
Plant Layout

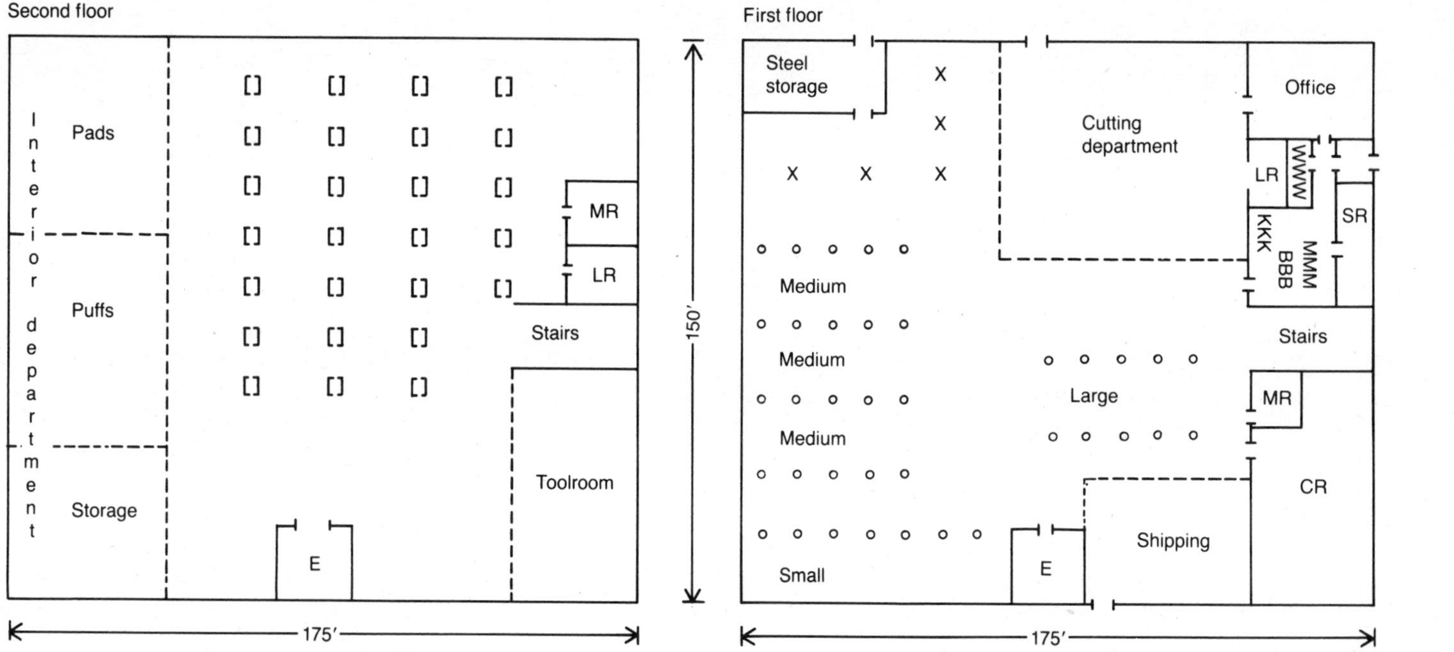

Second floor

├─ 175' ─┤

MR
LR
Stairs

Toolroom

E

Pads
Interior

Puffs
Interior

Storage
ment

|← 150' →|

First floor

Office

WWW
LR
KKK

SR
MMM
BBB

Stairs

MR

CR

Cutting
department

Large

Shipping

E

Steel
storage

X   X   X

X

X   X

Medium

Medium

Medium

Small

├─ 175' ─┤

LEGEND

o—Wrapping machine.
X—Stamping press.
[ ]—Assembly table.
E—Elevator.
Source: Blueprints of factory.

WWW—Wilson's desk.
KKK—Kurtz's desk.
MMM—Morvan's desk.
BBB—Bourn's desk.

MR—Men's room.
LR—Ladies' room.
SR—Showroom.
CR—Cafeteria.

The owners' explicit goals focused on maintaining their independence and style. In particular, they did not want to become a "captive" supplier to a big company, nor did they, for example, want to run a second shift for which they would be "absentee managers."

Ed Kurtz and Eric Wilson ran the day-to-day business. Kurtz was responsible for operations, and Wilson for staff functions. Kurtz had joined the company in 1957 and was a storehouse of information about the product, process, and customers. Wilson, son-in-law of Bourns, had come to the company in 1974 with a MBA from Wharton and experience as an Air Force pilot and in public accounting work.

THE PRODUCTION PROCESS

The SRB factory housed five production departments on the two floors (Exhibit 3). A breakdown of labor and material costs by department is presented in Exhibit 4. A simplified diagram of the production process is shown in Exhibit 5.

In the *stamping department,* 2,000-pound coils of sheet steel were converted into the metal shells with five large, noisy cold-stamp presses. Machine output depended upon box size: each press could stamp top and bottom shells for 1,800 small, 1,500 medium, or 1,200 large boxes per hour. The five operators set up the machines (which took about half an hour) and adjusted them during the run as necessary. Classified as heavy machine operators, all had been on the job at least five years.

EXHIBIT 4
Material and Labor Cost Breakdown ($ per 1,000 boxes)

Department	Box Size					
	Small		Medium		Large	
	Material	Labor	Material	Labor	Material	Labor
Stamping	$ 56.74	$ 3.71	$133.80	$ 4.41	$340.00	$ 5.50
Cutting:						
Exterior	33.87	1.18	80.01	1.18	203.24	1.18
Interior	31.70	3.87	74.68	3.87	189.87	3.87
Interior	5.39	9.53	5.43	9.53	5.43	9.53
Covering	—	11.68	—	15.61	—	31.29
Assembly	—	43.92	—	43.92	—	87.84
	127.70	73.89	293.92	78.52	738.54	139.21
Total	$201.59		$372.44		$ 877.75	
Average selling price	300.00		500.00		1,100.00	

Source: The company did not maintain "standards" such as the above. These figures are based upon relationships described by Kurtz.

EXHIBIT 5

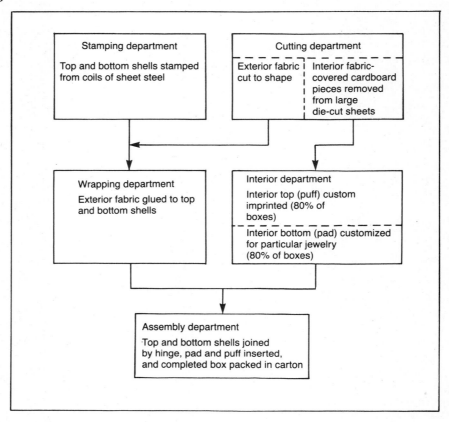

In the *cutting department,* the six types and many colors of exterior fabric were cut into shaped pieces. Twelve to twenty-four layers of the fabric were aligned on a long table and cut with a power "cookie cutter." Maximum hourly output was fabric for 8,000 boxes. Classified as heavy machine operators, the two workers were the most skilled workers in the plant: each cut required careful positioning of the cutter to minimize waste.

In addition, the department cut the interior parts, called puffs (tops) and pads (bottoms). Both were fabric-covered cardboard pieces that fit tightly inside the metal shells. They were die-cut from purchased sheets (2 by 2 feet) on an automatic machine with an output of 7,500 box interiors per hour. Several unskilled workers removed the pads and puffs from the die-cut sheets, a very repetitive job. Wilson had noted considerable turnover among these workers; in late 1976, he had begun to fill the positions exclusively with temps. A temp could remove about 1,250 interiors per hour.

In the *wrapping department*, the exterior fabric pieces were glued to the metal shells. A wrapping machine heated the shell and stretched the fabric, coated with a heat-sensitive glue, tightly over it. The company had 37 machines, but each would wrap only one box size. The machines were positioned within the department by size.

Box Size	Number of Machines	Average Hourly Output per Machine (boxes; tops and bottoms)
Small	7	400
Medium ...	20	300
Large	10	150

A worker, classified as a light machine operator, sat in front of the machine. S/he loaded shells and fabric pieces into stack trays and activated the dual hand controls. While physically near each other, operators spent the work day focused on a machine.

In the *interior department*, pads and puffs were customized for about 80 percent of the boxes. The workers operated the simple imprinting machines and did handwork such as the insertion of a jewelry-holding elastic loop into the pad. While several employees might work on the same order, each completed the full task independently; output for the department averaged 360 box interiors per hour per worker. They were classified as bench workers.

In the *assembly department*, the several components of the box were brought together and assembled. Work was done by four-person teams. A "hinger," the most skilled team member, sat on one side of a table. S/he operated the machine that hinged the top and bottom shells together and, in essence, paced the group (Exhibit 6). Across the table, the second worker inserted the puff, the third inserted the pad, and the fourth packed the completed box into a shipping carton. On the average, a team could assemble 400 medium or small boxes, or 200 large boxes (which required two hinges and a more complex insertion procedure), per hour. The job was quite social in nature, with the workers depending on each other for assistance and conversation.

Box quality was primarily judged by appearance. The company had no formal quality control procedures. However, it did expect the workers, in general, to be quality conscious and the assemblers, in particular, to inspect each box before it was packed. "This," Kurtz noted, "is one reason we want permanent employees who identify with and care about the company."

Filled cartons were moved to the *shipping room*. Completed orders were shipped by truck every afternoon.

EXHIBIT 6
Hinged Box Prior to Pad
and Puff Insertion

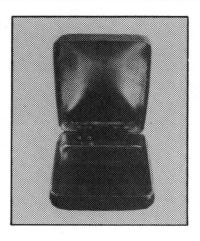

A crucial support department was the *tool room.* This group of 10 men was responsible for the construction, maintenance, and repair of the many machines in the plant, most of which had been designed and made in-house.

INFORMATION AND MATERIAL FLOW

SRB tried to maintain a six- to eight-week order backlog as a good balance between necessary lead times (primarily for fabric orders) and competitive delivery performance. As the backlog built above that level, the company began to schedule overtime and bring on more temps; as the backlog fell, it reduced temps and worked ahead on large, annual orders.

Forecasted mix and volume had proved reasonably accurate (Exhibit 7). As a result, the company produced the metal shells and unfinished satin pads and puffs in large batches at a reasonably level rate.[1] Production in these two departments was modified over the year by trends in actual orders received, by specific shortages, and by storage limits of about 1.2 million boxes (boxes were bulky and space in the factory was at a premium). The company maintained a two-week steel inventory (order lead time was three days) and a four-week satin inventory (lead time was one week).

The metal shells were ejected by the presses into "shell boxes"—cardboard cartons about the size of a laundry basket. Filled shell boxes were stored adjacent to the appropriate sized wrapping machines. Pads and puffs were segregated by color and size and placed on edge in stiff cardboard trays. The trays were stored on shelves in the interior department. SRB maintained at least a two-week inventory of each standard shell size and interior color; supervisors could visually check for shortages.

---

[1] Experience had shown that satin interiors in one of four colors accounted for about 65 percent of demand; it was these 12 size/color combinations that were "standard."

EXHIBIT 7
Summary of 1977

Month	Shipments (000s of boxes)			Average Number of Workers											
				Stamping		Cutting		Wrapping		Interior		Assembly		Total	
	Forecast	Actual per Month	Actual per day	Perms	Temps	Perms	Temps	Perms	Temps	Perms	Temps	Perms	Temps	Perms	Temps
January	1,000	996	49.8	5	0	3	5	21	0	13	3	70	0	112	8
February	959	968	48.4	5	0	3	5	21	0	13	2	70	0	112	7
March	1,375	1,509	65.6	5	0	3	6	22	8	13	9	70	21	113	44
April	1,475	1,562	71.0	5	0	3	6	22	10	14	8	75	23	119	47
May	1,400	1,450	72.5	5	0	7	3	22	12	14	8	77	22	121	48
June	1,200	999	45.4	5	0	6	3	21	0	14	0	70	0	116	3
July	580	462	38.5	5	0	7	0	21	0	13	0	69	0	115	0
August	1,200	1,166	58.3	5	0	4	3	21	6	13	6	72	8	115	23
September	1,350	1,294	61.6	5	0	3	6	21	7	13	6	73	10	115	29
October	1,450	1,402	70.1	5	0	3	6*	21	12*	13	8*	74	23*	116	49
November	1,350	—	—	—	—	—	—	—	—	—	—	—	—	—	—
December	1,000	—	—	—	—	—	—	—	—	—	—	—	—	—	—

* Included in these numbers were the following workers on evalution.

Cutting........ 0	Interior........ 2
Wrapping...... 3	Assembly...... 6

Source: Company documents.

Box Shipments (millions)

	1972	1973	1974	1975	1976
Forecast	11.4	12.3	14.0	13.0	13.2
Actual	11.7	12.5	13.8	11.7	13.3

Product Mix

	Small	Medium	Large
Forecast........	25%	60%	15%
Actual........	23	63	14

The remaining operations were done strictly to order. Exterior fabric purchase required a lead time of four to six weeks; herein lay the incentive for the annual orders that enabled SRB to dampen seasonality. The company purchased fabric upon order receipt. Then, with the material on hand, SRB could respond quickly to a customer's request for a change in box mix or volume; for example, a 10,000-box order could be run through the plant in about a week. Exterior fabric inventory averaged about 20,000 yards, though this dropped significantly by the end of the year.

An incoming purchase order typically included several different finished boxes. For production purposes, the order for each type (a size/fabric/custom-feature combination) was handled as a batch; quantities ranged from 500 to 50,000 boxes (larger orders were split into two or more batches). A detailed instruction sheet was completed for each batch and sent to the supervisors.

Subject to component availability and to shipping deadlines, orders were processed on a first-in, first-out basis; exterior fabric cutting was the trigger operation. Each supervisor scheduled the work in his own department. This was most complex in assembly; the supervisor faced "a constant juggling act," according to Kurtz, as he matched work teams and ready-to-go orders a number of times each day. Work-in-process awaiting assembly was typically kept at the one- to three-day level.

Each supervisor circulated a daily summary of the orders completed by his department to the other supervisors and to Kurtz. At the end of the day, Kurtz updated his order log (Exhibit 8). He explained:

> I've developed this system over the 21 years I've been here. I won't let *anyone* write on my charts because as I fill them in, I absorb the status of each order and get a sense of what is happening in the plant. As we grow, however, it is becoming increasingly difficult to find the time to do this.

PERSONNEL POLICIES

The New York area was the center of the precious jewelry industry in the United States. While the industry was seasonal (24 percent of retail sales were made in December, 10 percent in November) and the "Christmas pink slip" typical, SRB, as a matter of owner philosophy and company strategy, sought to provide steady, long-term employment.[2] This commitment was also shared by the employees; in the spring recession of 1975, for example, they had shared the available work by working alternate weeks. The employees had soundly rejected a unionization attempt by the Amalgamated Clothing and Textile Workers in 1974.

Most of the workers in the interior, wrapping, and assembly departments were women. The majority were age 40 or over. Kurtz had found they preferred little overtime work; the practical limit was about two to

---

[2] A pink slip is a layoff notice.

EXHIBIT 8
Kurtz's Weekly Log

	THE SWIFT RIVER BOX COMPANY								
Week of: 9/13/76									
Order #	Customer	Qty.	Size-Fabric	Date entered	Fabric cut	Pads & puffs comp.	Wrapped	Assembled	Shipped
1068	AAA	25,000	M-3	9/13	10/13	10/19	10/18	10/22	10/22
1069	BBB	500	M-4		10/8	10/13	10/11	10/18	10/18
1070	BBB	1,000	L-3		10/13	10/20	10/20	10/22	10/22
1071	CCC	1,500	M-3		10/14	10/19	10/19	10/25	10/26
1072	DDD	500	M-2	9/14	10/21	10/26	10/25	10/29	10/29
1073	DDD	3,000	S-3		10/14	10/19	10/14	10/25	10/25
1074	DDD	500	M-4		10/19	13/25	10/27		
1075	EEE	2,500	M-3		10/14	10/20	10/19	10/22	10/22
1076	EEE	10,000	L-3		10/14	10/20	10/19	10/22	10/22
1077	EEE	500	L-5		10/20	10/25	10/26	10/29	10/29
1078	FFF	500	M-6		10/29				
1079	GGG	4,000	S-3		10/14	10/19	10/19	10/22	10/22
1080	GGG	5,000	M-4		10/21	10/26	10/27		
1081	HHH	10,000	S-3		10/14	10/20	10/21	10/26	10/26
1082	HHH	5,000	S-2		10/25				
1083	HHH	5,000	S-4		10/22	10/26	10/25	10/27	10/27
1084	HHH	5,000	M-2		10/27				
1085	HHH	20,000	M-3		10/15	10/19	10/21	10/25	10/26
1086	HHH	5,000	M-5		10/21	10/26	10/26	10/28	10/28
1087	HHH	10,000	L-3		10/14	10/19	10/19	10/21	10/21
1088	HHH	2,500	L-4		10/22	10/26	10/26	10/27	10/27
1089	III	4,000	L-3		10/14	10/19	10/21	10/25	10/25
1090	JJJ	2,500	S-2	9/15	10/23	10/28	10/27		
1091	JJJ	7,500	M-3		10/15	10/20	10/21	10/25	10/25
1092	JJJ	5,000	M-2		10/27				
1093	KKK	700	M-6						
1094	LLL	5,000	S-3		10/15	10/21	10/23	10/26	10/26
1095	LLL	10,000	M-3		10/15	10/21	10/22	10/26	10/26
1096	LLL	2,500	M-5		10/22	10/27	10/26	10/29	10/29
	(cont.)								

Size: S—small.   Fabric: 1—velvet.   4—cotton.
          M—medium.   2—velour.   5—leather.
          L—large.   3—leatherette. 6—other.
Source: Company document.

three hours per week for one to two months in the fall. The heavy machine operators, on the other hand, willingly accepted overtime.

All production workers were paid on an hourly basis (Exhibit 9). Top management established pay ranges for each job classification prior to the March and September pay reviews. While length of service had some impact upon a worker's wage rate (a good worker could move from the floor to the ceiling of a range in about three years), performance was the primary wage determinant. Supervisors recommended raises to top management based upon the following criteria and weights: productivity and quality—40 percent; absence/lateness record—40 percent; attitude, flexibility, and safety—10 percent; and work station neatness—10 percent. Top management reviewed these recommendations to ensure plantwide equity.

EXHIBIT 9
Job Classifications

		Heavy Machine Operators	*Light Machine Operators*	*Bench Workers*
Worker Classifications by Department	Stamping	All	—	—
	Cutting	Exterior	Die-cutter	Others
	Wrapping	—	All	—
	Interior	—	—	All
	Assembly	—	Hingers	Others
Hourly Wage Rates	Starting	$3.50	$2.95	$2.85
	Average	4.90	3.50	3.20
	Maximum	5.00	4.00	3.50
Calhoun Agency Rates	Billed to SRB	5.27	4.34	4.11
	Paid to worker	3.50	2.80	2.65
Productivity	Productivity of new worker as percent of trained worker	50%	60%	85%
	Time needed by average worker to reach full productivity	6 months	4 months	1 month

Source: Company documents and personnel.

The company had introduced an employee deferred profit sharing plan in 1976, in part to reward seniority. An employee's share was determined by his/her points (one for each $100 of gross earnings and one for each year of service) and by the "share point value" declared by top management at the end of the year (expected to be about $4 in 1977).

The benefit package included an individual medical plan, nine paid holidays, paid vacation (the plant shut down for the first two weeks of July each year), and a Christmas bonus. Wilson estimated the cost of benefits (including profit sharing) to run about 19 percent of an employee's gross earnings. In addition, the company paid taxes (FICA, Workman's Compensation, New Jersey Unemployment, and Federal Unemployment) amounting to about 15 percent of gross wages.

SRB obtained temporary workers from the Calhoun Temporary Service Agency of Newark. Jack Calhoun, agency head, described his operation:

> My job is really a delicate balancing act—I need to have workers for the jobs, and I need to have jobs for the workers. I make a real effort to understand the job a client has so that I can send a person with appropriate skills; and I deliver the workers with my own vans so I know they get there on time. On the other side, I consistently place over 95 percent of those who show up each day (at 6 A.M.!).
>
> Some people choose temporary work as a good introduction to several companies in the area; others like the freedom to take a day off, or only want to work two or three days per week; and some probably aren't ready for a regular full-time job. I would estimate that 50 percent of my workers are with me for more than three weeks, 30 percent for one to three weeks, and the remainder for less than a week.
>
> I charge clients an hourly rate based on what I will pay the worker (usually minimum wage), with a markup to cover payroll taxes, overhead, and profit.

Kurtz requested temps on a weekly basis and adjusted his order daily as employee absences or latenesses occurred or bottlenecks developed. While at least one temp had come to SRB every day for over two years, and several had come for three to six months, Kurtz explained that "from a practical point of view, each temp seems like a new worker."

Turnover was a continual problem for Wilson. To attract workers, SRB ran newspaper ads, worked with the State Employment Agency, paid a recruiting bonus ($50) to employees, and occasionally distributed flyers door to door in promising neighborhoods. However, getting a prospective worker to express an interest was only part of the problem. Wilson had tabulated turnover data for the 1973–76 period (Exhibit 10). About 80 percent of the turnover was "self-termination" usually due to an unwilling-

EXHIBIT 10
Turnover Data

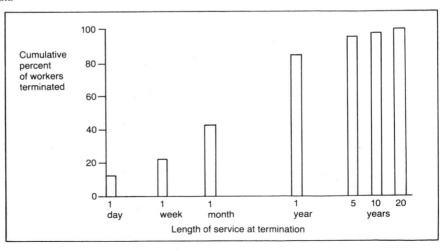

ness to meet attendance and work-pace expectations, but also for reasons such as "better job, back to school, child care, and medical." Company terminations were largely for a poor attendance record.

While Wilson interviewed all job applicants, he believed that "we need to see someone work to know whether he or she will fit here. We hire at the low end of the skill spectrum and do our own training, so we really seek attitude and reliability." In 1976, he had developed an evaluation program to provide such a work trial. After a quick initial screening, a job applicant was placed "on evaluation" for four weeks. During this time, s/he worked in the SRB plant but was technically an employee of the Calhoun Agency (which billed SRB at the usual rates). An applicant was let go at any time during the period if it became clear that s/he did not meet SRB expectations. At the end of the four weeks, the supervisors faced, according to Wilson, "the positive decision to hire rather than the negative decision to fire."

Wilson had found that the turnover relationship shown in Exhibit 10 had not changed noticeably with the evaluation program; however, the company's official turnover had declined markedly, since a worker did not appear on the SRB payroll until after "one month." Wilson believed that the program had reduced the administrative burden and cost of turnover.[3] In particular, it had enabled the company to reduce unemployment insurance taxes from 7 percent to 5 percent (on the first $4,800 of each employee's earnings). On the other hand, Kurtz felt that "this program gives me bodies, but it is talent that I need, and I don't think the shop floor should be the place where we do the work of finding it." Workers on evaluation, for their part, complained of having to go to the agency for their paychecks; it was common to hear comments such as "If I work here in the factory, I want to be paid here, too."

NOVEMBER 1977

As Wilson sat in his office, he realized that the issue of temps was complex, in part because the company used them for several quite different purposes. He reflected:

> We use temps to build the work force quickly to meet peaks and to protect our permanent employees in valleys. We use them for the really boring jobs, and as immediate fill-ins to cover daily absences and latenesses. They enable us to hire a good worker almost anytime, without overstaffing. And, of course, we use the temp agency in the evaluation program.

---

[3] Wilson summarized hiring and termination costs as follows:

Initial screening and advertising	$100
Placement on payroll	20
Termination by company	400
Termination by employee	50

Wilson looked at the forecast of shipments and work force requirements (Exhibit 11), and at the September 1977 data on the distribution of employees by service date (Exhibit 12):

> How many permanent people should we carry this coming year? I think I've got the numbers to determine this—but the practice is so much harder than the theory. How many of the current workers will we lose? How do we deal with the tremendous turnover during evaluation that makes the implementation of the decision to add a worker so subject to uncertainty? Can I develop good guidelines for hiring decisions? For example, I have three

EXHIBIT 11
1978 Forecast

Of box shipments:

| | Shipments (000s) | |
Month	Boxes per Month	Boxes per Day
January	1,050	50.0
February	1,100	55.0
March.............	1,330	57.8
April..............	1,365	65.0
May	1,200	57.1
June	1,055	48.0
July...............	595	54.1
August	1,345	61.1
September..........	1,365	65.0
October	1,500	75.0
November..........	1,330	70.0
December..........	1,115	61.9

Of workers required:*

| | Department | | | | | |
Month	Stamping	Cutting	Wrapping	Interior	Assembly	Total
January	4	8	21	14	68	115
February......	4	9	23	15	74	125
March	5	9	24	16	78	132
April	5	10	27	18	88	148
May	5	9	24	16	77	131
June.........	4	8	20	13	65	110
July	4	8	22	15	73	122
August.......	5	9	25	17	83	139
September	5	10	27	18	88	148
October.......	6	11	31	21	101	170
November.....	6	10	29	19	95	159
December.....	5	9	26	17	84	141

* Forecast developed by Ed Kurtz based upon forecast of box shipments reproduced above; average output rates; and forecast mix of 25 percent small, 60 percent medium, and 15 percent large boxes.
Source: Company documents.

292

EXHIBIT 12
Distribution of SRB Production Workers by Their Service Date (as of September 1977)

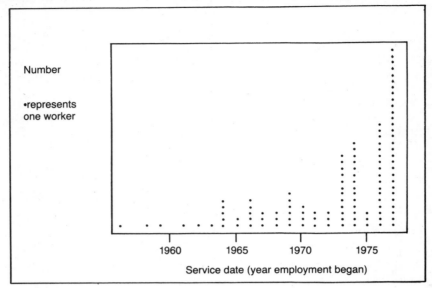

workers in wrapping who finish their evaluation on Friday. I hear they're okay, but not great. Do we hire them?

We're at our peak usage of temps right now, and I know Ed and the supervisors are sensitive. There is no question that their work is more difficult with nearly 50 temps out there. But do we have an option?

Usually the last to leave the office, Wilson locked the door and stepped out into the November darkness. "A busy week," he thought. "I've got to develop at least a rough plan for meeting our 1978 work force needs. With Ed's concerns, I'll have to present convincing arguments for the use of temps in that plan."

CASE 21

Kool King Division (A)

On the morning of September 4, 1979, Tom Stanley, marketing manager for Kool King air conditioners, called James Lewis, vice president of the Kool King Division, and requested he schedule a meeting with key division personnel to discuss the latest forecast for fiscal 1980.[1] This group had already met several times during the previous three months to discuss forecasts and production plans for the coming year.

Later in the day, Mr. Stanley drove to the Kool King plant in Melrose Park, Illinois, from corporate headquarters in Chicago. The meeting began in Mr. Lewis' office. Mr. Lewis, as division vice president, was responsible for manufacturing, engineering, and product development. Others at the meeting were:

Robert Irwin—plant manager.

Earl Williams—division controller.

Russell Frank—division materials manager.

John Victor—division personnel manager.

"I've just finished a careful review of the final figures for fiscal 1979," Mr. Stanley stated. "I've also spent four days in the field talking with three of our key distributors and one of our largest retail accounts.

"We lost far more sales this past year than any of us realized. We knew about the stockouts of 208-volt models that hurt us in New York City and we discussed them at our last meeting, but it now looks like we underestimated their total effect.

"As a result of this kind of information and other data that I've pulled together, I've raised the forecast for the coming year to a little over 120,000 units." (See Exhibit 1.).

---

[1] The fiscal year ran from September 1 to August 31.

EXHIBIT 1
Sales History and Forecasts

Fiscal Year	Actual Sales (units)
1976....	65,034
1977....	64,636 *8.7%*
1978....	70,272 *40%*
1979....	102,874 *19%*

100,000 ←

	Fiscal 1979 Forecast Sales (units)	Beginning Inventory, September 1, 1978 (units)	Fiscal 1979 Actual Sales (units)	Ending Inventory, August 29, 1979 (units)	Latest Fiscal 1980 Forecast Sales (units)
Midget	30,000	0	*30–40%* 36,482	0 *10–30%*	46,500
Mighty Midget ...	13,000	753	8,499	1,420	11,000
Breeze Queen....	33,000	6,136	*(5)* 38,620	2,165	*?641,000* 41,000
Breeze King.	4,000	1,320	6,647	0	8,000
Islander	7,000	2,049	4,215	2,604	5,000
Super	3,000	102	779	312	1,500
Slim Line........	10,000	9,144	7,632	1,512	10,000
Totals	100,000	19,504	102,874	8,013	123,000

"You've got to be kidding, Tom," replied Mr. Irwin. "Just three weeks ago we all sat around this table and talked about 114,000 units."

"That's right, Bob, but I'm telling you that our stockouts hurt more than we realized. Also, this year's early delivery orders are running well ahead of what we expected.[2] The economists say that we may be facing a mild recession this fall and winter, but by summer when our products sell, we should really be on the upswing. Our retailers want to be positioned to take advantage of this, and we can't let them down with stockouts."

"While I have the floor," Mr. Stanley continued, "I want to report that many of our distributors say that in addition to losing sales because retailers won't wait for factory shipments, they're getting an increasing number of quality complaints."

"I've heard some of these complaints myself," said Mr. Lewis, "You don't seem too worried about our product quality, Bob, but I'm concerned about our performance and about the possible negative effect of our quality on the image of other divisions."

Mr. Irwin addressed James Lewis: "I don't think quality is a big problem; we're doing as well as we ever have. The quality complaints I've heard are mostly nickel and dime oversights by new people on the line—getting the nameplate on crooked, not tightening the knobs, leaving the operations manual out of the carton, stuff like that. Our basic quality is still very good. Last year less than 0.5 percent of our production was returned for repair on warranty."

Tom Stanley broke into the conversation: "Look, what's important here is our increase in market share. Let's not kid ourselves. Sure, total sales have increased nicely lately, but the whole market is growing. We've got to do better than our competition in all respects. Crooked nameplates and loose knobs don't build a market."

Mr. Irwin turned to Mr. Stanley: "The discount policy is helping us level out production to some extent, but your forecasts don't help. If we stuck to your figure as a basis for production, we'd have to buy a new warehouse to cover for the mix and timing variations which we always have to deal with."

COMPANY HISTORY

Kool King was a division of the TIA Corporation (Television Industries of America). TIA, headquartered in Chicago, Illinois, was organized in the early 1930s to manufacture radios. After World War II, the company diversified into other electronic products including television sets.

In 1953, through an acquisition, TIA expanded its line to include oil and gas burners, room air conditioners, and central cooling systems. The acquired company was sold in 1959, but the room air conditioner portion of the business and the Kool King brand name were retained. In 1970, the

---

[2] Kool King's discount plan for early delivery orders is discussed later in the case.

Kool King Division was established in a new plant in Melrose Park, Illinois. Growth of this division was a source of pride to TIA executives. Unit sales for the division for four years are shown in Exhibit 1. The division produced seven model lines of air conditioners, as shown below:

Kool King Product Line

Chassis Series	Cooling Capacity BTU [a]	Voltage Rating	Mounting Hardware [b]		
			A	B	C
Midget	4,000	115		*	*
Slim Line [c]	5,500	115		*	
Mighty Midget	6,000	115		*	*
Breeze Queen [d]	9,300	208	*	*	*
Breeze King	11,000	208	*	*	*
Islander	17,000	230		*	
Super	24,000	230		*	

[a] BTU (British thermal unit) was the standard unit of cooling capacity to rate air conditioners. Manufacturers' ratings of their units were checked by representatives of the National Electrical Association (NEMA) at frequent intervals.

[b] Mounting hardware was available in three different designs. Available hardware shown by an asterisk.

[c] Slim Line units were designed to fit casement-type windows which in general were narrower than double-hung windows. The Slim Line units were also frequently sold for installation in double-hung windows too narrow to accomodate the regular units.

[d] The Breeze Queen series was available with a reverse cycle feature allowing the same unit to operate as a heater or an air conditioner.

All marketing of Kool King products was handled by TIA marketing people. TIA distributors in several large cities sold Kool King air conditioners as part of the full TIA line. Kool King products were also sold through TIA's field sales force to independent jobbers and to large retail accounts. Mr. Stanley had been with TIA for four years. He had assumed marketing responsibility for the Kool King product line, his first major responsibility with the firm, in December 1978. He was concerned primarily with marketing planning and advertising. Field sales for Kool King were headed by a colleague of Tom Stanley—both individuals reported to a marketing vice president who was responsible for a product group of which Kool King was a part.

PRODUCTION FACILITIES

The division production facilities in Melrose Park were located in a modern, one-story building with over 100,000 square feet of floor space. The division had no facilities for manufacturing any of the components used in its air conditioners—all component parts were purchased from outside suppliers. A typical room air conditioner had 200 parts, a few of which represented 85 percent of the material cost of an individual unit. Ten percent of the component parts were common to different chassis series. Within a given series, however, 75 percent of the parts were common.

Most models were assembled on a single assembly line. Differences in construction dictated that only one chassis type could be produced at a time. A large portion of the line consisted of a waist-high, roller conveyor along which partially assembled units riding on plywood pallets were pushed manually. Other portions of the line had a moving belt which moved the units along automatically at a preset speed. Most of the parts were screwed or bolted to the chassis by hand tools or small air-powered wrenches. Motors, compressors, and cooling coils, purchased already assembled, were easily mounted and wired to the chassis. The compressed gas charge required careful handling and frequent checking for leaks. Exhibit 2 shows the layout of the assembly line and describes the operations performed along its length.

SEASONAL SALES AND DISCOUNT STRATEGY

The sale of air conditioners involved a marked seasonal trend. In the early days of room air conditioners, the sales year ran from June 1 to August 1. As the industry developed, the sales year for room air conditioners lengthened. The company had attempted to broaden the production year by offering substantial discounts to distributors if they took delivery of air conditioners between October and February rather than between March and June. Discount and deferred payment plans had been recommended for several years by Mr. Irwin, Mr. Frank, and Mr. Lewis. In fiscal 1979, their suggestions had been adopted, and the following plans were again in effect for 1980.

I. *Early order discount plan:* All orders received after September 1, but before November 1, would receive an early-order discount off the regular manufacturers FOB Melrose Park, Illinois, prices. Deliveries on such early orders would be scheduled as follows:

One quarter of the order in October.

One quarter of the order in November.

One quarter of the order in December.

One quarter of the order in January.

II. *Deferred payment plan:* Payment for any orders received before February 1, 1980, would be due in three equal installments—May 10, 1980; June 10, 1980; and July 10, 1980.

Sixteen thousand units had been ordered in fiscal 1979 under the early-order discount plan. Mr. Stanley estimated that 24,000 units would qualify for early-order discounts in fiscal 1980.

EXHIBIT 2
Layout of Assembly Line

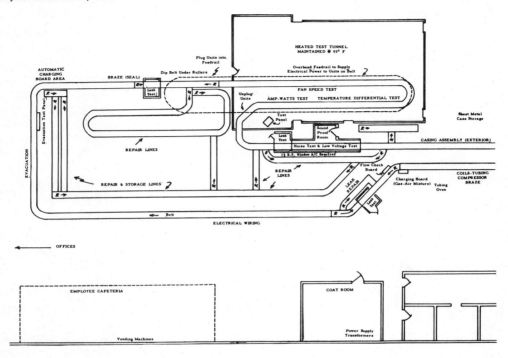

A growing consumer attitude that air conditioning was a necessity helped to lengthen out the sales year. With almost one half of the homes in the United States having at least one air conditioner, replacement sales were beginning to rise; these were made from early April to early September. The energy-efficient, quick installantion Midget unit was introduced in 1978 and sold for $300 retail.[3] In contrast, the 24,000 BTU unit, selling for $950 (at retail) and requiring professional installation, would typically be purchased in April or May. Seasonality was influenced somewhat by weather, but mainly at the extremes. A chilly April would reduce sales significantly, whereas a hot April led to very brisk sales.

PLANT WORK FORCE

In 1979, the Kool King Division employed 150 people of whom approximately 100 were classified as "direct labor." Included in the 150 employees was an executive group of six—the vice president of the division, the plant

---

[3] Typical retail markups were 100 percent.

EXHIBIT 2 (*concluded*)

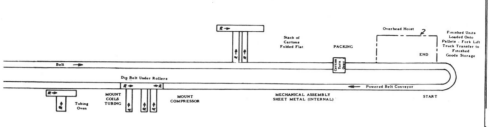

manager, the personnel manager, the accounting manager, the materials manager, and the director of engineering. Four other groups of employees were classed in categories other than hourly employees. These four groups were the plant supervisors (4); planning, materials, and administration staff (4); the engineering and design group (16); and the clerical staff (8).

The hourly employees were classified in eight grades as follows:

Grade 1 (70)   Assembly-line workers. No previous skills required. Approximately two-day training period.

Grade 2 (10)   Inspectors, janitors, and "spares"—people trained for any position on the line as replacement for absent workers or workers temporarily called away from the line.

Grade 3 (14)   People who repaired defective units discovered in the final test area of the assembly line, forklift truck drivers, station wagon driver, stock clerks, receiving and shipping department employees.

Grade 4 (1)   Group leader in the stockroom.

Grade 5 (8)	Refrigeration mechanic, employees who sealed the tubing used in air conditioners, mechanical inspector in the receiving area.
Grade 6 (5)	Maintenance people (a carpenter, an electrician, and a plumber), quality control spot checkers.
Grade 7 (3)	Line supervisors.
Grade 8 (1)	A machinist and model maker.

All direct labor was paid on an hourly basis with no incentive. New grade 1 employees were paid $4.80 per hour, a competitive wage in the Melrose Park area for unskilled labor. The union contract provided regular pay increases for grade 1 employees over a period of 18 months. After 18 months, grade 1 employees reached $6 per hour and could increase their hourly rate only by moving to a higher grade. The contract also provided a 30-day trial period for new employees. During this period, the company could discharge an employee without consulting the union. The reason for most dismissals during the trial period was the inability of some employees to maintain the relatively rapid pace required on the job.

Mr. Victor, the personnel manager, had estimated the cost of changing the size of the work force.[4] He stated: "The turnover of grade 1 employees, within the 30-day trial period, is quite large when compared to that of unskilled employees in other plants around here. Although this situation isn't too desirable, it's not serious because assembly-line operations are carefully laid out by our industrial engineers. We estimate that new employees are up to peak efficiency within two days."

Turnover of personnel in higher grades was another matter: "Skilled production employees are vital to maintaining our product quality and plant efficiency. We try to keep turnover in grades 2 through 8 as low as possible by avoiding a varying rate of production, which involves laying off and then rehiring skilled workers."

The plant had shut down for about 40 working days in 1976, 1977, and 1978. In 1979, this was cut to 30 days.

PLANNING

Planning for the Kool King Division had in past years started in May. In a series of meetings, Kool King and TIA executives laid out general guidelines for the division's sales and production budgets for the next fiscal year. Planning meetings in 1979 had begun with an aggregate forecast of air conditioner sales for the coming year presented by Mr. Stanley. Kool King executives usually questioned some features of the forecast. For example,

[4] See Exhibit 7.

the fiscal 1980 TIA forecast had been based on the assumption that the new Mighty Midget would not only take over a portion of the market of the smaller Midget unit but also increase total sales volume. Mr. Lewis had believed this assumption to be erroneous and had pointed out that the Mighty Midget's $350 price opened a new sales market in this price range in addition to the $300 Midget market.

Once the forecast was agreed upon, a large chart was prepared to facilitate the development of a production plan for the division (see Exhibit 3 for the plan which had been adopted one year ago for fiscal 1979). The number of units in a given series which could be produced in a week at the normal work force level was determined from the production rates shown in Exhibit 3.

In determining the production plan to be entered on the chart, division executives were guided by three policies which they believed to be very important: (1) the desire to minimize fluctuations in the size of the work force throughout the production year, (2) a preference for a large lot size since model changeover costs were estimated at $6,000 per change (a 10,000-unit run was considered optimal. If demand for a certain model was 20,000 units, the planners tried to schedule two runs during the year), and (3) a finished goods inventory containing almost all the division's products. Because distributors frequently order in truckload lots to minimize freight costs, most orders were for a mixture of large and small quantities of several different units. Production plans had to account for this product mix requirement.

The production plan (Exhibit 3) was not intended as a production schedule for the whole year. Production plans on the chart were for aggregated groups of product and did not show, for example, the BTU or voltage rating on products, the number of units to be made with or without the heating feature, etc. Detailed master schedules were issued frequently throughout the year by the materials manager, Mr. Frank. These schedules listed the production schedule for a 12-week period and showed in detail the number and type (voltage, accessories, etc.) of each model to be made each week. These schedules were reviewed and reissued at least once a month so the net effect of a series of these overlapping schedules was to reschedule production for a given period at least three times. As a production year progressed, information was received which tended to force changes in the original production plan. Because such changes were qutie frequent, Mr. Frank liked to keep the schedule flexible at all times. Information on actual production and shipments is shown in Exhibits 4 and 5.

Any changes from the original production plan meant a change in the planned pattern of component parts acquisition. In fiscal 1979, Kool King had processed over $11 million worth of purchased parts. Mr. Frank attempted to keep no more than two weeks components parts inventory on hand at any one time. For models running on the assembly line, the component parts inventory might be as low as one or two days' production

EXHIBIT 3
Planned Production by Week—Fiscal 1979

		Chassis Series						Total
	Midget	*Mighty Midget*	*Breeze Queen*	*Breeze King*	*Islander*	*Super**	*Slim†Line*	
Estimated FY 1979 sales	30,000	13,000	33,000	4,000	7,000	3,000	10,000	
Inventory, September 1, 1978	0	753	6,136	1,320	2,049	102	9,144	
Estimated FY 1979 production requirements	30,000	12,000	27,000	3,000	5,000	3,000	0	
Production rate (units per day)	550	550	325	325	275	65	550	
DAYS NEEDED	90	18.5	125.6	25.5	9.6	16.3		286 days
Week ending:								
September 8	550							
15	1,000							
22	2,750							
29	2,750							
October 6	2,750							
13	2,750							
20	1,450	1,300						
27		2,700						
November 3		2,000						
10			1,075					
17			1,625					
24			1,625					
December 1			1,300					
8			1,625					
15			1,625					

Month	Date						
January	22			1,625			
	29			1,300			
	5			200	975		
	12				1,625		
	19				400	975	
	26					1,375	
February	2					1,375	
	9	50				1,275	50
	16	2,200					250
	23	2,750					250
March	2	2,750					250
	9	2,750					250
	16	2,750					250
	23	2,750					250
	30		2,750				250
April	6		2,750				250
	13		500	1,200			250
	20			1,625			250
	27			1,625			250
May	4			1,625			200
	11			1,625			
	18			1,625			
	25			1,625			

EXHIBIT 3 (*concluded*)

| | | Chassis Series | | | | | |
	Midget	Mighty Midget	Breeze Queen	Breeze King	Islander	Super*	Slim† Line
June 1			1,625				
8			1,625				
15			800				
22							
29				Contemplated			
July 6							
13				inventory			
20							
27				and			
August 3							
10				vacation			
17				shutdown			
24							
31							

* The Super units were assembled on a small assembly line which was not part of the main assembly line.
† The Slim Line unit was scheduled for a complete redesign in FY 1979—no production was planned for the year.

EXHIBIT 4
Actual Production, Shipments, Inventories (Units) and Direct Labor Index by Week—Fiscal 1979

Week ending	Chassis Series						Total Production	Shipments	Finished Goods Inventory	Direct Labor Hours Index†
	Midget	Mighty Midget	Breeze Queen	Breeze King	Islander	Super				
			*				—		19,504	—
September 8			441				441	128	19,817	48.4
15	1,149						1,149	31	20,935	88.4
22	2,005						2,005	292	22,648	95.0
29	2,277						2,277	208	24,717	111.4
October 6	2,568	*					2,568	521	26,764	116.1
13	2,715	*					2,715	660	28,819	120.1
20	2,849	*					2,849	968	30,700	121.3
27	2,831	*					2,831	1,876	31,655	120.3
November 3		2,693					2,693	2,786	31,562	123.2
10		1,298					1,298	441	32,419	76.9[g]
17		301	1,300				1,601	1,503	32,517	112.0
24			1,685				1,685	469	33,733	111.2
December 1			1,043				1,043	651	34,125	66.7[b]
8			1,689				1,689	114	35,700	109.0
15			1,623				1,623	266	37,057	103.5
22			1,587				1,587	1,417	37,227	106.9
29			664				644	2,746	35,145	47.0[c]

EXHIBIT 4 (continued)

Week ending:	Chassis Series						Total Production	Shipments	Finished Goods Inventory	Direct Labor Hours Index[†]
	Midget	Mighty Midget	Breeze Queen	Breeze King	Islander	Super				
January 5			671				671	2,315	33,501	52.5[b]
12			1,155	360			1,515	285	34,731	115.6
19			442	400			842	1,031	34,542	58.9[d]
26				1,401			1,401	1,237	34,706	100.0
February 2				324	967		1,291	1,054	34,943	113.6
9					895		895	1,432	34,406	82.2
16					1,516		1,516	2,698	33,224	116.6
23					1,072		1,072	1,519	32,777	103.4
March 2			1,125	*	320		1,445	3,561	30,661	97.9[b]
9			1,155	480			1,635	1,413	30,883	126.4
16			1,684			130[h]	1,814	1,570	31,127	139.4
23			1,431			275[h]	1,706	2,326	30,507	137.4
30			1,237[f]	200		231[b]	1,668	1,830	30,345	121.3
April 6	*			1,582		287[h]	1,869	1,076	31,138	134.4
13	*		1,054	580		66[h]	1,700	2,423	30,415	131.4
20	100		1,540				1,640	3,344	28,711	135.9
27	2,334						2,334	5,613	25,432	134.3
May 4	2,925						2,925	4,146	24,211	129.0
11	2,917						2,917	2,771	24,357	130.2
18	2,893						2,893	3,694	23,556	129.2
25	2,762						2,762	3,225	23,093	127.4

	Week ending†									Index†
June	1	900		1,087				1,987	7,038	18,042	123.8
	8			1,985				1,985	4,898	15,129	143.9(e)
	15	*		2,117				2,117	2,198	15,048	136.1
	22	*		1,995				1,995	2,587	14,456	132.2
	29	*		1,985				1,985	5,061	11,380	131.4
July	6	*		2,019				2,019	2,354	11,045	132.7
	13	1,565		1,114				2,679	3,511	10,213	132.4(c)
	20	3,309		136				3,445	3,302	10,356	138.2
	27	3,329		45				3,374	4,538	9,192	135.0
August	3	1,928		577				2,505	2,981	8,716	130.1
	10			60				60	557	8,219	Inventory
	17	*		3				3	105	8,117	and
	24	*	*					—	51	8,066	vacation
	31	*	*					—	53	8,013	shutdown
	Totals	36,482	9,166	34,649	5,327	4,770	989	91,383	102,874		

* Stocked out.

† This index was calculated by dividing the actual direct labor-hours for each week by the direct labor-hours for the week ending January 15, i.e., index = 100 for week ending January 25.

(a) Stocked out of 9,300 BTU model only.

(b) One-day holiday this week—holidays often followed by substantial absenteeism.

(c) Two-day holiday this week.

(d) Two-day plant shutdown—snow storm delayed receipt of parts from a supplier in West Virginia.

(e) One-day holiday this week not taken—i.e., overtime paid for working on holiday.

(f) Parts shortage for Breeze Queen units.

(g) Two-day plant shutdown—election day and shortage of Mighty Midget motors.

(h) The Super units were not run on the main assembly line.

EXHIBIT 5
Monthly Summary of Production, Shipments, and Finished Goods Inventories

	Sept.	Oct.*	Nov.	Dec.	Jan.*	Feb.	Mar.	Apr.*	May	June	July*	Aug.	Total
Monthly Shipments	659	6,811	3,064†	4,543	5,922	9,210	7,139	16,602	16,728	14,744	16,686	766	102,874
	800	*8100*	*2700*	*5400*	*4100*	*11000*	*8600*	*18900*	*20000*	*13600*	*19900*	*900*	*102,500*
Percent of Year's Shipments Shipped This Month	0.64	6.62	2.98	4.42	5.76	8.95	6.94	16.14	16.26	14.33	16.22	0.74	100.00
Percent of Year's Shipments Cumulative	0.64	7.26	10.24	14.66	20.42	29.37	36.31	52.45	68.71	83.04	99.26	100.00	
Average Finished Goods Inventory during Month	22,029	29,900	33,198	36,282	34,485	32,767	30,715	27,981	22,262	14,003	9,904	8,104	

* For the months of October, January, April, and July, the shipments for the first day or two of the next month were included, e.g., October figures include data from week ending November 2.

† Commitments on the early order discount plan were not met in November due to shortages in the stock of several models.

EXHIBIT 5 *(concluded)*

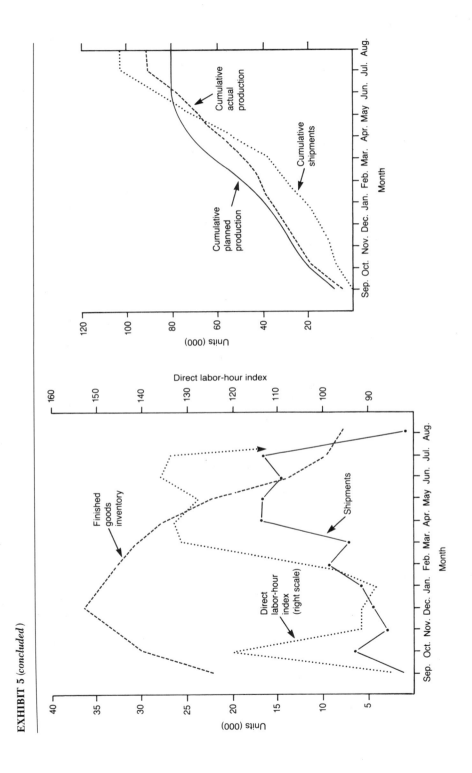

requirements, since material was being received regularly. For models which were not being produced currently, component parts inventory could be as much as one or two months ahead of scheduled production. This was particularly true when extreme changes were made in the schedule and during September and October.[5]

Mr. Frank hoped to plan schedules 12 weeks in advance. In actual practice some planning had to be done more than 12 weeks ahead. The purchasing of steel, for example, required planning up to four months in advance of production. On the other hand, many decisions could not be made and then held for 12 weeks. Developments in the market often forced the company to change the schedule with only one or two weeks' notice. The minimum advance notice required to make changes in the schedule was a function of the lead time of the suppliers of component parts. If all the parts were in inventory or on order, a one- or two-week lead time often caused no difficulty. If a major change in the schedule was contemplated, however, a number of suppliers could not furnish the required parts without a lengthy advanced warning. This was especially true when Kool King attempted to make major changes in the orders for motors or compressors.

* * * * *

Mr. Lewis stated, "There are obviously different points of view about what's important here. One thing I'm sure we all agree on is that we need a new plan and we need it fast. What do you think, Bob?"

Mr. Irwin replied, "Frankly, I wonder if we should really run with this new forecast. Tom is planning almost a 30 percent increase in sales of the Midget unit. Keep in mind that we're not the only ones in the market with a $300 unit any more. Also, I think this increase in the forecast will push us beyond one-shift capacity."

"This is a realistic forecast," Mr. Stanley said. "You fellows have to realize that we're in a rapidly growing market and just holding our market share will give us considerable growth."

"We'll have to evaluate this thing carefully," Mr. Irwin replied. "This may cause quite a bit of overtime or perhaps a second shift for part of the year. We've got the space for a second assembly line and I suppose, on a crash program, we could have it installed by Christmas."

The controller, Mr. Williams, said, "One of the problems that we face when annual demand begins to push against our capacity is that our finished goods inventories go up. I've got some figures on inventory costs for last year (Exhibit 6). Even at a 10 percent cost of capital we spent over $108,000 to carry excess inventory."

---

[5] During September and October, materials orders were generally based on the previous year's production schedule, plus a growth factor. This was due to the fact that orders for some materials to be used in September and October had to be placed in the late spring, before the next year's production plans and schedules were finalized.

EXHIBIT 6
Analysis of Inventory Carrying Costs—Fiscal 1979 (prepared by Mr. Williams)

I.   **Annual space cost:**
Space cost 9/1/78–8/29/79 (rent):

$$\frac{\$1,450,000}{100,000 \text{ square feet plant space}} = \$14.50 \text{ cost per square feet}$$

II. **Warehousing space:**

(1) Sum of weekly inventory 1,308,798 ÷ 52 weeks = 25,169 average units.
Less: Basic inventory quantity carried
weekly as part of manufacturing
operations 15,000*

Average excess warehousing weekly inventory 10,169 units per week.

(2) Average floor space required per unit = 0.725 square feet (units stacked in pallet loads)
Add 40 percent for idle space (aisles, etc.):
0.725 × 1.4 = 1.015 square feet per unit
(space occupied by average unit)

III. **Warehousing labor:**

One person full time 52 weeks @ $300 = $15,600 per year (including fringes)

IV. **Cost of finished goods:**

Standard cost of average unit produced 9/1/78–8/29/79 = $125.70 average unit cost.

V.   **Total dollars tied up in finished goods inventory:**

Space $14.50/square feet × 10,169 units × 1.015 square feet per unit.	$ 149,662
Labor	15,600
Finished good 10,169 units × $125.70 average cost per unit.	1,278,243
Total dollars	1,443,505

VI. **Cost of total dollars tied up in finished goods:**

$1,443,505 × 0.10 corporate interest rate × $\frac{39}{52}$ (finished goods inventory exceeds 15,000 units on 39 weeks only) = $\underline{\$108,263}$

---

* Manufacturing assumes that 15,000 units of finished goods inventory are required to permit long runs and to assist in leveling production. Inventory charges are assessed only against units over 15,000.

EXHIBIT 7

Memorandum   June 16, 1979

To: Bob Irwin

From: John Victor

Subject: Cost of Changing the Size of the Work Force

As I have previously mentioned, we have no exact data on the costs of changing the size of our work force. Since we cannot change the number of assembly workers on the main line without rebalancing the job assignments, we have not had much experience with more than two or three work force levels on the main assembly line.

The costs involved in hiring a new worker can be estimated as follows:

Application processing, interview, and selection
    (character reference check, etc.):
    Three hours employment office clerical time @ $18 per hour
      (including overhead) .... $ 54.00
    One hour interviewer's (personnel manager's) time @ $21
      per hour 21.00
    Physical examination 30.00
    Payroll entry preparation: 30 minutes per new employee
      @ $21 per hour for payroll clerk and overhead........... 10.50
    Training:
      Assume 2 days per worker @ $36 per day................ 72.00
        plus lost time for experienced worker-trainer, say,
        1 day @ $52 per day 52.00
      Plus lost time for foreman, say ½ day @ $90 per day 45.00
        Total 284.50

In addition to these costs, any significant increase in the number of employees would require more supervisory personnel, more indirect labor (order clerks, receiving clerks, stockroom clerks, materials handlers, etc.) and perhaps extra costs for maintenance and repair.

Decreasing the size of the work force involves costs that are even more difficult to estimate. In some cases, laying off a grade 1 employee and replacing him or her with a new worker actually would result in a saving because of the automatic wage increase feature of the union contract. However, our unemployment compensation costs are tied to the stability of our work force. Our maximum contribution is 2.7 percent of the employee's pay up to the first $3,000. This contribution can drop to as low as 0.1 percent if the cumulative amounts of withdrawals from the compensation fund by employees laid off is small for the past three years.

Wide swings in our employment level may be costly in terms of bad will in the community and may also adversely affect the quality of our product.

John Victor, personnel manager, added: "Don't forget though, Earl, that inventory buys us something. The work force can't be counted on to stick with us when we change things around. As a good example, yesterday morning when we opened the plant after our annual shutdown, 30 workers didn't show up. Even though a number of our skilled workers received two or three weeks of paid vacation during the shutdown, seven workers from grades 3 and 5 didn't come back." (See Exhibit 7 for John Victor's memorandum to Bob Irwin about the costs of changing the size of the work force.)

CASE 22

Sorenson Research Company

Early in December 1976, James L. Sorenson, president and founder of Sorenson Research Company of Salt Lake City, reviewed his firm's year-to-date financial statements (Exhibit 1). Sales were 50 percent higher than those of the previous year, and net income had grown at a slightly faster pace. Moreover, market reaction to two recently introduced products—REGUFLO and TRUSET—was such that this already rapid growth might well accelerate in 1977 and beyond. Sorenson was concerned, however, with the even faster rate of inventory expansion that was tying up funds that were needed to enlarge the firm's productive capacity and react to competitive challenges. He was anxious to reduce inventories as much as possible while maintaining customer service levels.

BACKGROUND

As a young man, Sorenson had sold medical supplies throughout the Intermountain West (primarily Utah and Idaho) for several large pharmaceutical concerns. He was thereby exposed to a wide variety of hospitals and became well acquainted with the technological needs of the medical community. Naturally inventive, Sorenson had developed and patented several disposable catheter devices that ideally complemented the advancing medical hardware. After quitting his sales job and briefly experimenting with a partnership, he had formed his own corporation to produce and market the new products.

Within 10 years of incorporation, Sorenson Research Company was nationally known as a major producer of catheters (INTRASET), catheter-support devices (REGUFLO), and fluid-suction systems (VACUFLO, COLLECTAL). (See Exhibits 2A, 2B, and 2C.) Catheters are small plastic tubes introduced into the circulatory system through a metal needle placed

EXHIBIT 1

SORENSON RESEARCH COMPANY
Financial Summary Report
Year to Date November 1976*
($000)

	1976	1975
Current assets:		
Cash......................	$ 180	$ (−50)
Deposits	1	2
Receivables...............	4,200	2,800
Inventories net...........	7,100	3,700
Prepaid expense..........	35	49
Total current assets.......	11,516	6,501
Current liabilities:		
Trade accounts payable........	2,000	400
Accrued liabilities	1,100	(10)
Total current liabilities.....	3,100	390
Net working capital.............	8,416	6,111
Fixed assets—net.............	1,500	1,000
Miscellaneous assets	10	21
Deferred charges/credits—net ..	250	300
Total investment	$10,176	$ 7,431
Financed by:		
Interplant control[†]...........	$ 2,300	$ 2,000
Debt......................	2,420	1,300
Equity	5,456	4,131
Total capitalization........	$10,176	$ 7,431
October sales (annualized).......	$24,100	$15,500
Cost of goods sold	12,773	8,225
Contribution to sales commissions, overhead, and profit..................	11,327	7,275

* All data have been disguised but reflect pertinent trends.
† Line of credit extended by other Sorenson controlled corporations.

in the arm, leg, or chest. Catheter-support devices keep such catheters free of blood clots and help regulate infusion of drugs. Fluid-suction systems are plastic canisters and/or lines attached to suction pumps which evacuate excess body fluids (Exhibit 2).

A nationwide distribution and sales network was responsible for annual sales of more than $24 million (Exhibit 3); 15 percent of sales were in Europe and Latin America. Sorenson was one of the top four firms in terms

EXHIBIT 2A
Product Literature—INTRASET (catheter device)

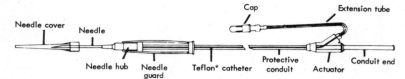

"A Safe, Simple and Sterile Technique for Central Arterial Pressure."

The C.A.P. INTRASET is a 100 cm. (39.37 in.) long Teflon* catheter that allows safe peripheral arterial puncture for central arterial pressure monitoring and blood chemistries.

The Central Arterial Pressure Catheter C.A.P. (Intraset) is a 100 cm. (39.37 in.) long, Teflon* catheter for central arterial pressure monitoring and blood chemistries. Arterial puncture may be performed in an accessible artery such as the radial, brachial, ulnar or femoral. The catheter may be advanced to the intrathoracic arteries for pressure measurements.

The C.A.P. INTRASET may be positioned the day before a surgical procedure, used again for measurement at the time of surgery, and then later for measurement in the post-operative recovery area. If the percutaneous route is not feasible, the catheter can be placed in position during surgery by the surgeon in the operating room directly into the thoracic vessels or advanced after peripheral arterial cutdown.

1. Remove plastic cap from extension end and attach to pressure transducer flushing system.

2. Flush catheter and allow solution to completely fill catheter for high fidelity pressure recording. This will remove air from catheter. Needle cover may be left in place or removed during flushing.

3. Perform arterial puncture with oscilloscope monitoring to assure proper entry into vessel lumen. FIGURE 3.

IMPORTANT: Grasp Needle Hub, not needle guard during arterial puncture.

4. When certain that the lumen of the artery has been properly entered, the Teflon* catheter may be advanced. Hold needle firmly in the artery. The third, fourth and fifth fingers of the right hand grip the conduit end while the thumb and forefinger walk the actuator in a forward direction along the protective conduit advancing the catheter to desired position. Position of catheter tip can be determined by measuring distance actuator has been advanced from starting point on conduit. FIGURE 4. To assure free passage of the catheter up the artery, it is important to observe the pulse contour on the oscilloscope to determine any damping due to obstruction of the catheter tip against the artery wall. If damping occurs (not due to clotting in the catheter tip), very careful manipulation must be observed to by-pass this point (Instruction 6).

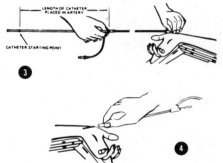

of market share in the catheter market and was the leading firm in catheter-support devices and fluid-suction systems.

Unlike many of its competitors, Sorenson Research did not make "staple" hospital commodities such as scrub brushes, gowns, and surgical masks. Instead, product development and marketing were focused on specialized, high-technology items with relatively high margins that generated the funds for further research and innovation. This was particularly essential as Sorenson, a privately held corporation, had no ready access to equity markets.

SALES AND DISTRIBUTION

Before 1969, Sorenson products had been distributed through independent national and regional medical-supply dealers; they, in turn, were serviced by independent sales reps. The dealers commanded a 40 percent

EXHIBIT 2B
Product Literature—REGUFLO (catheter-support device)

CATALOG NO. DAF-30

SCALE: A NORMAL CONTROL RANGE OF 5 TO 250 MILLILITERS (CC) PER HOUR
MAXIMUM UNRESTRICTED FLOW RATE: APPROX. 2,600 CC HR.

REGUFLO Instructions

1. Hang solution container approximately 76.2 cm. (30 inches) above patient.

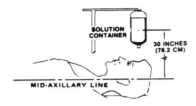

2. Look at the I.V. infusion set package to determine the number of drops/cc of the drip chamber.

3. Connect standard I.V. infusion set to solution container.

4. Connect **REGUFLO** to infusion set.

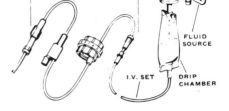

5. Open clamp on infusion set to maximum flow position.

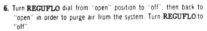

6. Turn **REGUFLO** dial from "open" position to "off", then back to "open" in order to purge air from the system. Turn **REGUFLO** to "off".

margin on retail hospital sales; the sales reps received an additional 12 percent of sales. However, Sorenson had discovered that dealers allocated most sales time to products with an established volume of sales. In the words of Sorenson's marketing director, "Dealers simply supply existing markets and do not really attempt to create new markets or educate the market in the value of new products." Moreover, the sales reps made no effort to provide the type of feedback from the hospitals that was so essential to a firm whose primary competitive advantage was identifying and satisfying needs for new products.

After experimenting briefly with special franchise distribution plans where dealers marketed Sorenson products exclusively, the company began to build up its own direct sales force in 1970. Ties with all dealers were eliminated. Each company salesperson was paid on a straight commission equal to 20 percent of the sales revenues of each order obtained. As a practical matter, each member of the sales force was assigned a geographical region and paid a sales commission on all revenues coming from customers in that region.

EXHIBIT 2C
Product Literature—VACUFLO (fluid-suction device)

"A Vacuum Suction Collection System Offering Aseptic Disposal."

Suctioned fluids are contained entirely within an unbroken fluid path. After use, the disposable liner and contents are removed from the reusable canister and can be disposed of intact.

SIGNIFICANT ADVANTAGES

1. Disposable — Complete throw-away of Liner and contents.
2. Simple — Easy to use. Reduced handling means time and money saved.
3. Closed system offers aseptic handling of all aspirated fluids.
4. Compact, requires minimum storage space.
5. Instant suction. Readily adaptable to most steady or intermittent suction systems.
6. Highly durable, reusable canister.
7. Affords improved patient care.
8. 25cc graduations.

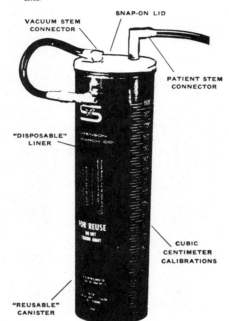

VACUUM STEM CONNECTOR

SNAP-ON LID

PATIENT STEM CONNECTOR

"DISPOSABLE" LINER

FOR REUSE

CUBIC CENTIMETER CALIBRATIONS

"REUSABLE" CANISTER

CATALOG NUMBER

KG-1600-C
A 1500 cubic centimeter impact resistant polymer Canister graduated every 25 cubic centimeters, numbered every 100 cubic centimeters (includes CV14PC vacuum line assembly).

KG-2100-C
A 2000 cubic centimeter impact resistant polymer Canister graduated every 25 cubic centimeters, numbered every 100 cubic centimeters (includes CV14PC vacuum line assembly).

KGV-1600-L
A 1500 cubic centimeter, flexible, disposable liner including lid and shutoff valve.   (five units per box - 50 units per case)

KGV-2100-L
A 2000 cubic centimeter, flexible, disposable liner including lid and shutoff valve.   (five units per box - 50 units per case)

Because Sorenson emphasized specialized, high-technology products rather than standard commodity items, the sales effort tended to bypass the traditional hospital purchasing channels. Rather than calling mainly on hospital purchasing agents, the Sorenson sales force called on doctors and professional staff, introducing them to Sorenson products and demonstrating their use. Once such "users" agreed to try the products it was a relatively simple matter to get a purchase order from the purchasing agent.

Because of the nature of Sorenson's products and the company's selling approach, demand was not very price sensitive. In the catheter line, Sorenson did feel compelled to meet the market prices of its competitors. However, since Sorenson was the major factor in both catheter-support devices and fluid-suction devices, these products were value priced by the company. The company was also helped by the fact that hospitals could gener-

EXHIBIT 3
Sales Breakdown*

	Units	Volume	Product Type
INTRASET	1,000,000	$ 2,500,000	Catheters
SUBCLAVIAN II.........	250,000	137,000	Catheters
SUBCLAVIAN...........	150,000	975,000	Catheters
JUGULAR II	300,000	300,000	Catheters
CATHASPEC............	100,000	150,000	Catheters
IV-SET	700,000	1,000,000	Catheters
CENTRI-CATH..........	500,000	3,500,000	Catheters
IV-12	15,000	74,700	Catheters
CSP	1,000,000	750,000	Catheters
Pressure cuff.............	600,000	972,000	Catheter support
Pressure tubing	25,000	825,000	Catheter support
EZE-FLO	4,200	65,100	Catheter support
REGUFLO..............	1,000,000	5,000,000	Catheter support
TRUSET	2,850,000	7,115,000	Catheter support
INTRAVAL..............	10,000	8,300	Catheter support
VACUFLO	355,000	350,000	Fluid suction
COLLECTAL canisters	40,000	54,800	Fluid suction
COLLECTAL liners	393,000	727,000	Fluid suction
	9,292,200	24,503,900	

* All data have been disguised. Unit and dollar volumes shown above are for entire product lines. Within any one product category, such as REGUFLO, the company made several variations of the basic item. The firm manufactured about 160 different product variations within these 18 general categories.

ally pass the cost of Sorenson products on to individual patients since they were all disposable items for one-time use.

Concurrent with the buildup of a direct sales force, regional and "garage" warehouses were established (Exhibit 4). The "garage" warehouses were often located in the salesman's garage or simply kept in the salesman's car. These warehouses were considered necessary for two reasons. First, most hospitals had not been designed to store large inventories. This factor, along with a shortage of capital for inventory investments, had prompted hospitals to shift storage onto their suppliers. Most of Sorenson's competitors provided such storage. Second, to secure a competitive market position upon instituting its own direct sales force, Sorenson had heavily promoted a comprehensive service program; this included an assurance of prompt delivery—within 24 hours if need be—to most major hospitals.

The regional warehouses were supplemented by "emergency" stocks maintained by individual sales representatives to ensure immediate delivery of critical products to hospitals. Sales and marketing people were confident that such ready availability was a crucial sales advantage; others in the firm, including the treasurer, had expressed doubts, however.

EXHIBIT 4
Field Warehouses

LEGEND

Type	Average Inventory at Factory Cost
■ Major	$165,000
● Minor	$ 40,000
▲ Garage	$ 10,000

Number indicates full-time salesmen drawing on that warehouse.
Heavy lines indicate sales regions.

It was observed that many hospitals—particularly substantial accounts with established reorder patterns—could, and often did, order directly from Salt Lake City. Delivery was about two weeks after the receipt of such orders, depending on the distance from Salt Lake. (Delivery from regional warehouses, in comparison, varied from one to seven days, depending on a variety of factors.) Sorenson had customarily paid all shipping expenses. Sorenson would ship any quantity or mix of products ordered; there were no minimum order quantities.

Many Sorenson executives, particularly those not in sales and marketing, saw little need for regional warehouses whose annual rental and order-processing costs were about 10 percent of the average field inventory investment. (The firm's estimated cost of capital was 15 percent.) Moreover, many felt that the warehouse network further complicated the already difficult task of allocating field stocks of back-ordered products to regions where shortages existed (Exhibit 5).

In spite of such objections, marketing and sales managers had prevailed and the firm had gradually developed a system of 23 major, minor, and garage field warehouses. The difference between "major" and "minor" was one of degree. Major warehouses had more complete inventories of the product line and more sophisticated communications equipment. (For ex-

EXHIBIT 5
Inventory Situation (November 1976) (manufactured cost $000)

Total inventory...................	$7,100
Total finished goods inventory.....	4,350
Raw materials...................	2,750
In-house finished goods	1,400
Field finished goods	2,950
Total current back orders.........	1,395
Hospital back orders.............	653
Regional back orders.............	742

Back-Ordered Products*

	Back Orders		Sales Last	Field	Inventory
	Hospital	Regional	Week	Inventory	Total†
COLLECTAL					
liners	$ 3.8		$ 14.0	$ 5.3	$ 7.4
CATHASPEC	8.8	$ 10.3	1.5	14.6	14.7
VACUFLO.........	2.9		2.9	4.6	5.0
REGUFLO.........	515.9	358.5	102.0	118.3	192.9
INTRASET........	34.7	5.4	82.0	444.0	448.0
Pressure cuff	6.9	12.0	5.5	132.2	134.5
CENTRI-CATH	19.9	248.7	60.0	127.4	215.1
S-C II	26.8	6.2	3.9	14.9	15.2
CSP..............	14.5	95.8	15.2	252.0	309.9
Others............	18.7	5.8	9.3	69.7	98.9
Total	652.9	742.7	296.3	1,178.4	1,434.4

* The table contains only product categories with products in back order. Not all product categories have products in back order; and furthermore, not all products in the above product categories are in back order.

† Field inventory plus central warehouse inventory at Salt Lake.

ample, most major sites had Telex.) Garage warehouses were glorified emergency stocks.

INVENTORY CONTROL SYSTEM

Throughout 1976, the policy in field inventory control had been outlined by the marketing and accounting departments in an evolving fashion (Exhibit 6). Under this policy, each major warehouse was permitted an inventory whose value was equivalent to 45 days of sales in the region served by the warehouse. The regional sales managers were instructed to compute this stock level on the basis of sales activity over the preceding two to four months. (Sales were not seasonal, making these calculations relatively straightforward.) They also decided on the quantities of each product in the stock.

EXHIBIT 6

January 20, 1976

To: Bill Johnson, Office Manager, Salt Lake City Factory

From: Larry Harmer, Special Assistant, National Sales and Marketing

Subject: Inventory Control/Warehousing

In recent weeks we have discussed the need for a monthly summary to each manager or salesman charged with finished goods inventory identifying movements in and out. Such a summary seems essential if the factory is going to be able to maintain accurate records as well as to permit the field representative a means of identification and control for his inventories.

As soon as the above program is ready, please let us know so that we may inform our field people.

Also, as discussed, there needs to be a confirmation document of some kind sent to all parties involved where there is an interwarehouse field transfer of merchandise. This is to ensure a record of movement that will tie the communication together for the shipping warehouse, the receiving warehouse, and factory control.

It appears our back-order notification and advice of expected shipping dates of back-order merchandise has fallen into arrears. It is important the customer as well as the salesman know when to expect fulfillment of an order for future shipment incident to current back-order conditions. At one time we had a mimeograph postcard notice prepared to be sent to all customers and/or salesmen involved if an order could not move within three days after receipt.*

Thanks Bill.

* As a practical matter, when a product became back-ordered it was put on allocation. Generally, those who needed it most were then shipped the next available units.

EXHIBIT 6 (*continued*)

March 17, 1976

To: Regional Managers and Sales Representatives

From: Office Manager, Salt Lake City Factory

Subject: Monthly Warehouse Inventory Report

Included in the package of computer listings this month is a warehouse inventory report showing inventory balances, shipments, and receipts of inventory for each catalog number held by your warehouse.

This report is reconciled to our perpetual inventory card for your warehouse each month. Our reconciliation is done after your copy is mailed so there will be no corrections noted on it. Thus, we feel this represents accurately the inventory you should have in your warehouse.

We ask that you review this report monthly with your perpetual inventory cards by the following methods:

1. Add to your balance on your inventory card shipments made during the month but not shown as a shipment on warehouse inventory report.
2. Add samples to your inventory card not yet reported to SLC.
3. Add to your inventory shipments made to your warehouse by SLC but not yet received before month-end.

When above procedures are followed, inventories should balance. If a difference occurs, effort should be made to determine why. Perhaps the following suggestions may help:

1. Shipments made to hospitals but not recorded on inventory card.
2. Shipments made to hospitals, recorded on card, but delivery receipt not sent to SLC.
3. Sample invoices, no-charge, and warehouse transfers not recorded.
4. Extension errors or wrong amount recorded.
5. Shipments from SLC in quantities not specified on invoice.
6. Invoiced in different quantities than shipped.

Careful attention should be given in the review of inventories monthly. Should you have any questions or problems we will be happy to discuss them with you.

Thank you,

EXHIBIT 6 (*continued*)

May 10, 1976

To: All Regional Managers

From: Larry Harmer, Special Assistant, National Sales and Marketing

Subject: Warehousing/Inventory Control

Incident to our mushrooming growth as a company, our field warehousing and distribution system, as now constituted, is very inefficient and economically burdensome. We have given this problem considerable in-depth thought and engaged in possible solution discussions with most of you.

Outlined herein is our current planned approach to the problem, with the following parameters to be accomplished:

1.   To improve and/or maintain adequate and competitively effective hospital support service.
2.   To improve utilization of our finished goods inventory with reduction of incidence of back-order conditions.
3.   To reduce frequency of physical involvement by field sales personnel in handling of orders, thus making maximum time available for sales and service support efforts.
4.   To effectively utilize company financial resources to the maximum which includes doubling the rate of inventory turnover.

The above effort will involve two major segments:

1.   Strategic location of storage warehouses across the nation, each situated for maximum/prompt distribution capabilities to our hospital customers.
2.   Identification and distribution of finished goods to be used as product samples separate and apart from sales stocks of inventory.

Warehouse locations:

All field warehouse locations to be designated as major, minor, or garage. Major warehouses will be those serving all of the greater portion of a particular distribution area. Minor warehouses are those so designated because of limited service coverage incident to geographic location. A garage location is one with inventory drawn from major warehouse stock and charged thereto, where proper servicing of hospital accounts in isolated areas is necessary.

Responsibility for selection, communication, and control of all major warehouses to be assigned to our Salt Lake City factory, Mr. Bill Johnson, office manager. Selection and determination of each warehouse facility to be in conjunction with the regional managers. Matters to be kept in mind in selection of such warehouses should include, but not necessarily limited to, accessibility; ability to receive and process orders direct from the customers to maintain and be able to identify stock levels on a daily basis; an ability to process and fill orders, including shipping notices and advice to all concerned;

EXHIBIT 6 (*continued*)

All Regional Managers
May 10, 1976
Page 2

security from damage, theft, or vandalism; bonded; repackaging if or when necessary, etc.

Communications in a prompt and accurate manner between the warehouse and factory will be essential. This may include Telex, telephone, or air mail. The factory will maintain adequate and necessary control procedures to ensure maintenance of proper inventory levels.

Warehouse stock levels:

A total dollar value equivalent to 45 days' sales will be allowed for each major warehouse. The dollar value to be determined by an average of the preceding 120 days' sales volume. Selection of items to be maintained at the warehouse and within the dollar structure identified to be the responsibility of the regional manager. As warehouse stocks are depleted on an on-going basis, it will be the factory's responsibility, in close communication with the warehouse, to maintain inventory stocks as designated by the regional manager. Any changes in stocking items to be designated by the regional manager. All inventory movement to and from each warehouse to be controlled by invoice. There must be no movement of inventory, for emergency purposes or otherwise, without adequate adherence to established controls.

Implementation:

We suggest the first steps to be taken are:

1. Return of all inventory stocks consigned to individual salesmen and maintained in their local garages or from existing warehouses.
2. Consolidation of existing stocks to one location within the region the total of which should not exceed the dollar value of 45 days' sales. Details in this effort should be worked out in discussion with Bill Johnson or his assistant, Mr. Marvin Billings.
3. It is essential the total paperwork accompany each movement of goods to ensure proper accounting credits.

Emergency stocks:

If, in the regional manager's opinion, an emergency stock of inventory should be kept by an individual salesman at a location other than the above designated warehouse, he may issue stock to the salesman up to a maximum value of $1,000. Such stock transfer to be covered by invoice and consigned to the salesman for resale purposes. Such emergency stock issues to be included within the 45-day total dollar value allowed for the major warehouse.

Sampling procedures:

In lieu of using resale stock merchandise for demonstration samples and customer evaluation, products marked as samples to be available and fur-

EXHIBIT 6 (*concluded*)

> All Regional Managers
> May 10, 1976
> Page 3
>
> nished direct to each salesman involved. Each sample item to be so labeled and marked as "samples only, not for resale." Such samples will move from the factory to the salesman and/or customer and will not be stocked at a field warehouse facility.
>
> **Implementation of samplimg program:**
>
> Initially a selection of samples, as above described, covering a broad range of our products will be sent to each individual salesman without solicitation. We do not contemplate supplying slow-moving product samples in the initial effort. A supply of the form "request for sample" will be forwarded to each salesman that he may requisition additional items to those initially offered. If a need arises for an item not in hand, the "request for sample" form should be filled out and mailed direct to the factory. The sample product will be sent to the individual salesman or customer as designated on the order. As additional sample supplies are needed, they may be requisitioned by using the "request for sample" form.
>
> With inception of the new sampling procedures, "salesman's weekly sample distribution report" form currently in use will be discontinued. It will not be necessary for the salesman to identify sample distribution in this new effort. Should, however, an occasion arise that will necessitate knowledge as to distribution of a particular lot of product samples, we will resort to the salesman's daily call reports for specific information.
>
> To the extent possible we recommend filling orders in less than case quantities be from Salt Lake City. Installation of our new WATS line service, plus nationwide distribution from Salt Lake City by UPS, should make this very feasible.
>
> Inauguration and maintenance of this program to be under the direction of and the responsibility of Mr. Bill Johnson and his staff. Any questions or recommendations in this matter should be directed to Mr. Johnson.
>
> Thanks and regards,
>
> L. H.

Minimum stock levels were established for each product in every warehouse; if the stock fell below this point, a restock order was sent to Salt Lake City. Maximum levels were also set on the total amount of on-hand plus in-transit inventory permitted to any one region. Since all products were sterilized after packaging, they had a shelf life of several years, and the maximum inventory level reflected cash constraints and the need to minimize losses from theft and damage and poor physical inventory control.

EXHIBIT 7
Reorder Points for Typical Major Warehouse

	Actual Monthly Sales Volume (units)					Order* Point Max/Min
	Preceding Four Months				Average per Month	
	4	3	2	1		
TRUSET-03F	4,900	5,200	3,700	3,950	4,438	6,300/2,500
TRUSET-03............	3,700	2,900	4,200	2,800	3,400	5,000/1,500
TRUSET-06F	1,950	2,050	2,300	2,000	2,075	3,200/1,000
TRUSET-30............	1,300	2,700	1,400	1,200	1,650	2,300/700
REGUFLO-30..........	6,000	6,400	7,100	7,200	6,675	11,500/3,500
COLLECTAL2100......	19,500	18,000	18,500	20,000	19,000	32,000/10,000
COLLECTAL2100V	11,000	12,500	12,000	14,200	12,425	20,000/7,000
COLLECTAL1600......	8,300	8,000	9,500	9,000	8,700	14,500/4,500
COLLECTAL1600V	6,500	7,000	4,100	5,600	5,800	8,500/2,500

* As a starting point, the minimum was 2 weeks' worth and the maximum was 45 days' worth of demand. These were modified somewhat to reflect management judgments as to how future demand would differ from the preceding four months.

(Such losses in the systems had never been tracked; management estimated they were as high as 5–8 percent of factory cost.)

He had not specifically stated it in his policy memos, but the national sales manager had informed all regional managers that it was their responsibility to determine the appropriate max/min levels for all products in their regions. Moreover, it was the regional manager's job to inform Salt Lake when reorder minimums were reached so that the inventory could be immediately replenished (Exhibit 7). Warehouse replenishment orders, as well as hospital orders taken by salesmen but to be filled direct from Salt Lake, were placed by phone, Telex, or mail. On average, it took two weeks from the time an order was received in Salt Lake until the hospital or field warehouse received the items ordered. Half of this time was required under existing order-processing procedures; the other half represented transit time. Most warehouse orders were shipped by common carrier as less than carload lots (LCL). Annual shipping tonnage to each of the 23 warehouses did not justify full carloads.

PROBLEMS WITH THE SYSTEM

To complement the reorder-point replenishment procedure, the central office in Salt Lake continually monitored all transfers of inventory from the central warehouse to the field warehouses and from the central warehouse to the hospitals. Shipments from Salt Lake to a field inventory were credited to the regional account on inventory-history cards in the accounting department. Similarly, when orders were filled from a warehouse, the warehouse sent an order receipt to Salt Lake. The receipt served Salt Lake as the basis for customer billing invoices; these in turn were used for compiling data for commission allotments, for sales analysis, and for inventory records.

In June 1976, it was generally believed that the home office's field-inventory records provided, at best, only an estimate of actual regional inventories. The accounting department supervisor had found that errors were occasionally made in crediting shipment of stock from Salt Lake to a given warehouse and in transcribing depletions of field stocks due to hospital sales. The usefulness of the inventory records was also mitigated by the lag between the arrival of a warehouse's field-order receipt and the actual field stock depletion; there was another lag between the arrival of the order receipt and its posting on the central warehouse history cards. The total lag ranged from five days to as much as two weeks. Thus, the records of the home office inventory comptroller who received restock requests from regional managers did not always match the actual inventory in the field.

During June 1976, in an attempt to remedy this situation, all inventory movements were to be compiled and monitored by a new computerized control system. It was hoped that the new system would reduce the probability of human posting errors in tabulating regional inventory totals. The system was to be complemented by expanded use of the Telex to reduce lag in the system and to provide the comptrollers with more current records. By late November, however, the new system had still not gone beyond the debugging stages. Moreover, the old control system had not been effectively maintained, and the home office had essentially lost track of field inventories. Reliable figures were obtainable for total field inventory (as surmised from central warehouse shipments and order records from hospital sales); however, there was no way of knowing the stock level of a given product in a given field warehouse. In late September, the regional managers had taken a physical inventory; however, these figures had become rapidly outdated and could not generally be used by the comptroller to assess the reasonableness of reorder requests from the field.

BACK-ORDER PROBLEMS

As 1976 progressed, James Sorenson became increasingly concerned with the accumlation of back orders. In large measure, the problem resulted from serious production delays on one of the firm's best-selling items. Several other products, however, were also back ordered (Exhibit 5). These unfilled orders included both regional restock requests and direct hospital replenishment requests. In most instances, Sorenson had observed that the firm was incurring hospital ill will because of these regional stock-outs, although the net field inventory of the back-ordered items was often substantial. Any progress in rectifying production delays was rapidly obscured by booming sales demand.

On the basis of the September physical inventory, the central comptroller sometimes contacted warehouses which had reported fairly large stocks of a back-ordered item. However, these regional managers often reported that their stocks had since been depleted. And even if the comptroller was able to locate sufficient amounts of the back-ordered item, the time required to track it down plus the time and cost of the interwarehouse transfer absorbed much of the profit from the sale. (Gross margins were about 47 percent of the price paid by a typical hospital. Payment of the 20 percent sales commission gave the company a 27 percent contribution to general overhead and profit.)

THE SITUATION IN DECEMBER 1976

Sorenson and many of his top managers knew they could not afford to remain heavily back ordered throughout the nation. Several medical-products conglomerates had been thinking of expanding their entries in the disposable-catheter and suction-system markets. Sorenson realized that the efforts to expand productive capacity would have to be coupled with a more effective distribution/control system. Indeed, the severity of the production problems simply highlighted the importance of distributing available inventory as efficiently as possible.

In late December, Larry Harmer, special assistant, national sales and marketing, had proposed a policy revision to alleviate the back-order problems. In addition to designating a new head for field-warehousing and inventory systems, he proposed a five-step plan:

1. To achieve a total inventory turnover rate (Cost of goods sold ÷ Finished goods inventory) of six or more, all regional managers would have to ensure that warehouse stocks of any given catalog item did not exceed a 60-day supply, based upon sales history.
2. Merchandise in excess of specified inventory limitations would be reshipped to the factory or another field warehouse as designated by the new systems head. If there was a second instance of excess supply of a given product at a given warehouse, the reshipping cost would be charged to the regional manager.
3. All emergency stocks in garage warehouses would be discontinued.
4. The new systems head would expedite daily order processing via Telex and would constantly keep track of inventory movement involving any individual warehouse.
5. Periodic physical audits and control procedures for all field-warehouse stocks would be initiated under the direction of a home office representative.

The national sales manager also observed that it would be relatively simple to implement his proposals. They would require little if any change, since they were already in force in many of the warehouses. Currently, stock was being transported by United Parcel Service and occasionally by leased truck. Typical shipping weights, values per pound, and costs of shipping products from the Salt Lake warehouse to a regional warehouse or hospital (e.g., Salt Lake to Boston) are shown in Exhibit 8A.

Sorenson had also considered a departure from the field-warehouse concept—airfreight distribution from one central site. In particular, he was aware that Federal Express of Memphis, Tennessee, had instituted a new "parts-bank" program that provided clients with centralized warehousing in Memphis, next to a fleet of small jets. All order-processing and inventory-control functions were administered by parts-bank personnel and were included in Federal's quoted rates. Federal Express had assured Sorenson representatives that the company's lightweight, high-margin products were ideally suited to airfreight. Moreover, in light of the daily volume of orders, Federal Express offered to cover all Memphis warehouse rental charges. Thus, the only cost to Sorenson would be airfreight charges (Exhibit 8B).

EXHIBIT 8A
Weight and Value Data for Typical Products

Product	Pounds per Case	Units per Case	Price per Case
CATHETER (INTRASET)	10	100	$300.00
CATHETER-SUPPORT DEVICE (REGUFLO)	4	100	500.00
FLUID-SUCTION LINER (COLLECTAL)...................	11	50	92.50

EXHIBIT 8B
Examples of Existing shipping Costs (United Parcel Service) and Proposed Shipping Costs (Federal Express)

Weight (pounds)	United Parcel Service*	Federal Express†
4 ..	$1.71	$ 7.53
8 ..	2.77	9.88
10 ..	3.29	10.94
15 ..	4.61	13.59
20 ..	5.93	16.24
25 ..	7.25	18.88
30 ..	8.57	21.53

* These UPS costs are for Salt Lake City to Boston, one of the longest shipments presently made on a regular basis.

† These Federal Express costs, which include a $2.50 per unit processing fee that might well be negotiable, are from Memphis to Boston. Bulk shipments from Salt Lake City to Memphis would cost about 15 cents per pound. Aside from the capital cost to carry inventory in Memphis, Sorenson would *not* experience any operating costs for the Memphis inventory, since the Federal Express rates covered warehousing and insurance as well as delivery costs.

These Federal Express prices were for guaranteed two-day delivery. For a substantial premium, one-day delivery could also be arranged.

To assess the impact of this alternative, Sorenson calculated the cost per unit of transporting the REGUFLO device. Each case of REGUFLO weighed 4 pounds and held 100 units. Referring to the Federal Express rate schedule (Exhibit 8B), Sorenson figured that if two cases were ordered by a hospital in Boston (a typical order size to a city representative of the average shipping distance from Memphis), the cost per order would be $9.88 + $1.20 or 5½ cents per unit.[1] Aside from pressure tubing, however, other catheters and support devices weighed about twice as much per unit as REGUFLO devices. Fluid-suction devices (canisters and liners) were much heavier and might best be ground freighted in any case. The feasibility of the Federal Express option was diminished by the fact that all goods airfreighted from Memphis would first have to be shipped there from the Salt Lake factory. This would require one week in transit and cost about 15 cents per pound.

Sorenson wondered which of the two approaches, if either, he should pursue. He realized that Federal Express was eager to develop large-volume accounts and might well negotiate the processing fee or other auxiliary costs.

---

[1] The $9.88 is for 8 pounds from Memphis to Boston (Exhibit 8B); the $1.20 is for 8 pounds bulk shipped from Salt Lake to Memphis; and the 5½ cents is simply ($9.88 + $1.20) ÷ (200 units).

CASE 23

Hank Kolb, Director, Quality Assurance

Hank Kolb was whistling as he walked toward his office, still feeling a bit like a stranger since he had been hired four weeks ago as director, quality assurance. All last week he had been away from the plant at an interesting seminar entitled "Quality in the 80s" given for quality managers of manufacturing plants by the corporate training department. He was not looking forward to really digging into the quality problems at this industrial products plant employing 1,200 people.

Hank poked his head into Mark Hamler's office, his immediate subordinate, the quality control manager, and asked him how things had gone last week. Mark's muted smile and an "Oh, fine" stopped Hank in his tracks. He didn't know Mark very well and was unsure pursuing this reply any further. Hank was still uncertain of how to start building his relationship with him since Mark had been passed over for the promotion to Hank's job—Mark's evaluation form had stated "superb technical knowledge; managerial skills lacking." Hank decided to inquire a little further and asked Mark what had happened. Mark replied:

> Oh, just another typical quality snafu. We had a little problem on the Greasex line last week (a specialized degreasing solvent packed in a spray can for the high-technology sector). A little high pressure was found in some cans on the second shift, but a supervisor vented them so that we could ship them out. We met our delivery schedule!

Since Hank was still relatively unfamiliar with the plant and the products he asked Mark to elaborate. Painfully, Mark continued:

> We've been having some trouble with the new filling equipment, and some of the cans were pressurized beyond our acceptable standard on a psi (pounds per square inch) rating scale. The production rate is still 50 percent of standard, about 14 cases per shift, and we caught it halfway into the shift. Mac Evans (the inspector for that line) picked it up, tagged the cases "Hold"

and went on about his duties. When he returned at the end of the shift to write up the rejects, Wayne Simmons, first-line supervisor, was by a pallet of finished goods finishing sealing up a carton of the rejected Greasex; the reject "Hold" tags had been removed. He told Mac that he had heard about the high pressure from another inspector at coffee break, had come back, taken off the tags, individually turned the cans upside down and vented every one of them in the rejected eight cartons. He told Mac that production planning was really pushing for the stuff, and they couldn't delay by having it sent through the rework area. He told Mac that he would get on the operator to run the equipment right next time. Mac didn't write it up but came in about three days ago to tell me about it. Oh, it happens every once in a while, and I told him to make sure to check with maintenance to make sure the filling machine was adjusted; and I saw Wayne in the hall and told him that he ought to send the stuff through rework next time.

Hank was a bit dumbfounded at this and didn't say much—he didn't know if this was a "big deal" or not. When he got to his office he thought again what Mr. Morganthal, general manager, had said when he had hired Hank. He warned Hank about the "lack of a quality attitude" in the plant and said that Hank "should try to do something about this." He had further emphasized the quality problems in the plant; "We have to improve our quality, it's costing us a lot of money, I'm sure of it, but I can't prove it! Hank, you have my full support in this matter; you're in charge of these quality problems. This downward quality-productivity-turnover spiral has to end!"

The incident had happened a week ago; the goods were probably out in the customer's hands by now; everyone had forgotten about it (or wanted to!); and there seemed to be more pressing problems than this for Hank to spend his time on; but this continued to nag at him. He felt like the quality department was being treated as a joke, and it also felt to him like a personal slap from manufacturing. He didn't want to start a war with the production people but what could he do? He was troubled enough to cancel his appointments and spend the morning talking to a few people. After a long and very tactful morning, he learned the following:

A. From personnel—the operator for the filling equipment had just been transferred from shipping two weeks ago. He had had no formal training in this job but was being trained by Wayne, on the job, to run the equipment. When Mac had tested the high-pressure cans, the operator was nowhere to be found and had only learned of the rejected material from Wayne after the shift was over.

B. From plant maintenance—this particular piece of automated filling equipment had been purchased two years ago for use on another product. It had been switched to the Greasex line six months ago, and maintenance had had 12 work orders during the last month for repairs or adjustments on it. The equipment had been adapted by plant maintenance for handling the lower viscosity Greasex, which it had not originally been designed for. This included designing a special filling head. There was no scheduled preventive maintenance for this equipment, and the parts for the sensitive filling head, replaced three times in the last six months, had to be made at a nearby machine shop. Nonstandard downtime was running at 15 percent of actual running times.

C.   From purchasing—the plastic nozzle heads for the Greasex can, recently designed by a vendor for this new product on a rush order, were often found with slight burrs on the inside rim, and this caused some trouble in fitting the top to the can. An increase in application pressure at the filling head by maintenance adjustment had solved the burr application problem or had at least "forced" the nozzle heads on despite burrs. Purchasing said that they were going to talk to the sales representative of the nozzle head supplier about this the next time he came in.

D.   From product design and packaging—the can, designed especially for Greasex, had been contoured to allow better gripping by the user. This change, instigated by marketing research, set Greasex apart from the appearance of its competitors and was seen by the designers to be "significant." There had been no test of the effects of the contoured can on filling speed or filling hydrodynamics from a high-pressured filling head. Hank had a hunch that the new design was acting as a venturi when being filled, but the packaging designer thought that "unlikely."

E.   From manufacturing manager—he had heard about the problem; in fact, Wayne had made a joke about it, bragging about how he beat his production quota to the other foremen and shift supervisors. Wayne was thought by the manufacturing manager to be one of the "best foremen we have . . . he always gets his production out." His promotion papers were actually on the manufacturing manager's desk when Hank dropped by. Wayne was being "strongly considered" for promotion to shift supervisor. The manufacturing manager, under pressure from Mr. Morganthal for cost improvements and reduced delivery times, sympathized with Hank but said that the rework area would have just vented with their pressure gauges that Wayne did by hand. "But, I'll speak with Wayne about the incident."

F.   From marketing—the introduction of Greasex had been rushed to beat competitors to market and a major promotional/advertising campaign was now underway to increase consumer awareness. A deluge of orders was swamping the order-taking department right now and putting Greasex high on the back-order list. Production "had to turn the stuff out"; even a little off spec was tolerable because "it would be better to have it on the shelf than not there at all. Who cares if the label is a little crooked or the stuff comes out with a little too much pressure. We need market share now in that high-tech segment."

What bothered Hank the most was the safety issue of the high pressure in the cans. He had no way of knowing how much of a hazard the high pressure was or if Wayne had vented them enough to effectively reduce the hazard. The data from the can manufacturer which Mark had showed him indicated that the high pressure which the inspector had found was not in the danger area; but then again the inspector had only used a sample testing procedure to reject the eight cases. Even if he could morally accept that there was no product safety hazard, could he make sure that this never happened again?

Hank, skipping lunch, sat in his office and thought about the morning's events. Last week's seminar had talked about "the role of quality," "productivity and quality," "creating a new attitude," and the "quality challenge" but where had they told him what to do when this happens? He had left a very good job to come here because he thought the company was serious about the importance of quality, and he wanted a challenge. Hank had demanded and received a salary equal to the manufacturing, marketing, and R&D directors and was one of the direct reports to the general manager. Yet he still didn't know exactly what he should or shouldn't do or even what he could or couldn't do.

Fabritek Corporation

One afternoon in March of 1969, Frank Deere, milling department foreman of the Fabritek Corporation, was approached by Stewart Baker, Fabritek's automotive products manager.

> Hi, Frank. I hope that you've got good news for me about this week's Pilgrim order. I don't think that my nerves can take a repeat of last week.

Fabritek Corporation was organized in 1938 and in its early years had specialized in machining castings for the packaging machinery industry. In recent years, the company had developed a strong position in the high-quality machined parts market. In 1968, Fabritek sold $15 million worth of parts to 130 machinery and equipment manufacturers in several different industries. The Fabritek plant and offices were in Columbus, Indiana, in a modern, single-story building with 150,000 square feet of floor space.

The company had worked hard to develop a reputation for rapid, on-time delivery and competitive prices for its high-quality machine work. The president (the son-in-law of Fabritek's founder) stressed four key elements of the company's strategy for meeting these objectives: (1) a highly skilled and well-paid work force: (2) a large number of general-purpose machine tools, readily adaptable to a wide variety of precision machinery operations; (3) an engineering department capable of developing imaginative approaches to machining problems to produce quality parts at low cost; and (4) a strong emphasis on inspection and quality control at several stages of the machining operations.

The company employed 250 workers, 200 of whom were engaged in production and maintenance activities. The United Auto Workers represented Fabritek workers. In 1952, the UAW had waged an intensive organization drive at a nearby diesel engine plant; the union had subsequently signed an agreement with Fabritek without a vote by Fabritek employees. Relations with the union had been cordial, due in part to the fact that Fabritek's wage level had been consistently higher than those of other companies in the area.

Stewart Baker had joined the marketing department of Fabritek in June 1968, following his graduation from a graduate school of business. He had personally obtained Fabritek's first automotive parts contract early in January, after learning that one of the suppliers to the Pilgrim Corporation (a major auto manufacturer) was having delivery problems because of labor difficulties. The contract with Pilgrim required delivery of 17,000 units of a major engine part over a period of about six months. Specifically, weekly shipments of 650 units were to be made each Friday, starting January 31 and continuing until the contract was fulfilled. The part required machining a purchased casting to close tolerance since it was to be assembled into an engine where high temperature and friction stresses would occur.

Pilgrim officials had made it clear that this was a trial contract; if Fabritek's quality and delivery performance were satisfactory, larger and more permanent contracts were likely to follow. In mid-January, Mr. Baker was designated automotive products manager and given responsibility for establishing Fabritek in the automotive market.

Most of the company's machine tool operators were paid on incentive piece rates based on stop-watch time studies. In the event that an operator failed to meet standard performance, he was paid at a base rate equal to the piece rate times the standard output rate. However, when an operator exceeded standard pace, his earnings increased in direct proportion to his output. Actual experience with the incentive plan over a period of years showed that Fabritek machinists, on the average, performed at about 133 percent of standard. Most operators were able to earn considerable premium pay above their base rates, in some instances well over the 133 percent average. As a result the company assumed operation at 133 percent of standard for scheduling production and for balancing machine time and operator time.

Fabritek executives were anxious to prevent "machine interference" (forced idleness while an operator waited for a machine to complete its operation) from limiting the productive effectiveness of any operator who was capable of exceeding the standard. If there was machine interference on a job, any time saved by a proficient operator on his own operations would merely result in increased idle time per cycle for the operator, rather than in increased production. To avoid this, company executives had adopted a policy of attempting to assign enough machines to each operator to prevent machine interference from limiting an operator's productivity, even if the operator would thus exceed standard work pace by a considerable margin. In this way workers were assured that within broad limits, their ability to earn premium pay would be determined by their own ability and willingness to maintain a premium work pace, and would not be impeded by machine interference.

At normal operating volume, sufficient numbers of the various machine tools were available to allow this policy of assigning a liberal ratio of machines to workers. When the volume of production rose, however, additional operators had to be hired to permit tighter scheduling of machine capacity. Under such circumstances the demands on setup workers were heavy. When Stewart Baker obtained the Pilgrim contract in early 1969, the overall plant volume was well above normal. Specifications for the Pilgrim part required eight operations:

1. Unpack and visually inspect purchased casting.[1]
2. Rough mill bearing surface.
3. Finish mill bearing surface.
4. Mill face.
5. Mill keyway.
6. Drill eight holes.
7. Finish grind bearing surface.
8. Final inspection and pack.

Because of design characteristics, it was essential that all four milling cuts be made in fixed sequence (cut 1 before cut 2, etc.). At the time the job was undertaken, there was considerable demand for milling machine capacity in the shop and the engineering department believed that it would not be possible to assign more than four milling machines to this sequence of operations without seriously disrupting the scheduling of other work in the milling department. It was anticipated that the demand for milling machine capacity would remain extremely high for some time to come, and that this fact would prevent even a subsequent assignment of more than four milling machines to this order. The four available machines were located in close proximity to each other, and since they were equipped for automatic feed, it was possible for a single operator to run all four of them.

The method which the engineering department developed for the four milling operations required that each of the four milling machines be set up to make one of the required cuts. Other possibilities, such as combining cuts by using specially formed milling cutters or changing the design of the casting, were explored but were rejected on technical grounds. Setup time averaged two hours for each milling machine; setup workers were paid $4.20 per hour.

Exhibit 1 shows the type of milling machine used for each of the four milling operations. The set up workers mount the appropriate cutters, adjust the table for proper depth of cut, and set cams and stops which determine the direction and limits of table movement. Feed and speed rates (see footnote†, Exhibit 2) are set by moving levers to point to appropriate readings on indicator dials. In practice these levers are often missing and adjustments are made with a wrench.

---

[1] Castings which contained pits, scars, or excess flash, or which failed to meet other quality criteria were returned to the vendor.

EXHIBIT 1
Diagrammatic Sketch of a Milling Machine

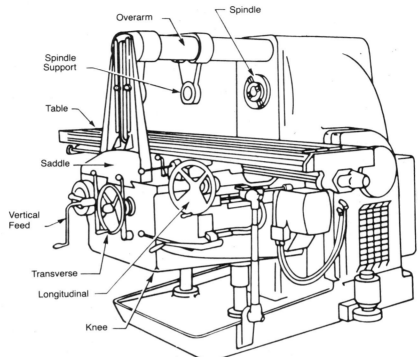

This sketch is of a general-purpose milling machine of the type used on the Pilgrim part. Fabritek generally uses this type of machine for production work rather than depending on higher speed, special-purpose machinery.

Three table movement hand controls are shown. Each of these movements is also provided with power feed in either direction. The table can be set up to follow an automatic cycle when it is to be used for a production job. The speed of table movement and the rotational speed of the cutter are set on indicator dials on the back of the machine.

The piece to be milled is clamped to the table. Cutters are mounted on a horizontal shaft which is rigidly supported by the spindle and spindle support. Table movement then feeds the work into the rotating cutters.

The machining processes to produce the Pilgrim part were set up in January 1969. A drill press and a grinder were moved close to the four milling machines. Two inspector/material handlers and two experienced machine operators, all of whom had been working together on another order, were transferred to the new job. One operator was assigned to the four milling machines, the other to the drilling and grinding operations. On their previous job the two machine operators had been paid on an individual incentive basis: the inspector/material handlers had been paid an hourly rate. These pay arrangements were continued on the new job. Since it was often difficult to trace the responsibility for quality problems or rejects, workers were paid on the basis of total output, rather than total good output.

std shop
feed &

EXHIBIT 2
Cycle Analysis for Milling Operations on Pilgrim Part No. 37906 (all times in minutes—
operation at the rate shown results in standard production of 100 pieces per day*)

	Total Cycle Time	Machine Time	Total Operator Time†	External Time†	Internal Time†
Milling cut 1.....	3.594 =	2.600	1.139	0.994	0.145
Milling cut 2.....	2.964	2.220	.992	0.744	0.248
Milling cut 3.....	3.301	2.420	1.244	0.881	0.363
Milling cut 4.....	1.725	1.118	1.035	0.607	0.428

3.23   4.41

* The operator has allowances of 39 minutes per day for personal time, fatigue, etc.
† Total operator time for each milling cut was divided between "internal time" (i.e., the time required for operations which the operator was expected to perform during the machine cutting time) and "external time" (i.e., the time required for operations which the operator was not expected to perform or could not perform during the machine cutting time). Load and unload operations, for example, always required external time. Total cycle time equalled machine time plus external time. The operator times shown are summaries of observed element times (adjusted for pace). Machine times shown are derived from standard shop feed and speed tables. Feed rate is the rate at which the workpiece is fed against the milling cutter. Speed rate is the rotational speed of the milling cutter. Setting the machine at the proper feed and speed rates was important for several reasons—to minimize undue stress and wear and tear on the motor and drive mechanism of the machine, to prevent rapid wear and damage to the cutting tool, and to ensure a proper finish by preventing "tool chatter" or skips and jumps of the tool which would leave a rough, scratched, or bumpy surface finish on the piece being milled.

The standard was set at 100 completely milled pieces per day for the milling operations. However, since an experienced worker was assigned to the milling machines, an output of at least 133 percent of standard was expected. Assuming the 133 percent output, a small cushion of 15 pieces per week would exist. Stewart Baker thought this was a bit tight, but was reluctant to add more workers to the job because of the limited profit margin on the order.

Soon after production started, a smooth flow of material was obtained and no unacceptably large in-process inventories accumulated between operations.

The first shipment of 650 pieces was made on schedule on January 31. The group settled down to an average performance of 135 percent of standard. Frank Deere reported to Stu Baker that the group was continuing to work as well on this product as they had on their previous job. The group took rest and lunch breaks together as they had before moving to the Pilgrim part job.

After two deliveries had been made to Pilgrim, the milling machines operator was involved in a weekend automobile accident. He was hospitalized with severe injuries, and although the exact time of his return could not be predicted, it was clear that he would be unable to return to work for several months.

On Monday morning, Frank Deere assigned a particularly skilled operator, Arthur Moreno, to the milling job. Moreno started the Pilgrim job after lunch. This assignment meant transferring Moreno from another job on which he had been earning substantial premium pay. His typical weekly take-home pay on that job—where he worked alone—had been $215, of which approximately $85 was premium pay attributable to working in excess of standard pace. The foreman believed, however, that production on Moreno's present job was coming to an end and that it would work out well to transfer him to the new job which would continue for several months.

Frank Deere and Stu Baker were pleased that the group had little difficulty in meeting the February 14 delivery. Moreno had learned the job well by the middle of the week, and except for an occasional buildup of inventory ahead of the drill and grinder, the transition seemed to be smooth and successful.

On Thursday, February 13, Moreno had mentioned to Frank that he thought he wouldn't be able to make as much money on the milling job as he had been making on his last job. Frank felt this mild discontent was to be expected from someone who had recently changed jobs.

On Tuesday, February 18, Arthur Moreno received his pay for the first full week's work on the new job. He burst in on Frank Deere waving a check for $174.14. "I told you this was a bum job, Frank, and here's the proof. I just can't go fast enough to make out on this job."

Frank thought that Moreno simply was used to working faster than the other members of his group, but realized that Moreno had raised a strong enough objection to have the job checked.

Just before lunch on Wednesday a time-study man evaluated the milling job. Moreno, the foreman, and the time-study man agreed that this study indicated that the original study (shown in Exhibit 2) was technically sound. Even though Moreno agreed with the figures shown in Exhibit 2, he restated to Frank that he was annoyed at not being able to make more than a 33 percent bonus. Frank admitted that all jobs in the line had been balanced for average work rates and told Moreno, ". . . Don't worry about piling up work ahead of the next operation. If you want to go faster, go ahead."

By Thursday afternoon Moreno was upset again. He had run out of work and couldn't find the inspector/material handler who prepared the workpieces for the milling operations. The inspector had other duties as well as the Pilgrim auto part castings job and was working in another part of the plant. The other workers told Moreno they didn't know where he was.

The next day, the Pilgrim shipment was made on schedule and although work was beginning to pile up ahead of the drilling and grinding operation, there appeared to be no problems.

During the next week, a new problem developed. The final inspector, who checked the parts before packing, rejected 38 pieces of Monday's and Tuesday's output. Since the critical bearing surface on the part was out of tolerance and rough, the problem seemed to lie with the grinding operation. Frank Deere asked the drill and grinder operator, Paul Clark, to work three hours overtime on Wednesday to regrind some of the defective pieces and to cut into the accumulated backlog ahead of his machines. Clark was delighted with the opportunity for overtime work but made it clear to Frank that he felt he was *not* responsible for the unacceptable bearing surfaces, commenting, "If you want to find trouble, ask Moreno. He's feeding me a lot of crap, and I've got to slow down the grinder feed to get a decent finish."

Moreno was now producing milled castings at a rate of 167 per day (167 percent of standard).

The February 28 shipment was made, but the company truck was delayed for an hour waiting for the last few parts to be finished, inspected, and packed.

By Tuesday, March 4, it was clear to Frank Deere that the quality problem was not solved and that even with considerable overtime for Paul Clark, they were going to have difficulty making the Pilgrim shipment on Friday. During the afternoon, Stewart Baker came to check on the Pilgrim run. (See Exhibit 3 for a summary of the above events.)

"Stu, we've got a real problem. It looks as though I'll have to add more people, replace someone, work overtime, or put on another grinder. Of course, I'll have to talk with the superintendent before I decide what I'm going to do here."

EXHIBIT 3
Chronology

Jan.	31	Friday	First shipment
Feb.	3		
	4		
	5		
	6		
	7	Friday	Second shipment
Feb.	10	Monday	Moreno assigned to milling operations
	11		
	12		
	13	Thursday	Moreno's first complaint
	14	Friday	Third shipment
Feb.	17		
	18	Tuesday	Moreno's first paycheck for this job
	19	Wednesday	Time-study reevaluation
	20	Thursday	Moreno runs out of work
	21	Friday	Fourth shipment
Feb.	24		
	25		
	26	Wednesday	38 pieces rejected—Clark works overtime
	27		
	28	Friday	Fifth shipment—truck delayed
Mar.	3		
	4	Tuesday	Discussion between Baker and Deere

"Wait a minute," Stu replied. "We don't know what's causing those rejects yet. If we sweep this problem under the rug with something like overtime, we'll lose our shirts on this order."

"What else can I do, Stu? You want that order out on time, don't you?"

"Well, we were doing all right until a week or so ago. I think that Moreno must have something to do with it. It must bother Clark to see that pile of work ahead of him getting bigger every day. And Moreno's rushing may mean that Clark's grinding operation is slowing down. You know, I've never seen Moreno with that group except when they're on the job."

"I suppose you want me to take Moreno off the job. He's one of my best men. Look, Stu, you'll get your Pilgrim order on time. Now I've got other things to do. I've got 23 other millers to keep busy, you know."

CASE 25

FBO, Inc.

In July of 1977, John Reiling, general manager of FBO, Inc., was pondering a problem: scheduling the contract refueling operations for the commercial airline flights that FBO serviced at Metro Airport in Metropolis, Illesota. Mr. Reiling felt that the present refueling operations were inefficient. Although the problem had been a long-standing one, Mr. Reiling was particularly concerned at this time because costs had been increasing rapidly while revenues had remained level. As a result, profit margins had been dropping.

To complicate matters, FBO employees at Metro were unionized and they were satisfied with the present refueling operations. Since FBO had experienced union problems concerning work changes in the past, Mr. Reiling felt that the union and the individual employees might resist changes in the refueling operations. However, he also felt that improved scheduling in the refueling operations could yield considerable cost savings. Mr. Reiling summarized his opinion: "Since the union is pleased with the present mode of operations, there must be a better way to do them."

BACKGROUND

Services. FBO operated its facilities at Metro Airport under terms of a 15-year permit (to expire in 1980), with the Metropolis Airport Commission. Under the terms of the permit, FBO provided both commercial and retail services. The commercial services consisted of refueling commercial airline flights under contracts made with the airlines. The retail operations consisted of services to private and corporate aircraft, including fueling services, collection of aircraft parking fees (as agent for the Airport Commission), maintenance and avionic services, hangar/aircraft storage, and other services such as office cleaning, baggage handling, and vehicle maintenance.

Competition.   At Metro, FBO had one other competitor, Acme Aviation. The two firms were the only aviation services licensed to operate at the airport. Corporate and private aircraft were required to use one of the two firms for all necessary services, while commercial airlines were usually required to use FBO or Acme for refueling services. There were a few exceptions in the case of commercial airlines, however. Commercial airlines had the option of using one of the airport's licensed aviation services or of doing their own refueling. FBO refueled 9 of the 18 airlines serving Metro; Acme refueled 6; and three airlines did their own.

Financial Performance.   The commercial operations provided about 40 percent of FBO's revenue at Metro, while the retail operations provided the other 60 percent. Total revenues had been steady for the past few years at about $3.2 million per year.

Facilities.   FBO operated out of three locations at the Metro Airport proper: hanger 6, hanger 8, and the central terminal building.

FBO's administrative offices and its corporate/private aircraft services lobby, dispatch counter, and pilots lounge were located in hanger 6, Aircraft hangar/storage space, maintenance, and avionics services were also provided in hanger 6. In hanger 8, FBO maintained its fleet of aircraft refueling vehicles plus its other automotive ground handling equipment. FBO maintained a small "line shack" in the main terminal building as a ready room for its commercial airline refueling staff.

Employees.   FBO employed 82 people to perform its activities at the airport. Nine of these were managerial personnel, and the remaining 73 were union employees who were divided into two basic groups: the hangar group and the nonhangar group.

The nonhangar group included the following: (1) refuelers who could fuel either corporate and private aircraft or commercial aircraft, depending on their assignment; (2) towmen who maneuvered private and corporate vehicles; and (3) ramp attendants who used station wagons to transport FBO's retail customers to and from their aircraft and various other locations. The hangar group included the following: (1) auto mechanics who did maintenance work on all of FBO's vehicles (whether FBO owned or leased the vehicles); (2) aircraft mechanics who did maintenance and repair work on corporate and private aircraft; and (3) avionics technicians who did maintenance and repair work on corporate and private aircraft instruments.

UNION-MANAGEMENT RELATIONS

FBO's employees were represented by the International Brotherhood of Teamsters, Chauffeurs, Warehousemen, and Helpers of America, Local #999. Management felt that the union contract (which was renegotiated every two years) was cumbersome and costly to the company because of specific work rules, restrictive employee classifications, and especially the method of awarding overtime.

The seniority system was important in scheduling shifts and overtime at FBO. When new shift schedules were made, they were given to the employees for the purpose of bidding. The most senior employees within each classification had the first option of the shift schedule they wanted. Overtime was also offered according to seniority. However, if overtime assign-

EXHIBIT 1
Excerpts from 1976 Union Agreement

HOURS OF WORK AND OVERTIME

A. Eight (8) consecutive hours in the twenty-four- (24) hour period following the time an employee starts his scheduled shift, exclusive of an unpaid lunch period, will constitute a regular workday.

B. Forty (40) hours consisting of five (5) days of eight (8) hours each, worked within seven (7) consecutive days will constitute a regular workweek for an employee.

C. Overtime at the rate of time and one half shall be paid for all hours worked in excess of eight (8) in a workday.

D. Overtime at the rate of time and one half shall be paid for all hours worked in excess of forty (40) in an employee's scheduled workweek, and for all hours worked on his regularly scheduled first day off and overtime at the rate of double time for all hours worked on his regularly scheduled second day off, if he also worked on his scheduled first day off.

F. Lunch periods shall be completed between three and one half (3½) and five and one half (5½) hours on each shift. If the employer requires an employee to work through such lunch period, he will be paid at the rate of time and one half for time worked during such lunch period and, in addition, will be given fifteen (15) minutes for lunch at least two hours (2) hours before his quitting time.

H. An employee called back to perform work after completion of his scheduled hours on a workday and after he has left the employer's premises shall be paid at the applicable overtime rate for not less than four (4) hours.

An employee who reports for work as scheduled without having been notified in advance by the employer not to report shall receive not less than eight (8) hours of pay at his regular straight-time rate, unless the employee on his own initiative fails to complete his scheduled hours, is sent home for just cause, is excused from such hours at his own request, or no work is available as a result of a work stoppage or interference with operations in connection with a labor dispute.

Q. An employee who works overtime will be allowed eight (8) hours off duty between the time of completion of his overtime assignment and the start of his next scheduled shift, and will not suffer a loss of regular pay for reporting late for such next shift as a result of this allowance.

ments were not accepted by senior employees, the most junior employees on the shift were required to accept the assignments. (See Exhibit 1 for the sections of the contract regarding hours of work and overtime.).

The union had organized FBO in 1961. Since that time, relations with the union had not been cordial. The company had suffered a strike during two of the last three contract negotiations. In the 1972 negotiations, one of the main issues concerned the number of refuelers that should be used to refuel a plane. Previously, two refuelers had been used, but management felt that only one person was necessary. This issue was eventually granted to management after a nine-week strike; but the settlement included annual wage increases of about 8 percent. In the 1974 contract negotiations, one of the major issues concerned employee classifications. The company wanted to eliminate all nonhangar group classifications (refueler, towmen, and ramp attendant) so that any employee could perform all three tasks, but the union wanted to maintain classifications as they had previously existed. After a two-week strike, management withdrew this demand and signed a contract which included another 8 percent annual wage increase. There had been no strike in 1976 when a settlement was reached which included a 7 percent annual wage increase.

CONTRACT REFUELING—COMMERCIAL SERVICES

Contract Arrangements.   The airlines serviced by FBO arranged contracts both with FBO and an oil company. The oil company supplied the fuel at an agreed-upon price while FBO acted as a "mediator," picking up fuel from the oil company's pumps and dispensing it into the planes. FBO's contract with an airline included the total gallonage to be dispensed during the year and a fixed into-planing fee which FBO received for each gallon pumped. The into-planing fee averaged about 2.56 cents per gallon, and FBO had contracts to deliver a total of about 50 million gallons during 1977.

The refueling arrangements were complicated by the fact that each oil company required FBO to dispense fuel utilizing trucks with that oil company's markings. This requirement had not been a problem in the past since all the airlines FBO serviced had contracts with National Oil. But, recently, Gamma Airlines had contracted with Continental Oil to supply their fuel. FBO estimated that starting in September, two or three Continental trucks would be needed to perform Gamma's refueling operations.

Equipment.   FBO used 11 fuel trucks in the commercial refueling operations. Nine had capacities of 8,400 gallons, while two had capacities of 5,100 gallons. The larger trucks were leased from the oil companies at a cost of $1,200 per truck per month. FBO owned its smaller trucks, but could lease additional 5,100 gallon trucks at a cost of $800 per truck per month. Operating and maintenance costs amounted to about $5,000 per year for the larger trucks and about $3,000 per year for the smaller trucks. This included fuel and oil for operating the trucks and parts and labor for maintaining them. It did not include the costs of the refuelers.

Fuel Requirements. While the total number of gallons to be pumped during the year was contracted, the specific amount of fuel to be pumped into a plane each day was decided daily by the airlines. The amount of fuel required depended on the type of plane, its destination, its passenger load, and weather conditions. Since passenger loads and weather had only a limited effect on fuel requirements, the amount of fuel a particular flight took from day to day varied within narrow limits, because the plane type and destination was almost always the same for a particular flight.

The airlines usually waited until a few hours before departure time before determining the exact amount of fuel they wanted for each flight. By so doing, they took advantage of the most current information about the weather and passenger loads. Occasionally, fuel requests were even changed while passengers were boarding the plane. Once airline personnel had determined the amount of fuel they wanted for a particular flight, the amount was written on a card that was held by the airline dispatchers until someone from FBO picked it up. (Although FBO serviced nine airlines, there were only four dispatch counters because some of the larger airlines handled the dispatching and the arrival and departure information for the smaller airlines.) A refueler could not fuel a plane until he had the proper card, which was prepared in triplicate. One copy was left with the dispatcher, one copy was for FBO's use, and one copy was usually left either with personnel at the plane's gate or with the pilot after refueling had been completed. Exhibit 2 shows the various types of planes that FBO refueled and the amounts of fuel each type took.

EXHIBIT 2
Contract Airline Refueling (fuel gallonage uplifts)

Airline	Type of Aircraft	Uplift Gallonage Range
Alpha	DC-9	1,000–1,500
	CONV-580	300–500
Beta	DC-9	1,500–2,400
	B727	2,500–4,500
	DC-10	2,000–3,000
Gamma.	B727	2,500–3,500
	L-1011	3,500–5,000
Delta	B737	1,000–1,300
Epsilon.	B727	1,600–2,000
Zeta	B727	3,000–3,500
Eta	DC-9	1,500–2,200
Theta	DC-9	1,000
Iota.	DC-9	1,000

Flight Schedules.   In the contract refueling operation, FBO serviced 98 commercial flights per day, Monday through Friday. Some of the flights were not scheduled on Saturdays and Sundays, so fewer flights were serviced on those two days (81 on Saturdays and 85 on Sundays). Two large boards (coinciding with FBO's two daily shifts) were maintained at the pool with a complete schedule of the estimated time of arrival (ETA) and estimated time of departure (ETD) for all the flights that FBO serviced. Airline schedules changed about two or three times a year. The Monday–Friday schedule of airline arrivals and departures for the summer of 1977, including aircraft type, is provided in Exhibit 3.

Several planes serviced by FBO were on the ground overnight. However, these planes could not be refueled until morning since the airlines wanted as much time as possible to determine passenger loads and weather conditions. The refueling cards for these planes were usually available at 6 A.M., and the refuelers generally began refueling these planes about 7 A.M.

Performance Criteria.   The essential performance criteria for the refueling operation were on-time service, safety, and quality fuel.

1. *On-time service.*   FBO's policy was to meet a plane as soon as it arrived at its gate and complete the refueling operation as quickly as possible. They could, however, actually continue pumping fuel into a plane until just before it was ready to pull away from the gate without causing any delay. But FBO's management preferred that the refuelers complete the refueling at least five minutes before departure time.
2. *Safety.*   Refuelers maneuvered the trucks carefully to avoid collisions with the planes. When refuelers backed their trucks into or out of fueling positions, they were required to have someone assist them. However, if a refueler could maneuver in and pull away from a plane by driving straight forward, he was allowed to do so on his own.
3. *Quality fuel.*   The refuelers had to make sure that the proper fuel was dispensed into the plane, and that the fuel had no contaminants in it. This meant that fuel trucks had to be emptied every morning to remove any water that may have condensed inside the tanks overnight.

In addition to the major criteria outlined above, FBO's management also wanted the refuelers to provide their services in a courteous manner.

Organization of Refueling Operations.   The contract refueling operations were performed utilizing a pooling concept. Both manpower and trucks were assigned to a pool. The "pool" for the refuelers was the small 8 by 18 feet line shack located in the airport terminal. Parking for the fuel trucks was provided out near the taxiways about 700 yards from the pool. FBO had been unable to secure permission from the Airport Commission to move the truck parking nearer the terminals. However, a driver could stop his truck momentarily at the pool to see if it would be needed again

EXHIBIT 3
Airline Schedule—Monday through Friday

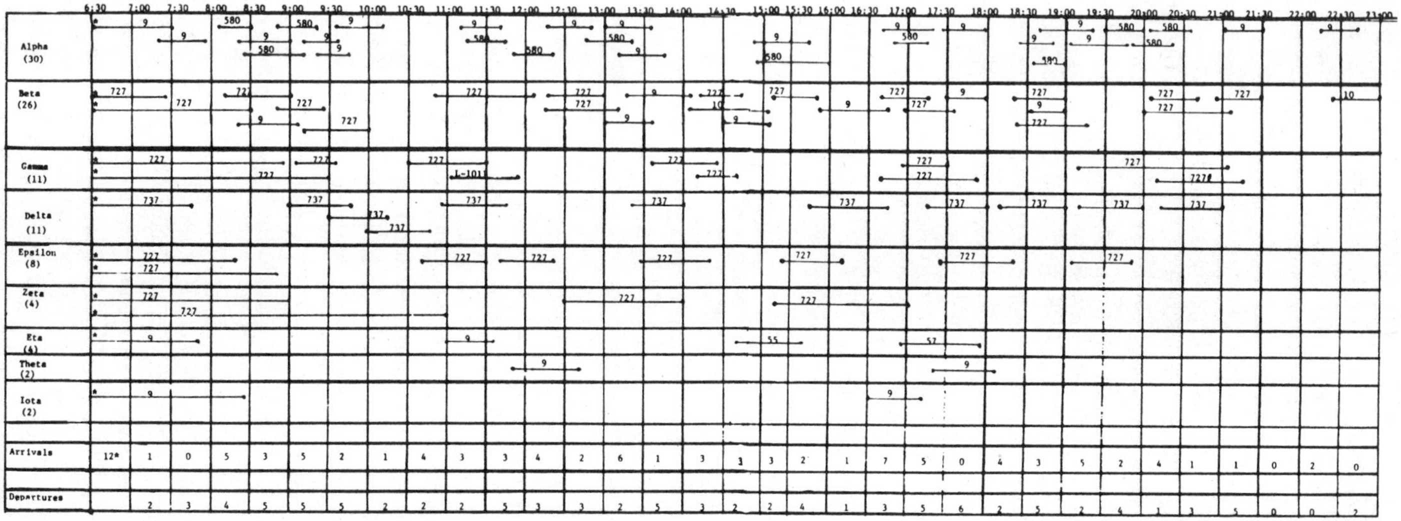

* On the ground overnight

Type of aircraft
arrival   departure
time   time

@L-1011 on Monday and Friday

Alpha (30)																																		
Beta (26)																																		
Gamma (11)																																		
Delta (11)																																		
Epsilon (8)																																		
Zeta (4)																																		
Eta (4)																																		
Theta (2)																																		
Iota (2)																																		
Arrivals	12*	1	0	5	2	5	3	4	3	2	4	2	6	1	3	3	2	1	7	5	0	4	3	5	2	1	2	4	2	5	2	1	0	2
Departures	2	3	4	5	3	5	2	2	4	5	2	3	2	5	2	3	3	5	6	1	5	2	5	3	2	2	1	4	5	2	2	4		

immediately. In addition, one or two spots were used near the pool (about 50 yards away) for trucks that would be needed within two or three minutes.

In the refueling operations, one lead refueler, one "floater," and several regular refuelers were used. The lead refueler was responsible for giving the refuelers assignments throughout the day. The work had to be coordinated so that the planes were serviced without delay and so that the fuel trucks were filled again (topped) when they became too low on fuel for further refueling. The lead refueler could also refuel planes. He did not top trucks, however, because this assignment would take him away from the pool for too long a period.

The floater was a refueler assigned to drive a station wagon throughout his shift. He was responsible for picking up the fueling cards from the dispatchers, for driving refuelers to and from fuel trucks, and for helping refuelers back the fuel trucks into and out of position near the planes.

The regular refuelers reported to the pool and waited for assignments from the lead. A refueler might be assigned to refuel a plane, or top a truck that was too low on fuel to be used in another refueling. Often the lead gave a refueler a series of assignments (two or three) at one time. In 1977, a lead refueler earned approximately $7.50 an hour; a refueler earned $6.50 an hour. In addition to regular pay, fringe benefits amounted to about 25 percent of straight-time pay.

Communications with the Airlines. The refuelers had no contact with the tower and no formal communication system with the individual airlines to learn in advance whether the planes would arrive on schedule. FBO previously had communication systems in the pool for all the airlines, but these were eliminated when the airlines switched to closed-circuit televisions to show arrival and departure times. FBO had not tapped into the television communication system because facilities would have had to be provided for four separate channels. (The larger airlines handled arrival and departure information in addition to dispatching for the smaller airlines.) Management estimated that these channels would cost about $4,000 to $5,000 each to install. Furthermore, the system was often not updated soon enough to be of use and did not provide information about when planes were cleared to land or when they had actually landed.

Normally, however, FBO knew that a plane was on the ground before a refueler was dispatched to the plane's gate. Airline personnel often (but not always) contacted the lead refueler in the ready room by phone if planes were behind schedule. In addition, the dispatchers usually knew when planes would arrive late, and they so informed the person from FBO who picked up the fuel cards. This information reduced the number of times refuelers made trips to a gate to discover that the flight had not yet arrived.

Communication among the Refuelers. The lead refueler and the floater used walkie talkies in communicating with each other. The floater frequently used the walkie talkie to inform the lead of the flights for which he had fueling cards, the amount of fuel the planes would need, and whether the planes would arrive on schedule. This allowed the lead to make assignments to the refuelers without always having to wait for the floater to bring him the fuel cards. By driving around, the floater kept track of the refueling of each plane and knew when it was time to help a refueler back a truck near an aircraft. In this way he also knew when a refueler needed to be driven to the ready room from the fuel truck parking area. He also used his walkie talkie to inform the lead when refuelers had finished their assignments. The lead, in turn, used the walkie talkie to ask the floater to pick up refuelers and drive them out to the fuel trucks. He could also request the floater to give a refueler another assignment.

FBO's management had considered installing radios in the fuel trucks to improve the efficiency of the refueling operation but had decided against it, "simply because the radios would be stolen."

The lead refueler used the airline schedule, information from the floater, and information obtained by phone to determine when to dispatch refuelers. The lead used the fueling cards plus information obtained directly from the refuelers and the floater to keep track of the amount of fuel in each truck to determine when a truck needed to be topped. The lead was not always able to keep track of the fuel in each truck, especially during peak times or when the lead had given a refueler a series of assignments.

Refueling Process. When a refueler was assigned to refuel a plane, he first checked to see if a truck was already available at or near the pool. Frequently, however, all the trucks were in the regular parking area. In that case, the lead assigned the floater to drive the refueler out to the trucks. The refueler picked up the necessary fuel card either from the lead or the floater.

After the refueler had been driven to the parked trucks, he drove a truck to the gate where his assigned plane was scheduled to arrive to refuel the plane. Occasionally, however, the plane was not at the gate when the refueler arrived with the truck. In that case he checked with personnel at the gate to ascertain the plane's expected arrival time. If the plane was to arrive in less than five minutes, he waited and then refueled the plane. If the wait was to be longer than five minutes, however, he drove the truck back to the pool to see whether it would be needed immediately elsewhere. If the truck would not be needed immediately but would be needed within two or three minutes, he parked in a spot near the pool (if space was available). Otherwise he took the truck back to the regular parking area, usually after requesting that the floater come out to pick him up.

Sometimes a refueler was using a fuel truck that did not have enough fuel to supply his assigned plane and the lead was unaware of it. Ideally, under those circumstances, the refueler would start pumping fuel into the plane and then phone the lead from the gate to request a backup truck. Occasionally, however, the refueler did not check in advance to see if he had enough fuel to refuel the plane, so he had to call the lead after he had run out of fuel. When this happened, it sometimes caused a departure delay.

Often, however, the lead assigned a truck to be used that he already knew was too low on fuel to refuel the assigned plane. In this case he also assigned a backup truck. This type of assignment was made to reduce the number of times the fuel trucks needed to be topped with fuel.

Topping Trucks.   Once a refueling operation had been completed, the driver checked to see if enough fuel remained in the truck to do further refueling. (The fuel farm was located on the far side of the airport. The fuel farm consisted of several large fuel pumps that supplied various kinds of aviation fuel. The fuel farm was maintained by the oil companies.) The lead had kept track of the amount of fuel in each truck, and he already knew whether the fuel truck would need to be refilled after the refueler finished the assignment. In this case, he usually assigned a driver to drive the fuel truck immediately to the fuel farm to be topped. If the truck needed to be refilled and the lead was not aware of it, the refueler drove the truck back to the pool and informed the lead, who either assigned this driver or another one to take the truck to the fuel farm to be topped. But if the truck still had enough fuel to refuel another plane, the refueler either went to another refueling assignment or drove the truck back to the pool or directly to the regular parking area, depending upon the assignment the lead had given him.

Time Requirements.   The time required for the various assignments was as follows: about two to three minutes were required to ride out to the trucks in the regular parking; another two to three minutes were required to drive to the plane's gate where the refueling operations could commence. Refueling could usually be completed in about 15–20 minutes. Following the refueling, another two to three minutes were required to drive the truck back to the parking area. If the refueler had to walk in from the regular parking area (this occurred rarely), it took him about 10 minutes. Topping off a truck took about 40 minutes. About half the time was spent simply driving the 2½ miles (each way) to and from the fuel farm.

Staffing and Shift Schedules.   The contract refueling operations used a total staff of 23 refuelers. Each refueler served five shifts per week. The shifts were 8⅓ hours each (eight paid hours) with a half hour for a meal, two 10-minute breaks and a 10-minute cleanup period at the end of the shift. However, since the employees had a considerable amount of idle time during their shifts, breaks were not formally scheduled. The union contract required that the meal break be given between the third and fifth hours of the employee's shift. The aggregate shift schedule is shown in Exhibit 4 while the schedule for the individual shifts (which the refuelers bid for by

EXHIBIT 4
Aggregate Staffing Schedule—Commercial Refueling

	Number of Refuelers per Shift						
Shift	M	Tu	W	Th	F	Sa	Su
A₁ (6:30–14:50)	7	7	7	7	7	8	7
A₂ (7:30–15:50)	2	2	2	2	2	—	—
B₁ (14:30–22:50)	6	6	6	6	6	5	6
B₂ (15:30–23:50)	2	2	2	2	2	2	2

seniority) is shown in Exhibit 5. The refuelers ranged in age from about 20 to 60 and in lengths of employment from 2 to 25 years. The average length of employment was about 8½ years.

Overtime. FBO did not schedule any shifts to exceed 8⅓ hours, but they budgeted for overtime wages at about 10 percent of the straight-time wages paid during the year. Overtime was caused by three main factors: (1) the airline schedules were thrown off occasionally by bad weather and slowdowns by pilots and flight controllers. When this happened, the flights began arriving late and the entire schedule was usually delayed by several hours. This often meant that refuelers had to remain at the airport to handle the later flights. Bad weather disrupted the flight schedules approximately 36 days a year. (2) Overtime had to be paid on holidays at 2½ times the straight-time rate. (There were 11 paid holidays each year.) (3) Overtime was also incurred to cover unscheduled absences by refuelers. The absenteeism rate (currently about 8 percent) had increased substantially in recent years and was seen as one of the main contributors to the excessive overtime wages which currently amounted to about 14 percent of straight-time wages.

ALTERNATIVES UNDER CONSIDERATION

In rescheduling the refueling operations, Mr. Reiling was considering several alternatives: Refuelers could be assigned to specific trucks, to specific airlines, to top fuel trucks only, or a combination of these alternatives. Mr. Reiling's goals were to achieve maximum utilization of manpower and to improve cost control. He hoped to be able to reduce maintenance costs and the number of trucks and people required. If changes meant that fewer

EXHIBIT 5
Individual Shift Schedule—Commercial Refueling

		Schedule						
	Title	M	Tu	W	Th	F	Sa	Su
A₁ Shift —6:30–14:50								
1.	Lead Refueler.....	A₁	A₁	A₁	A₁			A₁
2.	Refueler........	A₁	A₁	A₁			A₁	A₁
3.	Refueler........		A₁	A₁	A₁	A₁	A₁	
4.	Refueler........			A₁	A₁	A₁	A₁	A₁
5.	Refueler........	A₁	A₁			A₁	A₁	A₁
6.	Refueler........	A₁			A₁	A₁	A₁	A₁
7.	Refueler........			A₁	A₁	A₁	A₁	*
8.	Refueler........	A₁	A₁	A₁	A₁	A₁		
9.	Refueler........	A₁	A₁	A₁			A₁	A₁
A₂ Shift —7:30–15:50								
10.	Refueler........	A₂	A₂	A₂	A₂	A₂		
11.	Refueler........	A₂	A₂	A₂	A₂	A₂		
B₁ Shift —14:30–22:50								
12.	Lead refueler		B₁	B₁	B₁	B₁	B₁	
13.	Refueler........	A₁	A₁	B₁	B₁			A₁
14.	Refueler........			B₁	B₁	B₁	B₁	B₁
15.	Refueler........	B₁	B₁			B₁	B₁	B₁
16.	Refueler........	B₁	B₁	B₁	B₁			B₁
17.	Refueler........	B₁	B₁	B₁	B₁	B₁		
18.	Refueler........	B₁	B₁			B₁	B₁	B₁
19.	Refueler........			B₁	B₁	B₁	B₁	B₁
B₂ Shift —15:30–23:50								
20.	Refueler........	B₁	B₂	B₂	B₂	B₂		
21.	Refueler........	B₂		B₂		B₂	B₂	B₂
22.	Refueler........	B₂	B₂	B₂			B₂	B₂
23.	Alternate lead.....	B₁	B₁			A₁	A₁	B₁
	Refueler........	*		A₁		*	*	*

* Works shift on the retail side of the field.

people would be required, employees would not be laid off, however, but the work force could be reduced through attrition.

Mr. Reiling felt that by assigning men to specific trucks, the men would develop pride in their vehicles and would take better care of them. Management would also have greater control since they would know who was responsible for a given truck in case any damage or other problem occurred. Mr. Reiling felt that this plan would reduce truck maintenance costs by 5 to 10 percent. By assigning specific people to airlines, he hoped to provide better service to the airlines and hoped that refuelers would get to know the flight schedule for the planes they were assigned to refuel.

Mr. Reiling felt that one of the options would improve the refueling operations significantly. He based this on the experience during the last strike, when FBO used its managers to do all the servicing. These men, who had previously done strike work together, worked 12-hour shifts, usually 7 days a week. During this time the commercial refueling operations were not organized under the pool concept. Rather, teams were assigned to specific airlines. Management felt that under this system they were able to give better service to the airlines and complete the work more efficiently. During the strike 14 members of management handled the commercial refueling operations instead of the 23 union employees that were normally used.

Mr. Reiling realized, of course, that there were risks in assigning people to trucks and to airlines because FBO would lose some of the flexibility the pool provided; and workers might refuse even in emergencies to do refueling for planes other than their own assigned airlines. So he wondered whether he should simply try to utilize the pool concept better. He knew that on several occasions the refuelers had been able to accomplish the refueling of all planes with ease when an unscheduled absence occurred and a replacement was not called in.

IMPLEMENTATION

Mr. Reiling was not only concerned about how to reschedule the refueling operations but also about how to implement whatever decision was made. He felt that implementation would be the biggest problem. He first had to decide whether the changes should be made on a piecemeal basis or all at once. He favored making the changes on a piecemeal basis because he could experiment a little and try to determine the best system. Furthermore, he could present the problem and some of his ideas to the union and the employees and perhaps get their support. He felt that if the union and the employees had the opportunity to influence the final decision, they might not resist the changes so much. Moreover, they might make some good suggestions about improving the operations. On the other hand, Mr. Reiling felt that the union believed that management was only trying to lay people off whenever any changes were made, so cooperation might be difficult to get.

At any rate, the decision needed to be made soon, because new schedules were coming up for bidding in September and the decision had to be worked out before then. Mr. Reiling felt that any changes had to be made in the summer, because employees could slow down the operations if they didn't like a change that management had made, causing delays to the airlines. Mr. Reiling stated that if changes were made in the winter and employees didn't like them, they could probably shut FBO down. Delays were much more serious and difficult to handle in the winter than in the summer. If enough delays were caused, the airlines might petition the commission, who could give FBO 30 days' notice to vacate the airport.

With all the foregoing facts and considerations in mind, Mr. Reiling sat down to work out both the changes that should be made in the contract refueling operations and the methods that should be used in implementing those changes.

Sunshine Builders, Inc.

In the five years since its founding, Sunshine Builders, Inc., had grown to be one of Florida's larger home builders. In the opinion of the company's management, major credit for Sunshine's growth and success was due to customer-oriented service and guarantee policies which, in combination with good construction, reasonable prices, and on-time completions, had enabled the firm to acquire an excellent reputation.

The founders of the company, Charles and Arthur Root, had come to Florida in 1953 at the ages of 28 and 26, respectively, after five years in the furniture business in Chicago. Charles Root had majored in economics at the University of Chicago, and Arthur Root in chemical engineering at Northwestern. While their furniture business had been moderately successful, they felt that the potential margin of profit was becoming increasingly narrow and that the personal time and effort required was out of proportion to the return attainable.

The Root brothers were attracted to Florida as a state which offered rapid growth and above-average business opportunities. They spent their first several months becoming familiar with the metropolitan area which included a population of nearly 500,000 within a 10-mile radius. During this period, realizing that land was appreciating in value, they bought eight lots for speculation. Shortly thereafter, encouraged by their father, who had had some experience in contracting, they decided to build houses on the lots. These homes were built and sold by early 1954, subcontracting the construction work to different local contractors.

Since this operation had been profitable, population growth was accelerating, land was relatively cheap, and there was some evidence of industrial movement to Florida, the Root brothers became convinced that the home construction business in Florida offered excellent prospects.

CONSTRUCTION OPERATIONS 1954–1958

Following the completion and sale of the first eight homes, the Root brothers built a model home and sold 40 very quickly. These homes were located on customers' lots and were entirely subcontracted. Since the customer made regular progress payments as the house progressed, beginning with an initial payment of 15 percent, the net effect of these arrangements was that relatively little capital was required. The company was hard-pressed during 1954 and 1955 to build enough houses to meet the demand.

During this period, Charles Root found that his greatest interest was in the development of land and formed a separate corporation (Root Land Development Corporation) for this purpose. Their father took no active part in either Sunshine Builders, headed by Arthur, or the land development operations under Charles. Each brother devoted nearly all of his time to his own operations and only assisted the other as requested or when dealing with major policy issues. A third corporation, Root Associates, was established by Arthur to handle sales for Sunshine Builders. Cooperative selling arrangements were also established with local real estate firms.

From 1954 to 1958, Sunshine expanded each year. Operating data for this period and for the first four months of 1959 are shown in Exhibit 1. During the years 1954–58, management operations, while extremely hectic and requiring consistently long hours on the part of both brothers, had been essentially simple in concept. With very few exceptions, the land on which Sunshine Builders constructed homes was owned by the customer, who had purchased it from either the Root Land Development Corporation or some other source. All construction work had been subcontracted to local subcontractors who by mutual consent had chosen to concentrate their efforts largely on work for Sunshine Builders.

From late 1954 through 1956, Arthur Root was assisted in the job of managing the construction end of the business by Herbert Playford. Mr. Playford had known the Root brothers in Chicago and had come to Florida at their request in September of 1954. Mr. Playford had had a high school education and then had worked successively as a shipping clerk, a neon glass blower, and in his father's junk business. On his arrival in Florida, Mr. Playford, 25, was taken by Arthur Root to visit 13 home sites which were in various stages of construction and given immediate responsibility for their completion with the instruction "Build them." In carrying out this assignment, Mr. Playford acted as superintendent, working with the various contractors, scheduling, coordinating, and supervising their various efforts.

As the business grew, four other superintendents were hired. In 1956, Mr. Playford was moved into the office to serve as an expediter and coordinator of the four superintendents and to take care of the mounting volume of paperwork associated with the construction end of the business. In this capacity he set up the systems of scheduling and cost control described later.

EXHIBIT 1
Operating Profit Data (expressed as a percentage of sales)

	1956	1957	1958	1959 (4 months)
Sales*	100.00	100.00	100.00	100.00
Construction costs†	85.20	86.60	83.33	84.80
Gross profit	14.80	13.40	16.67	15.20
Expenses:				
Sales expense	5.00	5.00	5.00	5.00
Salaries and wages‡	3.15	3.85	5.23	5.20
Sales promotion and advertising	0.63	0.27	0.78	1.38
Depreciation	0.10	0.21	0.40	0.61
First-year house maintenance ("punch work")	0.13	0.45	0.38	0.37
Auto and aircraft expense	—	0.17	0.33	0.33
Office expenses	0.37	0.18	0.18	0.32
Radio expenses	—	—	0.10	0.19
Production office §	0.37	—	0.16	0.70
Equipment rental	—	—	—	0.36
Maintenance of model homes	0.07	0.10	—	0.02
Maintenance of trucks, tools and equipment	—	—	—	0.66
Legal and accounting	—	0.04	0.16	0.04
Taxes and licenses	0.46	0.15	0.13	0.69
Travel and entertainment	0.10	0.08	0.20	0.34
Telephone and postage	0.08	0.09	0.10	0.14
Warehouse expense	—	—	—	0.81
Insurance	0.19	0.10	0.09	0.23
Christmas gifts to employees	0.19	0.07	0.09	0.12
Plans and designs	—	0.10	0.08	0.12
Discounts and collection fees on mortgages	—	—	0.04	0.46
Rent	0.10	0.10	0.08	0.21
Miscellaneous	0.08	0.11	0.05	0.11
Total expenses	11.02	11.07	13.58	18.41
Operating profit [( ) = loss]	3.78	2.33	3.09	(3.21)
Number of houses built	124	134	151	52 (4 months)
Average selling price	$13,500	$14,250	$15,000	$15,250
Average number of construction workers#	94	114	113	124

* Based on completed houses. A "sale" was made only when a house was completed, and construction costs were charged to work-in-process inventory until the home was completed. Expenses were charged monthly as they occurred.

† Construction costs include direct labor, material, subcontracting cost, and the salaries and wages of foremen, superintendents, warehousemen, draftsmen, blueprint operators, messengers, and the service department, plus fringe benefits for those salaries and wages included.

‡ Includes all other salaries and wages not included under construction costs.

§ General-purpose production requirements, such as blueprint paper, steel tapes, forms, office supplies, and small hand tools.

For the years 1956, 1957, and 1958, these figures represent the total of the subcontractors' men working on Sunshine houses. For 1959, the 124 men were on Sunshine's payroll.

Mr. Playford's assumption of many of the daily details of construction left Arthur Root free for sales, purchasing, and managing the company's finances. In late 1956, he was joined in the firm by a younger brother, Daniel Root, 25, who until that time had been pursuing graduate studies in history.

On December 1, 1956, Mr. Playford resigned from the company to enter the building business for himself. He founded a new firm, Meadowlark Builders, aided with a substantial investment by the Root brothers. Meadowlark was successful from the start, building a total of 200 low-cost homes in 1957 and 1958. In December 1958, Arthur Root persuaded Mr. Playford to return to Sunshine as treasurer, assistant secretary, and manager of production and service, and the Meadowlark operation was discontinued.

By the end of 1958, Daniel Root, as vice president and secretary, had taken up full responsibility for sales, broker relations, customer relations, advertising, and the developing and merchandising of new models. Arthur Root, as president, handled all financing and purchasing. Charles Root continued to devote his time principally to the Root Land Development Corporation.

The construction work, under Mr. Playford, was handled by eight subcontractors who performed the following functions:

Plumbing	Plastering
Electrical	Carpentry
Painting	Heating
Masonry	Cleaning

Each contractor sent in a weekly bill for the wages he had paid, plus 8 percent for equipment. His own time was included at an hourly rate approximately 15 percent above his highest paid man. Material was purchased and supplied by the contractor at cost. The contractor hired and fired as he felt necessary, but Sunshine Builders had the right to approve any wage increases. Arthur Root and Herbert Playford made it a practice to question the subcontractors on jobs on which their costs appeared out of line with previous cost experience. Total costs for each contractor were tabulated for each job to furnish this information. Except for the masonry crew, the workers were not unionized, but the wages for each trade were approximately equal to the appropriate general community average.

The contractors each had a number of crews whose activities were arranged and assigned by the four superintendents previously mentioned. The superintendents were paid about the same or slightly more than top construction craftsmen. Each superintendent covered the Sunshine Builders' homes in the geographic territory assigned to him, the bulk of the homes being located within a 7-mile radius.

By late 1958, Arthur Root had become increasingly concerned about the effectiveness of this entire arrangement. In discussions with his brothers and Mr. Playford, he made the following observations and criticisms of the existing operation:

1. The superintendents were spending most of their time competing with each other for crews to work on the houses in their territory. They were "high-grade expediters" but made no attempt to coordinate the crew requirements between each other.
2. Seven of the contractors were personally receiving \$11,000–\$12,000 per year, working solely for Sunshine.[1] In effect, they were acting not so much as independent contractors but rather as foremen who could be hired for less to perform such work.
3. The subcontractors were not buying labor-saving equipment but tended to "run old equipment into the ground."
4. It should be possible to centralize controls and scheduling and to eliminate conflicts, delays, and superintendents.

After considerable discussion, a unanimous management decision was made to absorb all of the subcontractors' organizations into the Sunshine firm and to eliminate the use of superintendents. As planned, the various subcontractor crews would be placed on the Sunshine payroll, with the previous subcontractors as Sunshine foremen.

Individual meetings were held with each contractor in December 1958. The proposed changes were explained, and each contractor was offered a salary reflecting his experience and ability. A reasonable price was to be negotiated for his equipment. In spite of the fact that the salaries offered were 10–25 percent below their recent annual earnings (the masonry contractor, for example, had been making \$12,000 and was offered \$9,250), the offers were accepted by the entire group. Arthur Root felt that the offers were higher than the men could earn elsewhere and that the men realized they had been overpaid previously and that it was "a gravy train that might stop suddenly any time. They were also glad to be freed of the payroll paperwork and to give up some responsibility." Under the new arrangements the foremen were to continue to do the hiring, as necessary. The foremen were also told that they would be given year-end bonuses, dependent on the company's annual operating profit.

The four superintendents were dismissed, and the new method of operation was installed on January 1, 1959. Three of the superintendents were rehired as tradesmen on the various crews, and an additional eight construction workers (who had been on the payroll of certain of the subcontractors, working on jobs other than Sunshine houses) were also absorbed, bringing the construction crew to 124.

OPERATIONS IN EARLY 1959

The Sunshine Builders' organization as of May 1, 1959, is shown in Exhibit 2. The numbers of personnel working in the various functional areas are shown in parentheses after each descriptive title. Each construction

---

[1] The eighth, the cleaning contractor, had been receiving approximately \$5,000 per year.

EXHIBIT 2
Organization as of May 1, 1959

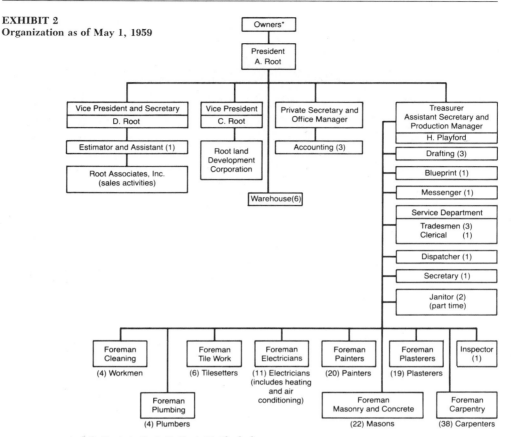

* C. Root, A. Root, D. Root, H. Playford.

crew consisted of nearly equal numbers of skilled tradesmen and helpers with the exception of the cleaning crew which included only unskilled general labor. The total personnel on the regular payroll at that time numbered 161, of which 124 were direct labor on construction. Following the organizational change, there had been no significant change in construction crew levels during the past four months.

In April 1959, Arthur Root and Herbert Playford both felt enthusiastic about the results of the new organization thus far. They stated, for example, that without the superintendents there was "now a closer, more direct line of communication between the office and the crews." Further, fewer mistakes were now being made, according to Mr. Playford. The foremen appeared to be taking a broader point of view which Mr. Root pointed out was demonstrated, for example, by their keeping the office better informed as to their own stage of progress on each job.

Herbert Playford ran the production end of the business with an apparent assurance and good humor despite the constant rush of decisions and problems to solve. The basic approaches to planning and controlling production employed in April 1959 were essentially the same as those he had set up himself during the years 1955–56.

The dispatching office and the "production boards" on two walls in that office served as a central nucleus of information in Mr. Playford's system. While no formal scheduling was attempted, the "boards" aided the dispatcher in keeping up to date on where each job stood. The "boards" themselves consisted of wallboard material on which was tacked blueprint-type paper with a 2-inch grid. Across the top (along the horizontal scale) were these headings: (*a*) the owner's name; (*b*) the address where the house was to be built; (*c*) the model number of the house; and (*d*) the 65 individual steps, operations, or phases of the construction work. These are described in Exhibit 3. The houses were then listed vertically, adding new homes at the bottom as orders were received. The board's appearance is depicted below:

Jobs			Construction steps								
OWNER	LOCATION	MODEL	1 SIGN CLEAR LOT	2 DELIVER	3 POWER	4 STAKE	5 DIG	6 POUR	7 ORDER	8 LAY	9 FILL
E.K. Williams	14 Coral St.	69									
D.W. Onan	262 Beach Rd.	14									
A. T. Bovril	69 Hacienda	190	L								

The dispatcher, Mabel Roark, 35, posted the information to the boards. She was energetic and personable, and had nearly one year of experience in her job. She placed her initials in the box after she had called the foreman requesting the performance of each construction step. The foreman, of course, knew what work was required for each step but relied on Ms. Roark for instructions as to what house and which step should be his crew's next assignment. She wrote in the date when the operation had been promised for completion and noted "OK" when the step was completed.

Ms. Roark also used five colored pins to assist in calling her attention to an operation as follows:

Black—indicated "on order."
Red—indicated "did not arrive or get completed as promised."
White—indicated "crew is there, on the job."
Yellow—indicated "Roark should call."
Blue—indicated "have a question for the foreman."

From the visual standpoint, since the jobs were added at the bottom of the sheet as they were taken on and the construction steps proceeded from left to right, the completed steps made a slightly irregular diagonal line, slanting downwards from right to left. Thus, any house that had fallen behind showed up as an indent to the left in the diagonal line of completed boxes.

By and large, Mr. Playford stated during the last 12 months all houses had been taking the same length of time to complete, namely, 80–85 calendar days from the date construction work was started. Customers were promised delivery in no more than 100 calendar days from the signing of the purchase agreement. Because so many purchasers were new residents moving south and therefore had many moving details to schedule, any delays in house completions were felt to significantly jeopardize customer relations.

In addition to assigning the work to the foremen, Ms. Roark's activity as dispatcher included maintaining the production "boards" and serving as a communication and recording center for all reports and instructions. In this duty she made use of a two-way radio system. Each foreman, Mr. Playford, and the warehouse supervisor had a two-way radio in his car or truck. The radio system had been installed in mid-1958 on a lease basis, and cost the company a monthly rental of $375.

Ms. Roark talked with each foreman intermittently three to six or more times daily. In a typical conversation the masonry foreman might call in and tell her that the footings operation his crew had been working on at the Kelly house was now completed, but that the ironwork for the Kent job hadn't arrived and that Mr. and Mrs. Kent had been around that morning and asked if they could change the dimensions of their back patio from 12 by 15 feet to 12 by 20 feet. He might then ask where Ms. Roark wanted his crew the next day and would she check her paperwork to see whether the Larsen house was to have a front planter and whether the plumbers should be through with the O'Leary house so that the slab could be laid by the masons.

Ms. Roark independently made the innumerable decisions as to the operations and jobs which would be done next, receiving little or no aid from Mr. Playford, whose office was next door. While he came in to see the "boards" once or twice a week, he did not attempt to participate in the hour-by-hour job of scheduling and directing the crews.

To prevent delays and idle crews, Ms. Roark had to have a clear understanding of the various operations and their interrelationships. It was essential, for instance, for her to know that the electricians couldn't do their rough in until the studs were up, that the heating work could be done while the carpenters were trimming, that the electricians and plumbers could go on ahead or behind the painters on certain operations but could not work at the same time in the house with them, etc. Ms. Roark stated, "I still make some mistakes, but I've learned a lot about house building during this past year."

In scheduling the crews, she used as guidelines the time and crew requirements shown on Exhibit 3. These guidelines had been established

EXHIBIT 3

Steps of the Construction Job as Used on the Company's Production Boards / Work Force and Time Estimates for Dispatcher

Step Number	Operation Required	Explanation	Crew	Normal Crew No. Workers	Worker Days of Work	Elapsed Time Allowed (Days)	Remarks
1	Sign posted, lot cleared.		Masonry	1	1	1	In typical subdivision lot already cleared.
2	Deliver stakes, material, and steel.		Warehouse	—	—	—	
3	Power pole and water meter in.	Done by utilities.	Power Co.	—	—	—	
4	Stake out.		Masonry	{3	{3	}2	Includes a day for checking by foreman.
5	Dig footing.	Footing only 12–18" below the surface.	Masonry	2	1	½	
6	Pour footing.		Masonry	2	1	½	
7	Order sliding glass doors.		(Roark)	—	—	—	
8	Lay foundation.	Set reinforcing steel and pour concrete.	Masonry	2	1	½	
9	Fill foundation.	Fill and pack dirt within foundation for slab.	Subcontracted	SC*	—	1	Done during no. 11.
10	Tie in foundation.	Plumbing for water and sewer connections.	Plumbing	2	{5	}1	
11	Plumbing rough in.	Set plumbing for slab.	Plumbing	3	3	2½	Includes a day for city inspection.
12	Grade slab.		Masonry	2	2	2	Includes a day for city inspection.
13	Pour slab.		Masonry	3	1½	1½	Includes a day after pouring for slab to set.
14	Strip for terrazzo.	Place strips for sills or sliding doors.	Subcontracted	SC	—	1	
15	Pour terrazzo.		Subcontracted	SC	—	1½	Includes a day for terrazzo to set.
16	Deliver blocks, steel, sills.		Vendor and warehouse	—	—	—	
17	Lay block walls.		Masonry	5	10	2	
18	Form and pour lintels.		Masonry	2	1	½	Must be inspected.
19	First grind, terrazzo.		Subcontracted	SC	—	2	
20	Carpenter's frame.	Frame up interior wall studs and roof.	Carpenters (Roark)	4	20	5	
21	Order cabinets.		(Roark)	—	—	—	
22	Dry in.	First layer of lumber on the roof.	Carpenters	4	1	—	Included in time allowance for no. 20.
23	Flue and/or ductwork.		Masonry	2	4	2	Done during framing.
24	Set tub.		Subcontracted	SC	—	½	Done during framing.
25	Electrical rough in.	Place most of electrical wiring.	Electricians	2	4	2	Done during framing (after studs in).
26	Prime cornice.	Paint under overhang of roof.	Painters	2	1	½	
27	Order lath.		(Roark)	—	—	1	One day necessary for framing and electrical inspection.
28	Lath.		Plaster	4	4	1	
29	Order vanity.		(Roark)	—	—	—	

Step	Operation	Detail	Performed by				Remarks
30	Ceiling heat.	Electrical radiant heating usually used.	Electricians	2	2	⎱2	
31	Roof complete.	Pitch and gravel built up roof.	Subcontracted	SC	—	⎰	
32	Scratch for tile.	Preparation for tiling.	Plaster	2	3	2	
33	Brown coat plaster and stucco.	First coat.	Plaster	4	4	2	Includes a day for drying.
34	Second grind, terrazzo.		Subcontracted	SC	1	½	
35	Ironwork	Any decorative ironwork.	Carpenters	2	6	½	
36	Tile walls.	Bathrooms and sometimes kitchen areas.	Tile	4		1½	
37	Plaster and stucco complete.		Plaster	4	4	1	Need two-day notice.
38	Glaze.	Install window glass.	Subcontracted	SC	—	1	
39	Install sliding glass doors.		Subcontracted	SC	—	1	Does not interfere with any other work.
40	Insulation.		Subcontracted	SC	—	1	
41	Clean and rough grade lot.	Remove debris and grade.	Subcontracted	SC	—	1	
42	Front stoop.		Masonry	2	1	½	Usually done while framing.
43	Pour outside concrete.		Masonry	2	2	1	
44	Form outside concrete.		Masonry	2	2	1	Need good weather.
45	Outside gravel or asphalt.		Subcontracted	SC	—	2	
46	Order trim material.	Moldings, door frames, etc.	(Roark)	—	—	—	
47	Carpenter's trim.		Carpenters	5	20	4	Done by vendor during trim operation.
48	Glaze jalousie doors.		Subcontracted	SC	—	½	
49	Install cabinets.		Subcontracted	SC	—	1	
50	Septic tank.		Plumbers	2	2	1	
51	Plumber's trim.	Final plumbing work.	Plumbers	2	2	1	
52	Heating.	Install and/or complete heating system.	Electricians	3	6	2	Done while carpenters are trimming.
53	Paint.		Painters	4	16	4	Must be alone in house.
54	Install operators and deliver screens.	Window mechanisms.	Carpenters	1	½	½	Now done before glazing.
55	Electrical trim.	Install lamps, outlet plates, etc.	Electricians	3	3	1	Must be alone in house.
56	Polish terrazzo.		Subcontracted	SC	—	2	
57	Clean windows and interior.		Cleaning	2	2	1	
58	Grass.		Subcontracted	SC	—	1	
59	Install screens.		Carpenters	1	½	½	
60	Painters complete, inspect.		Painters	5	15	3	Including time for company inspection, final adjustments and odds and ends.
61	Wallpaper and mirror.		Painters	2	2	1	
62	Plumbing inspection.	By city inspector.		—	—	1	City inspection.
63	Electrical inspection.	By city inspector.		—	—	1	City inspection.
64	Permanent electrical connection.	By power company.	Power Co.	—	—	1	
65	Production inspection.		Co. inspector	1	1	1	Note also inspection at step no. 60.

* SC (subcontracted). In 1959, the average house required $2,500 of subcontracted work.

by Herbert Playford and Ms. Roark out of their combined experience as to how many men and how much time were necessary for the completion of each step. They had learned, for example, that it was entirely reasonable to expect a crew of four carpenters to frame up an average house (Exhibit 3, step no. 20) in five days working at an ordinary pace.

Ms. Roark's purchasing activities were confined to ordering specific items for delivery from vendors selected previously by Arthur Root. Arthur Root handled all negotiations with suppliers and arranged for prices, delivery, and payment terms. This work occupied a significant portion of his time. He regularly "shopped" for better values in windows, fixtures, lumber, appliances, etc., and had accomplished considerable standardization of purchased items.

In late 1958, Sunshine Builders had leased a 6,000-square-foot warehouse in order to be able to stock various purchased materials. Five men were hired to receive, stock, and deliver items stocked. A sixth employee, who had previously acted as a truck driver and errand runner, was also assigned to the warehouse group. The arrangement was intended to allow the company to buy in larger volumes at lower prices. It was also intended that this new approach would give Sunshine more direct and closer control over the delivery of items to building sites. Mr. Root estimated that he could negotiate volume purchases covering about 75 percent of the material used (based on cost), which could secure for Sunshine a 4 percent saving in cost if the company would purchase and take deliveries no more frequently than three times per year.

While Sunshine Builders did not attempt to maintain a breakdown between material and labor costs, Mr. Root pointed out that costs had been rising steadily, citing *Engineering News —Record* statistics which showed that on a national basis material costs had been rising at a rate of 2 percent per year over the past four years. Construction labor costs on the same survey showed increases at an annual rate of about 4 percent.

The foremen were responsible for ordering all material from the warehouse with the exception of the staking-out material which Ms. Roark ordered. The warehouse truck then delivered the material ordered to each building site.

Sunshine Builders encouraged prospective buyers to make any non-structural changes which they desired. Daniel Root pointed out that "different models are built in each Sunshine subdivision, allowing a considerable freedom of choice for the buyer which, coupled with the further variations which Sunshine offers at a nominal price, results in a low-cost house with considerable individuality." The exceptions and additions to a typical contract shown in Exhibit 4 were not unusual in either nature or quantity.

Ms. Roark and the foremen were given copies of each customer's plans, together with the agreed-upon changes. She kept a "customer detail sheet" for each customer which contained this information and the frequent addi-

EXHIBIT 4
Excerpt from Building Agreement with Customer

Third: All details of material and construction will be identical with those used in the model home located at

. . . Lot #4, Belle Lake Subdivision . . . with the following exceptions:

1.	Model 190L.	$10,990
2.	Place wrought iron shutters with oak leaf design on kitchen windows, front bedroom windows, and left side bedroom window. Retain stucco decoration.	90
3.	Substitute screen patio with terrazzo floor at house level, full foundation, one waterproof electric outlet, light fixture centered over sliding glass doors. Floor area 16 by 10 feet. Roof to extend 2 feet past floor area with screening to be canted toward floor. Roof to be aluminum with styrofoam insulation.	740
4.	Install glass shower door in bath no. 2.	50
5.	Substitute American Standard Bildor cast-iron tub for present steel tub.	n/c
6.	Erect tile wainscot in bath no. 2 to 3 feet, 8 inches height.	145
7.	Install air-conditioning aperture centered under front windows to bedroom no. 1, with 220-volt outlet on separate circuit for same.	28
8.	Install tile backsplash above base cabinets in kitchen.	50
9.	Install gutter and downspout over front entrance, left side of bedroom wing, kitchen, and garage.	50
10.	Eliminate Walltex in baths no. 1 and no. 2.	n/c
11.	Install bookshelves between living room and dinette in lieu of present planter and wrought iron. Shelves to be placed at 42-inch, 54-inch, and 74-inch height.	n/c
12.	Raise 1-by 4-inch pressure-treated drapery hanger above sliding glass doors in living room to ceiling height.	n/c
		12,143

n/c = No charge.

tional changes. Such further changes were written up and priced by the estimator at the time they were requested. A "customer request for extra work" form was filled out and signed by the customer, with the original copy being sent to the office for the final bill, the customer keeping the second copy, the foreman receiving the third copy, and the fourth being sent to Ms. Roark.

Before actual construction could begin on a specific house, about two or three weeks were required to complete the steps shown on the start chart (Exhibit 5). Commencing with the signing of the contract, Mr. Playford personally handled the preproduction phase of each job, covering steps 1 through 25 on the start chart.

EXHIBIT 5
Start Chart

Customer's name _____
Address: _____

Phone: _____

Broker: _____
Legal description: _____

_____

1. Contract signed or on file ☐
2. Detail Sheet #1 received ☐
3. Plans ordered ☐
4. Survey ordered ☐
5. Detail Sheet #2 received (if there is more than 48 hour lag between #3 and #5, report to A.R.) ☐
6. Plans returned ☐
7. Plans inspected (if there is more than a 24 hour lag between #6 and #9, report to A.R.) ☐
8. Plans returned for correction ☐
9. Corrected plans returned ☐
10. Plans inspected for correction ☐
11. Plans sent to _____ ☐
12. Plans received from _____ ☐
13. Building permit applied for ☐

14. Plans and letter to customer (air mail special delivery with enclosed return envelope) ☐
15. Send loan plans ☐
16. Submit plans for subdivision approval (special messenger) ☐
17. Subdivision approval received ☐
18. Survey received ☐
19. Notify supervisor and production to check lot for clearing and for errors in lot line ☐
20. Customer's approval ☐
21. Notify accounting of loan approval and of who holds the loan ☐
22. Construction loan ☐
23. Add name to production chart ☐
24. Building permit picked up ☐
25. Water meter permit picked up ☐

In explaining his methods of managing the production operation, Mr. Playford made the following points:

1. Two employees have been added in drafting since the first of the year in an attempt to eliminate the subcontracting of drafting work. The drafting is necessary in order to have separate plans for every house because of the large number of changes usually incorporated for each customer.

2. The major change in operations without the four superintendents is that the various foremen now have responsibility for the construction of the house at different phases. These responsibilities are as follows:

Operations	Supervisor or Foreman Responsible
1–2	Mr. Playford
3	Electrical
4	Carpenter
5–10	Mason
11	Plumber

Operations	Supervisor or Foreman Responsible
12–18.	Mason
19–23.	Carpenter
24.	Plumber
25.	Electrician
26–30.	Plasterer
31.	Carpenter
32–34.	Plasterer
35.	Carpenter
36–37.	Plasterer
38–49.	Carpenter
50–51.	Plumber
52–55.	Electrician
56–65.	Inspector

3. Low-cost construction comes from doing jobs conventionally. The only good approach to cost cutting comes from making operations fast and smooth. Sunshine has cut two weeks off of building homes in recent years and should eventually be able to cut one or two more. I made a study at Meadowlark which showed that a home comparable to Sunshine's $15,000 models could be built in 52 calendar days if everything worked out well.

Our men use the same methods for each step in every house. It's all pretty much standardized—the block work, slab, framing, electrical wiring, plastering—they do each house the same way as the others. We use only the most elementary common tools and equipment, such as power saws and cement mixers, and have very little else.

By and large, most prefabbing does not pay unless the customer is not allowed to make any changes. If Sunshine adopted that approach, we would lose sales. For instance, prefabbed roof trusses so commonly used by other construction firms are more expensive for Sunshine than on-site building of the roof structure, probably because we have so many models. We visited Levittown, Pennsylvania, in 1956 to see if we could pick up any ideas and found that they permit no changes whatever. Building houses block by block, they can do more precutting and standardizing than we can since our houses are usually not adjacent.

One way we save time is to get foremen to make suggestions. For instance, our masonry foreman has learned that a mason will lay blocks faster if his helper will keep the blocks piled up ahead of him. And we have discovered that it is a good idea to supply about 10 percent extra material to each job in order to prevent any picking and hunting for material. Any extra material left over is sent back to the warehouse. But the conventional methods of building are cheapest for us.

4. Our workers are picked by the foremen. They usually hear about good people in the trade, and many that they hire are friends or have been sent by friends. The foremen can hire and lay off as needed. Crews work a 5-day week, 9 hours a day, which gives them 45 hours of pay per week. The masons

are unionized, but the others are not. The workers tend to work in teams, a journeyman and a helper. They also tend to specialize. For instance, on a carpenter crew the foreman has separate workers for door jambs and window frames, for rafter cutting, and for cornices for general framing, as well as a saw specialist. Helpers are paid $1.25–$1.75 per hour. We pay no overtime, just straight time. The wage structure for the craftsmen is masons, $2.75; plumbers, $3; carpenters, $2.45; tile setters, $3; plasterers, $3, electricians, $2.25; painters, $2.40. There is no wage progression, no future, no security, and no benefits other than those required by law, social security, etc., which add up to about 8 percent over these rates. But we've had no major layoffs ever and have a darn good crew.

5.   Up until January, Arthur used the six charts on my office wall—which I started—to control costs. These showed the dollar-per-square-foot cost for each phase (corresponding to the foreman's areas of operations) for each house when it was completed, the point being plotted on the horizontal axis by date of completion. This would have revealed any trends and any house that was out of line. No clear trends were shown, though.

Now these charts have been discontinued because they were too much work to keep up. Instead, about once a month we spot-check costs by studying the accumulated costs on several completed jobs quite closely and figuring out the total cost per square foot on various operations such as electrical, plumbing, etc. Every three months I'll make a still more detailed check on 12 houses. I control material costs by controlling the amount sent out to each house, depending on its size. Arthur, of course, keeps check on supply sources.

If any costs get looking high, I talk to the foreman. Recently tile costs had moved up about 15–20 percent, and upon investigating I found that the foreman was driving 20 miles for supplies every day. I showed him how to order in advance and stock more in our warehouse. He had also guaranteed his crew 10 hours of pay regardless of the actual time worked. And some of his crew were driving to our warehouse instead of getting material delivered.

As long as I'm out watching and the men are working and Ms. Roark keeps things moving, the costs will be OK.

6.   We are still too lax in our attitude toward delay. I want more flow and speed, better customer relationships, lower work in process. I am getting out in the field more now that I've got things set up better here, and getting my eyes opened finding jobs where no action is taking place. Ms. Roark gets along well with the foremen, but she is not firm enough with them or with outsiders. She can learn to do her job even better.

7.   Crews are instructed to work an extra hour to finish up on a house and whenever possible to make moves to the next house on an overnight basis. If a house really needs only eight hours of plastering, it gets nine because we work on a nine-hour day. However, if it has what we might consider 10 hours of plastering, it is usually done in 9 also in order to finish it in one day.

Houses were priced by estimating construction costs (Exhibit 1) and then adding 5 percent for expenses and 15 percent for selling costs and profit together. The estimating was performed by Daniel Root's assistant, who served as the company's estimator. He had had some architectural training and spent a large portion of his time working with customers on their changes from standard plans. The average house in 1959 included approximately $2,500 of subcontracting. Exhibits 6 and 7 show one-page brochures illustrating the cheapest and the most expensive houses in the line. Once a price was set on a model it was not changed, though its costs tended to rise slightly as new improvements of a minor nature were gradually added. Arthur Root and Herbert Playford agreed with Daniel Root that Sunshine Builders' prices in 1959 could not be increased if Sunshine's product was to remain competitive.

Considerable emphasis was placed on customer satisfaction after the house was completed. Sunshine's policy was that during the first year they would repair any item that the customer did not consider satisfactory. As long as the request was in any way reasonable (and often when it did not appear so), they did the work at no charge and with a willing and pleasant attitude. The service department (Exhibit 2) handled this work. In the Sunshine organization it was referred to as "punch work," meaning that it was to be "punched out, without delay." In April 1959, the clerical worker

EXHIBIT 6
Sales Promotional Material (for a two-bedroom model)

$10,990 on your lot   With 2-car garage $11,840

- 2 master bedrooms
- 2 "decorator" baths
- cement tile roof over 2x8 rafters
- 15 ft. sliding glass wall to patio
- Sunshine kitchen; Coronet cabinets and Nu-Tone ventilating hood; Moen single-mix faucet
- General Electric wall oven, cook top, 40 gallon water heater
- radiant electric ceiling heat—silent, clean, maintenance-free, economical; individual room-thermostats
- 6" Fiberglas insulation for cooler summers, warmer winters
- Minneapolis-Honeywell tap switches; clothes dryer outlet; circuit-breakers (eliminating fuses); 200 ampere service
- Hall-Mack bathroom accessories
- spacious garage plus utility "ell"
- spot sodded lawn
- square footage: living area   1073
  utility   63
  garage   249
  TOTAL   1385
- Sunshine guarantee of satisfaction

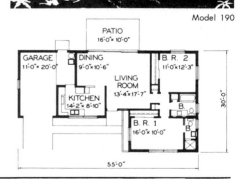

Model 190

1202 Hacienda Ave. • Minneapolis, Florida • Phone 6-4602

it's a SUNSHINE home

Model Home on Poinsettia Rd. — 2 Miles South of Key Drive

EXHIBIT 7
Sales Promotional Material (for a three-bedroom model)

$18,500 on your lot

- 3 bedrooms • 3 "decorator" baths
- cement tile roof over 2x8 rafters
- tile foyer entrance with guest closet
- spacious family room with serving bar
- sliding glass walls from living and
  dining rooms to
- 18 ft. screened porch
- 20 ft. free-form patio
- Coronet cabinets in solid maple or solid
  walnut; Nu-Tone ventilating hood;
  Moen single-mix faucet
- General Electric dishwasher, wall oven,
  cook top, 52 gallon water heater
- radiant electric ceiling heat—silent, clean,
  maintenance-free, economical;
  individual room-thermostats
- 6" Fiberglas insulation for cooler
  summers, winter warmth
- Minneapolis-Honeywell tap switches;
  clothes dryer outlet; circuit breakers
  (eliminates fuses); 200 ampere service
- Hall-Mack bathroom accessories;
  "relaxation unit" in master bath
- 2-car garage plus utility "ell"
- spot sodded lawn
- square footage: living area   1656
  porch   180
  garage and utility   505
  TOTAL   2341
- Sunshine   guarantee of satisfaction

Model 215

1202 Hacienda Ave. • Minneapolis, Florida • Phone 6-4602

it's a **SUNSHINE** home

overseeing punch work was moved into Mr. Playford's office in order to provide better supervision of her activities. The biggest single item requiring punch work was ceiling cracks. In pricing a house, about 2 percent of the expected price was allowed for punch work and included in construction cost estimates.

On May 1, 1959, the production "boards" listed a total of 42 houses, consisting of 12 different models ranging from $10,990 to $18,500 in price. Comparable figures for October 1958 and April 1, 1959, showed 35 and 36 houses under construction, respectively. Nine units of the most popular model were under way, five models had three to six units in process, and the six other models listed three or less units each.

The April increase in houses in process—from 36 to 42—was due to a heavy influx of orders received in late March and in the month of April. This improvement in sales had caused Mr. Playford to gradually increase the houses started each week from three during the first week of April to six in the last week of that month. Sales prospects for the balance of 1959 appeared to be excellent, and Mr. Playford expected to be able to continue starting five to six houses weekly. Mr. Playford noted that he liked to make any changes in starts on a gradual basis in order to maintain a smooth flow of work to all crews. "This approach," he said, "paces the whole operation."

Arthur Root stated five principles which he felt represented the key to Sunshine Builders' success and to its future:

1. Our houses must be completely livable.
2. They must have eye appeal.
3. As builders we must develop and hold a reputation for honesty, integrity, skill, and on-time completion.
4. We must offer exceptional value.
5. Our houses must be properly presented and promoted.

"Any one factor that is not up to standard would hurt us badly. We must do a top job on all five."

CASE 27

Sof-Optics, Inc.

> What an unpleasant surprise! We had thought about 20 percent of our callers waited more than 10 seconds to get one of our customer service reps—but I looked at the first data from our new call monitoring system this morning and found that 76 percent of our callers waited more than 10 seconds yesterday, with the average wait more than 80 seconds. And, although we can't measure it, I wonder how many customers get a busy signal; and how many just get fed up and call a competitor.

Nancy Langstaff was director of marketing of Sof-Optics, Inc., a San Francisco manufacturer of a high-quality soft contact lens. The company had been founded in early August 1977. Sales had grown to $5.8 million in FY 1980 (financial year ending July 31, 1980) and were forecasted to nearly double in FY 1981 in a rapidly expanding marketplace. However, Sof-Optics had yet to show a profit and was under increasing pressure from its major stockholder, a San Francisco venture capital firm, to do so. As Langstaff continued to look at the data she had received that morning (Wednesday, October 22, 1980), she thought:

> Dan [national sales manager] has been telling me for several months that we have a real problem with the waits in our customer service department. I'll collect a couple more days' data, but will have to have some recommendations ready for my meeting with George [president] on Monday.

THE SOFT CONTACT LENS INDUSTRY

While spectacles date at least to 1270 AD, and the principle of contact lenses can be traced to Leonardo da Vinci, the history of the soft contact lens is brief indeed. A new plastic material (HEMA), developed in Czechoslovakia in the early 60s, was similar to other plastics in that it was hard, transparent, and machinable, but was strikingly different when placed in water—it became soft and pliable. Bausch and Lomb (B&L), the leading company in the U.S. vision care products industry, obtained a license to manufacture contact lenses of the material in 1966 and received FDA approval to market the "Soflens" in 1971.

The soft contact lens market was a small but rapidly growing segment of an industry that included eyeglasses, frames, and hard contact lenses as well (Exhibit 1). By 1980, it was estimated that only 10 percent of the more that 50 million Americans whose vision problems could be helped with soft contact lenses had tried them; and it had been found that the contact lens replacement (lost or broken) market (about 30 percent of sales) and contact lens care supply market (about $50 per user per year) were also strong. Contact lenses offered primarily a cosmetic advantage over eyeglasses. As B&L's soft contact lens marketing manager stated, "What we're really selling is an improvement in visual performance and appearance, things near and dear to people's hearts."[1] Soft contact lenses were easier and more comfortable to wear than hard lenses, although they fit a smaller range of eyes and eye problems.

EXHIBIT 1
The Vision Care Products Industry ($ millions)

	1977 Sales	1987 Estimated Sales (1977/$)
Eyeglasses............	$226.0	$ 438.5
Frames..............	222.5	443.3
Hard contact lenses....	27.2	28.9
Soft contact lenses.....	70.0	502.5
	545.7	1,413.2

Source: Frost & Sullivan Report #564.

Soft contact lenses were sold through the private practices of the more than 15,000 ophthalmologists and optometrists and through optical retailers (such as Pearle Vision Centers). It was projected that the retailers, with a 25 percent market share in 1979, would continue to take business from the private practitioners, but that the higher quality service and products available from the private practitioners would continue to attract the top end of the market. As one executive said, "It's the same in the car market. Some people want to buy a Mercedes, some want a VW."[2]

The $155 million (1979) soft lens market was dominated by Bausch & Lomb (51 percent market share), American Optical (14 percent), and Con-

---

[1] "Eyeball to Eyeball," *Barron's* August 25, 1980, p. 21.

[2] Ibid., p. 23.

tinuous Curve (10 percent). More than 20 other companies were active in the market, including Sof-Optics (3 percent share) and several small, regional firms. This market represented 28 percent of B&L's sales and 56 percent of its profits. With a sales force of 225, the company sold both to the optical retailers, to take advantage of B&L's high-volume position, and to the private practioners, supported by a 1977 move to a "consignment" sales program, in which a larger number and variety of lenses were stored at the doctor's office, though not paid for until sold. "In essence, (we) moved our warehouse to the doctor's office," one B&L executive said.[3] B&L had also developed a markedly different, spin-casting manufacturing process that significantly reduced the traditionally labor-intensive finishing operation. With manufacturing costs that were reported to be 50 percent of those experienced by its competitors, B&L had chopped wholesale prices by 25 percent (to $25 per lens) in April 1979. Another recent development in the market was the acquisition of Continuous Curve by Revlon and the anticipated use of Revlon's marketing muscle in the optical retailer segment of the market. Observers expected a shakeout in the soft lens industry by the mid-80s, with perhaps six national companies to remain, due to the heavy R&D needs in the still young and innovative industry and an eventual slowing of the spectacular early growth rates.

THE COMPANY

In their spare time during 1976, San Francisco ophthalmologist Carl Wagner and his neighbor, University of California physics professor Johan Schmidt, developed a superior soft contact lens. Based upon Schmidt's expertise with exotic materials, and in his basement lab, the pair had made an unusually thin lens with excellent water absorption properties (both features important for corneal health) that was durable, comfortable, and resistant to discoloration. The inventors applied for patents on both the product and process in December 1976 (pending in 1980).

In early 1977, Wagner and Schmidt had asked George Powell to develop a business plan for presentation to the financial community. Powell, then 40, was a Wharton MBA who had spent 10 years with a large consulting company before starting his own practice, specializing in small business, in 1975. During the spring, Wagner and Schmidt, both of whom wanted to continue with their professions, had come to trust Powell's business judgment and personal integrity, and had found him easy to work with. For his part, Powell had become excited with the potential of the product so that when asked if he would head the proposed company, he quickly accepted. By July, he had raised $10 million in venture capital and long-term debt from a San Francisco firm, and Sof-Optics had been formed in August 1977. The new company had begun production in November in a small purchased plant. First (fiscal) year volume, which had totaled $1.3 million on 36,214

---

[3] Ibid., p. 21.

EXHIBIT 2

SOF-OPTICS, INC.
Financial summary

	FY 1978	FY 1979	FY 1980	FY 1981 (est.)*
Lens volume	36,214	103,974	211,422	400,000
Average price	$35.24	$33.74	$27.53	$26.38
Revenue:				
Lens	$ 1,276,181	$ 3,508,083	$5,820,448	$10,550,000
Supplies	18,122	69,701	121,239	300,000
Total revenue	1,294,303	3,577,784	5,941,687	10,850,000
Manufacturing cost:				
Lens	1,498,535	1,538,815	1,653,320	2,532,000
Supplies	15,205	61,283	103,117	250,000
Total manufacturing cost	1,513,740	1,600,098	1,756,437	2,782,000
Gross margin..............	(219,437)	1,977,686	4,185,250	8,068,000
Operating expenses:				
Research and development	221,187	236,411	243,135	250,000
Marketing:				
Market research	35,221	60,098	78,226	100,000
Advertising	54,321	178,215	530,669	1,000,000
Sales	446,716	827,349	1,126,879	1,500,000
Customer service	200,214	253,796	327,704	400,000
Returns.................	25,817	40,221	141,653	300,000
Shipping...............	55,698	127,216	338,275	700,000
Total marketing........	817,987	1,486,895	2,543,406	4,000,000
General and administration	826,444	1,334,799	1,763,299	2,500,000
Total operating expenses..........	1,865,618	3,058,105	4,549,840	6,750,000
Net profit or loss	$(2,085,055)	$(1,080,419)	$ (364,590)	$ 1,318,000

* Forecast includes the anticipated effect of the new warranty program but not the effect of the proposed consignment program.

lenses, had increased to $5.8 million on 211,422 units in FY 1980 (see Exhibit 2 for a summary of operating statistics).[4] However, with start-up expenses higher than expected, the company had not shown a profit in the first three years of operation, and an additional $3 million had been raised from the same venture capital firm in October 1979.

[4] Throughout this case, physical volume is expressed in terms of individual lenses, *not* pairs of lenses.

With its lenses perceived as of a higher quality than B&L's, Sof-Optics sold only to ophthalmologists and optometrists. The sales force had grown to 20 by the fall of 1980 and was concentrated in major cities across the United States. Salespersons, whose salaries and bonuses ranged from $22,000–$30,000, called on eye doctors to show the product, leave samples, and encourage a trial of Sof-Optics. Doctors placed lens orders over toll-free WATS lines. Sof-Optics mailed standard lenses from San Francisco on the day following order receipt, while custom lenses took three to four weeks. Although the company had over 2,800 customers and produced more than 2,000 different lens types, sales were concentrated with the top 80 customers accounting for 32 percent of sales.

Powell had hired Nancy Langstaff as director of marketing in August 1978. As she recalled:

> George was a good salesman. He convinced me to leave my job as an associate product manager with Procter & Gamble to join Sof-Optics. I was very happy at P&G, having learned a lot in my four years there following my 1974 graduation from Stanford's business school. But the opportunity for me, at age 31, to have complete marketing responsibility for an exciting new product, as well as to obtain a small equity position in a promising business, tipped the scales in favor of Sof-Optics.

Reporting to Langstaff were the sales, advertising, customer services, shipping, returns, and market research departments. Manufacturing was headed by Tony Rinaldo (43), who had joined the company in September 1977; while the finance function was directed by Deacon Upson (56) who had been hired in October 1979. Johan Schmidt had maintained a part-time involvement with the company as director of R&D. In October 1980, the company employed a total of 248 people. See Exhibit 3 for an organization chart.

THE PRODUCT

The human eye's lens has no oxygen-carrying blood vessels in it and so must get its oxygen directly from the atmosphere. Hard contact lenses are small enough that some oxygen reaches the eye around the lens edges. The much larger soft lenses allow oxygen to pass through the lens (if thin and porus enough) and/or to make oxygen available through water held by the lens. The Sof-Optics lens had particularly good oxygen transport and water absorption qualities (Exhibit 4).

The very thin lens also allowed one base curve to fit 90 percent of eyes; in addition, one diameter (14.8 mm.) had been found to fit 90 percent of eyes. The power curve was not quite as standard, however, with 40 power curves fitting 94 percent. Thus the company had found that 40 standard lenses fit approximately 75 percent of all wearers, and these, known as inventory lenses, were stocked. Other lenses, known as custom lenses,

EXHIBIT 3
Organizational Chart, October 1980

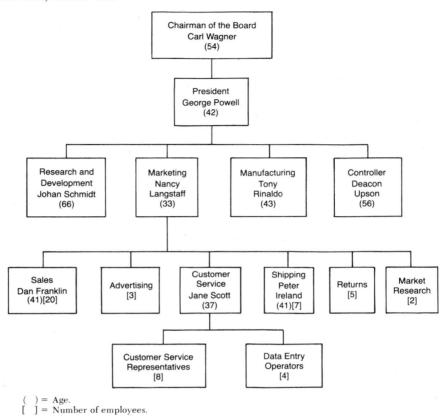

( ) = Age.
[ ] = Number of employees.

EXHIBIT 4
A Diagram of a Soft Contact Lens

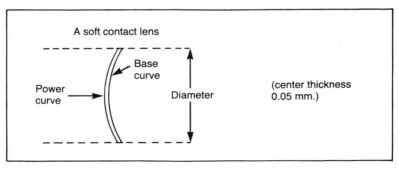

were made to order. Soft-Optics' price per lens was the same for standard and custom lens. Langstaff explained, "We established what is standard. Why should the patient pay more? The patient and the doctor pay a premium by waiting for up to three weeks for the custom order."

Sof-Optics also sold a small amount of contact lens supplies. These supplies were purchased from a manufacturer who packaged the supplies under the Sof-Optics label.

Sof-Optics' proprietary plastic material was manufactured in a capital-intensive chemical polymerization process. The plastic was formed as 15-inch long hard, transparent rods of 15 percent greater diameter than the finished lens. Because of long setup times, rods were produced in long runs of each diameter. Lens production, which was a labor-intensive machining operation, consisted of two major steps. First, a rod was sliced into "buttons" about 20 percent thicker than the finished lens. Second, the "buttons" were turned on lathes and finish ground on grinders to the exact size and shape required, both high-skill operations. Completed lenses were moved to the quality control area for inspection and on to the adjacent warehouse for inventory stocking (standard lenses) or immediate shipment (custom lenses). Warehouse inventory levels were updated daily. An inventory clerk initiated a production order for a batch of lenses when the stock of a particular lens fell below the indicated reorder point shown in Exhibit 5.

Custom orders triggered a manufacturing order for a batch size of one or two lenses depending upon whether both lenses on the typical order had the same parameters. Several skilled workers specialized in custom orders, slicing buttons from rod stock, and finishing the lenses according to the doctors' specifications.

The manufacturing facility consisted of a 50,000 square feet addition to the original building which was divided into a smaller rod production area and a larger lens production area. In October 1980, the plant was producing approximately 2,000 lenses per day, well under the capacity of 6,000 per day set by the rod production machines. Finishing capacity was largely set by the number of employees, and the company had not had difficulty in

EXHIBIT 5
Inventory Control

Category	Sales Volume (per week)	Number of Standard Lens Type	Batch Size (per lens type)	Reorder Point (months supply on hand)
A	50 or more lenses	16	500	1.5
B	20–49 lenses	3	250	2.0
C	Less than 20 lenses	21	200	2.5

EXHIBIT 6
Yield Data

	FY 1978	FY 1979	FY 1980	FY 1981 (est.)*
Variable cost (per good button).............	$12.00	$ 7.25	$5.00	$4.75
Average yield (button to lens)	29%	49%	64%	75%
Variable manufacturing cost (per good lens)............	$41.38	$14.80	$7.82	$6.33
Annual volume (000 units)................	36	104	211	400

attracting sufficient workers. Manufacturing employed 92 hourly workers (average wage $8.31 per hour including fringes) and 23 technical and supervisory employees (18,000 per year including fringes). Annual turnover had averaged under 10 percent.

Due to the very high quality standards and the significant difficulty of machining the tough plastic to close tolerances, the company had experienced low, but improving yields, as shown in Exhibit 6. Improvements in the yield had come through a new, nondestructive test technique, improved machines and procedures, and increased work-force skill.

THE CUSTOMER SERVICES DEPARTMENT

One of six departments reporting to Langstaff, the customer services department, was responsible for staffing the telephone system through which customers contacted Sof-Optics to place orders, and for entering order information into the on-line order entry/inventory control/shipping computer system. In October 1980, the department was supervised by Jane Scott who managed eight customer service representatives (CSRs) and four data entry operators (DEOs). Scott, 37, had joined Sof-Optics as a CSR in March 1979 after 12 years of work as a telephone operator for Pacific Bell. She had been promoted to department supervisor by Langstaff in September 1980 when her predecessor had resigned to enroll in San Francisco Bay College's MBA program.

The department was located in two adjacent rooms (Exhibit 7).

The CSR's room contained 10 work stations around the circumference, each with a telephone (which was connected to the 12 incoming WATS lines and had the capability of transferring calls to any other phone on the Sof-Optics system); a customer services policy manual (which detailed company policies on pricing, warranty, and returns, and outlined order-taking procedures); a U.S. map (which showed postal zones with expected delivery times from San Francisco); a list of customers and account numbers; a list of standard lenses; and a supply of order forms. The room also contained two CRTs (video terminals) with which order status could be checked.

EXHIBIT 7

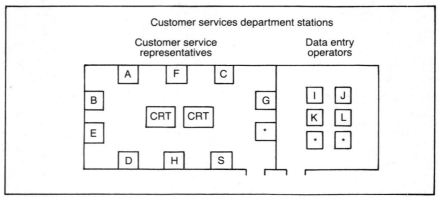

Customer services department stations

Letters A–L represent individual workers.
S = Supervisor.
* = Vacant (October 1980).
CRT = Cathode ray tube (video display terminal).

The Sof-Optics phone system assigned incoming callers to available CSRs. If none were available, the caller received a recorded message ("Thank you for calling Sof-Optics. We are sorry that all CSRs are tied up at the present time. Your call will be answered by the first available representative.") followed by background music. The message was repeated every 60 seconds during a caller's wait. If all 12 incoming lines were full, the caller received a busy signal. When a CSR became available, the system automatically switched the first call in the queue to his or her phone.

Six different kinds of calls were received by the CSRs: inventory order, custom order, status check, new account creation, lens care supply order, and miscellaneous requests for information. The overall work flow and specific tasks for each of these are presented in Exhibit 8. Jane Scott, describing the process, the department, and her job, said:

> The first step is usually to get the customer's name and account number. About 25 percent of the time we end up having to look part of this information up because they don't have the account number handy or because the account is in a clinic's name rather than an individual doctor-within-the-clinic's name, for example. We have a list of the standard lenses and can tell from the three basic parameters if the order is a standard one. If it isn't, we have to take another eight parameters. Most of our orders are for a pair of lens, but 90 percent of these pairs require lens with different parameters. We have to get the shipping information because a replacement lens is often sent direct to the patient; and with replacement lenses, we often have to get the name of the insurance company for billing purposes. We estimate the arrival time with the zone maps, knowing that the order will be in the mail the next day.
>
> On a status check, we have to go over to the CRT and punch up the customer's patient list. Most of the time, the lenses are in the mail and

EXHIBIT 8

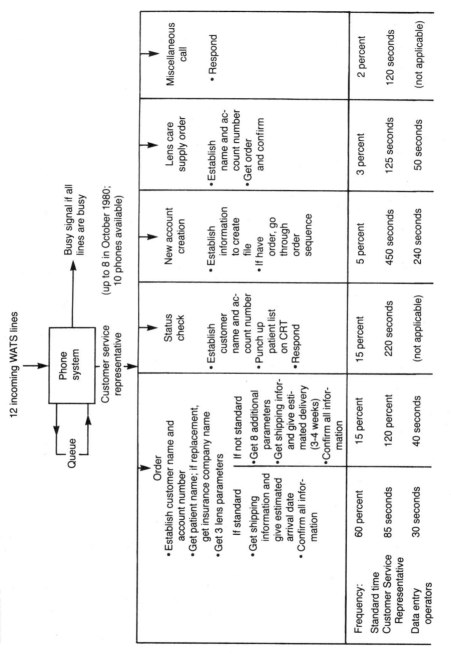

12 incoming WATS lines → Phone system → Busy signal if all lines are busy (up to 8 in October 1980; 10 phones available)

Queue

Customer service representative

Order
- Establish customer name and account number
- Get patient name; if replacement, get insurance company name
- Get 3 lens parameters

If standard
- Get shipping information and give estimated arrival date
- Confirm all information

If not standard
- Get 8 additional parameters
- Get shipping information and give estimated delivery (3-4 weeks)
- Confirm all information

Status check
- Establish customer name and account number
- Punch up patient list on CRT
- Respond

New account creation
- Establish information to create file
- If have order, go through order sequence

Lens care supply order
- Establish name and account number
- Get order and confirm

Miscellaneous call
- Respond

	Order (If standard)	Order (If not standard)	Status check	New account creation	Lens care supply order	Miscellaneous call
Frequency:	60 percent	15 percent	15 percent	5 percent	3 percent	2 percent
Standard time Customer Service Representative	85 seconds	120 percent	220 seconds	450 seconds	125 seconds	120 seconds
Data entry operators	30 seconds	40 seconds	(not applicable)	240 seconds	50 seconds	(not applicable)

someone recently suggested that we just respond to that effect automatically. But occasionally, an order does get dropped, or a doctor may have forgotten to place it, so we have to check each one. The new account calls take quite a while since we need a lot of information and they usually have an order on top of it.

We have been surprised at how many doctors place their own orders, over 40 percent. And they are often steaming if they have been in the queue for long or think their order should have arrived. So our people have to take some pretty grating abuse. And during the busy times, the pressure can get pretty high—a constant stream of calls. I figure each of the reps takes about 10 minutes during the 10 to 1 period just to stand up and stretch, get a cup of coffee, or put his or her head down on the table.

As the department supervisor, I'm responsible for hiring, scheduling, training, and evaluting the workers, for interfacing with the telephone company and our computer facility, for order forms from the CSRs to the DEOs, and for dealing with the many small problems that come up. And, of course, in a real crunch, I'll take some calls. I love the chance to learn the supervisory skills and, desite the pressures and ornery customers, really like working here. But a lot of the CSRs are pretty frutrated, and I;m not sure quite how to address that.

CSRs started at $5.50 per hour and were increased to a maximum of $7.20 over two years. Benefits included medical and life insurance, paid holidays, a two-week paid vacation—about a 25 percent increment to the salary. The CSRs worked an 8-hour day that included two 15-minute paid breaks and a 1-hour unpaid lunch period. Their schedules were staggered across the workday from 6 A.M. to 6 P.M. (the phones had to be attended at the start of the business day on the East Coast) as shown in Exhibit 9. CSR turnover had been very high: of the eight CSRs working in October 1980, one had been hired in 1978, two in 1979, two in the first half of 1980, and three in the last three months. As one of the longer term CSRs (designated as "G" in exhibits) noted:

> The position has always been stressful, and not too many people are willing to put up with the pace and the abuse. But it has grown worse over the past few months as the volume has increased without additional staffing.[5] They talk of getting more lines in, but I haven't seen anything happen. And Scott is a problem—she's just not managing the department, and I think I'm more qualified to do it than she is.

Training for new employees consisted of a one-day orientation with the supervisor and a series of four two-hour training courses spread over the first month. The company had found that it typically took a new worker six months to get up to the standard of 159 calls per day (see Exhibit 10 for standards and for recent CSR performances, and Exhibit 11 for a CSR job description).

---

[5] Eight CSR positions had been filled since June 1980; for the first half of 1980, six positions had been filled.

EXHIBIT 9
Daily Schedule for Customer Service and Entry Departments (week of October 20–24, 1980)

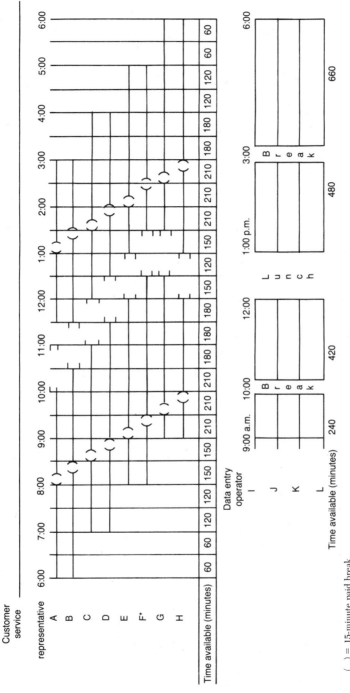

( ) = 15-minute paid break.
[ ] = 60-minute unpaid lunch break.
* Customer service representative **F** was sick on October 21, 22, 23.

388

EXHIBIT 10
Actual versus Standard Performance

	Customer Service Representative Performance Standards *Time on Job (months)*						
	<1	*1*	*2*	*3*	*4*	*5*	*6*
Calls per day*	68	114	123	132	141	150	159

* Based on 7½-hour day with 4 hours of little or no idle time and 3½ hours with some idle time (management estimates).

Actuals (October 21–23)

		Calls			
Customer Service Representative	*Months on Job*	*Tue. Oct. 21*	*Wed. Oct. 22*	*Thurs. Oct. 23*	*Average*
A.............	16	227	176	198	200.3
B.............	1	118	88	91	99.0
C.............	5	205	180	197	194.0
D.............	19	254	243	185	227.3
E.............	2	109	118	145	124.0
F.............	½	Sick	Sick	Sick	—
G.............	32	189	167	221	192.3
H.............	6	114	127	141	127.3
		1,216	1,099	1,178	1,164.3
Average per CSR		173.7	157.0	168.3	166.3

The data entry operation was located in the adjacent room (see Exhibit 6), which contained six CRT work stations arranged in the middle of the room such that the four DEOs (in October 1980) could see and talk with one another.[6] The DEOs entered the order and new account data generated by the CSRs during the day into the computer system by the end of the working day. The order forms were collected by the customer service supervisor from the "out" bins on the CSRs' desks and delivered to the DEOs. Overtime was sometimes required to meet this target, but it seldom exceeded three hours per week for one or two DEOs, and was most typically due to system downtime (see Exhibit 12 for a DEO job description, Exhibit 9 for the DEOs' daily schedule, and Exhibit 8 for DEO task times and frequencies).

---

[6] The number of CRTs connected to the on-line computer system could not be increased without substantially reducing the response time of the existing CRTs. CRTs were leased for $70 per month.

EXHIBIT 11
Position Description

Title: Customer Service Representative   Date: August 21, 1980

Department: Customer Service   Reports to: Customer Service
                                                     Supervisor

General statement:

Responsible for taking telephone orders for contact lenses and supplies and general communication with customers regarding Sof-Optics policies.

Duties and responsibilities:

1. Receive telephone orders for contact lenses and supplies.
2. Discuss company policies, lens availability, and pricing with customers.
3. Check status of orders, handle customer complaints, and take messages for other company personnel.
4. Set up new accounts.

Contacts:

Constant daily contact with Sof-Optics accounts, prospective customers, and Sof-Optics corporate, shipping, and production personnel.

Preferred skills and qualifications:

1. High school graduate.
2. Knowledge of basic office machines, including CRT, typewriter, and 10-key calculator.
3. Pleasant and cooperative telephone technique and personality, excellent verbal communication skills, mathematical ability with a high degree of accuracy, and typing ability.
4. Enthusiasm towards working in a high-pressure environment.

Although their pay was comparable to the CSRs, the DEOs strongly preferred their work to that of the CSRs. As one said:

> We have a small congenial group working in order entry. Three of us have been working together for about a year now. And, Susan, who was hired to fill the newly budgeted fourth position last July, fits in nicely with our group. In fact, we had a say in selecting her. The four of us have lunch together almost every day. I wouldn't trade jobs with a CSR for 50 percent more money. They are always on the spot and have very little freedom. And the stories they tell about disgruntled customers! I don't need that kind of abuse.

EXHIBIT 12
Position Description

Title: Data Entry Operator   Date: August 21, 1980

Department: Customer Service   Reports to: Customer Service
                                                                            Supervisor

General statement:

   Responsible for CRT entry of orders.

Duties and responsibilities:

1.   Set up for new accounts.
2.   CRT entry of orders for contact lenses and supplies.
3.   Entry of file maintenance documents, credit and debit documents, and
     diagnostic indicators.
4.   CRT information retrieval, including invoice research and parameter de-
     tail.
5.   When necessary, enters changes to existing orders.
6.   Other duties related to order taking/entry processes.

Contact:

   Constant daily contact with Sof-Optics corporate, data processing, shipping and production personnel.

Preferred skills and qualifications:

1.   High school graduate.
2.   One-year data entry experience.
3.   Knowledge of basic office machines, including CRT, typewriter, and
     10-key calculator.

SHIPPING

   Each morning, Peter Ireland, the shipping department supervisor, received a list of computer-generated invoices for all of the previous day's
orders. The work of the department consisted of picking, packing, and
shipping the standard lens (and lens care supply) orders (about 10 percent
were shipped Rush, as per customer order, and the remainder mailed first
class); of generating shop orders for manufacturing on standard lenses that
had fallen below the reorder point; and of generating and monitoring shop
orders for custom lenses (and shipping them when completed).[7] The department employed seven clerks under Ireland, all of whom felt that the

---

[7] The customer paid the shipping charges for a rush order.

department functioned smoothly within a cooperative atmosphere. The warehouse was kept neat and orderly, and few shipping errors were made. Frustrations centered on the U.S. mail. As Ireland said:

> We get the product out the next day without fail. But the postal service often seems to take a year and a day—and we get the brunt of the customer's dissatisfaction.

NEW MARKETING PROGRAMS

In March 1980, Sof-Optics had introduced an expanded warranty policy under which the company agreed to accept any standard lenses returned within six months of shipment. Returns, handled by the returns department, had increased significantly. Langstaff had recently analyzed the returns for March and April sales. The results are shown in Exhibit 13.

In addition to the warranty program, Langstaff had been studying a consignment program, similar to B&L's, during the summer and had instituted a trial with three large customers in early September. She noted:

> We've been successful with our present distribution strategy, but I think we've got enough sizable customers now to make use of the consignment approach. Of course, we hope that such a program would lock doctors in to us, but we see real advantages for them—they will be able to fit most patients in one visit and largely avoid returns, for example. In this first month, we've been pleased to find a 7 percent sales increase at the test customers that we can attribute to the program. I anticipate expanding the program in January 1981, and am now grappling with how many customers we should offer it to.

Under the test program, each doctor was supplied with a four-week supply of each of the 40 standard lenses (including at least one pair of each configuration), known as the "base stock," and a $30 sterilizer kit used to resterilize a lens that had been tried on a customer.[8] Once a week, a doctor

EXHIBIT 13
Warranty Policy Data

Customers' responses had been very positive.

Sixteen percent of standard lenses were returned.

Of these.

74 percent cited misfits.

20 percent cited manufacturing defect or shipping damage.

6 percent cited error in order taking.

Clerical cost to process a return and send a replacement lens was about $4.50.

Approximately 10 percent of the good lenses that were returned had been damaged during return shipping due to inadequate packaging by the customer.

---

[8] Paid for by Sof-Optics.

ordered replacements for all lenses sold during the week. While Langstaff anticipated that a significant consignment program would reduce inventory levels in the warehouse at some point in the future, she expected to keep reorder points as they had been during the early stages of the program so that the consignment inventory would represent additional inventory that Sof-Optics carried (at a 25 percent annual carrying charge with lenses on consignment valued at $15). With additional handling of inventory at the doctor's office, the increase in product damage was estimated to be 4 percent. In addition, she anticipated that the decreased order entry costs (due to the less frequent, consolidated orders) would be balanced by increased inventory monitoring needs.

THE CALL MONITORING SYSTEM

In late September, Langstaff had talked with Dan Franklin (national sales manager) who had described the sense of frustration experienced by the sales force when eye doctors whom they had convinced of the merits of the Sof-Optics lens were unable to place their orders because all incoming WATS lines were busy when they tried to call Sof-Optics. He added:

> I think it will be almost impossible to get the doctors to call back if their first experience is a negative one. Our product and company is still on trial, and I don't like the verdict that many of our new customers are handing down. I realize that we are trying to curb spending this year, but the cost of adding people and equipment in the customer service department seems very cheap when compared to the contribution we receive from selling additional lenses.

In addition, George Powell had received complaints from several high-volume customers about the difficulty of placing an order with Sof-Optics. As a result Langstaff had had a $500 per month call monitoring system installed on Monday, October 20, 1980. She had been distressed by the results from the first day, and the subsequent two days' data had not proved better (see Exhibit 14 for half-hourly call, delay, and abandonment data, and Exhibit 15 for distribution of sales by day of week, by customer, and by time zone).

As Langstaff left the office on Friday, October 24, she anticipated a busy weekend:

> George asked me to meet with him on Monday with the first cut of a plan to address our order-taking problem. We're under so much pressure to turn a profit this year that more people and/or equipment will be hard to justify. But can we afford not to? We've forecast almost a 100 percent increase in volume this year (see Exhibit 16), and Rinaldo expects to have this level of product available—but can we provide the service? If we do want to add equipment, we run into the interminable Bell System lead time on WATS lines. It's up to six months now, though we have two costing $1,700 per month each, scheduled to be added in late December. We ordered them last July. And I'm concerned about morale among the CSRs. I got a very unhappy note from one rep earlier this week, and the last thing I need is a revolt among the

EXHIBIT 14
Call Statistics (daily average for October 21–23)

Half Hour Ending	Number of Calls Handled	Number Delayed	Average Delay (seconds)	Number † Abandoned
6:30 A.M.	22.7	5.7	21.2	1.3
7:00.	26.7	10.7	28.6	2.7
7:30.	52.3	41.7	35.7	4.7
8:00.	54.0	47.7	49.3	5.0
8:30.	55.7	49.7	61.4	6.3
9:00.	58.3	57.3	73.8	7.7
9:30.	75.7	56.4	75.1	5.7
10:00.	75.3	60.0	82.4	8.3
10:30.	74.7	68.7	96.7	8.7
11:00.	67.0	60.3	103.5	10.7
11:30.	65.3	61.7	106.2	12.7
12:00 noon. . . .	62.7	58.0	102.1	10.3
12:30 P.M.	63.7	59.7	115.2	11.3
1:00.	47.7	46.3	127.2	16.3
1:30.	71.3	62.0	105.0	9.3
2:00.	72.3	60.3	66.2	7.0
2:30.	65.3	59.3	56.4	6.3
3:00.	47.7	12.3	22.3	2.0
3:30.	41.3	7.7	15.8	0
4:00.	22.0	4.7	14.2	0
4:30.	16.3	2.3	11.2	0
5:00.	15.3	0.3	5.0	0
5:30.	6.0	0	0	0
6:00.	5.0	0	0	0
Totals	1,164.3	892.8	81.0*	136.3

* Weighted average.
† Voluntarily disconnected by caller.

EXHIBIT 15A
Distribution of Sales by Customer (based on August and September 1980)

Lenses Per Week	Number of Customers	Cumulative Percent	Lenses	Cumulative Percent
50 or more	6	0.2	600	7.9
40–49	14	0.7	620	16.1
30–39	16	1.3	530	23.1
20–29	10	1.6	230	26.1
15–19	15	2.1	250	29.4
10–14	20	2.8	240	32.6
8–9	112	6.7	950	45.2
5–7	207	13.9	1,240	61.5
3–4	388	27.4	1,480	81.1
2	178	33.5	356	85.8
1	628	55.3	628	94.1
Less than 1 . . .	1,286	100.0	450	100.0
	2,880		7,574	

EXHIBIT 15B
Distribution of Sales by Day
of Week

	Index	Percent of Week
Monday	119.2	23.8
Tuesday	95.4	19.1
Wednesday	89.2	17.8
Thursday	92.8	18.6
Friday	103.4	20.7

EXHIBIT 15C
Distribution of Sales by Time Zone

	Percent Sales	Typical Mail Service
Eastern standard time	35	4–5 days
Central standard time	20	2–4
Mountain standard time	15	1–3
Pacific standard time	30	1–2

EXHIBIT 16
Fiscal 1981 Forecast (prepared by marketing department)

	Units	Actual	Unit Price	Forecast
August	30,000	32,400	$27.00	810,000
September	30,000	33,600	27.00	810,000
October	30,000		27.00	810,000
November	30,000		27.00	810,000
December	30,000		27.00	810,000
January	30,000		26.00*	780,000
February	25,000		26.00	650,000
March	30,000		26.00	780,000
April	35,000		26.00	910,000
May	40,000		26.00	1,040,000
June	45,000		26.00	1,170,000
July	45,000		26.00	1,170,000
	400,000		26.38	10,550,000

* To meet expected price reduction by Baush & Lomb.

few experienced reps we have. It's always tough there, and I think Jane is doing a creditable job. I wonder if I should involve her in developing a plan for the customer service department or do it all by myself. Finally, I have to keep prodding myself to look longer term, because we're growing so fast, and introducing so many new programs, that I don't want to make a decision now that will be out of date in three or six months.

CASE 28

University Health Service: Walk-in Clinic

Kathryn Angell stared out her office picture window, oblivious to the bustle on Mount Auburn Street. In July 1979, shortly after receiving her master's degree in health policy and management from the Harvard School of Public Health, Angell was hired into a new University Health Service position as assistant director for ambulatory care. A major objective of the new position was the reorganization of the Walk-In Clinic—the exact topic of Angell's thesis.

As the chief administrator of the clinic, responsible for its daily functioning, the organization of medical and support services, and its overall planning, the emphasis of Angell's position was clearly placed on the improvement of the delivery of medical care through better services coordination and the implementation of new programs. Soon after assuming her duties in July 1979, Angell implemented a triage system in the Walk-In Clinic, whereby arriving patients were screened by a triage coordinator to determine whether they should be treated by a nurse practitioner or a physician. After almost a year's operation under the new system, Angell's concern shifted from implementation to evaluation of the clinic's performance.

THE UNIVERSITY HEALTH SERVICES

The University Health Services offered medical care to Harvard University students, staff, faculty, and their dependents who elected certain health care plans in which the services of UHS were included. Since the system was prepaid for over 90 percent of the potential users, UHS operated primarily as a health maintenance organization.

The medical services provided to patients by UHS included surgical and 24-hour emergency facilities, an inpatient infirmary, four outpatient clinics (including the Walk-In and three primary care clinics associated with specific Harvard professional schools), mental health services, laboratory and X-ray facilities, and a variety of other specialized services. Patients were free to choose a personal physician, who could be seen by appointment and who would, if necessary, refer the patient to an appropriate specialist. Ailments of an acute or emergency nature were treated by the outpatient clinics.

For the 1979–80 fiscal year, UHS was budgeted approximately $10 million to meet its total health care expenses (Exhibit 1). Of the $10 million, the Walk-In Clinic, including its emergency facilities, expended approximately 20 percent for salaries to its medical professionals and clerical staff as well as for its portion of overhead and supplies. Physicians worked 46 forty-hour weeks in the year. Of the 40 hours, approximately 12 were spent in the Walk-In Clinic, 16 hours in meeting patients by appointment in the physician's office, 5 hours on duty at the UHS infirmary, and 7 hours on admininistrative and other matters. Included in the time for appointments (which were normally scheduled by the physician's secretary in ½-hour intervals) were two ½-hour periods per week known as "reserve time." These were periods when the doctor might ask patients to come to see her or him in the office, perhaps to check on the progress of treatment. Reserve time differed from regular appointments in that patients could not, by themselves, book appointments at these times—only the physician could schedule them. The physician could sometimes see up to four patients in one half hour of reserve time. By well-established precedent, all UHS doctors were required to undertake duty in the Walk-In Clinic. Doctors who were associated with UHS on a part-time basis were normally allocated a proportionate share of their time in the clinic. While exceptions existed, most doctors preferred seeing patients in their office to Walk-In Clinic duty—partly because of the hectic pace of the Walk-In Clinic, but also because in their appointments they could deal with patients they knew and with whose medical record they were familiar. Salaries for physicians ranged from $35,000 for new primary care physicians to over $69,000 for a specialist physician. A range of $16,000 to $26,000 were paid nurses, depending upon their level of practical experience. For both physicians and nurses, UHS incurred additional costs of 18.5 percent of salary in the form of benefits.

THE WALK-IN CLINIC

The Walk-In Clinic at the Holyoke Center provided the most comprehensive ambulatory care of the four walk-in clinics by offering the patient a portion of the total available UHS services. Patients with acute medical and surgical problems, who had not chosen a UHS personal physician or who were unable to wait for appointments with their personal physicians, were served on a first-come, first-serve basis Monday through Friday,

EXHIBIT 1
Income and Expense Statistics

	Income		Expenses	
	1978–79	*1979–80*	*1978–79*	*1979–80*
Unrestricted............	$7,951,202	$9,471,290	$8,028,554	$9,359,768
Restricted..............	149,426	188,025	149,426	188,025
Gifts..................	416,465	173,467	416,465	173,467
Total	8,517,093	9,832,782	8,594,445	9,721,260

	1979–80	*Percent 1978–79*	*Percent 1979–80*
Income:			
Student health fee......................	$3,390,023	38.2	34.4
Student insurance	1,636,925	17.3	16.6
Harvard University			
Group Health Program	900,212	7.0	9.1
Payroll assessment......................	1,589,497	16.9	16.1
Care for medicare	252,074	1.6	2.5
Radiation protection	435,603	3.8	4.4
Other services	1,628,448	15.2	16.9
Total..........................	9,832,782	100.0	100.0
Expense:			
Salaries, wages, and benefits..............	5,223,685	53.5	53.7
Student insurance	1,636,925	17.2	16.8
Building operations and maintenance	388,870	4.3	4.0
Medical/dental supplies	278,987	2.3	2.8
Outside laboratories	176,309	2.2	1.8
Malpractice insurance...................	49,048	1.1	.5
All other	1,967,436	19.4	20.4
Total	9,721,260	100.0	100.0

8 A.M. to 5:30 P.M. The clinic was also open on Saturday mornings, 8 A.M. to 12:45 P.M. Emergencies, of which there were relatively few, were of course treated immediately.

In 1979, over 37,400 patients visited the Walk-In Clinic for treatment of problems ranging from common ailments such as colds, nausea, and respiratory illnesses to those with more serious problems such as acute appendicitis and chest pains. Of the patients who visited the clinic, 67 percent were students, 23 percent staff, and 10 percent dependents and Medex and medicare subscribers. One UHS study conducted in 1980 over a three-week period demonstrated that an average of 143 patients were seen per day at an average rate of 14 patients per hour (Exhibit 2). The study further suggested that for the majority of patients who visited the clinic, this was their first visit for the particular medical problem they came in with (Exhibit 3).

398

EXHIBIT 2
Daily Average of Patient Visits by Day of the Week

Monday	163
Tuesday	151
Wednesday	136
Thursday	137
Friday	128
Average total	715

Average Number of Patient Arrivals per Hour

7–8 A.M.	1.7
8–9 A.M.	16.4
9–10 A.M.	17.5
10–11 A.M.	16.7
11–12 noon	15.1
12–1 P.M.	11.7
1–2 P.M.	16.9
2–3 P.M.	16.1
3–4 P.M.	15.8
4–5 P.M.	11.5
5–6 P.M.	2.7

EXHIBIT 3
Patient Distribution by Reason for Visit*

Reason	Daily Average	Percent of Total
Emergency	10	1.4
Medical: initial visit	270	41.3
Medical: Return visit	81	11.3
Medical; Specific provider	179	24.0
Surgical: Initial visit	1	0.1
Surgical: Return visit	6	0.8
Lab result	14	2.0
Premarital test	3	0.4
Blood pressure	13	2.2
Prescription: Confirmed diagnosis	6	0.8
Prescription refill	15	2.0
Administrative	7	1.0
Other	12	1.7
Unspecified (missing)	64	9.0

*As indicated by the patient.

Staffing levels for the Walk-In Clinic were scheduled on the basis of past experience with peak periods of patient visits, which typically occurred between 10 A.M. and 4 P.M., according to the generally accepted impression of the UHS staff (Exhibit 4). No set criteria existed for establishing staffing levels; only minor adjustments were made year to year, at times that were

EXHIBIT 4
Medical Professional Scheduling 1979 Walk-In Clinic

	Monday		Tuesday		Wednesday		Thursday		Friday	
	No. MDs	No. NPs	No. MDs	No. NPS	No. MDs	No. NPS	No. MDs	No. NPs	No. MDs	No. NPs
8–9 A.M.	2	2	2	2	2	2	2	2	2	2
9–10 A.M.	2.5	4	3	4	2.5	4	2	4	2.5	4
10–11 A.M.	5	4	4	4	5	4	5	4	5	4
11–12 noon	3	4	3	4	3	4	3	4	4	4
12–1 P.M.	3	2.5	2	2.5	2.5	2.5	3	2.5	2.5	2.5
1–2 P.M.	3	2.5	3	2.5	3	2.5	2	2.5	3	2.5
2–3 P.M.	3	4	4	4	3	4	3	4	4	4
3–4 P.M.	4	4	4	4	4	4	4	4	4	4
4–5 P.M.	3	2.5	2	2.5	2	2.5	3.5	2.5	3	2.5
5–6* P.M.	1	2	1	2	1	2	1	2	1	2

MD = Medical doctor.
NP = Nurse practitioner.
*The clinic admitted its last patient at 5:30 P.M. Staff were required to stay until 6 P.M.

felt to be too busy. Twenty-two physicians treated all patients in the clinic as part of their overall UHS responsibilities, and were scheduled by Ms. Angell for specific hours throughout the week, usually in blocks of three to four hours at a time. The Walk-In Clinic was also staffed by two registered nurses and 11 nurse practitioners, the latter being registered nurses with additional medical training capable of treating minor ailments without direct consultation with a physician. In a small number of cases, nurse practitioners also treated patients by appointment. Nurses and nurse practitioners worked eight-hour shifts, including one hour for lunch.

The Walk-In Clinic had 12 rooms available for seeing patients, 4 for nurses and 8 for doctors. However, three of the doctors' rooms were permanently assigned to individuals as their UHS office, and were only available for Walk-In Clinic use at the times when those three individual physicians were scheduled for Walk-In Clinic duty.

PRE-TRIAGE ORGANIZATION

Before the triage system was instituted, a typical patient's visit to the Walk-In Clinic proceeded in the following way. On arrival, the patient signed in at the front desk by providing basic identification information on a small, sequentially numbered sheet, and was then asked by a receptionist to take a seat in the waiting area. The receptionist next requested the patient's record from the medical records department. That department retrieved and sent down the record to the Walk-In Clinic in approximately eight to nine minutes. The receptionist then brought the record to the "medical desk" where a clerk checked to ensure that the patient's address and phone number were current and that all recent lab reports were present. When checking was completed, which took approximately five minutes, the clerk placed the record and the numbered sheet in a pile ordered according to the arrival of patients. Each patient was subsequently seen by the first available nurse when his or her medical record reached the top of the pile. If the problem was minor (such as a cold), the nurse would treat the patient definitively. However, if, after the nurse had done all she or he could, it was still necessary for the patient to see a physician, the patient would return to the waiting area and the nurse would put the record in a pile for the physicians, again according to the order of initial arrival. The patient would be seen, in turn, by the first available physician.

Widespread dissatisfaction had developed concerning the Walk-In Clinic. Waiting time between sign-in and treatment constituted the major complaint, specifically the waiting time to the first contact with a professional staff member capable of assessing the patient's problem. This time period averaged 23 minutes; however, as many as 22 percent of all patients who saw a nurse had to wait over 35 minutes for this first contact. A study of the Walk-In Clinic done in November 1978 found that patients who requested specific nurses or physicians at sign-in waited an average of 40 minutes before seeing the desired staff member; this group comprised approximately 19 percent of the total patient load. If a nurse had to refer a patient on to a doctor, an average of 10 minutes elapsed between the end of the nurse visit and the meeting with the doctor. Some patients complained that the length of their wait often had no relation to the nature of the visit, such as a 55-minute wait for a prescription renewal. Other patients reportedly decided to avoid potential visits to the Walk-In Clinic because of the anticipated wait. Consequently, patients viewed the Walk-In Clinic as cold, inefficient, and impersonal since there was such a time gap between sign-in and treatment.

Members of the UHS administrative and medical staff also expressed feelings that the Walk-In Clinic could function better than it had. Sholem Postel, M.D., the deputy director and chief of professional services (physicians and nurses) at UHS, and the person to whom Angell reported with respect to the Walk-In Clinic, commented on the pre-triage system's problems:

> All the nurses were involved in seeing all the patients initially. This created a bottleneck as each nurse independently decided the extent of care for a patient and then provided as much of that care as possible before, if necessary, having the patient wait to be seen by a physician for the rest of the care. This led to inconsistency and too much variation in treatment, given the different skills and experience levels of individual nurses. Furthermore, though nurses saw 100 percent of the patients, they treated only 40 percent definitively. The result: duplicated efforts (time, questions, and examinations) for 60 percent of our patients.

THE TRIAGE SYSTEM

To overcome these problems, a "triage system" was introduced in September 1979 by the UHS administration. The system was defined as "the preliminary evaluation and referral of patients to the necessary health resource, based on decisions about the nature of the patients' problems and knowledge of the priorities and capabilities of the available health care resources."

Under the triage system, the patient upon arrival filled out an ambulatory visit form (AVF) which requested the patient's reason for visit as well as identification information (Exhibit 5). If the patient checked off "emergency care," the front desk personnel immediately notified a physician, nurse practitioner, or triage coordinator who then more thoroughly assessed the patient's condition. In most cases, however, the front desk simply reviewed the AVF for completeness and requested the patient's record from Medical Records. Upon arrival of the record in eight to nine minutes, the appropriate clerical personnel matched the record with the AVF, ensured that all personal information and prior tests were properly filed and updated in the record, and then placed them chronologically in a "triage pile."

In turn, one of two "triage coordinators" called for the patient and provided the initial contact. The two triage coordinators were both highly experienced registered nurses. It was felt that experience was necessary so that they could make accurate assessments and preliminary diagnoses. The triage coordinator visited with the patient in a private room and, on the basis of the immediately available information and a brief discussion with the patient, summarized the nature of the patient's problem. If the triage nurse, in determining the severity of the patient's problem, decided the ailment warranted more immediate care, she would then put the patient ahead of others waiting to see a physician.

As one triage coordinator explained:

> My duties are to determine the chief complaint of the patient and to triage him or her to an MD or nurse practitioner. I'll spend three to four minutes per patient in an average encounter, and I rarely have to deviate from this— only when people are unable to clearly describe their symptoms or when they overestimate the severity of their illness. However, there is no time constraint in determining the status of a patient.

The triage coordinator did not treat the patient but determined, according to guidelines and her discretion, whether the patient needed to see a nurse practitioner or a physician in the Walk-In Clinic and whether the problem could be better handled by an appointment or referral to another service within UHS. Patients were triaged to a nurse practitioner if their ailments fell under one of 13 categories (Exhibit 6). All (other) ailments outside the guidelines required the attention of a physician, unless the

EXHIBIT 5

AMBULATORY VISIT FORM

FOR PATIENT USE: PLEASE FILL OUT THIS SECTION COMPLETELY

TIME & DATE

UHS/
HARVARD
I.D. NO.

NAME:
PLEASE
PRINT
First   Middle   Last

BIRTHDATE _____ MALE □
Mo.   Day   Yr.   FEMALE □

LOCATION OF VISIT:
□ Holyoke Center □ Law School
□ Business School □ Medical Area

LOCAL ADDRESS

PHONE DURING THE DAY

IS THIS YOUR FIRST VISIT TO
A UHS FACILITY? YES □

IF YOUR MEDICAL RECORD IS KEPT AT A UHS FACILITY OTHER THAN
HOLYOKE CENTER, PLEASE CHECK HERE: BUSINESS □ LAW □ MEDICAL AREA □

STATUS

□ H/R UNDERGRAD, CLASS
□ GRAD. SCHOOL (Name)
□ LESLEY COLLEGE
□ EPISCOPAL DIVINITY SCHOOL
□ STAFF WITH HARVARD DC/BS
□ STAFF WITH HARVARD UNIVERSITY
□ GROUP HEALTH PROGRAM (HUGHP)
□ STAFF WITH NO HARVARD INSURANCE
□ HARVARD MEDEX
□ MEDICARE (ONLY)

□ STUDENT DEPENDENT WITH UHS COVERAGE
□ STUDENT DEPENDENT WITH UHS COVERAGE
        — UNDER 14 YEARS OLD
□ HUGHP DEPENDENT
□ HUGHP DEPENDENT — UNDER 14 YEARS OLD
□ MEDEX DEPENDENT
□ SUMMER SCHOOL: STUDENT
        FACULTY _____ FAC. DEPENDENT _____
□ NONMEMBER OF HARVARD UNIVERSITY
□ OTHER

FOR WALK-IN PATIENTS ONLY

The following information is designed to help us treat you promptly and efficiently.
All information will be kept confidential. If you do not wish to complete the rest of
the form, please check "personal" and you will be seen in turn.

WHAT IS THE REASON FOR YOUR VISIT? PLEASE CHECK:

□ I NEED **EMERGENCY** CARE.   □ BLOOD PRESSURE CHECK ONLY

GENERAL MEDICAL PROBLEM   PRESCRIPTION(S) ONLY
□ FIRST VISIT FOR THIS PROBLEM   □ DIAGNOSIS CONFIRMED; INSTRUCTED
□ RETURN (REPEAT) VISIT FOR THIS   TO OBTAIN PRESCRIPTION
    PROBLEM   □ PRESCRIPTION REFILL:
□ TOLD TO SEE: UHS _____ OTHER _____

NURSE OR DOCTOR   ADMINISTRATIVE PROBLEM
                                    □ SPORTS CLEARANCE
GENERAL SURGICAL PROBLEM   □ MEDICAL EXCUSE FOR EXAM
□ FIRST VISIT FOR THIS PROBLEM   □ MEDICAL FORMS TO BE COMPLETED
□ RETURN (REPEAT) VISIT FOR THIS
    PROBLEM   □ PERSONAL
□ TOLD TO SEE:
                                    □ OTHER
NURSE OR DOCTOR

LABORATORY PROCEDURES ONLY
□ LAB RESULTS DESIRED
□ PREMARITAL TESTS DESIRED
□ PREGNANCY TEST REQUISITION

FOR UHS USE ONLY

TRIAGE TIME   TIME PT. SEEN

PROVIDER 1 NUMBER
NAME

PROVIDER 2 NUMBER
NAME

TYPE OF CONTACT
□ WALK-IN
□ APPOINTMENT
□ BROKEN APPOINTMENT
□ CANCELLED BY UHS
□ CANCELLED BY PATIENT
□ LEFT BEFORE BEING SEEN
□ RESERVE
□ OTHER

SERVICE
□ MEDICAL   □ IMMUNIZATION
□ SURGICAL   □ MENTAL HEALTH
□ EMERGENCY   □ NEUROLOGY
□ ALLERGY   □ NUTRITION
□ DENTAL   □ OBSTETRICS
□ DERMATOLOGY   □ ORTHOPEDICS
□ EAR, NOSE, & THROAT □ PEDIATRICS
□ EYE   □ PHYSICAL THERAPY
□ GASTROENTEROLOGY □ UROLOGY
□ GYNECOLOGY   □ OTHER

□ INITIAL VISIT FOR THIS PROBLEM

□ RETURN VISIT

Please circle as many lab test boxes as apply.

HEMATOLOGY
PROVIDER NO.:
1 2
□ □ COULTER CBC
□ □ DIFFERENTIAL
□ □ OCCULT BLOOD (GUAIAC)
□ □ PLATELET COUNT
□ □ PROTHROMBIN TIME
□ □ RETICULOCYTE COUNT
□ □ SEDIMENTATION RATE
□ □ OTHER

CHEMISTRY
PROVIDER NO.:
1 2
□ □ BILIRUBIN
□ □ BLOOD GLUCOSE
□ □ BLOOD UREA NITROGEN (BUN)
□ □ CHOLESTEROL
□ □ CREATININE
□ □ ELECTROLYTES
□ □ SGOT
□ □ SMA 12/60
□ □ T3 UPTAKE
□ □ T4
□ □ TRIGLYCERIDES
□ □ URIC ACID
□ □ OTHER:

SEROLOGY
PROVIDER NO.:
1 2
□ □ HETEROPHILE
□ □ RPR
□ □ RUBELLA
□ □ OTHER:

BACTERIOLOGY
PROVIDER NO.:
1 2
□ □ CERVICAL/URETHRAL CULTURE
        & GRAM STAIN
□ □ STOOL FOR CULTURE
□ □ STOOL FOR OVA & PARASITES
□ □ THROAT CULTURE
□ □ URINE CULTURE
□ □ OTHER:

MISCELLANEOUS
PROVIDER NO.:
1 2
□ □ BLOOD TYPE & RH
□ □ ELECTROCARDIOGRAM
□ □ MONILIA
□ □ PAP SMEAR
□ □ PATHOLOGY
□ □ PREGNANCY TEST
□ □ PULMONARY FUNCTION
□ □ TRICHOMONAS (WET PREP)
□ □ URINALYSIS
□ □ OTHER:

triage nurse, by using her discretion, felt a nurse practitioner could treat the problem. If, however, the nurse practitioner attended a problem which was not included under the 13 categories, a physician was required to countersign the treatment. This required the nurse to find a doctor who would sign the medical record, thereby authorizing the treatment recommended by the nurse. In some cases, the doctor might choose to meet with or examine the patient before signing. Other doctors would sign without examining further. Expansion of the guidelines beyond the 13 specific ailments would, by state law, require the drafting of detailed treatment guides so that a nurse practitioner could be allowed to treat the patient without consulting a physician. The UHS planned on such expansion in the near future. However, it was not known how many patients this might affect.

EXHIBIT 6
Categories Treatable under Guidelines by Nurse Practitioners

1. Acute viral respiratory illness (primarily colds).
2. Amenorrhea (missed menstruation).
3. Cerumen (wax in ears).
4. Enterobiasis (pinworms).
5. Lower urinary tract infection (females).
6. Mononucleosis.
7. Nausea, vomiting, diarrhea.
8. Pediculosis capitus (lice).
9. Pediculosis pubis (lice).
10. Pharyngitis (sore throat).
11. Rubella (German measles).
12. Seasonal rhinitis (hayfever).
13. Vaginitis (vaginal infection).

After the visit with the triage coordinator, the patient returned to the waiting area while his/her record was placed by the triage nurse chronologically in either the nurse practitioner or the physician "pile," unless more immediate care was deemed necessary by the triage coordinator. As physicians and nurse practitioners then finished with their previous patient, they summoned the next patient in their respective piles for treatment. In less than 10 percent of cases was it necessary for a patient triaged to a nurse practitioner to be seen subsequently by a doctor during that visit. Although significant variation existed, average treatment time by doctors was 20 minutes per patient, and 30 minutes per patient by nurse practitioners.

When the triage system was instituted, it was expected that the waiting time to see a triage coordinator would be about 15 minutes and waiting time to be seen by a nurse practitioner or a physician would be less than 10 minutes. A 1980 UHS study reported, however, that patients waited a mean length of 19.7 minutes to the point of being triaged and a mean time of 18.6 minutes from the start of the patient's visit with the triage coordinator to the point of being seen by either a nurse practitioner or a physician. The average total waiting time was 37.5 minutes, including the actual time to be triaged (Exhibit 7). Approximately 67 percent of the patients were triaged to a physician, whereas 33 percent were triaged to a nurse practitioner. Ms. Angell commented:

> When we introduced the triage system, we thought the nurse practitioners would accept more of the patient load and leave the physicians more time on a per patient basis. Unfortunately, it has not worked out that way. Among the reasons for this might be the fact that, as we discovered, the triage coordinators are sometimes classifying patients as "MD/NP" (physician/nurse practitioner) to maintain the flow when they feel the practitioners are backed up. The MD's share of patients thus gets increased in overload situations. We did not want to have "MD/NP" as a classification, and have asked the triage coordinators to stop using it. When in doubt, they are to triage the patient to a nurse practitioner.

Among the patients who were initially seen by a nurse practitioner, about 5 percent were then referred to a second provider, usually a physician. Though the mean times to be triaged were relatively equal (approximately 19 minutes), as would be expected, the mean waiting time to see a physician was much longer (25.2 minutes) than the mean waiting time to see a nurse practitioner (6.7 minutes).

It was suspected that one of the factors creating differences in the waiting time to be seen by a physician versus a nurse practitioner was the per-

EXHIBIT 7
Percentage of Patients Waiting, by Time Waited

Interval (minutes)	Waiting Time to Be Triaged	Waiting Time to Be Seen (after triage)	Total Waiting Time
0–4......	1%	24%	0%
5–9......	8	14	3
10–14.....	24	12	7
15–19.....	25	11	10
20–24.....	19	9	10
25–29.....	11	8	14
30–34.....	6	7	11
35–39.....	2	4	10
40–44.....	1	3	8
45–49.....	1	3	6
50–54.....	1	2	7
55+	1	0	14
	100	100	100

EXHIBIT 8
Summary of Patients Seen and Waiting Time to First Available Appointment, by Physician

Physician*	Total Patients Seen	Patients Who Asked to See Specific MD (Percent)	Total Hours	Patients Seen per Hour	Calendar Days to First Available Appointment
Zuromskis.....	113	33 (29.2)	36	3.14	9
Bogota........	50	23 (46.0)	17	2.94	24
Wellington	89	— —	18	4.94	5
Byrd.........	76	26 (34.2)	33	2.30	15
Recife	78	48 (61.5)	24	3.25	25
Brunei........	113	45 (39.8)	36	3.14	17
Lobito	28	10 (35.7)	6	4.67	21
Santiago	91	43 (47.3)	29	3.14	3
Hobart........	59	27 (45.8)	24	2.46	28
Seoul.........	90	34 (37.8)	28	3.21	5
Kingston	113	26 (23.0)	25	4.52	7
Java	78	16 (20.5)	27	2.89	13
Rome.........	74	32 (43.2)	19	3.89	7
Ottawa........	82	31 (37.8)	26	3.15	5
Caracus.......	53	17 (32.1)	18	2.94	7
Manila........	25	18 (72)	9	2.78	23
Durban	48	41 (85.4)	18	2.67	29
Luanda	61	5 (8.2)	21	2.90	8
Papua.........	34	— —	9	3.78	—
Glasgow	35	2 —	9	3.89	12
Cristobal......	33	3 (9.1)	19.5	1.69	2
Aukland.......	16	1 (6.3)	12.5	1.28	
	1,439	481	464	3.11	

*Some names in this exhibit have been disguised.

centage of patients who asked to see a specific provider of medical care. This percentage increased, for physicians in particular, after the institution of the triage system. Whereas 33 percent of the patients asked to see a specific physician, only approximately 8 percent asked to see a specific nurse practitioner. For almost one third of the physicians, more than 40 percent of the patients they saw in the Walk-In Clinic specifically asked for them. Perhaps as a consequence, the average number of patients seen per hour by these physicians was much lower than the overall average for all physicians of 3.11 (Exhibit 8). In contrast, approximately 1.83 patients per hour were seen by a nurse practitioner.

Though the waiting time for triage was the same for the patients who asked for a specific physician or nurse practitioner and for patients who did not, the waiting time to be seen by the specific provider requested was 8.6 minutes longer on average for the patients who asked. But as Mary Dineen, nurse, nurse practitioner, and supervisor of outpatient nursing, commented:

It seems doctors are allowed "walk-in appointments" with their own regular patients. Patients whose doctors have heavily booked appointment schedules become aware of the doctor's walk-in schedule and come into the Walk-In Clinic at prearranged times. This may be a necessary evil to some degree, but today, for example, two of the five doctors on duty are 100 percent occupied with "walk-in appointments." This decreases our available MD resources by 40 percent for true walk-in patients today and fills up our waiting room.

Peter Zuromskis, M.D., a physician in the Walk-In Clinic, also suggested reasons for the misuse of the walk-in operation:

My evaluation of the dissatisfaction our patients have sometimes expressed with this system is that it represents an approach to acute ambulatory care which is quite different from that which they have previously experienced. Patients understandably find appealing the nostalgic image of the general practitioner who knows his patients well and is able to provide advice and treatment of minor illnesses in his office with an apparent minimum of clerical encumbrances. This is clearly impossible in a clinic which provides the volume and variety of medical care services that UHS offers to a large and heterogeneous population with a wide variety of diseases, from relatively minor complaints to major medical emergencies. Our aim is not and should not be to provide an atmosphere reminiscent of the country doctor's office, but rather to provide the best possible care to all our patients, particularly to those whose medical needs are most urgent.

Although people, for the first time ever, had been giving unsolicited praise to the new system, Angell knew that it still had problems and didn't always work as it had been designed. Some patient complaints still noted "excessive" waiting times and misunderstanding of the triage systems illustrated by the following specific, though not average, opinion submitted to the UHS Patient Advocate:

In order to see a doctor about a very simple problem (a mild sore throat), I have seen a "triage nurse" (who stamped my form and passed me on) and a "nurse practioner" (who looked, felt, and probed, but dared not offer an opinion). I am now 30 minutes into my visit, much handled, but not within sight of a doctor.

The medical, clerical, and administrative staff within the Walk-In Clinic, however, felt that although the efficiency of the clinic was still at less than a desirable level, the triage system was an improvement. As Warren Wacker, M.D., the director of UHS commented:

Right now, I'm satisfied with the results of the triage system, and I expect the system to be operating very well in another year. Of course, we'll have to resolve some sticky issues in the meantime. For instance, we need to expand the 13 nurse practitioner guidelines and further define the roles of nurse practitioner and physician within the Walk-In Clinic. Another item is how do we educate students in the Walk-In Clinic concept? Expectations of traditional medicine don't fit with the walk-in concept.

ANGELL'S DILEMMA

Angell now had the difficulty of sorting through a year's performance data, the concerns raised by several distinct groups associated with the clinic, and her own subjective observations. What changes needed to be made, if any? Were waiting times now acceptable? What, after all, acceptable? Ms. Angell knew that work was in progress to expand the 13 nurse practitioner guidelines, but would this be enough to solve any remaining problems?

Among her biggest concerns was the issue of "walk-in appointments." She commented:

> We have tried in the past to ask the doctors to refrain from encouraging their patients to meet them in the Walk-In Clinic. However, we have not had very much success, since the practice continues. Some of the doctors feel that they want *their* patients to see only them. Part of this is for medical reasons (the doctors wish to check on their patient's progress), and part of it is a general philosophy that medical care involves more than just treatment, and that personal relationships add to both the quality of health care and the patient's perception of good service. Many patients, perhaps appropriately, have the attitude of wanting to see "*my* doctor." Apart from the fact that you can never dictate to doctors, the UHS has always had a philosophy of not trying to tell physicians how to practice medicine.
>
> Part of the problem is the general availability of appointment time. All our patients have the freedom to select their own "personal physician" from among any of our doctors. However, this often means that some are overloaded. Our overall staffing level at UHS is set approximately to provide one physician per 2,000 people covered by our various health plans. At the moment, the only way we try to limit the number of patients "assigned" to any given doctor, is by pointing out to the potential patient the difficulty of getting an appointment with an overloaded physician, and this is generally only done if the patient asks about it. We do not know how many patients each doctor is seeing as the patient's "personal physician," since this is an arrangement made by the doctor and the patient and not a formal "assignment."
>
> There are a number of potential alternatives for dealing with this problem. We could try to educate our patient public on the separate purposes and missions of doctor appointments and the Walk-In Clinic—try to get them to use each appropriately. We could ask the triage coordinators to be a little more aggressive in asking patients who request a specific physician whether they really need to see that person and suggest alternatives. Ultimately, we could establish a firm policy of not accepting specific physician requests in the Walk-In Clinic.

Angell had these questions and more to consider over the next two weeks. At that time, she would share her findings and proposals with Ms. Dineen and Dr. Postel, since they would all have to agree on necessary changes and be involved in their implementation if any changes were to succeed.

CASE 29

Kalamazoo Plant Parts Division— Acme Motors

Bob Moore, supervisor, salaried personnel, returned to his office after a management development discussion with the plant manager, Rich Howards. During the discussion, Bob had informed Howards of the year-end figures for supervisory turnover. Out of a total of approximately 170 supervisory positions at Kalamazoo, the industrial relations department had placed (hired) 78 supervisors during 1978. The plant manager had asked Bob to look into the problem, find out the reasons for the high turnover, and make recommendations. With increasing pressure for cost reductions and improved productivity from division, the high supervisory turnover was seen by Moore and Howards as a critical problem.

The Kalamazoo Plant of the Parts Division of Acme Motors (one of the big three auto manufacturers) was one of the largest plastic molding and injection assembly plants in the country. It produced a variety of plastic parts used in an automobile including grilles, instrument panels, instrument clusters and gauges, fender aprons, fan shrouds, turn panels, and so forth. Kalamazoo was one of seven plants in the Parts Division, each of which was a profit center with a fully autonomous organization. Sales at Kalamazoo were about $400 million annually. With the trend toward fuel economy and energy conservation, the use of plastics had been increasing, taking on strategic importance. The Kalamazoo Plant was the major supplier of plastic parts to the Acme Assembly Division; the operation of the assembly lines was highly dependent on the Kalamazoo production.

The Kalamazoo Plant, located in Kalamazoo, Michigan, employed about 3,600 people in early 1979. Of this total, 3,100 were hourly and 500 were salaried employees. The hourly personnel at the plant were unionized (UAW). The plant operated three shifts on most lines. Six- and seven-day weeks for many of the supervisors and management were commonplace.

EXHIBIT 1
Organization Chart*

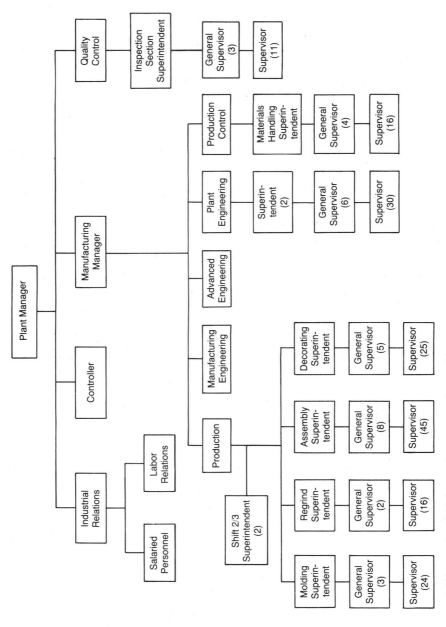

* Abbreviated to highlight manufacturing supervisory positions.

The manufacturing supervisors constituted the largest group of salaried employees at Kalamazoo. There were 167 supervisors, 31 general supervisors, and 10 superintendents. Supervisors were employed primarily in four main areas: production, quality control, maintenance (plant engineering), and production control (materials handling). (See Exhibits 1 and 2.)

Bob Moore had prepared a table (Exhibit 3) showing the placement (accessions) of manufacturing supervisors for 1978. Twenty-three of the new supervisors had been attributed to increasing production and line expansion ("volume"). The volume accessions were distributed as follows: production control (1), maintenance (2), decorating (5), molding (2), assembly (5), and regrind and panel assembly (2); the remaining supervisors had been temporary hires for the new model changeover and start-up ("79 launch").

Approximately 75 percent of the supervisors had been promoted through the ranks from hourly, and the remaining 25 percent moved into manufacturing supervision as new hires from several local colleges and from other parts of the plant as part of a development program. Divisional industrial relations and division management have been pressing Kalamazoo to increase the ratio of college graduates (CG) to those promoted through the

EXHIBIT 2
Plant Distribution of Hourly Supervisors

	Supervisors	General Supervisors	Superintendents
Production............	110	18	6
Maintenance..........	30	6	2
Quality control........	11	3	1
Production control.....	16	4	1
Totals..........	167	31	10

EXHIBIT 3
Manufacturing Supervisory Accessions (Kalamazoo, 1978)

Department	College Grads	Nongrads	Total
Production control.......	0	5	5
Quality control..........	0	2	2
Maintenance............	0	11	11
Production:			
Decorating............	18	11	29
Molding..............	3	1	4
Assembly.............	5	10	15
Regrind and panels....	5	7	12
Totals............	31	47	78
	(39.7%)	(60.3%)	(100%)

hourly ranks (PTR) to 50:50. From Bob Moore's perspective, the rationale for this policy seemed to be:

> that they don't think there are enough people in general supervisory positions with potential to move further into superintendent or production manager slots. There are too many blockers in the general supervisory category. . . . I personally feel that, though we might need more college graduates, to go to a 50:50 split is too far. The college grads come in with very high expectations, and we just aren't able to offer them movement and development activities, in manufacturing or elsewhere.

At Kalamazoo, the general supervisors had almost always been promoted from the first-line supervisory position. Further, the superintendents had almost always been promoted from general supervisor, being "products of the manufacturing system." During 1978, two supervisors had been promoted to general supervisor (one retirement, one death), and no general supervisors had been promoted to superintendent. Bob Moore stated:

> Unless someone is on the fast track, has high potential, and has talent outside manufacturing, they may be best suited to stay in production . . . production people are best there, they just can't compete in other areas; the best opportunities for them are in manufacturing—it uses their skills to the best advantage . . . however, manufacturing is an excellent area for developing good managers and engineers; a year in there gives them good experience.

The job of manufacturing supervisor at Kalamazoo was considered to be one of extreme difficulty and high pressure. It involved dealing with up to 45 people on a line, absenteeism, tardiness, union officials, grievances, scheduling, checking time sheets, equipment maintenance, obtaining parts, inspecting purchased parts, maintaining quality, keeping down health and safety violations, making performance goals, negotiating work standards, identifying and solving production problems, and disciplining employees, to name a few. Supervisors were caught between the often conflicting demands of management, the union, labor relations, and the workers. Due to increased organizational and technological specialization, they were dependent on a series of specialists over whom they had little control, such as maintenance, quality control, industrial engineering, and industrial relations. Every day a printout was sent to the production departments with the previous day's results. On this were the profit (loss) for each supervisor, number of pieces produced, rejects, and number of machine cycles.

The supervisors were evaluated annually with a performance appraisal. As seen by a superintendent, the major criteria for this evaluation (and subsequent salary increases) were "performance" and "how they handle their employees." Performance was measured by the ability to "run black" (high-quality production with standard amount of labor—standards set by industrial engineering). The ability to handle people was a more subjective measure, but, in the words of one general supervisor, "It's how they get the job done without lots of grievances and without getting . . . runover." The general supervisors evaluated ("wrote up") the supervisors under them and the superintendents evaluated the general supervisors.

Bob Moore commented:

> The measures on which supervisors are evaluated in their annual performance appraisal are budget performance, labor control, housekeeping, absenteeism, and training. It's pretty informal though—the underlying question is how well did they perform.

A management development package, updated twice yearly, was kept on most salaried people, particularly those thought to have "potential." Individuals had "potential" at Kalamazoo if they were considered to be capable of advancing at least one level of management (general supervisors were in the level above supervisors, middle managers were at the next level). This management development package consisted of a folder with information on an individual's history (including education, Acme experience, and other experience), an evaluation of their potential by the immediate supervisor, specific plans and job assignments for promotions, and specific qualified replacements for their present job. This package was widely used in moving, rotating, promoting, and developing people with potential. In early 1979, a development folder was maintained on very few supervisors or general supervisors.

An MBO system was used for middle and upper plant management. It was fairly well regarded as a development tool at Kalamazoo. Each manager, from superintendent on up, set annual goals and objectives and was evaluated on their level of attainment. Although managers did not see the comments which went into the management development package, the content, particularly the evaluation of their potential, was expected to be discussed with them at the MBO appraisal.

One superintendent commented on supervisory promotions:

> Our supervisors are really frustrated—an opening at the general or superintendent level comes up, I make recommendations to the front office (industrial relations) on who I want in there—one of my best people—and it always comes back with someone else in the job. IR usually sticks some college grad or developmental in there and my people just don't see any hope of their getting bumped up.

The range of base salary for a new supervisor was $1,465–$2,008 per month plus $180 a month for a cost-of-living allowance. Afternoon shift carried a five percent premium, and midnight shift a 10 percent premium. Overtime varied according to the area of the plant but averaged about four to eight hours per week of paid ("compensable") and four to eight hours per week of unpaid ("casual") overtime. Annual merit raises ranged from 0–8 percent of base salary. General supervisors' base salary range was $1,640–$2,500 per month.

In addition to base compensation, new supervisors received special merit raises; a "B" increase at 4–6 months of 4–6 percent and an "F" increase at 15–18 months. These raises were historically based. They were intended to accelerate the supervisors' salary progress since supervisors had traditionally lagged behind their administrative counterparts in increases. The supervisors were pegged, initially, at 15 percent above the average hourly pay. Almost all supervisors, if they stayed in the job, received the "B" and "F" increases.

In recruiting and selecting new supervisors from outside the plant ("walk-ins," local colleges, and referrals), there were four main criteria: (1) desire for a career in manufacturing, (2) appropriate education (equivalent of a B.B.A.), (3) favorable reactions from interviews with the production manager and two general supervisors, and (4) successful completion of the first line supervisory selection system (FLSSS).

The FLSSS was a companywide, day-long written and oral examination. It included a written portion (½ day) consisting of an in-basket exercise, a production scheduling problem, and an interpersonal skills section. The oral, done by three trained assessors, one for each of the three parts, was designed to probe the decision-making process and judgment of the applicants in regard to the written answers.

Applicants were evaluated on six dimensions. With priority weightings, these were problem solving (1), short-range planning (1), task structuring (1), interpersonal skills (2), personal work standards (3), and long-range planning (4). The first three, considered the most important, were all given an equal weighting in importance. Two out of five applicants passed the FLSSS.

Hourly people applying for a supervisor's position also had to take the FLSSS. Their selection process began with a posting of the available positions twice a year. The respondents to this posting, if their employee records were good, were sent to the FLSSS. Those that passed were put into a pool and randomly selected for the available jobs. The system was set up so that anyone applying for a supervisor's job who passed the FLSSS and was placed into the pool of applicants was never passed over more than twice. The third time someone made it to the pool they were selected automatically.

Of the 55 supervisors placed in 1978, Bob Moore estimated that roughly half of them had left voluntarily and half of them "failed" and were asked to step down. Part of the total returned to hourly, part went to other jobs in the plant, and part left the Kalamazoo plant altogether. When asked about the ones that failed, Bob replied:

> They failed because of three main reasons—inability to control the work force, inadequate training, and the self-fulfilling prophecy. In regard to the first, you have to be aggressive to make it on the floor. If the hourlys feel they can get away with something—they'll do it. You have to be able, as a supervisor, to step up to it, set limits, and maintain respect.

Secondly, a lot of our supervisors are put on a line after a few hours training. The general supervisors expect them to just walk in and hit it. They don't have the time to spend three to four months training them. Some supervisors don't know what industrial engineering is; they don't know how to fill out a time sheet; they don't know how to handle a hearing or a grievance; they don't even know their rights from the union contract. Some of the union people, whom they have to deal with, have been to school to study their contract rights.

Finally, I think there is a self-fulfilling prophecy operating out there. I think that when general supervisors or superintendents think someone is no good, then they end up failing in the end. When they don't think someone has what it takes to make it, then it is hard for them to justify spending limited, precious time training, guiding, assisting, or protecting the new supervisor. Especially when it comes to handling the work force—the general supervisors and superintendents have a tendency to dictate those methods that were successful for them when they were supervisors; they don't want to see the supervisors doing anything different.

In 1978, Bob Moore had instituted a new training program for new supervisors. Under this program, industrial relations paid the supervisors' salary and trained them for the first month. This month-long training included rotating through all the main functions in the plant, spending a day with the timekeeper on common time/pay errors, working with the supervisors on their lines, sitting in grievance hearings, and having a day with labor relations on contract, discipline, and hearing procedures. This special program, available only to college graduates, handled two people a month; six supervisors completed the program in 1978. Of those six supervisors, all were still on the job and "getting up to speed." Because of budget cutbacks this program was taken out of the 1979 budget. However, the plant manager was in the process of trying to get it reinstated.

Bob also conducted an exit interview with one of the supervisors who had left voluntarily. The reason he gave for leaving was that he was just not trained for the job. His general supervisor had just said, "do it," and sent him out on the line. In addition, when it came to labor control, his general supervisor had imposed his will on how "things were to be done around here." The departing supervisor summed up the exit session by stating that he was effectively left alone, without the required skills and tools, and expected to act toward the hourly employees the way the general supervisor wanted.

In spring 1978, the division had taken a salaried opinion survey of all the salaried employees at all locations. This survey confirmed the suspicions of Rich Howards and Bob Moore that there was a "morale problem" among some of the salaried people. In particular, on those questions where the responses of supervisors could be separated from other personnel, there seemed to be particular dissatisfaction in the areas of career development, communication, and supervisory and management practices. Bob Moore said that he thought that a "lack of recognition" was a critical part of that dissatisfaction.

> They are not feeling part of the team, they're alienated; they are the lowest rung on the ladder and no one is paying attention to them—just putting demands on them. Communications is a big key to this. A recent breakfast meeting of all salaried people was very well received, I'm getting good feedback. . . . But you just can't tell a general supervisor to communicate with his people. . . . On top of this they feel that management is selling out to the union, giving the plant away.

This last statement referred to some labor unrest which had been smoldering for the last few months. Although the exact causes of the unrest were vague and complicated to Bob, he said that it seemed to involve several incidents where decisions around the supervisor's authority were reversed in the grievance hearings, a manufacturing superintendent had been threatened, and a particularly troublesome employee reinstated after termination. Most recently, in early February, under the threat of a strike and with the full involvement of divisional and corporate labor relations people, there had been a settlement around a deluge of industrial safety and health grievances.

In discussions with superintendents and general supervisors about the supervisor's job and the high turnover of supervisors, the following comments were emphatically conveyed:

> Our people are being asked to do more, get more performance, and to be responsible for things that they have no control over (i.e., attendance, parts availability, maintenance, etc.). The attitude that we get from management if there's a problem is "fix it—make it go away." No matter what happens you're expected to run black or get yelled at. They don't accept any reasons as being realistic or valid . . . they just don't have any authority anymore and yet they still have all the responsibility for production . . . no one responds to them as supervisors, no one reacts . . . you used to be able to pick up a phone and make engineering jump . . . now they do things when they get around to them . . . we just don't get any support anymore from anyone.

> The workers out on the line just don't want to work anymore, they just don't give a rip about their job . . . most of the younger workers are happy with three days a week, enough for their car payment and a nickel bag . . . the women are usually the second breadwinner and if one of the kids is sick, if it snows, or something comes up they just take off . . . you always have to keep on your toes or they will stick it to you; it's a jungle out there . . . let's face it, since they all are getting paid the same, if they can come to work and stick it to a supervisor, that's a bonus for the day.

> To make it out there you have to know what factory life is about, how the system works, how to beat the local agreement, and how to get revenge . . . you can't be afraid to speak with or confront people . . . you have to be able to deal with people who don't want to work—the 5 percent—you have to be willing to offend someone, to be unpleasant, to be aggressive to get the job

done . . . this Maslow stuff and counseling jazz is garbage . . . it takes intestinal fortitude. . . .

And when it comes down to keeping that line going you have to do something—if you come into work and half of your people are absent, if you don't find replacements, matching the right people for the right jobs; get your line started within 15 minutes you have lost it for the day—you're running red . . . management just doesn't understand what we have to deal with.

A labor relations person at the plant offered the following viewpoint on the supervisor turnover problem:

The younger supervisors are sharp and aggressive, but they just aren't given sufficient training—especially in how to deal with the union and how to treat people. It is hard for them to accept that they don't have the power and authority that they used to have . . . let's face it, the union does have power now.

A lot of labor problems and lost production all focus on the supervisor— the supervisor is the one who interacts with the employee and is responsible for the company hourly interface. Most of the problems that cross my desk could be prevented if the supervisors knew how to get along with hourly people. They seem incapable of being able to understand the needs and wants of their people, to care about them. The union calls it, "treating us like human beings." Supervisors would be more successful if they could treat their people with respect, courtesy, and recognition and not have such negative attitudes about them.

They also get very frustrated because they think that we [labor relations] are down here undermining their authority. They don't understand about compromise and negotiation. They don't see that often I have to give in to the union in one thing if we want to get something else in another part of the plant or in another part of the company. Those are hard things to explain— sometimes you can't explain them. All the supervisors see is one of their disciplines being sent back to the line, laughing at him, waving a check for the lost time in the supervisor's face.

We have to do a better job of communicating with the supervisor, of letting him know, when we make a decision or reverse one, why we did it. Right now they hear it as rumors, secondhand reports, or from the union. We have to do a better job of training our foremen—they often are out there working with little knowledge of the correct way to handle labor situations and they are up against veteran committeemen who have been to long training workshops on the contract, their rights, and their bargaining levers.

Bob Moore knew that he was not faced with a simple problem in trying to solve the supervisory turnover. The ramifications went way beyond the cost of turnover—they infected the morale of half of the salaried work force, productivity, the development of future management, and company-union relations. There seemed to be no simple key to unlock this.

By the end of March he wanted to have recommendations on what could be done about this on the plant manager's desk. He also had to have a specific action plan for implementing them. With this deadline in mind, and the end of February approaching, Bob pondered what could be done.

CASE 30

Boise Cascade Manufactured Housing Division: The Lafayette Region (B)

At 7:30 P.M. on October 28, 1978, Fred Beech, manager of Boise Cascade's manufactured housing plant in Lafayette, Colorado, poured himself another cup of coffee and sat down on one of the chairs just outside the regional general manager's office. For the last hour he had been waiting to hear the results of the union representation election held that day. He was joined by Mike Nabors, production superintendent, and Bill Ash, materials manager.[1] As they talked about the campaign and speculated on the outcome, Bill Newton, general manager for the Lafayette Region of Boise Cascade's Manufactured Housing Division/West, came through the door.

"It looks like we've won the election," he exclaimed. "The preliminary count gave us 122 to 65."

"Bill, that's great news," Beech said, as he rose to shake Newton's hand. "I can't believe the support we got. This is a vindication of the things we've been trying to do."

Mike Nabors slapped Beech on the shoulder and said: "It looks like all the hard work on the campaign really paid off."[2]

As the group turned to leave, Bill Newton remarked: "You know, I'm glad we won, but I think the victory could be temporary. There are still a lot of problems in the plant, and we don't have much time to deal with them. The last few months we have spent a lot of time getting the new work force schedule up to speed and dealing with the union election. We've got to take a good hard look at the operation and develop a plan for turning it

---

[1] Hank Cherry the former superintendent had been terminated the first week of the union campaign and Mike Nabors, a supervisor from the Laurel, Montana, plant, was brought in.

[2] Newton had been particularly pleased with the cooperation Beech and Mike Nabors had given him and the corporate personnel staff. Both had put in long hours in the last three weeks.

around in the next three to five months. Let's get together Monday morning and review the situation."

MANUFACTURED HOUSING IN BOISE CASCADE[3]

The Manufactured Housing Division of Boise Cascade was part of its building materials group and was divided into an eastern (MHD/E) and a western (MHD/W) operation (Exhibit 1). The eastern operation produced house panels, while the western operation manufactured modular houses. In late 1978, MHD/W was organized into five regions, each of which was headed by a regional general manager (RGM) who was responsible for production, sales, customer service, and other general management functions. Bill Newton took over as RGM of the Lafayette region in December of 1977, after serving for five months as an assistant to the senior vice president of the building materials groups.[4]

Newton inherited a plant which had a history of poor performance and a reputation for troubled employee relations. At the end of 1977, he found a management team in a state of flux. During the previous summer, the entire system of supervision had been changed. The original "general foreman–leadmen" organization, with hourly workers serving as crew chiefs ("leadmen"), was replaced by a "plant superintendent–supervisor" setup with supervisors treated as part of management. Hank Cherry was promoted to production superintendent from another plant with little experience, and six leadmen from Lafayette were made supervisors. By the time Newton arrived, 10 of the remaining 11 leadmen had quit. Fred Beech had been transferred to Lafayette in October of 1977 after the former plant manager had been fired.

The personnel situation was no more tranquil in the dealer and sales organizations. Newton found poor attitudes, bad feelings, and demoralization among the dealers. He felt that many had joined Boise Cascade just to get their own house at wholesale. Almost all of the dealers had other sources of income and felt very little commitment to the Lafayette region. After some digging, Newton discovered that the dealers generally had been poorly treated by the sales and production people at Lafayette. Unfilled delivery promises, inadequate response to dealer requests, a general dis-

---

[3] The next five sections (manufactured housing in Boise Cascade, the market and the product, the production process, inside operations, and outside operations) are summaries of material found in Boise Cascade, Manufactured Housing Division, the Lafayette Region (A), written by David C. Rikert under the supervision of Professor W. Earl Sasser.

[4] Newton received an M.B.A. from the Harvard Business School in June of 1977. He had graduated from the Naval Academy in 1969 where he was president of his sophomore, junior, and senior classes. Prior to entering the M.B.A. program at Harvard he served six years in the Navy and had been decorated several times while flying 280 combat missions. Newton had chosen to work for Boise Cascade after considering a position with a leading Wall Street investment banking firm.

EXHIBIT 1
Manufactured Housing Division Organization

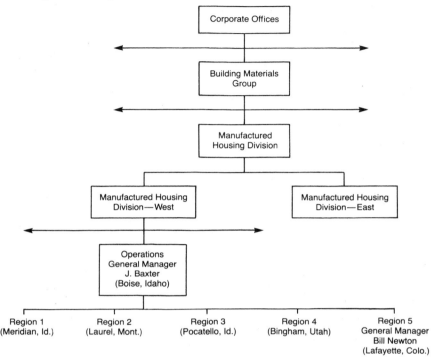

regard for the dealer's importance to the business, all combined to sour the relationship between dealers and the plant.

Sales and the dealer organization dominated Bill Newton's first four months at Lafayette.

> I knew the plant needed attention, but I felt we had to strengthen sales and the dealer network. Given the kind of competition we face and the type of product we sell, the dealers play a critical role in our success. The dealer not only sells our product but provides the land and a foundation, obtains all the permits, connects the utilities and is responsible for final placement of the house at the site.

THE MARKET AND THE PRODUCT

Once on the site, a modular home was essentially indistinguishable from a conventional house. "Within the basic box shape determined by the size limits of our production line, we'll build anything," Newton said.[5] The

---

[5] A house could be up to 60 feet long, and either 24 or 28 feet wide.

Boise Cascade catalog offered three series of two- to four-bedroom ranch house designs, with 38 floor plans and 12 types of exteriors. A number of standard options was available, ranging from appliances for the kitchen to cedar shakes for the roof. Further, MHD/W was willing to make custom changes in a house, such as moving the location of an interior partition, if requested by a customer. Customers were charged both for options and custom changes, and Newton felt that the margins on these items were higher than the margin on the basic house.

The housing industry had traditionally consisted of small, local "stick builders" who constructed on-site homes with conventional methods. While these small stick builders accounted for a large percentage of single-family starts in 1977, they faced competition from many different sources. One was large, regional, or national home builders such as U.S. Homes, Inc., who had become very efficient builders of standard, conventional houses, usually in large metropolitan areas. In 1977, large builders held a small market share nationally, but up to a 40 percent share in a metropolitan area such as Denver. The second was industrialized housing, which ranged from *panels,* such as walls, that were produced in a plant and assembled on the site, to *modular houses,* which were constructed in a plant and trucked in two halves to the site and "stitched" together, and to *mobile homes,* which were constructed of metal and ready to live in as they left the plant.

In late 1977, Boise Cascade planners had forecast total U.S. housing starts to range from just over 2 million in 1978, to just under 1.7 million in 1980. While growth in the Lafayette region might well exceed the national average, Newton felt that a sustained period of real growth in modular housing would probably require taking share away from other industry segments.[6]

> The economics of the business favor the big stick builder in the metropolitan area. But as we go 30–50 miles away from that area, it becomes more expensive to transport workers to the site, and deal with the resulting scheduling problems, than it does to transport the house. Building on a production line allows us to use lower skilled labor, and makes possible tighter scheduling of crews and better control over costs. And, of course, we have advantages over the small town builders who don't have access to skilled workers and subcontractors.
>
> We thus focus on rural areas, with a sales message that depends on the particular area. For example, over in Aspen, we sell mostly on price, since labor cost is so high there. To an energy company supplying employee housing near a Wyoming project, we sell our dependability—we're not going to go bankrupt in the midst of their project as might a small, local contractor. Nearer to Denver, we sell our delivery. In general, our real competitive advantage lies in lower costs and reliability.

------

[6] In 1977, the Lafayette Region's market share was 1.2 percent, well below the 2.7 percent MHD/W average.

The sales effort launched in early 1978 was successful. By April, firm orders had increased from 37 to 89 units. Training programs for dealers had been implemented, and a new commission structure had been devised which Newton felt would increase sales productivity. As his attention turned to the problems in the plant, Newton discovered that the break-even volume of production was somewhat higher than the plant's traditional peak capacity (eight units per week). Probing further, he also found bottlenecks in the operation which would limit output to about eight units per week unless changes were made in process design or staffing.

THE PRODUCTION PROCESS

The Lafayette plant, a 51,300-square-foot steel frame building, was organized around a 500-foot production line. (The plant layout and process organization are presented in Exhibit 2, and standard labor-hours for the various operations are given in Exhibit 3.) The modular houses were built in two separate halves, or pods, that moved sideways, at intervals, down the line. They were carried on low, wheeled cradles which ran on three parallel steel rails embedded in the floor. The cradles made it possible to move the houses manually from station to station. A pod remained in the plant until its exterior and roof were finished. It was then placed beside its mate and moved outside through a huge, overhead door.[7]

INSIDE OPERATIONS

The floor, walls, and roof were built in the subassembly area using specially designed jigs and fixtures. The roof jig, for example, was a 7-foot high, 66 by 20 foot platform which included a 3-foot wide walkway all around it. Sheetrock was first laid on the jig, with prefabricated trusses (rigid frames that supported the ceiling and roof) then positioned on the sheetrock.[8] While plywood was nailed to the top of the trusses to form the roof undersurface, the sheetrock was screw-gunned to the bottom of the trusses, forming the ceiling. Finally, exterior trim, such as eaves, was attached as were the gable ends.

The completed subassemblies entered the main assembly process at specified stations. The floor was placed on the cradles at station A (Exhibit 2) after underfloor plumbing and insulation had been installed. Interior walls were installed at station C, while exterior walls were nailed into place at station E. The roof was fastened to the walls at station G. Plumbing, electrical work, exterior plumbing, and insulating and roofing were com-

---

[7] A 15-acre (1 acre = 43,560 square feet) paved and gravel yard surrounded the building and was used to store raw materials and partially or fully completed house units.

[8] As with all tasks in the production process, workers consulted blueprints that traveled with each house for exact dimensions.

EXHIBIT 2
Plant Layout and Planned Staffing—October, 1978 (assignment of crews is given in parentheses by each work station)

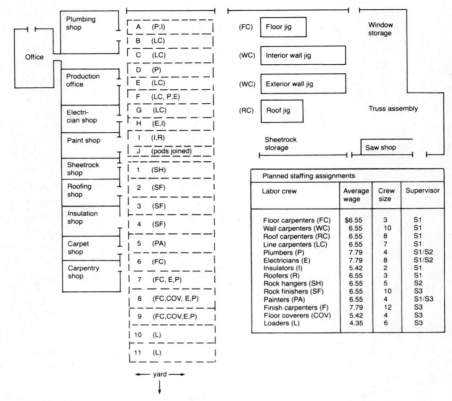

Note: Staffing and supervisory assignments are for one shift under the "4+4" plan.
   * The outside shops were used for storing tools, equipment, and supplies and for carrying out preparatory work.

EXHIBIT 3
Standard Labor-Hours for a Typical Small, Medium, and Large House Including Options

	JIGS			
	Standard Labor-Hours Hours per House			
	Small	Medium	Large	Average*
Floor carpenters	10.4	13.8	18.0	13.2
Wall carpenters	41.0	49.4	64.6	49.0
Roof carpenters	22.4	30.4	40.0	29.0

EXHIBIT 3 (*concluded*)

INSIDE PLANT

	Standard Labor-Hours Hours per House			
	Small	*Medium*	*Large*	*Average**
Line carpenters........	34.6	42.2	61.0	42.0
Plumbers	8.4	15.8	17.4	12.8
Electricians	26.6	31.2	34.0	29.8
Insulators	6.4	8.8	11.6	8.4
Roofers	10.6	13.8	17.6	13.2
Painters..............	6.0	7.4	9.2	7.2

OUTSIDE PLANT

	Standard Labor-Hours Hours per House			
	Small	*Medium*	*Large*	*Average**
Sheetrock hangers......	22.5	28.5	37.3	27.8
Sheetrock finishers	50.1	62.4	80.0	60.8
Plumbers	4.1	7.3	10.6	6.6
Electricians	12.9	17.2	20.6	16.0
Painters..............	9.3	11.7	14.6	11.3
Finish carpenters	48.5	66.5	85.7	62.8
Floor coverers	17.0	25.7	31.3	23.1
Loaders..............	30.9	30.9	30.9	30.9
Total hours per house..	361.7	463.0	584.6	444.9

* Assuming the present mix of four small, three medium, and two large houses per week.

pleted at the other stations. Completed matched pods were joined at station J, and the whole house moved outside.

OUTSIDE OPERATIONS

The outside operations were divided into four categories. At stations 1–4, the interior sheetrock was hung, taped, and coated with compound. At station 5, the painters applied two coats of latex paint to the walls and ceilings. An hour's drying time was required between coats. The interior finish work was done at stations 6, 7, 8, and 9: finish carpenters installed doors, cabinets, shelves, countertops, and trim; electricians and plumbers attached and connected fixtures; and floor coverers laid linoleum, carpeting, and tile. Much of this work had to be sequenced (countertops had to go in before sinks could be set into the countertop and connected), although some could be done independently (ceiling light fixtures could be attached at anytime). Finally, at station 10, the loaders stocked the house with "loose parts," such as optional kitchen appliances, and the house was inspected. Any defects were repaired at station 11. The loaders then thoroughly cleaned each pod and sealed it with plastic for shipment.

During his first tour of the plant after arriving at Lafayette, Bill Newton heard Fred Beech explain the difference between inside and outside operations:

> Within the plant, the crews at the jigs and stations work with individual pods. Timing is essential since the subassembly jigs feed into the line at specific points. A pod has to be ready, for example, to receive its roof when it gets to station G. Outside the plant, the two pods, temporarily joined, move down the line together as a house. There is no fixed equipment outside, so that timing is less critical.

BOTTLENECKS AND CAPACITY DECISIONS

In the spring of 1978, houses were not being finished on schedule but were being moved to the yard with work still to be done. Newton recalled the problem:

> We were getting the work done inside the plant, but outside we often slipped behind schedule. I asked Fred to look into the problem, and he concluded we had a bottleneck at sheetrock finishing. Given our product mix, and the fact that only 12 people could work in a house at one time, we could just about finish a house in five hours. But with a start rate of nine units per week we had a cycle time of about 4.5 hours. We were starting nine and finishing about eight per week.[9]

Realizing he had to increase capacity Newton considered several options, but finally decided on a new shift schedule which he called "4+4." The plant work force would consist of two crews, each of which would work four 10-hour days and then would be off for four consecutive days.[10] Thus, for example, the A crew would begin on Monday and work through Thursday; the B crew would then begin on Friday and work through the following Monday. Although this scheme radically changed the nature of the workweek, Newton felt it was superior to a second shift. Begun on May 1, 1978, he expected capacity to increase to 12–14 starts per week.

MONDAY MORNING

Bill Newton looked quickly through his in-box on the Monday morning following the union election. He was particularly interested in a memo (Exhibit 4) from a private investigator he had hired to work in the plant.

---

[9] The cycle time of the line (for a house) was determined by dividing the length of the workweek by the number of houses to be started that week.

[10] The day under "4+4" began at 7:30 A.M. and ended at 6 P.M., with an unpaid lunch break from 12 to 12:30.

EXHIBIT 4

HARRISON INVESTIGATIONS INC.
1042 Paine Street
Boulder, Colorado

Investigation Report

To: Bill Newton

Re: Plant Assignment

This is a preliminary report covering my first week on the job. I will summarize the results briefly and follow up with a complete report after the assignment has been completed.

Drugs:

a. Based on observation I estimate (conservatively) that 20–25 percent of the work force uses some kind of hard drug on the job (cocaine, heroin, speed, angel dust etc.).

b. If you include marijuana and alcohol (a beer at lunch, liquor), along with hard drugs, I estimate 75–80 percent of the work force uses some kind of drug during working hours.

Stealing:

a. It's hard to tell but there's probably some petty theft (small hand tools). There certainly is every opportunity—no control over tools and supplies that I could see.

b. If the people wanted to, they could steal you blind, especially in outside work. It's pretty hard to find anything or anyone out in the yard.

General atmosphere:

a. The people I worked with were pretty cynical. Two of the guys on my crew had really negative attitudes about the company. There is little respect for supervisors or other management types. I got the impression they felt they had been lied to and mistreated in the past.

b. It's hard for a new employee to know what management expects. I was just introduced to the crew chief and told to work with two other guys on sheetrock hanging. I was told what my pay was, but not much else. For example, as far as I could tell from talking to people, there are no rules on absenteeism or tardiness. I was also told that supervisors promote without posting jobs like they're supposed to. There are some bad feelings about this.

Roger Harrison
Roger Harrison

EXHIBIT 5
Lafayette Region Income and Expense Statement, 1978 ($000)

Category	First Quarter		Second Quarter		Third Quarter		September	
	Actual	Budget	Actual	Budget	Actual	Budget	Actual	Budget
Sales	$1,589.0	$994.0	$2,041.2	$2,974.8	$2,566.1	$3,752.9	$716.3	$1,271.9
Units	75	48	97	143	116	172	34	57
Direct manufacturing expenses	$1,421.6	$874.9	$1,622.3	$2,328.6	$2,105.0	$2,709.4	$612.1	$872.1
Materials	1,002.2*	614.3	1,130.0	1,635.7	1,402.3	1,950.2	400.9	643.4
Labor (direct production)	326.4	221.2	410.0	586.8	605.4†	637.3	183.0	188.9
Field (skid crews, trucks etc.)	93.0	39.4	82.3	106.1	97.3	121.9	28.2	39.8
Gross profit	167.4	119.2	418.9	646.2	461.1	1,043.5	104.2	399.8
Manufacturing overhead	254.6	218.8	241.0	234.9	279.2	261.2	92.6	87.0
Fixed‡	162.4	172.4	165.3	178.4	171.2	185.7	60.5	62.1
Variable§	92.2	46.4	75.7	56.5	108.0	75.5	32.1	24.9
Administrative expenses	123.7	114.2	114.4	126.2	122.1	129.5	34.0	41.8
Plant	77.4	85.5	85.0	93.1	98.6	93.9	26.3	30.9
Region	46.3	28.7	29.4	33.1	23.5	35.1	7.7	10.9
Selling expenses	36.2	56.1	32.7	66.7	31.2	62.1	9.6	22.0
Region profit	$ (247.1)	$(269.9)	$ 30.8	$ 218.4	$ 28.6	$ 591.2	$ (32.0)	$ 249.0

* Includes a one-time write-off of $120,000 in scrap.
† Includes a $56,780 for subcontractors (no subcontractors were hired in September).
‡ Includes utilities, depreciation, insurance, taxes, supervision, and maintenance.
§ Includes employee fringe benefits, workers compensation, indirect labor, and tools and supplies.

Newton had spent much of the weekend reviewing a report on the plant and going over the third quarter financial statements for the Lafayette Region (see Exhibit 5 for a summary of the first three quarters of 1978), and the year-to-date financial comparison of all regions in the division (Exhibit 6).

Two months earlier he had received permission to bring in Max Donovan, a plant manager at the Bingham, Utah, plant, to study the operation and prepare a report (see Exhibit 7). Newton was not surprised by Donovan's initial report; many of the problems had been identified in discussions he had held in June with Fred Beech. Although Newton had made it clear that he expected Beech to take steps to deal with the problems, the report confirmed Newton's assessment that little substantive change had been made.

As he prepared for the staff meeting scheduled to begin in a few minutes, Newton decided not to take an active role in the discussion. He wanted to hear what his managers thought without taking a strong position himself. On his way out the door, his secretary handed him a special delivery letter from Jack Hickman, the Lafayette region's largest dealer (Exhibit 8). Newton read the letter while walking down the hall to the conference room; it was the third such letter he had received in the last three weeks.

EXHIBIT 6
Manufactured Housing Division/West Year-to-Date Plant Income and Expenses, October 1, 1978*
(based on first three quarters of 1978; except where noted data are in $000)

	Region				
Category	*Meridian*	*Laurel*	*Pocatello*	*Bingham*	*Lafayette*
Capacity† (units)...............	900	1,000	650	1,000	350
Sales........................	$11,240.9	$9,595.6	$9,082.8	$8,273.7	$6,196.3
Units........................	590	506	462	401	288
Direct manufacturing expenses‡ ..	$ 8,464.4	$7,225.5	$6,380.6	$6,184.7	$5,148.9
Materials	5,925.1	5,058.0	4,614.7	4,386.2	3,534.2
Labor	2,115.8	1,806.4	1,510.7	1,552.6	1,341.8
Gross profit	2,776.5	2,370.1	2,702.1	2,089.0	1,047.4
Manufacturing overhead.........	1,326.4	1,046.4	984.2	789.4	774.8
Plant administration............	377.0	293.2	285.6	248.1	261.0
Plant profit	$ 1,073.1	$1,030.5	$1,432.3	$1,051.5	$ 11.6

* 1977 results:

	Sales ($000)	*Units*	*Plant Profit ($000)*
Meridian	$12,100	696	$1,016
Laurel.........	10,319	545	995
Pocatello	9,772	525	1,575
Bingham.......	8,906	455	1,445
Lafayette	6,668	276	637

† One-shift, 40-hour per week nominal capacity.
‡ Includes expenses for field work (skid crews, trucks, etc.) that are not shown separately.

EXHIBIT 7

Interoffice Memo

Boise Cascade Corporation

To: Bill Newton   Location: Lafayette

From: Max Donovan   Location: Bingham

Subject: Lafayette

Date: October 27, 1978

Attached you will find an outline as to the problems that I see in the Lafayette organization.

While it seems easy for an "outsider" to pick things apart, seldom does that "outsider" offer the workable solution to correct the problems. In my next memo I will attempt to offer methods to help correct the problems. There are some sensitive areas that I want to reserve comment on until I have an opportunity to study these areas closer.

As I view the situation, it appears there are three major areas of concern.

1. Supervisory strengths.
2. Systems disorganized and/or missing.
3. Staff communications/support.

Max

Max Donovan
Plant Manager
Bingham Plant

EXHIBIT 7 (*concluded*)

PROBLEMS

I. **Supervision:**

Supervisors are inexperienced and timid; follow-up and follow-through are weak. They have no sense of urgency, even though they are spread too thin. There is not enough time for them to do administrative work (e.g., hiring, time keeping), and these are neglected. Job description and authority may be   unclear. They are unable to delegate to group I's. They are reacting and fighting fires.

II. **Systems disorganized and or lacking:**

Materials.   There is no material-handling system: no system of requisitions, no limits to access, inadequate methods for accounting for material picked and used. Few people are careful; few feel responsible. Storage areas are small and disorganized. Housekeeping is awful. Materials flow is haphazard; skilled/semiskilled people do a lot of traveling.

Production.   Computer is not being used to schedule; there really isn't a schedule that people can plan on. The only part of the plant running well is the inside operations. Outside, station/task definition has broken down; can't tell what is being worked on where. Supervisors are not using formal check-off for work done. No feedback about weekly results (percent of schedule completed, efficiency) is provided to supervisors or workers.

III. **Staff support:**

Staff lacks team spirit, no sense of urgency, not enough cooperation. People don't understand each other (e.g. materials/production). Problems are not being solved. Answers/solutions given in generalities. Supervisors (and others) may be saying what they think management wants to hear. In general, people are protecting themselves.

IV. **Work force:**

Work force is poorly motivated (too many bull sessions, too little work, too much traveling). New people (and some older) are not trained (use of skill saw, material retrieval, etc.). Group I's lack responsibility and accountability. Safety is worst in division (over $90,000 in Worker's Compensation and 300 days lost—average is more like $15,000, and 40–50 days lost). Housekeeping discipline is poor (general problem). Morale is below average, and attitudes are bad. Not operating efficiently—not working very hard, especially outside. Unfair treatment in past may have poisoned the atmosphere.

EXHIBIT 8

> Hickman Realty
> 1437 Broadview Drive
> Colorado Springs, Colorado
>
> Mr. William Newton
> Boise Cascade
> P.O. Box 4743
> Lafayette, Colorado
>
> Dear Bill:
>
> I don't usually come to you with delivery problems, but this one is serious. I've got five houses that were supposed to be ready a month ago and they still haven't been shipped. I talked to Art about it, but all I get is some fairy tale about a shortage of windows. I finally decided to write to you to see if I could find out what is going on. This deal is an important one to me and could mean big business if this energy thing kicks off. Could you look into it for me?
>
> Regards, 
>
> *Jack Hickman*
>
> Jack Hickman
> President
>
> P.S. Some of the houses you're shipping are pretty dirty when they get to us. I've had to hire contract cleaners on the last two shipments. The last time I found some empty beer cans in the master bath!

STAFF MEETING

The staff meeting was attended by the people who reported directly to Newton (Fred Beech [plant manager], Bill Ash [materials manager], Bill Palmer [sales manager], Art Budd [service manager], and Tom Thorne [manager of quality control]). (An organization chart is presented in Exhibit 9.)

Newton opened the meeting by recognizing the effort each of the participants had made in the union election campaign. He then turned to the third-quarter financial statements.

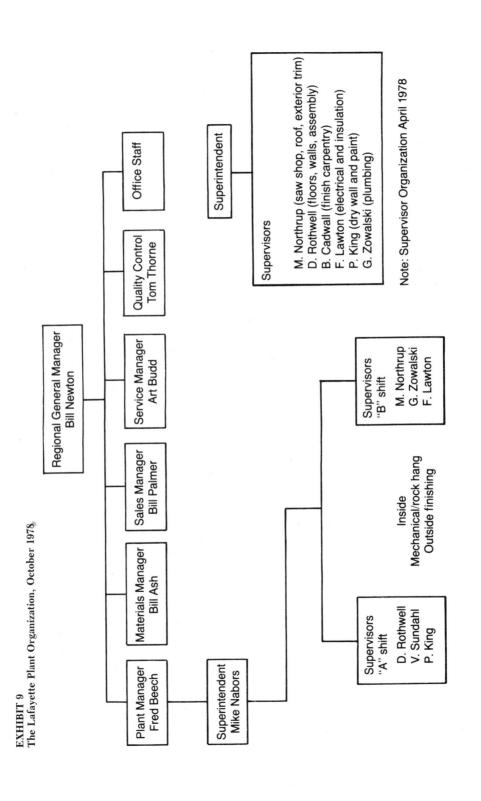

EXHIBIT 9
The Lafayette Plant Organization, October 1978

Regional General Manager
Bill Newton

Plant Manager
Fred Beech

Materials Manager
Bill Ash

Sales Manager
Bill Palmer

Service Manager
Art Budd

Quality Control
Tom Thorne

Office Staff

Superintendent
Mike Nabors

Superintendent

Supervisors
"A" shift
D. Rothwell
V. Sundahl
P. King

Supervisors
"B" shift
M. Northrup
G. Zowalski
F. Lawton

Inside
Mechanical/rock hang
Outside finishing

Supervisors

M. Northrup (saw shop, roof, exterior trim)
D. Rothwell (floors, walls, assembly)
B. Cadwall (finish carpentry)
F. Lawton (electrical and insulation)
P. King (dry wall and paint)
G. Zowalski (plumbing)

Note: Supervisor Organization April 1978

Newton: As we expected, the results for September were not good, and the third quarter showed only a small profit for the region. In July, we thought that our profitability problems might be due to everyone getting used to the "4+4" system. But we've had six months to get the bugs worked out, and our results are still not where they should be. I think the problems may be more fundamental than we have realized, and I'd like to hear your thoughts.

Budd: I think one of our biggest problems has been lack of volume. We just haven't had the kind of throughput we need to cover our fixed costs.

Palmer: Well the volume problem is not due to lack of sales. We've had good success all summer long, and our firm backlog has been solid (see Exhibit 10 for sales and production data). Look, we can sell houses; we just can't make 'em fast enough.

Beech: Bill, I know we've got our problems in production, but you just can't expect to have a smooth operation when there are so many shortages of material and parts. Do you realize that we have several houses sitting on the lot ready to be shipped except for one problem—we ran out of windows. Stuff like that happens all the time.

Palmer: Yea, the shortages have really hurt our delivery schedules. It's something we've got to improve before it really starts hurting our sales.

Newton (turning to Bill Ash): Bill, what's your assessment of the situation.

Ash: Everytime there's a shortage, everyone assumes there's something wrong in the materials department. Well, a shortage is a two-way street. I can only order based on what the production guys tell me they need and what's on hand. Besides the fact our schedule is never met; the only other thing I can figure out is that the crews are taking stuff that's not recorded. Look, with the kind of people we've been hiring lately I wouldn't be surprised if half the stuff was going out the gate at 6 o'clock.

Thorne: I think Bill's right. The work force has really gone downhill. It's starting to show up in quality, and with all the subcontractors we've had to hire, efficiency must be terrible. Fred, this is not a criticism, but the workers seem to be giving you guys the run around.

Beech: Tom, that's really not an accurate view of the situation. Mike and I are working as hard as we know how to get the situation under control. We're down on the floor almost all the time, working with the people trying to solve problems. But it's like the kid with his finger in the dike. It seems like we get one problem solved and another leak springs. And I don't think our people are all that bad. Basically, the production workers do a pretty good job.

Budd: I agree with Fred. I don't think the problem is that we've got bad people. It's just difficult to overcome four or five years of bad relations in a few months. And besides, the new schedule hasn't worked as well as we hoped. These people are working 10-hour days, and in the last five months they've been putting in 45 minutes to an hour overtime. Bill, I think we've got to take a look at this "4+4" system. It's causing a lot of problems.

Newton: Fred, you've operated under both the old setup and the "4+4," what do you think?

Beech: I hate to say this Bill, because I supported the idea. But I'm starting to think the "4+4" just isn't going to work. We don't have accountability of work

EXHIBIT 10
Summary of Monthly Activity, April–October 1978

Month	Monthly Activity				Plant Status at Month's End			
	Starts* (units)	Completions (units)	Units Shipped	Days to† Completion	WIP§ Units	FG‖ Units	Firm Backlog	Direct Production Employees‡
April.........	34	30	35	18	30	17	89	112
May..........	33	26	24	23	37	19	97	124
June	47	43	38	31	41	24	131	136
July..........	35	33	36	33	43	21	85	161
August	45	44	43	34	44	22	81	163
September.....	38	36	37	34	46	21	64	162
October:								
Week 1......	9	11	4	33	44	28	64	167
Week 2......	11	7	9	35	48	26	75	169
Week 3......	8	4	7	37	52	23	80	172

* Includes all types of houses; for the period shown, the size mix averaged four small, three medium, and two large houses per week.
† Days to completion is defined as number of elapsed working days from start to finish.
‡ This does not include material handlers, clean-up crew, or saw shop carpenters. The count is based on the payroll as of the end of time period; it is not adjusted for absences, either excused or unexcused.
§ WIP indicates work-in-process inventory.
‖ FG indicates finished goods inventory.

done; people get tired, and the last two hours of every day are basically wasted; and it's causing some personal and family problems, particularly with the supervisors.

Ash: We talked about all those things before the decision was made. I don't think the "4+4" or any other schedule is going to solve our production problems. But, one thing we haven't mentioned is the quality of supervision. Fred, if you had better supervisors you wouldn't have to be solving problems on the floor so much.

Budd: I think you're being a little harsh, Bill. Those guys are in a pretty tough position. All of them used to be hourly workers and now they're management, but we really haven't done very much to help them make the transition. They may not be the greatest managers in the world, but they know how to make houses and I think they ought to get more support.

Beech: I think that's a good point. The situation is really impossible. Right now sheetrock operations are taking up most of the outside line stations. That means that Pete King and Foster Lawton have to cover all those stations plus try to keep up with painting and finish carpentry. I think they're doing pretty well given the job they've got.

WORK FORCE CHARACTERISTICS AND PERSONNEL POLICY

Following the staff meeting Newton reviewed a report (Exhibit 11) on recent new hires and promotions prepared by Mary Stanton of the office staff. The work force at Lafayette was younger and less skilled than a regular builder would employ. The average age was 27, 92 percent were male, and over 25 percent had some college experience. Most new hires came from Boulder, Lafayette, or several other small towns within a 15-mile radius of the plant.

When he arrived in late 1977, Newton had been surprised to find that the plant had no written personnel policies. In the spring of 1978, Newton had been concerned about the level of absenteeism and turnover (Exhibit 12). With assistance from the corporate staff he had introduced a job posting and bidding system for the promotion of production workers. As in the past, the decision was the supervisor's, but workers were to be given information about openings and an opportunity to apply for them. Ability, seniority, and general attitude were the criteria to be used in making selections.

Because houses were certified to both state and local building codes in the design stage, licensed journeymen were not required in the plant. None of the workers was a journeyman, and almost all had come to the plant with little meaningful building experience. Fred Beech believed, however, that any carpentry experience, however slight, was much more important than attitude, work history, or past performance:

> While we build top-quality houses, and we have jigs and fixtures, we need a worker who has prior carpentry experience. A lot of our knowledge and ability must be in our heads and our ability to read blueprints. Thus, I instruct

EXHIBIT 11

MEMORANDUM

To: Bill Newton   October, 1978

From: Mary Stanton

New Hires and Promotions June–September 1978

I.   New Hires:

	Number of New Hires	Number with Construction Experience	Average Years of Work Experience	Average Age	Education	
					High School Graduates	Number with Some College
June........	26	3	3½	22	12	10
July	40	4	3¼	24	24	9
August	32	2*	3⅔*	23	15	11
September..	17	2*	3⅔*	22	9	8

    * These numbers partly are guesses. I couldn't find the information for very many of the new people. A lot of the forms weren't filled out.

II.   Promotions:

    We don't keep records on the things you wanted so I went back and did a little checking myself. I used the files for July, August, and September. I could only find two promotions (out of about 35) that looked somewhat questionable. In one case, Bud Casper was promoted from grade IV to grade III carpenter even though he was absent a lot. If I remember right, though, he's the one with a little girl that was sick. The other one was Jimmy Novack. He was almost fired for fighting last May. Then, in September he was made a grade III electrician. I couldn't tell from the records whether these jobs or any of the others were posted like they are supposed to be.

our supervisors to look for hammer and nail experience. I don't care if they've been in six jobs over the past year. In fact that may mean they have more varied experience. These kinds of people take less training and are better at producing a quality product with little supervision.

    Nine job classifications had been established based on the usual building trades. Workers were paid at one of four pay grades, depending upon job classification. New hires were paid about $1 per hour less than scale during their first six months on the job. Wage rates were average for manufacturing in the Boulder area, but Boise Cascade benefits made the total compensation package "very competitive," according to Newton.

    Each of the 14 direct production crews was responsible for specific tasks in the production process (see Exhibit 2 for a listing of crews). Beech felt that

EXHIBIT 12
Absenteeism, New Hires, and Termination of Direct Production Workers, April–September 1978

Month	Percent Absenteeism*	Applicants Hired	Terminations†	Tenure at Termination (months)					
				0–3	4–8	8–12	12–24	24–48	48+
April.........	7.2	23	11	5	3	1	0	2	0
May..........	9.1	23	11	5	4	1	0	0	1
June..........	9.2	26	14	9	3	0	2	0	0
July..........	10.1	40	15	8	2	1	0	3	1
August.......	9.6	32	30	18	2	3	0	4	3
September....	10.3	17	18	10	2	1	1	2	2

* Percent absenteeism is an average of the daily figures; it is defined as the ratio of number absent to number employed. Absentees were not paid for time not worked.

† Includes terminations for all reasons (quits, discharge, layoff, etc.); on average quits accounted for 40–50 percent of terminations within the first three months, and 85–90 percent of terminations thereafter.

the workers generally identified more closely with their crew than with their job classification and the workers resisted movement among crews. However, crews were changed to handle temporary bottleneck operations and to cover for absenteeism and vacations. On rare occasions, workers from one job classification were assigned work in another, i.e., carpenters did electrical or plumbing tasks.

THE BASKETBALL GAME

That evening, Newton played in a basketball game with the plant team. Since his move to Lafayette, he had made an effort to participate on the sports teams at the plant. He felt athletics was a good way to stay in shape while keeping in touch with the workers. It also helped the team: Newton had been an Academic All-American in football at the Naval Academy. After the game he walked to the parking lot with Phil Wexler, a group I roof carpenter, who was leaving the plant in December to go back to school; he had one year left in a masters degree program in chemical engineering at the University of Wyoming.[11] His older brother had served with Bill Newton in Vietnam.

As they reached their cars, the conversation turned to the plant.

Newton: When are you going up to Laramie?

Wexler: About the 28th of December, I want to get settled before classes start on the 6th.

Newton: Well, I'm glad you're going to finish your degree, but we're sure going to miss you. You've really kept that roof crew humming.

Wexler: Yes, we've done all right, but I can't say that I'll miss it. It's a pretty tough place to work right now. Beech is on the supervisors all the time to do something, and the supervisors are after us, but they don't really know what they are supposed to be doing. People are pretty frustrated.

Newton: I know, Phil. Just the fact we had the union election showed that. We have our work cut out for us, but we can all make it better if we work together. I hope you get a chance to come back and visit next summer to see if we've made any progress.

Wexler: I hope you're right, but I don't see how you can change it that fast. I mean, a lot of the guys hope you do. Besides the fact that the carpenter's union was pretty incompetent; I think they didn't vote in the union because they wanted to give you a chance. But after the hassles with Matthews and now all the problems lately, some of the people just don't give a rip about their work or the company.[12]

---

[11] The workers on production crews were classified into one of four skill/responsibility groups. Group I's were the most skilled and were supposed to oversee technical performance and assist other members of the crew with technical problems. In the old supervisory setup, group I's had been called leadmen.

[12] Ed Matthews was the plant manager before Beech. He had a reputation (well deserved according to Newton) as a tough, hard-nosed, theory X manager.

BREAKFAST WITH MAX DONOVAN

The next morning Newton had breakfast with Max Donovan and discussed Donovan's report on the plant. Donovan emphasized the lack of supervisory strength and the importance of getting a materials system in place. He then raised a new issue:

Donovan: I think I told you there were some other things I wanted to look at. I was talking about the management team. I'm convinced it's a very weak group. If I were you, I'd put Beech on a short leash. He has very little credibility, and he won't listen to me.

Newton: Max, I've tried to work through Beech all summer long. I met with him, went over problems, and gave him assignments and warnings. But by August little had changed.

Donovan: That must have been about the time I came over.

Newton: That's right. You're the best plant manager we have. He can learn from you if he will just try. I told Fred what I was doing and why, and he even agreed with the idea. We've made some headway in the last two months, but there are things going on out there that have no place in a good operation. Since we started the "4+4," I've made it a point to be out in the plant more. Last Wednesday I was walking through some unfinished houses out in the yard and I found a guy asleep in the closet of the master bedroom!

Donovan: You know Bill, a year ago Fred Beech was thought to be one of the best plant managers in the division. But he just may be in over his head. If he's been warned, I think you ought to let him go right now. You probably ought to get some new supervisors too. Once you get some new people, you can start looking at your systems problems. The first thing I'd do, Bill, is take a real hard, objective look at the "4+4" setup. I think it's causing a lot of your problems.

Newton: I appreciate your advice. Your report and some other information I've received have convinced me that I've got to move quickly. But I want to be sure that the decisions I make will lay the foundation for sustained growth and profitability.

CASE 31

Sedalia Engine Plant (A)

The transition period for the Sedalia Engine Plant (SEP) would not be easy. Of that, SEP's newly appointed plant manager, Danney Goble, was certain. The plant had been manufacturing and assembling diesel engines in Sedalia, Minnesota, since 1974; and SEP's parent company, American Diesel, had allowed the plant to chart an exciting and innovative course. A bold venture not only in the redesign of work but also in the environment in which that work takes place, SEP had emphasized a participatory style of management. All SEP employees, from top managers to line workers, were salaried. All belonged to semiautonomous work teams in which team members were involved in establishing budgets, setting work schedules, and ordering equipment, as well as learning a wide variety of skills and performing a broad spectrum of functions. Although there was no union at SEP, workers could—and did—sit as representatives on numerous governance organizations.

Since its inception, SEP had been under the firm hand of the original plant manager, Donald St. Clair. Often described by co-workers as "charismatic," St. Clair had served as a sort of father figure for the new plant and its employees. He had become such an important part of the early life of SEP that the observation of one of his managers that "this place looked and smelled like Don St. Clair," met with near unanimous agreement.

But now, in the fall of 1979, St. Clair had just been promoted to vice president for domestic operations—responsible for the Sedalia plant among other American Diesel plants—and moved to American Diesel's corporate headquarters in Beacon, Illinois. His successor, Danney Goble, formerly SEP's director of assembly and testing, offered a sharp—and to some, quite disturbing—contrast to St. Clair's managerial style. He seemed to emphasize process—wanted to institutionalize that process and make it less personal than it had been under St. Clair's leadership. St. Clair liked to define his role in the plant as an "agitator," trying to encourage people to take upon themselves the responsibility to live up to the goals and ideals of the plant. Goble saw himself more strictly as a manager. Well aware of that contrast, Goble insisted that such a change was necessary for the future growth and health of SEP.

But Goble also knew that the leadership transition problem went beyond adjustments to a new plant manager. Not only St. Clair, but practically all of SEP's top-management team had left, saddling Goble with a massive rebuilding program. That turnover, although a quite normal step in the career development of those individuals involved, could not have come at a worse time. The declining national economy was forcing upon SEP its greatest challenges yet. The downturn of 1979 raised the real possibility of layoffs at SEP for the first time in the plant's brief history. Layoffs were surely coming to American Diesel's Beacon plant. Because Sedalia wages were linked to those at the Beacon plant, there could be a sharp reduction in the raises that had been coming regularly to SEP workers. How would these twin economic threats, coming as they did on the heels of a major change in the leadership of SEP, affect the level of commitment that had been from the beginning such a critical feature of life in the plant? Danney Goble could not be sure.

THE GUIDING PHILOSOPHY OF SEDALIA ENGINE PLANT

The notion of experimenting with innovative work systems had taken root at American Diesel in the early 1970s. Following a 60-day strike at the Beacon plant in 1972, American Diesel undertook several innovations in their new plants. In 1974, American Diesel decided to move into Sedalia, Minnesota, and opened the Sedalia Engine Plant. The SEP philosophy, unique within American Diesel, grew out of a series of discussions between Don St. Clair and his operating team. Because of the oil embargo of 1974, American Diesel's business had been reduced sharply. As a result, the company allowed St. Clair and his team considerable slack time in which to work through and carefully develop an operating philosophy.

After visiting a number of innovative plants throughout the country and working with an outside consultant, St. Clair and his operating team selected four words to help identify the type of organization they hoped to create: excellence, trust, growth, and equity (see Exhibit 1 for a detailed definition of these goals as provided by the organizing team). Essentially, he hoped to create an organization where the self-interest and creative talents of all employees would be directed to the general well-being of the plant. Allowed a maximum amount of freedom, responsibility, and flexibility, employees would dedicate themselves to a high level of performance. "People want to work hard, perform well, learn new skills, and be involved in the decision-making processes that affect their jobs," said St.

EXHIBIT 1

HOW WE DO BUSINESS

Our business goals are basically the same as those of any successful business:

Produce a quality product.

On-time shipment of our product to our customers.

Be effecient in our operations.

Be profitable.

Each of us has ideas on how we can best reach these overall goals, and on how we can do business to reach more specific goals which will contribute to reaching these overall general goals.

A way to do business can mean many different things, such as a way to run a machine, prepare a report, train an employee, solve a problem, evaluate plant performance, communicate an idea, arrange a work area, or practice safety. Each of these and all other ways to do business can be accomplished in many ways. Each different way to do business is assumed to have some advantages and some disadvantages and may be compared to other ways for accomplishing the same thing. The way with the strongest advantages and most acceptable disadvantages will be selected.

A good question to answer at this point is: "How do we decide?" Because we must do many things in unison as a single plant, we as a plant organization have come up with four basic guidelines to help us decide the *best* way of doing business or the way we think has the best chance of success. These guidelines or key questions which have served as the building blocks of our organization are:

Excellence: Does the way we do business allow every employee to perform to the best of his/her ability? Does the way to do business allow the plant to function as effectively as possible? Our assumption is that all people who belong to our organization will want to do their best and will expect the same of others even in the performance of many repetitive, routine tasks which are part of our work. We assume nothing less than such effort will allow us to be an effective competitor in the diesel engine business.

Trust: Does the way to do business reenforce the idea that employees are expected to behave as responsible adults, and, therefore, information, equipment, and materials are made accessible to them? If employees are assumed to be responsible adults, then the risks of abuse of information are low and the advantages of accessibility and openness are great. For example, it is assumed that we can solve any problem once it is raised and that all employees will bring us problems, issues, and sensitive information because they are confident that this information will be treated effectively with no harm coming to them simply because they raised an issue. Trust does not mean that information will be handled carelessly or that everything will be available to everyone. However, it

EXHIBIT 1 (*concluded*)

is assumed that ownership in and a commitment to accomplishing objectives is strongest when relevant information is available. Therefore, information will be made available as appropriate.

Growth: Does the way to do business encourage both the *learning and performing* of many tasks by said employees? We assume that human resources are too valuable to waste. People have been educated more and are capable of learning and performing more at work. It is assumed that work can be more interesting when people are challenged to perform a series of related tasks that add up to a measurable end product or service, rather than routinely performing only the smallest parts of total jobs. This does not mean that uninteresting or repetitive work is eliminated, for, in fact, many such tasks are required to make diesel engine parts, however we organize our work. It is assumed that as employees, we can recognize the need to continue to perform the skills that we have learned, even though without new learning, some tasks may eventually lose some of the initial excitement or interest they held. In our business, we must learn in order to perform. We do not learn for the sake of learning.

It is assumed that we can recognize the value of sharing the skills which we have learned with others even though our instincts and past experience may mislead us to think that protecting some unique skills which we have will make us more valuable employees. A valuable employee is capable of, and willing, to train others.

Equity: Does the way to do business treat all employees as adults and as fairly as possible? Our assumption is that we will tend to perform better as an organization to the extent that artificial differences in the way people are treated are eliminated. *Note that equity does not mean equality.* There are some differences in pay, benefits, and work areas, based on levels of responsibility and functional needs. However, equity does mean that *where there is no good business reason* to have differences, such as special parking privileges or less medical insurance, that there are no differences.

Our business is growing rapidly, and our ways of doing business are evolving as we learn from experience. Our experience in orienting new employees has taught us to be careful not to exaggerate the differences between our organization and other business organizations. It is our intention to do business in a few ways which we think will be effective, and these ways may be different from what some of us have experienced in the past.

However, we are part of a plant start-up situation. This means that many of the intentions that we have are to be found only partially in practice at this time. It is assumed that each of us is committed to devote the extra effort that it will take to make our organization work as it is intended. It is certain that this effort from each of us will succeed.

Clair in expressing the basic assumption of his operating team. The work ethic was a powerful force that could be released if the proper atmosphere was created. So, the main point of the organizational structure at SEP would be to release that full potential inherent in most workers.

Although American Diesel's main plant at Beacon was unionized, there was to be no union at SEP when it opened. There would be ample protection for the rights of employees, St. Clair's team believed, in an elaborate governance system which would allow all employees to air grievances freely, speak their minds, and seek remedies to perceived inequities. Unions would not be needed to perform such a task, the team hoped. Besides, the operating group felt that at SEP, individuals would represent themselves through their teams and other plant organization. The adversarial relationship which they thought would result from a unionized plant would get in the way of the experimentation in job design. As a result, there would be no union.

The basic unit of organization at SEP would be the team. All employees would be grouped into small teams, and within each team emphasis would be on self-management, learning new skills, and performance. Teams would be trusted to regulate themselves, keep track of their own performance, and encourage growth and the acquisition of new skills on the part of individual members.

Groups of between three and four teams would then be clustered into what were called "businesses." One of the basic assumptions of St. Clair's organizing group was that the maximum number of people any business unit ought to employ should range between 200 and 300 people. That size would allow the business manager to know personally each and every employee. Since it was assumed that SEP would quickly grow to 1,000 employees and eventually to 2,000, the plant was divided into five "businesses," each operating as autonomously as possible under its own business manager. Those business managers would oversee and direct the operations of various teams assigned to them.

As a reflection of their belief that, given the goal of creating an open and trusting environment, people would motivate themselves, St. Clair's organizing team replaced the traditional first-line supervisor with a "team advisor." While first-line supervisors usually represented company policy and policed the workers assigned to them, SEP's team advisors would work *with*, not above, their teams to facilitate performance and the acquisition of new skills. To fill these positions, St. Clair wanted to find individuals not just technically proficient but also able to work well with people in a nonauthoritarian, nonthreatening manner.

The compensation system at SEP would also reflect the organizing team's belief in growth and responsibility, and a shared commitment to the attainment of plant goals. To reduce the traditional gulf between workers and management, all SEP employees were to be salaried. Machine and assembly workers who traditionally were paid by the hour (as was the case in all other American Diesel plants) would be salaried along with management personnel. Everyone would be expected to work 40 hours a week and to make up any missed time. Further, the compensation system was based not on seniority but the acquisition of new skills and the willingness to perform varied tasks. Wages at SEP for machine and assembly workers would be relatively high compared to the prevailing wages of the community—in the 75th percentile—but, because of the generally depressed condition of the Sedalia area, low in comparison to other American Diesel plants. St. Clair and his team viewed pay not as a motivator but as a way of achieving equity among plant employees.

Participation at all levels; that was the key. "Participation," St. Clair said, "is a way of doing business effectively through achieving quality decisions or a commitment to carrying them out." St. Clair was adamant on the point that SEP was *not* a social experiment. "We are dealing with ways to develop and utilize the best skills and abilities of our human resources, while at the same time creating a more satisfying work environment."

INSIDE SEDALIA ENGINE PLANT

SEP's parent company, American Diesel, had been producing, manufacturing, and selling diesel engines, components, and parts since 1919. From corporate headquarters in Beacon, Illinois, American Diesel had constantly held onto a sizable share of the market—usually fluctuating between 40 percent and 50 percent—despite competition from such corporate giants as John Deere, Caterpillar, and even General Motors. Over the years, American Diesel has built its reputation on high-priced engines of excellent quality and exceptional service follow-up.

The town American Diesel selected in 1974 as the site for its new plant—Sedalia, Minnesota—was home to 55,000 people. The work force was both highly skilled and strongly union. Sedalia Engine Plant set up shop in a 930,000-square-foot plant vacated three years earlier. "Just to give you an idea of how enormous this place is," explained Connie Kelleher, one of SEP's directors, "they tell me you could put nine football fields on the roof. All you have to do is walk back and forth between the front office and the assembly lines once or twice, and you'll have no trouble believing that." (See Exhibit 2 for a floor design of the plant.)

Once it was operational, the physical layout of SEP reflected its operating philosophy. The south end of the plant was made up of compact, self-contained manufacturing lines for various components of the diesel engine: pistons, piston liners, camshafts, camboxes, flywheels, etc. The northern half of the facility housed the elongated assembly lines, added after the plant opened, small test rooms, and the loading docks.

The 24-foot-high building was open from top to bottom except for a core of offices dividing the plant down the middle. A few of those core offices

EXHIBIT 2
Plant Layout —May 1979

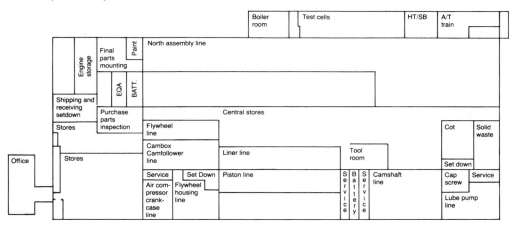

were built when the plant first opened. Later, in an effort to link staff support personnel more closely to the manufacturing functions, SEP began to enlarge those core offices so that even more of the support people could be placed right in the middle of the plant. When construction was completed on those offices, they stretched from the east to the west end of the plant, effectively shutting off the 10 manufacturing lines from the 2 assembly lines.

Sitting at the front of the plant in a small cluster of offices were the plant manager, his director of organizational development and training, and the finance department.

Internal Plant Structure

There was two separate but overlapping structures set up within SEP: the operating organization and the governance structure.

Operating Organization. The operating organization was divided into five levels: plant manager, directors, business managers, team advisors, and team members (see Exhibit 3). The plant manager, first St. Clair and then Goble, had overall responsibility for the operations at SEP. The seven directors served as the plant manager's team and were responsible for manufacturing and/or staff support functions. The combining of these two functions was done in order to create and maintain close ties between support and manufacturing operations, and to develop managerial talent. Thus, three of the directors—purchasing and materials, manufacturing services, and reliability—had both staff support and manufacturing functions under them. The director of purchasing and materials, for instance,

EXHIBIT 3

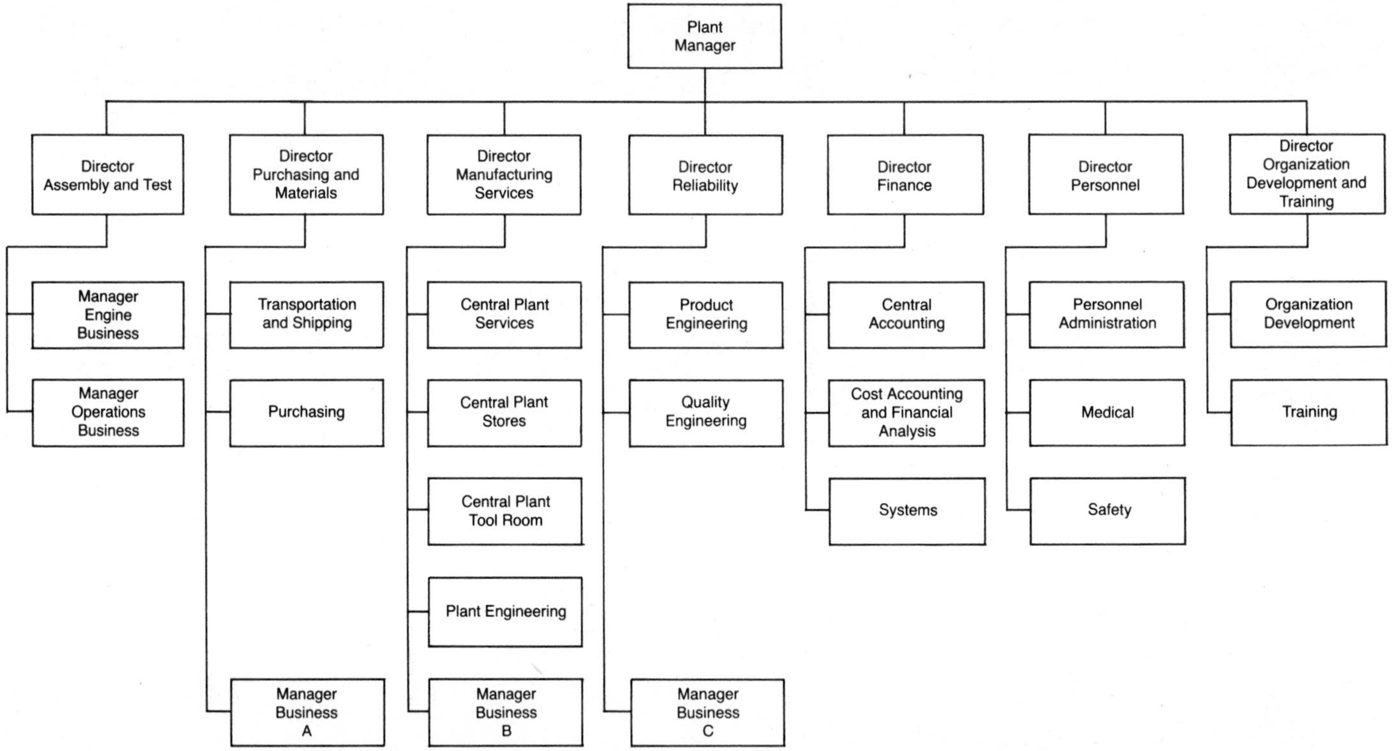

Plant Manager

- Director Assembly and Test
  - Manager Engine Business
  - Manager Operations Business
- Director Purchasing and Materials
  - Transportation and Shipping
  - Purchasing
  - Manager Business A
- Director Manufacturing Services
  - Central Plant Services
  - Central Plant Stores
  - Central Plant Tool Room
  - Plant Engineering
  - Manager Business B
- Director Reliability
  - Product Engineering
  - Quality Engineering
  - Manager Business C
- Director Finance
  - Central Accounting
  - Cost Accounting and Financial Analysis
  - Systems
- Director Personnel
  - Personnel Administration
  - Medical
  - Safety
- Director Organization Development and Training
  - Organization Development
  - Training

had responsibility not only for staff support functions like transportation, shipping, and purchasing, but also for one of the plant's manufacturing businesses. Three directors—finance, personnel, and organizational development and training—had only staff support functions under them; the director of assembly and test oversaw two manufacturing businesses.

Dropping down another level to business manager, the five managers in the plant reported on a direct line to their assigned director and served as heads of the five, semiautonomous "businesses" in the plant. The assembly-related businesses were named—engine business and operations business—and the other three merely were assigned letters "A," "B," and "C" (Exhibit 4). The business manager for operations had responsibility for seven assembly teams as well as a manufacturing support group made up of engineering services, specialized skills trainers, materials, finance, training, and order administration. In fact, every business within SEP had a number of staff support functions as well as a group of manufacturing teams (Exhibit 5).

In point of fact, during St. Clair's tenure as plant manager, the business managers became an important part of the plant's leadership.

Tom O'Donnell, business manager: We were a real tight-knit group when Don was here. The business managers spent a lot of time together and a lot of time with Don. I know the organization charts didn't show it, but we really reported on a direct line to St. Clair.

St. Clair relied heavily on his business managers for the day-to-day plant operations, while he and two or three of his directors—Danney Goble among them—provided the overall leadership. That close relationship between St. Clair and his business managers tended to blur the precise functions of the director level.

Next, there were team advisors—SEP's first-line supervisors—and, finally, team members. (Their functions will be defined below in the section on teams.)

Governance Structure.   St. Clair was convinced that the operating organization of SEP would not be enough to ensure a high level of commitment and participation. In addition, he felt the need for some sort of "safety valve" mechanism that would allow people to air grievances and work-related problems. There needed to be another structure that would allow people from all five levels to interact, and to work to resolve plantwide issues affecting the work environment. For that reason, his original organizing team developed a complex and multilevel governance structure to parallel the operating organization.

Atop the entire governance structure sat the plant operating team (POT). Made up of the plant manager and his directors, POT was charged with giving a general sense of direction to the plant. It worked with American Diesel on plant objectives and commitments, and was responsible for specific strategy and policy decisions, and other matters of plantwide concern.

EXHIBIT 4
Organization of "Business" at SEP

DIRECTOR OF ASSEMBLY AND TEST

Manager, Engine Business		*Manager, Operations Business*	
Manufacturing Teams	*Support Teams*	*Manufacturing Teams*	*Support Teams*
Final parts mounting	Engineering services	7 assembly teams	Engineering services
Test teams	Skilled tradesmen	Purchase parts inspection	Skilled tradesmen
Shipping	Materials		Materials
	Finance		Finance
	Training		Training
			Order administration

DIRECTOR OF PURCHASING AND MATERIALS

Manager, Business A

Manufacturing Teams	*Support Teams*
Flywheel	Engineering services
Flywheel housing	Skilled tradesmen
Air compressor crankcase	Materials
Cambox casting	Finance
Cambox kingsbury	Training
Cambox assembly	
Mechanical variable timing	

DIRECTOR OF MANUFACTURING SERVICES

Manager, Business B

Manufacturing Teams	*Support Teams*
Pistons	Engineering services
Piston liners	Skilled tradesmen
	Materials
	Finance
	Training

DIRECTOR OF RELIABILITY

Manufacturing Teams	*Support Teams*
Camshaft	Engineering services
Lube pump	Skilled tradesmen
Capscrews	Materials
Crankshaft	Finance
	Training

EXHIBIT 5
Representative Mature Manufacturing Business

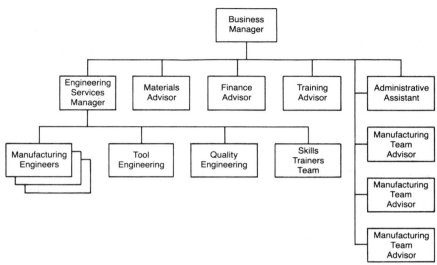

The second major governance organization was the board of representatives (BOR), made up of 20 elected representatives from all the plant's business and functional areas. BOR acted as a forum or sounding board for SEP employees. New ideas, unique viewpoints, and lingering complaints were aired at regular BOR meetings. Employees used BOR to debate matters ranging from concerns over the compensation system and layoffs, to complaints of petty thefts within the plant. BOR could then take suggestions, comments, or complaints to POT to seek some kind of resolution.

St. Clair had hoped that the atmosphere at BOR meetings would be such that all employees would feel free to speak their minds. But when Danney Goble became plant manager, he was somewhat surprised to find a considerable amount of dissatisfaction with the way BOR operated. Staff support personnel in BOR complained that manufacturing representatives often clogged BOR meetings with complaints about "petty" problems like overflowing toilets and disciplinary matters. Manufacturing team representatives responded by insisting that they had nowhere else to go with such problems. BOR was the only structure in SEP that offered them the opportunity to get together and jointly air their grievances and concerns. Besides, they countered, most BOR discussions were monopolized by staff support people.

Numerous other groups and task forces within the plant focused on specific issues. One informal safety valve mechanism begun by St. Clair and continued by Goble was the "fireside chat." Once or twice a week, the plant manager invited into his office a small group of employees representing a cross-section of the plant. St. Clair started the chats in order to keep "tuned in" to the plant. By speaking confidentially and keeping those confidences, he also hoped to create a feeling of trust that would allow any plant employee to come to him with their problems and concerns.

Plant Leadership

For five years, the personality of plant manager Don St. Clair galvanized SEP. The plant had been from its founding, an intimate and important part of St. Clair's life, and he in turn provided a model of enthusiasm and complete commitment to SEP employees. "He was a father figure to us," explained one of the original business managers. "Whatever 'charisma' means, Don had it," added an advisor.

Everyone, from directors to team members, leaned heavily on St. Clair during those start-up years, relying on the power of his personality and the force of his commitment to steer SEP through the hurdles of its early development. "This place looked and smelled like Don St. Clair," noted director Doug Pippy. "The whole thing was an extension of his personality."

St. Clair saw himself as a plantwide "agitator." Every day, he spent some time on the lines talking to people, questioning them, encouraging, prodding them to take responsibility and to live up to the expectations of the plant. "He was one hell of a guy," said a team member who had been with the plant from the beginning. "And we worked harder for him."

St. Clair's managerial style was wide open, Danney Goble observed of his predecessor:

> He was the kind of guy who liked to have his hand in everything. He liked to know everything that was going on. Because everybody in the plant—directors, managers, team members—trusted him, they would come to him with their problems. Anything they couldn't work out on the floor, they brought it right to Don. And he was glad to talk to them and work with them. His door was always open.

SEP's Teams

Manufacturing and staff support personnel at SEP were all organized into small teams, each with its own team advisor. Teams were usually made up of 20 people, although they occasionally grew to 50 or 80 people over three shifts. If a particular line or machine operated over three shifts, workers on all three shifts would belong to the same team, with only one team advisor. At least once a month, team meetings would have to be arranged so that members from all three shifts could gather at the same time. Since all decisions at SEP were meant to be made at the lowest possible level, each team was designed to be as functionally autonomous as possible.

Manufacturing Teams.   Each of the 40 manufacturing teams was clustered around a business manager, reporting to that manager through its own team advisor. Team members operated assigned machines or completed assembly tasks. However, at SEP a premium was placed on the ability of each team member to perform not just one but a variety of tasks. Thus, each team was expected to handle setup and maintenance as well as operation of the machines or assembly tasks assigned to it. Furthermore, each individual team member was expected, over the course of five years, to learn how to perform these functions on each of the machines. The members of a piston line team, for instance, should eventually be able to perform not just one but each job and support function assigned to the team as a whole. (See Exhibit 6 for a description of team responsibilities.) One of the signs of team maturity was the degree to which the team members did, in fact, encourage each other to learn and perform new tasks.

Out of necessity, the assembly teams operated somewhat differently than the machining teams. (See Exhibit 7 for assembly-line master plan.) Teams like the piston team were involved in the manufacturing of a "whole" product. Each of the seven assembly-line teams, however, was assigned just one stage in the assembly of a diesel engine. They completed that stage and then passed the engine along a conveyor to the next team. The line was constructed in such a way that each team could build up a surplus of from 8 to 10 engines. The plant manager, together with the director of assembly and the business managers from assembly and testing and shipping, set monthly rates of completion based on corporate demand. The entire assembly line was expected to schedule and pace their work in order to meet that monthly goal. Another, less formal motivator existed for assembly teams. If one team worked so much more slowly than the next that the faster team depleted its surplus, that second, quicker team would find itself with nothing to do. "If that happens," explained Dave Palmer, director of organizational development and training, "members from the faster team will walk over to the other group and not so politely ask, 'What the hell are you guys doing?' "

The functions of SEP's manufacturing teams went far beyond the operation and maintenance of machines, however. Each team was also expected to do its own administrative housekeeping. Team members kept track of their own team's inventory; ordered and inspected necessary materials; documented their team's production, costs, attendance, and performance; oversaw safety practices; and participated in budgeting and forecasting. In addition, each team was responsible for hiring its own members. Teams were to work with their advisor in performance appraisal, disciplinary actions, and even salary determination.

These administrative, housekeeping, and personnel functions were known in SEP as vertical tasks. Some members of the team were expected to devote some of their working time to a vertical task such as material ordering, budgeting, inventory control, or keeping cost records. Who does

EXHIBIT 6
Team Responsibilities

1. Participation in the selection of its members.
   a. Departing team members.
   b. Additional labor force requirements.
2. Participation in the setting and administering of rules governing behavior affecting the accomplishments of the teams and organization's objectives.
   a. Attendance.
   b. Housekeeping.
   c. Safety practices.
   d. Quality and quantity.
   e. Training and team participation.
3. Training of its members.
   a. Evaluation of competence levels of each member.
   b. Planning needs of team and individuals.
   c. Assume active role in training programs.
4. Distribution and assignment of tasks among its members.
   a. To cover for nonparticipation.
   b. To provide training opportunities.
   c. To assign individuals to committees.
5. Coping with production problems that occur within or between the teams' areas of responsibilites.
   a. Quality.
   b. Delivery.
   c. Service.
6. Regulation and control of process functions which cross crew boundaries, including planning and scheduling material requirements.
7. Participation in setting of organization's goals and objectives.
   a. Cost reduction.
   b. Quality levels.
   c. Budget control.
   d. Product ouptut.
8. Achievement of its objectives; ensuring that its members contribute toward the objectives.
9. Document and communicate the achievements and needs of the team to the necessary organizations in the systems.

Following will be provided to team:

1. All relevant resources and information needed to carry out its responsibilities.
2. Rewards according to the individual level of competence attained and contribution to the team achievement of its goals. These levels of competence will be based on objective measures of the ability to perform more than one combination of tasks.

Guarantees:

1. No difference in privileges between team members and other members of the organization except as required externally.
2. No barriers to attainment of higher competence levels.

EXHIBIT 7
Assembly-Line Master Plan

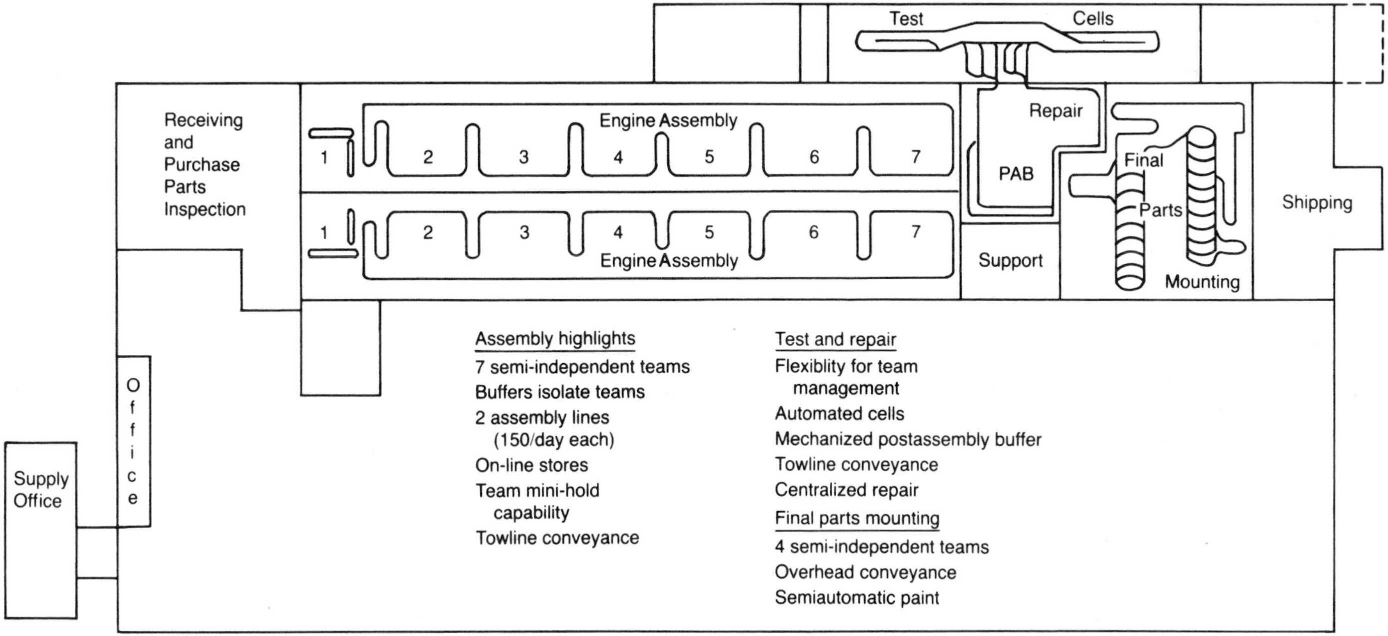

Receiving and Purchase Parts Inspection

Office

Supply Office

Engine Assembly
1 2 3 4 5 6 7

Engine Assembly
1 2 3 4 5 6 7

Assembly highlights
7 semi-independent teams
Buffers isolate teams
2 assembly lines
(150/day each)
On-line stores
Team mini-hold capability
Towline conveyance

Test

Cells

Repair

PAB

Support

Final Parts Mounting

Shipping

Test and repair
Flexibility for team management
Automated cells
Mechanized postassembly buffer
Towline conveyance
Centralized repair
Final parts mounting
4 semi-independent teams
Overhead conveyance
Semiautomatic paint

what vertical task? What percentage of the workday should be spent on a vertical task? These were decisions that each team was to make for itself. Such assignments usually lasted a year before being rotated to other team members.

The degree to which individual teams performed up to the ideal established by St. Clair's organizing team varied considerably. Mature teams encouraged individual members to learn new tasks and participate fully in devising ways to reduce costs, in evaluating performance of individual members, and in helping to correct the behavior of individuals that might be harmful to the team. The most mature teams—about one quarter of the teams, Dave Palmer estimated in 1979—were virtually self-managing and autonomous. The less mature teams depended almost entirely on the intervention of the team advisor to handle matters relating to training, housekeeping, and evaluation.

Perhaps the most dramatic example of a team handling its own affairs occurred in the cambox team in 1979. Cambox production had begun three years earlier and grown rapidly to 1,500 camboxes a day. The size of the team grew with the production rate: over 80 people spread over three shifts with one advisor. While the advisor felt the team was operating well, many team members thought otherwise. Said team member Sally Moore:

> Everything was chaos. There was absolutely no communication between shifts. You would leave a message for the next shift, telling them what needed to be done. They either didn't get the message, or would ignore it. Nobody really gave a damn.

Signs of poor performance seemed to spread. Low morale led to low efficiency, high turnover, and constant overtime. Quality suffered, and there was no way of knowing who or what was at fault. "There were so many people and so little communication," said Moore, "that there was no accountability." Finally, in one month American Diesel had to recall 35,000 camboxes, all made at SEP.

Even then, the team advisor refused to admit that he had a problem. But three months after the recall, Moore and fellow team member Dick Smith decided to take some action. With 80 people crowded into a meeting room for the regular team meeting, and with the advisor not present, the two stood up and expressed their feelings. Right in the middle of the meeting, Smith called St. Clair and asked him to join them. St. Clair did, and encouraged the team to develop, on their own, some plan for reorganization. Moore and Smith then called for an informal committee to consider the possibilities. Two representatives from each shift met every night after work, sometimes for five hours at a sitting, for five weeks.

Their first conclusion was that the team was too big and should be divided into four smaller teams. Recalled Dick Smith:

> Not everyone favored dividing us up like that. They said you'd lose product identification that way. But the committee decided that the number of

people on a team is more important than product identity. It's not looking at a cambox and saying "I made that" that gives me satisfaction. It's teamwork and cooperation that makes this place special.

In dividing up the tasks among the four teams—casting and drilling, assembly, variable machine timing, and inventory control—the committee made sure that each team still retained some variety of tasks. And to ensure better communications between shifts, a coordinator was appointed for the second and third shifts of each team.

The impact of the cambox reorganization was both immediate and dramatic. Averaging 920 camboxes per day for the year prior to reorganization, the reorganization cambox line upped its daily average to between 1,100 and 1,200 camboxes per day. Overtime dropped by 50 percent, scrap was reduced from 17 to 5 percent, turnover from 30 to 4 percent, while machine utilization increased from 42 to 56 percent (a measurement of the total time available over three shifts a machine is in use). Subjective assessments— team morale, communications, and problem solving—were all positive as well. "It seems that whenever we have a chaotic situation, and a team is able to deal with that chaos, then productivity rises," said St. Clair. "I'm not sure why that is, but it always happens."

While nobody at SEP could say for sure what made one team mature and another not, there seemed to be general agreement on the importance of three factors: the size of the team, the length of time the team had been together, and the willingness of the advisor to encourage team growth.

Staff Support Teams.   Like the manufacturing people, staff support personnel in the plant also worked as part of a team. Each team had its own advisor. Staff support teams provided specific services—quality and product engineering; financial analysis; materials planning, purchasing, and handling; maintenance duties; engineering, procurement, and installation of machine tools—in support of the manufacturing teams. A manufacturing team member assigned to the vertical task of forecasting and budgeting, for instance, could obtain expert consultation from staff support personnel.

Orientation.   St. Clair felt that in order to acclimate new employees to the drastically different work environment of SEP, all new employees should be subjected to an intensive orientation program. Therefore, once hired, each new team member went through an orientation program consisting of 13 sessions to be attended during the initial six months of employment. They discussed plant history, philosophy, goals, and practices. St. Clair candidly admitted, "As hard as we tried to keep these orientations realistic, we really ended up building unrealistic expectations of the amount of freedom they were going to find, of the excitement and the challenge of working here. When they went back out onto the floor, we hoped they'd turn whatever disappointment they might have felt into a determination to work twice as hard to change their expectations into reality."

The reaction of newly hired SEP personnel to the orientation program was decidedly mixed. Some complained about precisely what St. Clair talked about, building unrealistic expectations. Team member Dick Kirkendall said,

> We would be told all about teams, about how independent they are. But then I went to work and found out there were a lot of decisions we just weren't allowed to make as a team.

Others found the courses to be over their heads. Said team member Bob Reeds,

> They kept talking about "work systems." I know what that means now. But when I first got here, I was fresh off the streets. I had just barely finished high school, you know? They'd say "work systems," and I didn't know what the hell they were talking about.

How Did Teams Work?   Most of the workers at SEP came there after some experience in traditional, often unionized, plants. The idea of maximum flexibility, of responsibilities ranging far beyond the operation of a single machine, and of a commitment to learning new skills often struck them as rather alien when they first arrived at SEP. "I used to work in a plant," said Mike Cassity, whose experience was typical of most SEP workers. "There, I had a job to do and I did the same thing every day."

Still, the vast majority of the team members responded enthusiastically to the challenge of increased expectations:

Frank McCarthy, team member: Honest to God, I'm excited to get here every morning. I always hated work, but not now. I like living in Sedalia and raising my family here. But there weren't many good jobs around, and I thought I'd have to move. Then this came along. I'm as happy as can be about it.

Ed Purcell, team member: Before I came here, I was a clothing salesman. I made good money, but I was bored crazy. When I came here I took almost a $10,000 cut in pay! Can you believe that? And I've never regretted that decision for a minute. And if you think I'm nuts, I can tell you that there are plenty of people in this town who would give up a lot—maybe not as much as I did, but a lot—to work here.

Dave Thelen, team member: This is the best place I've ever worked, no doubt about it. A lot of the guys around here say they'd like to move up eventually, maybe become an advisor. But not me. As long as I can make enough money on this assembly line, this is where I'd like to stay.

One of the team problems that attracted Danney Goble's immediate attention had to do with discipline. St. Clair had created a mechanism, called the correction action process, for correcting "unacceptable" behavior—substandard performance, abuse of paid time off and property, disrespect for others. This involved informal counseling with the team's advisor. But some business managers complained that the process was not working. They identified absenteeism as a key concern, and heard reports of other disciplinary problems. Some team members on third shifts were sleeping on the job, and there were occasional outbreaks of fighting. In one case, the piston team decided to fire an unruly member, a dismissal upheld by the advisor, business manager, and director. The discharged team member, however, appealed directly to St. Clair who ordered him reinstated. (He lasted another month before being fired again, this time with no appeal.)

"One of the problems," thought director Connie Kelleher, "was that we just didn't have any common definitions. What *is* excessive absenteeism? What *is* disrespect for others? Nobody could say for sure, and many teams were asking for better definitions."

Stress: A Side Effect of High Commitment.   "I'm going to tell you something about this place you probably won't want to hear," said a team member. "There's a lot of stress here, a hell of a lot of stress."

By pushing down levels of responsibility and increasing expectations of commitment on the part of team members, SEP had introduced a new element into the lives of many line workers. Most team members had previously worked in traditional factory settings. Once they came to SEP, they were told to help set production and cost goals, maintain machines as well as run them, learn budgeting, and make up missed time on weekends. That high level of commitment had its rewards—enriched, interesting work—but also its cost—personal stress. There were no facts or figures on the level of stress among SEP's team members or the impact that stress had on their families. But most SEP team members recognized the problem after a few years of working there, and spoke candidly of it.

Mike Cassity, team member: My old job was pretty dull, but at least I knew what I was supposed to do, and did it, day in and day out. When I got interviewed for my job here, they told me all the things I would be expected to do: keep books, order materials, go to meetings, things like that. They asked me whether I could do that kind of work, whether I'd enjoy it? I said sure! I wanted the job, right? But when I got here and found out they really meant it. . . . My God! I do it, but it's hard. I worry a lot more now than I ever did before. I think you'll see a lot of high blood pressure and ulcers around here.

Ed Purcell, team member: Sometimes, to make sure we get everything done, our team will decide to work some extra hours or come in on the weekend. But my wife just can't understand why we do that. She gets really angry.

Henry Wallace, team member: We're always being taught and encouraged to talk things out and share our feelings. In team meetings, in BOR, we're always talking out things that are on our minds. That was all new to me at first, but eventually it became part of the way I did things. But then I'd go home and want to talk to my wife about things that were happening at the plant. I never did that at my other job. I'd just come home and forget about work. But there's something about this place that makes you want to share everything. And my wife would just look at me like I was nuts.

Harry Holmes, team member: We all work so hard together and spend so much time together that we become sort of a family. Maybe that's why there are so many romances and divorces here. People on my team call this "little Peyton Place." That's what happened to me. I got divorced last month.

Team Advisors. SEP's first-line supervisors, the team advisors, were given responsibility for the training of individual team members and the development of a mature, well-functioning, self-managing team. The SEP advisor was to act as a team builder, communicator, trainer, and occasional fill-in; but not as an autocratic overseer and decision maker. The plant sought advisors with a firm grounding in technical know-how, combined with interpersonal skills.

The team advisors sat in on the daily meetings of their teams, usually held in the first half hour of the workday, but their function there was to lead discussions rather than issue commands. They held personnel files for their teams, arranged for technical and professional advice from staff support personnel within the plant, and coordinated training for their teams.

When Goble became plant manager, he worried that several of his team advisors did not seem to be effective. The position had always been a difficult one to fill and maintain. While the original advisors came almost exclusively from supervisory positions in traditionally organized plants, their replacements came, for the most part, from within the plant. St. Clair felt tremendous pressure from team members to provide a place within the organization for them to rise to, and that place was the advisor position. But the practice of promotion from within was not entirely satisfactory. Between 25 percent and 50 percent of all the advisors who had been promoted from team members quit their position within a year or two to return to their team. Why?

Bob Kerr, team advisor: What I'm finding is that the more mature my team gets, the duller my job is. I used to help out on all the machines and teach people how to use them. Now, my team doesn't need my help, and they do their own training. So I spend most of my time settling arguments and talking to people about why they missed a day or two of work. That gets old fast.

Jim Gilbert, team advisor: When I think of all the extra hours I put in, coming around on second and third shift, attending meetings—I often get here at 5:30 in the morning and leave at 5:30 at night—I figure that I'm getting paid less on an hourly basis than when I was a team member.

Goble worried that while team advisors from the inside seemed to be somewhat dissatisfied, he was not getting new people to come in from the outside to fill new openings. Since advisors rarely rose to a higher rank at SEP, it seemed like a dead-end job. And the old problem of finding someone with both technical and people skills made it difficult to select the right person.

One of the constant complaints Goble heard from team members was the conflict between the demands of their advisor for maximum effort on the machine or assembly lines and the expectation that all team members would participate in vertical tasks. Time spent by a team member on budgeting and forecasting, ordering materials, or attending BOR meetings was time away from the line. Some advisors understood, even encouraged this as a necessary and significant part of the work day; others did not.

Mike Cassity, team member: Most advisors here put too much pressure on you. You go off to do a vertical task, and the advisor says to you, "Why the hell are you gone so often?" And then, when you're being evaluated, they say, "Why the hell haven't you done this or that vertical task?"

The pressure from some advisors for members to stay on the line was so great that a few members openly questioned whether the plant was really committed to their professed ideals. "I'll tell you this," said one disillusioned team member, "around here, production is number one. Quality of work life? That's two, three, or even four."

Performance Measurement.   The most significant continuing measurement of team performance came from cost-per-piece figures. St. Clair and his organizing team rejected a cost system based on standard costs established by industrial engineers. Instead SEP would establish a cost system based on improvements from previous performance. There would be a base cost for each piece that would be the real cost from the previous year. Each team in the plant would report monthly on its own cost per piece, and that figure would be measured against the base cost as well as the previous month's performance. Each manufacturing team would be responsible for computing its own cost per piece and for working to reduce that cost.

The monthly reports compiled by each manufacturing team were simple, yet complete. Costs were given for variable manufacturing expenses (broken down to such items as rework, maintenance, scrap, operating supplies, tools, and freight), semivariable expenses (salary, gas, travel, taxes, insurance) and total team costs. (See Exhibit 8 for a two-month cost-per-piece report of one SEP team.) Those figures were then compared to the previously supplied base costs. At the same time, the plant manager and the directors set plantwide goals for cost reductions on specific line items (direct materials, team expenses, etc.). In 1980, the primary goal was to reduce costs by the rate of inflation.

Dave Palmer explained the reasoning behind the continuing stress on this type of measurement: "The cost-per-piece computation is important because it gives each team a feeling of autonomy, a belief that they are key to our productivity." The cost-per-piece figures allowed St. Clair to assess the performance of teams at SEP in terms both of actual costs and cost reductions, and allowed teams access to the information necessary to make good economic decisions.

EXHIBIT 8
Cost per Piece, Cambox Camfollower (April 10, 1980)

	Base Cost	March		February		Cost Reduction (increase)	Total $	Y-T-D Reduction (increase)
Quantity—production		35,556		26,038				$70,356
Direct material at base cost	$25.193	$ 895,762	$25.193	$655,975	$25.193			
Direct labor at base rate	4.624	130,542	3.672	103,257	3.966	$0.952	$33,849	
Team manufacturing expense:								
Variable:								
Rework	0.009	155	0.004	53	0.002			
Premium	0.633	23,699	0.667	18,313	0.703			
Maintenance	1.138	45,409	1.277	39,920	1.533			
Manufacturing tools, gages	0.086	6,430	0.181	965	0.037			
Operating supplies	1.090	41,805	1.176	29,983	1.152			
Scrap—manufacturing	1.090	27,357	0.769	27,465	1.055			
Scrap—supplier	0.522	42,585	1.198	173,716	6.672			
Scrap recovery	(0.455)	(46,117)	(1.297)	(209,754)	(8.056)			
Others	0.047	3,519	0.099	14,314	.550			
Subtotal variable	4.160	144,842	4.074	94,975	3.648			
Freight	0.716	28,150	0.791	14,608	0.561			
Total variable	4.876	172,922	4.865	109,583	4.209			
Semivariable:								
Salaries, wages—fringes	1.287	42,071	1.183	38,162	1.465			
Power	0.268	21,535	.606	6,995	0.269			
Gas	0.011	535	.015	233	0.009			
Travel	0.011	305	.008	—	—			
Depreciation	1.210	29,892	.841	29,643	1.138			
Taxes, insurance	0.076	2,407	.068	1,980	.076			
Total semivariable	2.863	96,745	2.721	77,013	2.957			
Total team manufacturing expense	7.739	269,737	7.586	186,596	7.166	0.153	5,440	(44,555)
Total team cost	$37.556	$1,296,041	$36.451	$945,828	$36.325	$1.105	$39,289	$25,801

The Compensation System at SEP

The main distinction made in the plant was not the usual one between hourly and salaried employees but the legal one between those who must be paid extra for overtime work—nonexempt—and those who are not paid for working more than 40 hours—exempt.[1] Team members constituted the nonexempt employees, while advisors, business managers, directors, and the plant manager made up the exempt group.

In keeping with this attempt to minimize distinctions between workers, many of the status symbols typically associated with a plant hierarchy were nowhere in sight at SEP. Dress codes for exempt employees along with special parking spaces and dining facilities were never introduced. St. Clair was convinced that the removal of such artificial distinctions enhanced communications within the plant. At least some team members, however, found this attempt to downplay the gulf between management and workers to be somewhat superficial. "They wouldn't dream of wearing a coat and tie to work," said one veteran team member half-jokingly about the directors and plant manager. "I guess they think it makes them look like us. But after work, they go their way and we go ours."

Most team members, while appreciative of their salaried rather than hourly status, good-naturedly mocked any suggestion that there was no social distance within the plant. "It's as simple as this," commented one team member. "When we have plant athletic teams, they [exempts] sign up for the golf team and we sign up for the bowling team."

Exempt Compensation System.   Initially, SEP placed all exempt employees into 3 broad pay categories (as opposed to the 13 narrowly defined categories in place at American Diesel's Beacon plant). This, it was thought, would allow people to progress through a series of pay increases without quickly coming to the top rate for their category. "We hoped this would encourage stability and development," explained Dave Palmer. "People could get their raises without seeking other jobs and moving to different plants."

"That just didn't work," admitted Palmer. "People here were getting the same money as other executives within American Diesel, but they wanted the promotions as well. They complained that their careers were moving more slowly here than they would elsewhere in the American Diesel system." Just before St. Clair left in 1979, SEP moved to a seven-level exempt compensation system. Team advisors would be placed on one of the first three levels depending on a combination of education and job experience. Their annual salaries would range from $15,120 to $30,420. Staff support managers were assigned to level four ($21,840 to $34,920); business managers to level five ($26,220 to $41,940); plant directors to level six ($32,280 to

---

[1] For overtime work (work over 40 hours), SEP's nonexempt workers were paid on an hourly basis.

\$51,600), and the plant manager to level seven (\$40,680 to \$65,040). A progression matrix was then constructed by POT which would clarify the combination of skills, experience, and performance that would allow the individual to progress from the minimum through the midpoint to the maximum of the salary level.

Nonexempt Compensation System. The compensation of nonexempt employees was supposed to be based entirely on the acquisition of skills by individual team members, and the willingness of the individual to perform those skills. "It's a mistake to base pay solely on the acquisition of new skills," explained Dave Palmer. "People will learn something just to get more money, but then never put what they learned to use." There were five skill levels that each team member was expected to reach, one year at a time (there was also a six-month increment for the first year only, contingent on attendance at the 13 orientation sessions). All nonexempts worked out a yearly performance plan with their advisor, stating in writing what skills they would acquire and tasks they would perform during the year. At the end of each of the first five years, team members would be evaluated—by the team advisor, except in the case of an extremely mature team in which case the entire team would participate—on how well they had met those expectations. Promotion to a higher level depended on meeting expectations for performance and growth.

On some teams, members were reluctant to oppose openly the awarding of an increment to a fellow member. "Nobody wants to stand up at a meeting and say so-and-so shouldn't get a raise this year," said one team member. "If you do that, what's going to happen to you when it's time for your raise to be considered?" On those teams, the yearly increments designed to recognize the acquisition of skills became strictly seniority advances. Some team members, advisors, even business managers, insisted that they knew of no instances when a team member was denied a yearly raise. St. Clair acknowledged that while there were several instances when team members were denied a raise, compensation had indeed become a seniority-based system.

Another shortcoming of the five-level plan was the question of what happened after the fifth year. By the time Goble became plant manager, there were a number of five-year employees who wondered about that point. They could still receive general raises along with Beacon. They could not, however, receive increments based on the acquisition of new skills. "Do they expect our people to stop growing after five years?" asked one team advisor. "When I get a chance to talk to our new plant manager, I'd like to ask him that."

Each of the five levels was given a flat rate. At first, POT pegged that rate almost entirely to the prevailing wages in the Sedalia area. SEP's wages were competitive in comparison to similar workers in the community, but because it was a depressed area, they tended to be rather low when compared to American Diesel's Beacon employees. In order to achieve greater equity within the corporation, POT sought to upgrade nonexempt wages in 1977. (See Exhibit 9 for nonexempt wage scale, prior to and immediately following this upgrading.) According to plant policy, POT reviewed the entire compensation system twice a year. In the summer of 1977, POT decided to tie Sedalia's wages to the union-negotiated wage agreements in Beacon. Thus, a four-year employee at Sedalia was to be given a salary derived loosely from the average hourly rate for all four-year employees at Beacon. Fifth-year Sedalia employees, in recognition of their broader skills and responsibilities, would receive more than the average five-year Beacon employee. And because of that tie-in, any negotiated increase in the hourly wages at Beacon would result in an increase at Sedalia. Thus, SEP employees received raises in two ways: an annual advance in salary level for their first five years, and a negotiated increase in the Beacon contract. Between 1977 and 1979, those increases often reached 5 percent and 6 percent every six months. That shift moved SEP into the 90th percentile of wages in the Sedalia community.

EXHIBIT 9
Nonexempt Compensation System

Level	Weekly Salary	Hourly Equivalent
1976:		
Entry	$148	$3.70
6 months	154	3.85
1 year.	160	4.00
2 years	170	4.25
3 years	180	4.50
4 years	190	4.75
5 years	200	5.00
1977:		
Entry	186	4.65
6 months	198	4.95
1 year.	208	5.20
2 years	224	5.60
3 years	236	5.90
4 years	246	6.15
5 years	256	6.40

St. Clair hastened to add that the tie-in to the Beacon wage was not absolute. He and POT members felt no hesitation about adjusting wage rates up or down. "Compensation is one of those areas that I don't think should be too participatory," said St. Clair. "I tried to keep people informed about what we were doing, but me and my directors made final decisions ourselves. Seeking too much participation on compensation issues can get you in a lot of trouble."

One special category among SEP's nonexempt personnel was created for skilled trades people like electricians, or mechanics, who were hired to train team members in their skills. Because SEP was having a problem attracting skilled trades people, POT created a special wage scale for them in 1976. They were placed on a four-level wage scale considerably higher than the five-level scale used for other nonexempts. POT also tied Sedalia's 90 skilled trades people to the hourly wages for the skilled trades at Beacon. Thus, in 1977, the skilled trades entered at $246 a week and topped at $290.

From the beginning, that distinction caused resentment within the plant. Noted Dave Palmer:

> Some of our team members think the skilled trades shouldn't be getting any more than any other nonexempt. They figure they can do just about anything a skilled trades person can do. And for a few of our people in here, that's true. Some go as far as to say we don't need *any* skilled trades here. But the difference in pay between the regular nonexempts and the skilled trades has always been a sore point in the plant.

Concept and Reality at SEP

A minor but revealing example of tension between concept and reality occurred over the question of precisely how to translate into the reality of plant life one of the plant's key philosophical commitments, that of trusting all employees. Team advisor Ed Fremder explained the flap that occurred in the plant over the question of locks:

> We say we trust people around here to act like adults. Because of that, we give people access to whatever tools they need to do their jobs. Somehow, that got translated to mean no locks anywhere in the plant. Doors, equipment, files, everything was kept open. If Don saw a lock anywhere in the plant on *anything*, he'd rip it off. But that's not the real world, is it? People do steal things out there and in here.
>
> Now, at one point, the plant bought three-wheeled bicycles, one for each team, to be used by their members in getting around. Right away, those bikes started disappearing. One team would "borrow" a bike from another without asking, and then "forget" to return it. Teams started hiding their bikes so that others couldn't find them. It got a little ridiculous. Oh, we spent hours debating that one! Meetings all the time. You should have seen it. And we never really decided anything. The bikes just drifted away, and we never bothered replacing them.

That tension between the concept and the realities, and the danger of allowing one to blur the other, had always been a matter of concern at SEP.

PERFORMANCE AT SEDALIA ENGINE PLANT

"It may be too early to tell, but there are encouraging signs that our style of management is starting to pay off." That evaluation was offered in the fall of 1979 by Don St. Clair as he prepared to move on to corporate headquarters in Beacon and pass on managership of SEP to Danney Goble. St. Clair's hopeful appraisal of the plant's performance included the following specific points:

1. Absenteeism, including both excused and nonexcused, was down to about 3 percent, as opposed to about 6 percent at American Diesel's Beacon plant and 8 percent in the Sedalia community.
2. SEP's safety record, while poor at first, was improving steadily.
3. Initial warranty data on SEP's engines were extremely favorable.
4. Plantwide machine utilization usually ran between 60 percent and 70 percent, and sometimes as high as 75 percent, as compared to 50 percent at Beacon.
5. While technological differences existed between the two plants, indirect labor costs were significantly less at Sedalia than the Beacon plant. As the plant reached maturity, that savings could reach 20 percent. Because of the advanced skills of some team members, the need for skilled tradesmen at Sedalia was considerably less than for Beacon. Sedalia also operated with one half the first-line supervisors as Beacon.
6. Team members were continually performing major machine overhauls and minor maintenance.
7. Except for some start-up problems, quality seemed to be running high at Sedalia. For example, the number of engines rejected by testing at Sedalia was 25 percent of the Beacon number.
8. The general climate was positive and focused on plant excellence.
9. The work system and the governance system seemed to be working to the satisfaction of SEP employees. Job satisfaction seemed to be higher than at other American Diesel plants. To support that conclusion, St. Clair pointed to the fact that no serious union drive had been launched at SEP.
10. SEP enjoyed support from American Diesel's CEO, although there was still some skepticism and lack of understanding about SEP from some key people in upper management.

"By far," St. Clair concluded, "this has been the best plant start-up American Diesel has ever had."

Danney Goble Takes Over

"He really walked into a mess," said one of the business managers about Danney Goble's first months as plant manager. "You have to feel bad for the guy."

Goble himself spoke of the challenge not just to him but to the plant. "We now face our most serious test ever of our strength and moral fiber," he observed.

Leadership Turnover. The contrast in the personalities and styles of the old and new plant managers were dramatic and obvious to everyone in the plant.

Tom O'Donnell, business manager: I would characterize the difference this way. Don was people oriented, while Danney is process oriented. He seems to have less tolerance for ambiguity and more need for structure. Don looked at results, like most manufacturing people. Danney's background is engineering, and he seems more concerned with details than Don was. Don was a visionary; Danney is a tactical leader.

Some worried that Goble could not lead the plant in the same way St. Clair had been able to:

Doug Pippy, director: Danney seems to have a problem relating to other people. Like the other new management people he brought in with him, like me in fact, he's a little uncomfortable with other people.

Complicating matters even further was the fact that SEP was undergoing a large turnover among its top-management team. Directors, business managers, even some advisors were leaving SEP in large numbers. Out of its top 24 slots, SEP lost 15 people. Only three of those left American Diesel. The other 12 went to plants within the American Diesel system. "I can understand that," said Dave Palmer. "People left here because they wanted to get more attention from corporate headquarters. So they went to Beacon, or some of the new plants that American Diesel was opening." Moreover, it was customary for managers to move every several years. Also, American Diesel actively sought experienced SEP managers to help them start up new plants.

"The extent of the turnover and the short time in which it happened was completely unanticipated," said Goble. "I feel like I have to reinvent the wheel all over again, to teach these people from scratch what our operating philosophy is all about. This certainly won't make things any easier." (See Exhibit 10 for a history of the number of employees at Sedalia.)

Economic Downturn. "Our company business analysts still are projecting a major downturn 'soon.' Our company president stated two weeks ago we can expect it to be the second worst decline in the last 25 years for American Diesel (second only to 1974–75). All our planning is based on this assumption." (See Exhibit 11 for summary of American Diesel's economic picture.) That was Goble's gloomy assessment of economic conditions, communicated to SEP employees just after he became plant manager. Already, the indicators were unmistakable. In the six months prior to Goble's becoming plant manager, engine orders had declined 18 percent and projections indicated only a worsening of conditions.

"What we're faced with," said Goble, "is the possibility of our first layoffs

EXHIBIT 10
Total Employees

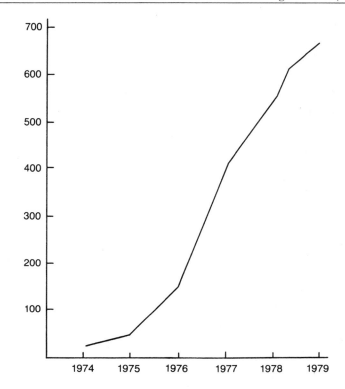

at SEP. The whole corporation is suffering, and we're going to have to shoulder our fair share of that suffering. I'm almost certain that there are layoffs coming, and that those layoffs will be sizable."

In considering the possibility of layoffs, Goble felt that he had an option of two broad policies. SEP could join other American Diesel plants in laying off workers. Although estimates of the extent of that reduction varied from week to week, Goble figured he would have to reduce SEP's work force by about 4 percent or 20 people. On the other hand, he could commit SEP to attempt at least to maintain current levels of employment. What layoffs would do to the high level of commitment that employees had built up over the years, he could not be sure. What layoffs would do to the fragile team member-management relationship of trust, already severely tested by the turnover, he was even less sure.

That second course—protecting all jobs—would still require sacrifice on the part of the plant, and a good deal of creativity in deciding how to absorb losses without cutting employment:

> If I go that route, I'm going to ask for even more commitment on the part of our employees. They're going to have to devote their energies to thinking of ways to cut costs. We might ask, for instance, that some people take

EXHIBIT 11
Economic Performance of American Diesel

	1973	1974	1975	1976	1977	1978	1979
Net sales*	$637,330	$801,566	$761,504	$1,030,532	$1,268,814	$1,520,742	$1,770,851
Profit on sales*	48,739	63,510	36,763	127,726	136,468	130,396	106,991
Net earnings*	26,592	23,775	491	58,622	67,022	64,399	57,938
Earnings per share....	$3.87	$3.31	$0.21	$7.66	$8.22	$7.62	$6.84

* Number in thousands.

temporary, voluntary layoffs. Perhaps we could all go on shorter workweeks. We might have to move people around from one team to another, maybe ask them to do work that we've previously contracted out for. We're getting ready to paint the plant, for instance. I wonder if we could get some of our teams to do that rather than hiring outside painters. But what will that do to our team structure?

Another question I've got to decide, and decide right away, is how much to tell people in the plant? Right now, all of this is speculation. I don't know for sure that we're going to have layoffs. Should I tell people now that it's a distinct possibility? I might be getting them upset over nothing. And with all the concern now with me and the other new people, that kind of bad news might be too unsettling. On the other hand, I'd like to get people involved in thinking about the alternatives. How do I do that unless I tell them everything?

Nonexempt Compensation.   "Danney keeps telling us that we're being paid fairly compared to the people at Beacon," said team member Bob Reed in the fall of 1979:

> Now, I'm getting paid well, but not for the kind of work that I do. I do a hell of a lot more than the people at Beacon. Do they have the vertical tasks that we do? No! Most of the guys here don't even look at Beacon for a comparison. Instead, we look at the auto workers over in Calhoun. They're getting $9 and $10 an hour, while we get $7 or $8.

With the enriched work and higher expectations of commitment, perhaps it was inevitable that nonexempt workers would begin to reconsider their compensation system. But the economic downturn brought the issue to a head just as Goble became plant manager.

Starting in 1977, nonexempt pay levels at SEP had been pegged loosely to the average wage of all four-year employees at Beacon. The economic downturn of 1979 had a dramatic impact on salaries, both at Beacon and Sedalia. Any large-scale layoff at Beacon could hurt Sedalia wages. If employees at Beacon were laid off in large numbers, quite a few employees there would find themselves bumped down to lower paying assignments. That would significantly reduce the average four-year wage at Beacon and if Goble and POT elected to adhere tightly to that average, negatively affect wages at Sedalia. Compounding the problem was the fact that the wages of the skilled trades at Beacon would not be affected by the downturn. Skilled trades people at Sedalia were tied independently to those at Beacon, which meant that they were still in line for significant raises.

Goble had an immediate question to consider in the fall of 1979. If he was to follow the formula of basing four-year Sedalia wages on the precise average of Beacon without making any adjustments, that would mean that team members would receive about two thirds of the increase they had received over the previous several years, while the skilled trades would receive a significantly higher raise. Team members were already concerned about the fact that overtime had been virtually eliminated in 1979, and might be even more upset by the enhanced inequity between themselves and the skilled trades. Could Goble's leadership withstand the disruption that might be caused by such unhappiness among team members?

Goble was clearly leaning toward the idea of sticking literally to the old formula for 1979 and then rethinking it the following year. He anticipated that such a course would raise some concern among team members, so he needed to devise some sort of a process for bringing them into the discussions. On the issue of equity between team members and the skilled trades, Goble figured that was an old problem that would cause no special concern now.

In fact, he worried more about the costs of suddenly abandoning the formula. Some POT directors were suggesting just that. "Let's make an exception in this case," one director argued, "and give the same raises to everyone." But Goble was skeptical:

> If POT went into a meeting and suddenly changed the formula, we would be setting a horrible precedent for the future. And I think that would really upset people. Sure, they would be happy if they got a little more money. But in the long run, they'd be suspicious of us. If we could change this long-held policy behind their backs, so to speak, what else would we change without asking them?

Besides, as one director told Goble, "Our people supported the old logic when it led to good raises. They should be willing to support it now that it means some sacrifice. Besides, people know what the economic situation is. They're not expecting much this time."

The possibility of opening up the process of compensation review to team members immediately after springing on them the news that raises would be reduced promised some disturbing times. Employees might come to view such participation as a kind of formal collective bargaining process over wages. There would be ticklish questions of deciding how employees should be brought into the process. Team members were dissatisfied with their representation in BOR, yet no other in-plant organization included nonexempts.

A Possible Organizing Campaign

Goble was aware of one final development. During the same week that he was considering what direction to take with the compensation system, the following article appeared in the *Sedalia Free Press:*

> Production and maintenance personnel of the Sedalia Engine Plant have been invited to attend an informal meeting at 7 P.M. Thursday at the Holiday Inn, being held by the Machine Workers of America Union.
> Robert Reinhold, a union representative, said his union represents about 6,800 workers in American Diesel's Beacon plant, and that the purpose of

Thursday's meeting is not to organize the workers in the nonunion plant here, but simply to provide information on wages and benefits being given union workers in Beacon.

"Of course, if the workers here wanted to organize a union, we would be interested," Reinhold said, "because we feel everyone would be better off if all the American Diesel workers were represented."

Index to Cases

This book has been set VIP, in 10 and 9 point Caledonia, leaded 2 points. Case numbers are 14 point Caledonia and case titles are 18 point Caledonia. The size of the type page is 31 by 47 picas.